*In commemoration of the centennials
of the Philippine Revolution (1896),
the Philippine Independence (1898), and
the Philippine-American War (1899)*

THE FILIPINO AMERICANS

FROM 1763 TO THE PRESENT

*Their History, Culture,
and Traditions*

VELTISEZAR BAUTISTA

Library of Congress Catalog Card Number 98-72131
International Standard Book Number 0-931613-14-0

Publisher's Cataloging in Publication
(Provided by Quality Books, Inc.)

Bautista, Veltisezar 1933 -
    The Filipino Americans: their history, culture, and
traditions / Veltisezar Bautista — 1st ed.
        p. cm.
    Includes bibliographical references and index.

    Preassigned LCCN: 98-72131
    ISBN: 0-931613-14-0

    1. Filipino Americans. 2. Filipino Americans—History
    I. Title.

E184.F4B38 1998   973'.049921
                            QBI98-224

Publisher's Note: Published in commemoration of the centennials of the Philippine Revolution (1896), the Philippine Independence (1898), and the Philippine-American War (1899).

Printed on acid-free paper.

Printed and bound in the United States of America

Bookhaus Publishers, P.O. Box 3277
Farmington Hills, MI 48333-3277 U.S.A
Phone: (248) 489-8640   Fax: (248) 489-8155
Credit card orders: Toll-Free 1-800-807-6908

ACKNOWLEDGMENTS

Researching, writing, and publishing a monumental book such as *The Filipino Americans: Their History, Culture, and Traditions* would not have been made possible without the support and encouragement of many people and institutions.

My special thanks go to the following:

To Lavinia Corpus-Guevara, a native of Caloocan City, Philippines, for helping me in an exhaustive research on the history of the Philippines and on the culture and traditions of the Filipino people.

To the librarians of the Farmington Community Library. Farmington Hills, Michigan, for helping me borrow, through their lending program, several books on early Filipino workers from other states, particularly California, Louisiana, Hawaii, and Alaska.

To the Washington State Archives for furnishing me with photographs of the pioneering Filipinos in America, particularly during the 1920s and the 1930s.

To the Hawaii State Archives for being kind enough to provide me copies of old photographs of Filipino *sakadas* on Hawaiian sugarcane plantations.

To the New Orleans Collections for making available to me copies of photographs of the Filipino fishermen who lived in the Manila Village on the bayous of Louisiana during the early migration of Filipinos to America.

To the National Archives for making available to me some photographs taken during the Philippine Revolution and the American Occupation of the Philippines.

To the Filipinas Heritage Library (through Maritoni Ortigas) in Makati, Metro Manila, Philippines, for providing me with pictures of the Filipinos and scenes during the early years of the Philippine Islands, particularly during the Spanish Occupation.

To Jim Zwick for allowing me to cull letters from the American soldiers who took part in the Philippine-American War (1899-1902) from his website on the Internet and for furnishing me with some historical photos during the Philippine Revolution.

To author Mariano Villarin, for permitting me to use excerpts from his book *We Remember Bataan and Corregidor: The Story of the American & Filipino Defenders of Bataan and Corregidor and Their Captivity* and for lending me some historical photographs.

To other book publishers who willingly permitted me to include in this volume excerpts from their books.

To many Filipinos, non-Filipinos, and public libraries who had faith in this book and who placed advance orders upon seeing it on the Internet, even when the book was still being written and not yet published.

To many other individuals and institutions, too many to cite on these pages, for their encouragement so that the publication of a comprehensive book on the Filipinos and Filipino Americans could be a reality.

Veltisezar "Velty" B. Bautista
Author
Farmington Hills, MI 48333 U.S.A.

DEDICATION

I dedicate this book to the light of my life,
Genoveva Abes-Bautista;
to my children,
Hubert, Lester, Melvin, Ronald, and Janet;
to my daughters-in-law,
Maria Cecilia Asi-Bautista and
Mary Joyce Icban-Bautista;
and to all Filipinos and Filipino Americans
who will read this book.

PREFACE

Although some Filipinos visited America many, many years ago, it was only in 1763 that Filipinos started to live in the United States. Seamen, called the *Manilamen*, jumped ship off New Orleans, Louisiana, and Acapulco, Mexico, during the Spanish galleon trade and settled in the bayous of Louisiana.

Since then, Filipino Americans quietly have made their indelible marks on America as politicians, doctors, judges, entrepreneurs, singers, scientists, professors, movie and television stars, etc. You name it, and there are many outstanding Filipino American achievers in every field of dreams.

Among the great Filipino American leaders are Ben Cayetano, governor of Hawaii; David Valderrama, delegate at the Maryland State Assembly; Velma Veloria, representative at the Washington State Assembly; Maria Luisa Mabilangan Haley, the highest ranking Filipino American official in the Clinton Administration; and Loida Nicolas Lewis, chair and CEO of TLC Beatrice International, a $1.8B business empire.

The Filipinos are expected to become the largest Asian American ethnic group by the year 2000. And yet, when many Americans refer to Asian Americans, they know more about the Japanese and the Chinese, than about the Filipinos. In fact,

the Filipinos are often mistaken for Japanese or Chinese. The Filipino Americans, indeed, in spite of their achievements and contributions to American culture and society, are still a little-known ethnic group, as far as the American mainstream is concerned.

It is, therefore, the purpose of this author to make known who the Filipinos are. With this book, people of all ages and backgrounds can learn about the values, beliefs, culture, traditions, and characteristics that have fueled the Filipinos' remarkable contributions to America.

Chapters on the Philippine Revolution (1896-1898), the Philippine-American War (1899-1902), and the Japanese Occupation of the Philippines (1942-1945) provide a historical backdrop for examining Philippine-American relations, and for commemorating the centennials of the Philippine Revolution (1896), the Philippine Independence (1898), and the Philippine-American War (1899).

It is also the purpose of this writer to correct "history." This pertains to the Philippine-American War that American authorities haven't recognized as a war, but as an insurrection, the Philippine Insurrection. While they recognized the three-month Spanish-American War as a war, they dismissed the Philippine-American war, that lasted three years (actually a number of years before resistance was totally stopped). Fighting between the Americans and the remaining armed groups of Filipinos, whom Americans branded as "bandits," lasted 16 years (1899-1914).

Commenting on this subject, James Loewen, a Washington, D.C.-based scholar and author of a forthcoming book entitled *Lies Across the Landscape: What Our Historical Markers and Monuments Get Wrong* said, "What we call the Philippine Insurrection should be called the Philippine War. We had never conquered the Philippines, so you can't call it as a revolt." That's why in history books, Americans call the Philippine soldiers "insurgents." The dictionary defines "insurgent" as "a person who rises in forcible opposition to lawful authority, especially a person who engages in armed resistance to a government."

The Filipino Americans, which took the author more than 20 years to think about and research and write, traces the Filipino history from the beginning of the peopling of the Philippines thousands of years ago to this present time in which they are still coming to America. A book of this kind—comprehensive, reader-friendly, and authoritative—should have been written and published a long time ago. But only a few dared to do an extensive research on the Filipino history, culture, traditions, and lives of outstanding Filipino Americans. Still, this author

decided to write and have it published, in spite of incredible odds.

To the non-Filipino American, may this book give you a panoramic view of the historical ties that have bound the Philippines and the United States for the past many years.

To the Filipino and Filipino American, may this volume become your guiding light to see the beauty and uniqueness of our history, culture, and traditions; thus, becoming proud of our own race.

If this book can help enhance the Filipino image in America and serve as an inspiration and enlightenment to the reader on the Filipinos' history, values, beliefs, customs, and characteristics, and promote understanding and goodwill among races, then the efforts of the writer and publisher and those who helped in the monumental task of the book's production, will not have been in vain. And, finally, one of my last major dreams in America—my real American Dream, to write a complete history of the Filipino people and the Filipino Americans, which other people had said was too difficult to accomplish—has been realized. Now I can face the world and proudly say, "This I've done!"

Veltisezar "Velty" B. Bautista
Author
Farmington Hills, Michigan 48333
United States of America
February 1998

TABLE OF CONTENTS

    (1899-1902)   61

    I. The Philippine-American War   62
    II. In the United States   63
    III. The War Goes On   65
    IV. The Writings of Mark Twain   69
    V. Other Happenings   70
    VI. Back to the Battlefields   72
    VII. Flashback: The Establishment of American Rule   77
    VIII. Epilogue   78

5. THE AMERICAN RULE AFTER THE 1899-1902 WAR   79

    I. Educational System   79
    II. Public Health and Sanitation   80
    III. Trade, Commerce, & Industry   81
    IV. Transportation and Communications   82
    V. Individual Freedoms   82
    VI. Introduction to Politics   83
    VII. Self-Government   83
    VIII. Agitations for Independence   84
    IX. The Commonwealth of the Philippines   85

6. THE JAPANESE OCCUPATION OF THE PHILIPPINES
    (1942-1945)   86

    I. Outbreak of War   87
    II. Bataan and Corregidor   88
    III. Establishment of Japanese Rule   93
    IV. Liberation of the Philippines   95
    V. The Third Philippine Republic   98

7. MANILAMEN: FILIPINO ROOTS IN AMERICA   100

    I. The Destination   101
    II. Their Way of Life   103
    III. Many Years After   105

8. THE FILIPINO IMMIGRATION TO THE UNITED STATES   107

    I. The Manilamen   108
    II. The Pensionados and the Nonsponsored Students   108
    III. The Workers   110
    IV. The Navy Men: 1903-1992   110
    V. The Military Personnel   112
    VI. The Professionals   113
    VII. The Population   115

Part I: Historical Background

THE PHILIPPINES: THEN AND NOW

The Philippines is located in the southeastern portion of Asia. Her neighbor on the north is the Republic of China (Taiwan or Formosa), while on the west is Communist Vietnam. Further west is Thailand. Immediately to the south of the Philippines is Indonesia and to the southwest are Malaysia and Singapore.

The Philippines is separated from her nearby Asian neighbors by several bodies of water. They are the Pacific Ocean on the east, the South China Sea on the north and west, and the Celebes Sea and the coastal waters of Borneo on the south.

I. LAND AND ITS PEOPLE

The Philippines is an archipelago of 7,107 islands and islets. The biggest islands are Luzon, with a land area of 40,530 square miles (105,000 square kilometers); Mindanao, 36,670 square miles (95,000 square kilometers); Palawan, 5,749.86 square miles (14,896 square kilometers); Negros, 5,278.55 square miles (13,675 square kilometers); and Samar, 5,183.59 square miles (13,429 square kilometers). She has a rugged land mass and, similarly, she has an irregular coastline, which is twice as long as that of the continental U.S.A. This irregularity has resulted in numerous fine harbors and landlocked straights that can accommodate large ships. They can also be a refuge of ships in distress during stormy weather.

The land surface is 115,800 square miles (300,000 square kilometers). Land forms include hills, plains, valleys, and mountains. Her mountain ranges, which are volcanic in origin, are drained by small river systems. There are seven major mountain ranges. The largest and longest is Sierra Madre, which faces the Pacific Ocean on the eastern coast of Luzon. The highest peak is Mt. Apo, a volcano in Davao del Sur Province. It has an elevation of 9,691.60 feet (2,954 meters).

Three Major Islands. The three major geographical groups in the country are Luzon,

A map showing a part of Southeast Asia, where the Philippines (center) is located.

Visayas, and Mindanao. Luzon comprises the northern portion of the archipelago. The Visayan region has about 6,000 islands including Leyte, Cebu, Samar, and Bohol. Mindanao is the second largest land and encompasses about 400 small islands.

These islands are divided into provinces, which are run like states in the United States. Each province is ruled by a governor, a vice governor, and members of the provincial board. Each province is composed of cities, towns, and barrios.

Several "Pinatubos." There are several volcanos in the Philippines. These have been one of the natural causes of destruction to life and property for centuries. At least 10 are considered active. The most famous are Iraya on Batanes Island; Taal in Batangas; Banahaw in Quezon; Mayon in Albay; and Hibok-Hibok on the Camiguin Islands; Makaturing in Lanao; Apo in Davao, and Mt. Pinatubo in Zambales.

Mt. Pinatubo has gained notoriety as being the most destructive volcano in the world. It lay dormant before it erupted in June 1991. It directly and indirectly caused damage to public and private property in the provinces of Zambales, Bataan, and Pampanga, including the Clark Air Force Base in Angeles City, Pampanga Province. Its ashes spread all over the world, causing global warming, damage to the ozone layer, and adverse effects on communications.

After six years of eruption, the lahar deposits along the volcano still cascade down the slopes after heavy rains. They continue to take lives, destroy bridges and roads, and defy billion-peso dikes built to contain lahar flows. These lahar flows are expected to last for five or more years, according to volcanologists. The Philippines lies within the Pacific seimic belt, which is why she experiences severer earthquakes.

Christian Groups. The people of the Philippines number about 73,265,584 (July 1995 estimate).

There are several ethnic groups and more than 65 so-called cultural minorities in the Philippines, which speak their own dialects or languages. Among these ethnic groups are the Tagalog, the Ilocano, the Pangasinanian, the Pampangueño, the Bicolano, the Cebuano, the Ilongo, and the Waray-Waray. They com-

Philippine Dept. of Tourism

Two youthful Filipinos in their formal traditional dresses.

prise more than 90 percent of all Filipinos and are the Christians. About 84 percent of Filipinos are Roman Catholics.

The Tagalogs live in Manila and in central and southern Luzon. Although they speak Tagalog, they have intonations of their own, as do the Batangueños from Batangas Province. The Tagalogs mostly live in such provinces as Nueva Ecija (the Ilocanos also live in some towns in the northern part of the province), Bulacan, Rizal, Batangas, Quezon, Laguna, and Mindoro (Oriental and Occidental). The Tagalogs dominate the people in Manila. There are, however, many people in the city who have come from different parts of the country, including Luzon, to live in the big city. Many also have come from the Bicol region and the Visayan islands.

The Ilocanos live in the Ilocos region in northern Luzon, particularly Ilocos Sur and Ilocos Norte, but many of them have migrated in large numbers to central Luzon, and, of course, to the United States. Most of the old-timers in the United States in the late 1920s and early 1930s came from the Ilocos region.

The Ilongos live in western Negros, in southern Mindoro, and on the island of Panay. The Cebuanos predominate in Cebu, western Leyte, Bohol, eastern Negros, and in some coastal areas of Mindanao.

The Bicolanos are in the southeastern Luzon and nearby islands, including the provinces of Albay, Camarines Norte, etc. The Pampangueños or Kapampangans live in central Luzon, particularly in Pampanga Province. The Pangasinanians live in the Lingayen Gulf region of Luzon, including Pangasinan Province; however, many Pangasinanians have migrated into other towns in central Luzon. The Waray-Warays are in the provinces of Samar and eastern Leyte.

Other Groups. Chinese and other groups also live in the

Philippines. The Chinese comprise 1.5 percent of the population, and are active in business.

Cultural Minorities. There are more than 65 cultural minorities, similar to the Indian tribes in the United States, who live in reservations and in the mountains.

They include the Muslim groups, which are comprised of the Maranao, the Samal, the Maguindanao, the Tausug, etc. They live in the Sulu Archipelago and southern Mindanao.

There are also the so-called upland tribal groups who live in the mountain regions of the country, such as in the Mountain Province of Luzon. In northern Luzon, the other ethnic groups include the Bontoc, the Kalinga, the Ifugao, the Kankanay, the Ibaloi, the

Philippine Department of Tourism

**Women members of
the Mandawi tribe, one of the cultural
minority groups in the Philippines.**

Isneg, the Ilongot, the Tinguian, and the Gadang.

The Mangyan group lives in Mindanao and the Batak and the Tagbanua live in Palawan. In Mindanao there are groups known as the Tiruray, the T'Boli, the Bagobo, the Mandaya, the Bukidnon, the Subanun, and the Manobo. The Negritoes, popularly known as the Agta or the Aeta live in the mountainous areas of Luzon, Negros, Panay, and Mindanao.

"I love You! *Iniibig Kita!"* Yes, "I love you" is said in about 87 dialects or languages in the Philippines. These include Tagalog, Kapampangan, Ilocano, Cebuano, Pangasinanian, Bicolano, Hiligaynon, Chabacano, and the different dialects spoken by other ethnic groups such as Muslims and cultural minorities.

The Filipino dialects belong to the so-called Malayo-Polynesian language family, which is said to be the largest language family throughout the world. Pilipino (not Filipino), which is based on Tagalog, is the national language in the Philippines, but both English and Pilipino, are the official languages in schools, in government, and in private institutions, especially in urban places. English serves as the official language used in communications and in business meetings, especially by Rotarians, Jaycees, and other organizations. That is, English and Pilipino both serve as the media of communications among the people who also speak their own dialects.

It is common that when a Filipino in the Philippines and a Filipino in America write to each other, they communicate in English. But in daily conversation, English and Pilipino are combined, which is called Taglish (meaning Tagalog (Pilipino) and English. For instance, one may say, "*Pupunta ako sa Maynila,* to enroll at the University of the Philippines, (I'll go to Manila to enroll at the....) or "*Okeng, okey ka,* you're so sweet!" (You're okay and you're so sweet!")

So whenever you meet Filipinos in the United States, they may be speaking their own dialects when not speaking in English. However, these groups know Pilipino. So if you want to know a Filipino language, it should be Tagalog or Pilipino so that you'll have more people whom you can converse with.

Government. The Philippines has a democratic form of government, like that of the United States. The government is divided into executive, legislative, and judicial branches.

Have Pesos and Enjoy! If you have the dollar, you can have it changed to the Philippine peso. The dollar when this book was about to go to press was equivalent to forty pesos (P40.00). The Philippine currency consists of the peso (P) and the centavo. One hundred centavos equal P1. Coin denominations are 1, 5, 10, 25, and 50 centavos, and P1, P2, and P5. Bill denominations consist of 5, 10, 20, 50, 100, 500, and 1,000 pesos. Foreign currency may be exchanged in banks, hotels, and most large department stores, which have authorized money-changing shops.

Charge It! Charge It! Most large hotels, stores, restaurants, and resort areas accept major credit cards, including Visa, Mastercard, and American Express. At hotels and other large stores, traveler's checks are accepted, preferably American Express.

How's the Weather? The weather in the Philippines is tropical, the country having only two seasons, the dry and rainy seasons. It's usually hot from April to July. The dry season is between November and June and the rainy season is between July and October. Filipinos consider December, January, and February as the cool months. But they may not be considered as winter without snow as in the United States; maybe it's milder or like spring or fall.

II. FLASHBACK: THE EARLY FILIPINOS

The Philippines, scientists believe, once was a part of Mainland China.

According to the scientists, during the Ice Age, the waters surrounding the Philippines dropped to about 156 feet below the present levels, exposing large bodies of land. These became land bridges connecting the Philippines to the Asian mainland.

The Philippines, Out from the Bottom of the Sea? In February 1976, Dr. Fritjof Voss, a German scientist who studied the geology of the Philippines, questioned the validity of this theory of land bridges. He maintained that the Philippines was never part of mainland Asia. He claimed that it arose from the bottom of the sea and, as the thin Pacific crust moved below it, continued to rise. It continues to rise today. The country lies along great Earth faults that extend to deep undersea trenches. The resulting violent earthquakes caused what is now the land masses forming the Philippines to rise to the surface of the sea.

Dr. Voss also pointed out that when scientific studies were done on the earth's crust from 1964 to 1967, it was discovered that the 35-kilometer-thick crust underneath China does not reach the Philippines. Thus, the latter could not have been a land bridge to the Asian mainland.

When They Came, How They Came. The traditional teaching of Philippine history in Filipino schools today has early Philippine habitants coming in waves.

In 1962, it was concluded that about 250,000 years ago, primitive men came to the Philippines from the Asian mainland. Then about 25,000 years ago came the pygmies, the small, black-skinned, squat-nosed, thick-lipped, and kinky-haired people from the south over the still remaining land bridges. (They are considered the ancestors of the Negritoes, who are, in turn, regarded as the aborigines of the Philippines.)

Around 12,000 to 15,000 years ago, another Negrito (or Aeta) migration occurred. They reached Luzon from Borneo over land bridges in Palawan and Mindoro. The submergence of the land bridges when the ice melted with the passing of time did not prevent other people from inhabiting the Philippines.

5,000 to 6,000 Years Ago? The first Indonesians arrived by boat from Southeast Asia some 5,000 to 6,000 years ago. Much later, around 1500 B.C., a second wave of

Indonesians arrived. Then came the Malays in two successive waves, the first between 800 and 500 B.C. and the second, between 300 and 200 B.C. From Borneo, they traveled by sailboats and settled in the three major islands of the Philippines: Luzon, Visayas, and Mindanao. Subsequent peoples who came from the start of Christianity until the present time include the Indians (Hindus), the Arabs, the Chinese, other Eastern Asians, the Europeans, and the Americans.

Who Came First? The matter of who the first settlers were has not been really resolved. This is being disputed by anthropologists, as well as the theory of Professor H. Otley Beyer that the first inhabitants of the Philippines came from the Malay Peninsula.

The Malays now constitute the largest portion of the populace and what Filipinos now have is a Malayan culture. Anthropologist F. Landa Jocano of the University of the Philippines contends that what fossil evidence of ancient men show is that they not only migrated to the Philippines, but also to New Guinea, Borneo, and Australia. He says that there is no way of determining if they were Negritoes at all. However, what is sure is that there is evidence the Philippines was inhabited as early as 21,000 or 22,000 years ago. In 1962, a skull cap and a portion of a jaw, presumed to be those of a human being, were found in a Tabon cave in Palawan Province.

The discovery proved that man came earlier to the Philippines than to the Malay Peninsula; therefore, the first inhabitants of the former did not come from the latter.

Jocano further believes that present Filipinos are products of the long process of evolutions and movements of people. This not only holds true for Filipinos, but for the Indonesians and the Malays of Malaysia, as well. No group among the three is culturally or racially dominant. Hence, Jocano says that it is not correct to attribute the Filipino culture as being Malay in orientation.

According to Jocano's findings, the peoples of the prehistoric islands of Southeast Asia were of the same population as the combination of human evolution that occurred in the islands of Southeast Asia about 1.9 million years ago. The proofs of this are fossil materials found in different parts of the region and the movements of other peoples from the Asian mainland during historic times.

He states that these ancient men cannot be categorized under any of the historically identified ethnic groups (Malays, Indonesians, Filipinos) of today.

Some Filipino ethnic groups were pagans while others were Muslims. The pagans were converted to Christianity by the Spaniards. The Americans later arrived and introduced further cultural changes, which made the Filipinos more and more different from the peoples of other Southeast Asian countries.

III. PRE-HISPANIC CULTURE

The Filipinos lived in settlements called *barangays* before the colonization of the Philippines by the Spaniards. As the unit of government, a *barangay* consisted from 30 to 100 families. It was headed by a *datu* and was independent from the other groups. (The Tagalog word *barangay* came from the Malay word *balangay*, a boat that transported them to the islands.)

Usually, several barangays settled near each other to help one another in case of war or any emergency. The position of datu was passed on by the holder of the position to the eldest son or, if none, the eldest daughter. However, later, any member of the barangay could be chieftain, based on his talent and ability. He had the usual responsibilities of leading and protecting the members of his barangay. In turn, they had to pay tribute to the *datu*, help him till the land, and help him fight for the barangay in case of war.

In the old days, a datu had a council of elders to advise him, especially whenever he wanted a law to be enacted. The law was written and announced to the whole barangay by a town crier, called the *umalohokan*.

The People's Commandments. Pre-college Filipino textbooks teach that the only written laws of pre-colonial Philippines that have survived are the Maragtas Code and the Code of Kalantiaw, both prepared in Panay. Some historians believe that the Maragtas Code was written by Datu Sumakwel, one of the chieftains from Borneo who settled there. As for the Code of Kalantiaw, it was said to have been promulgated by the third chief of Panay and possibly a descendant of Datu Sumakwel, Rajah Kalantiaw, in 1433. W. Henry Scott, however, has disputed the authenticity of the Code of Kalantiaw.

Classes of Society. There were four classes of society. They were the ruling class (datu), the freemen and notable persons (maharlika), the commoners (timawa), and the dependents and slaves (alipin). The alipin were of two kinds: the aliping namamahay, who were household servants, and the aliping saguiguilid, who were slave workers.

Clothing and Ornaments. The natives already wore clothes and personal ornaments. The men wore short-sleeved and collarless jackets, whose length reached slightly below the waist. The color of the jacket appeared to indicate the position of the wearer in society, e.g., red for the chief, and blue or black for those below him, depending on the societal class. For the lower part, they wore a bahag, a strip of cloth wrapped around the waist, passing between the thighs. Their thighs and legs were left exposed.

A piece of cloth wrapped around the head, called a putong, served as a head gear. The kind of putong one wore was important. For example, a red putong meant the wearer had killed a man in war while one who had killed at least seven people signified so by wearing an embroidered putong. They also wore necklaces, armlets or kalombiga, earrings, rings, and anklets, usually made of gold and precious stones.

The women's upper garment was a sleeved jacket, called a baro. Over their skirts (saya or patadyong) was wrapped a strip of cloth called tapis. They also wore gem-studded bracelets, necklaces, rings, and gold earrings.

Tattoos were part of the body ornaments of pre-Hispanic Filipinos, men and women alike. These were also sported as war "medals." The more tattoos, the more impressive was a man's war record.

The Filipinos from the Visayas Islands were the most tattooed, which was why early Spanish writers referred to them as Pintados or painted people. The writers referred to their Islands as Islas del Pintados or Islands of the Painted People.

Rice and More Rice. Agriculture was the early Filipinos' main means of livelihood. They also grew an abundance of rice, sugarcane, cotton, hemp, coconuts, bananas, and many other fruits and vegetables. Land cultivation was by tilling or by the kaingin system. With the kaingin system, the land was cleared by burning the shrubs and bushes. After that, it was planted with rice and other crops, which were watered by irrigation ditches.

The world-famous Ifugao rice terraces of Mountain Province, which have stone walls and run for thousands of feet on the mountain sides, are irrigated by a system of ditches. From afar, the terraces seem to be a giant stairway leading to the sky. From end to end, the length could be about 12,000 miles or halfway around the Earth.

There were public and private lands. Those along the mountainsides and less arable lands were public property. They were open to everyone who wanted to till them. Private lands were usually exclusively for nobles and datus.

Other Industries. Other industries were fishing, mining, lumbering, poultry raising, shipbuilding, and weaving. Fishing was particularly thriving for the settlements along rivers and seas.

Domestic trade existed among the barangays and the islands. The Filipinos' foreign trade was with China, Japan, Siam (now Thailand), Borneo, Sumatra, Cambodia, and other islands of old Malaysia. The barter system was used in business transactions because there was no currency.

Their God. Bathala was the supreme god of the pre-Spanish Filipinos. They attributed to Bathala the creation of the heavens, Earth, and man. There were lesser gods and goddesses, like a god of death, a god of agriculture, a goddess of harvest, sea gods, river gods, and the like. It was also believed that things found in nature were full of spirits more powerful than man. Spirits of dead relatives were also revered. Sacrifices were offered to all of them.

The ancient Filipinos believed in the immortality of the soul and in life after death. Disease or illness was attributed to the whims of the environmental spirits and the soul-spirits of the dead relatives.

The pre-Spanish Filipinos also revered idols, called *anitos* in Tagalog and *diwata* in Visayan. These seem to be the counterparts of the present saints, to whom Filipinos offer prayers and food, much like their ancestors did.

How Islam Conquered Parts of the Philippines. The Islamization of Southeast Asia was generally accomplished by peaceful means through Muslim traders, missionaries, and teachers. They went to Java, Sumatra, Jahore, Malacca, Borneo, and nearby islands to conduct their mission. To speed up the conversion process, these proselytizers usually married into the families of the rich and ruling class.

By the 13th century, most of the lands in Southeast Asia were Islamized. From there, Islam filtered to Mindanao and Sulu, the southern part of the Philippines, in the 14th century.

In 1380, an Arab teacher, Mukdum, arrived in Sulu from the Malay peninsula to preach Islam. He built the first mosque in Simunul, Sulu. Around 1390, he was followed by Raja Baginda, a minor ruler of Menangkabaw, Sumatra. About 1450, Abu Bakr, a Muslim scholar, came to Sulu and married Paramisuli, the daughter of Raja Baginda. After Baginda died, Abu Bakr established a sultanate form of government with himself as sultan. Islam then spread rapidly to all parts of Sulu.

Serif Kabungsuan was responsible for the spread of Islam in Mindanao. He led a force of Muslim Samals from Jahore that conquered the natives of what is now Cotabato and converted them to Islam. He also married into an influential family and founded the first sultanate of Mindanao, with himself as head.

On the other hand, Muslim Malay traders from Borneo spread Islam to the natives in Manila and in the provinces of Batangas, Mindoro, and Pampanga. When the Spaniards arrived in the Philippines during the first half of the 16th century, many parts of Luzon, including the large native kingdoms of Manila and Tondo, had already been Islamized.

However, the further spread and influence of Islam were cut short by the conquest and Spanish colonization of the Philippines starting in 1665.

Chinese and Indians. Chinese influences on Filipino life were mainly economic. However, at the same time, cultural influences were inevitable. Many words in the Philippine language have Chinese origins. The Chinese also taught the ancient Filipinos the use of gongs, umbrellas, lead, and porcelain, as well as the manufacture of gun powder, and metallurgy and mining methods. Filipinos also adopted customs from the Chinese.

Many words in the Philippine language also appear to have Sanskrit origins. In addition, ancient religious beliefs of the Filipinos show Indian influence. It is said that some elements of the Indian culture reached the Philippines through the Hinduized Malays who settled in the country permanently.

IV. UNDER FOREIGN INVADERS

The Philippines was colonized by the Spaniards for about 333 years and by the Americans for 48 years. Later, World War II broke out and the Japanese occupied the Philippines for three years. (See chapter 2: *The Spanish Colonization of the Philippines (1565-1898); chapter 4: *The Philippine-American War (1899-1902);* and chapter 5: *The Japanese Occupation of the Philippines, (1942-1945).*)

V. THE HUK REBELLION

After World War II, the bad relationship between landlords and farmers, who were seeking better conditions, became worse. The tenancy problem plagued the country, particularly in the provinces of Pampanga, Bulacan, Nueva Ecija, and Tarlac in central Luzon.

There was too much tension when the landlords who evacuated to urban areas during the war came to the rural areas to ask for back "rent" for their lands from the farmers. With the help of their own armed bands, they tried to force the peasants to give to them what they owed them.

At the same time, the Huks, or Hukbalahaps who fought against the Japanese as U.S.-supported Filipino guerillas did, were reluctant to give up their arms.

As a result, General Douglas MacArthur put to jail Luis Taruc and Casto Alejandro, the leading Huk leaders. Furthermore, the U.S. forces were ordered to disarmed the Huks. Instead, the Huks fled to the mountains. Still armed, they supported the *Pambansang Kaisahan ng mga Magbubukid-PKM* (National Peasant Union) in its fight against the landowners.

By that time, the peasants' movement represented about 500,000 members. The PKM, as part of the left-wing Democratic Alliance, which also included other groups, had supported Sergio Osmeña as the Nacionalista Party's presidential candidate against Manuel Roxas during the 1946 election campaign. Osmeña was the president of the Philippine Commonwealth, who replaced President Manuel Quezon after he died in the U.S. in 1944.

Osmeña got the support of the labor movement. He promised the farmers that a new law giving 60 percent of the harvest, instead of the then 50 percent or less, would be passed. At that time, Taruc, who was released from jail, and five other candidates of the Democratic Alliance won congressional seats during the 1946 elections which elected Roxas to the presidency.

However, Taruc and the other Democratic Alliance winners were not allowed to be installed into their positions. They were accused of having used terrorist acts during the campaign. Violence by landlords with the help of the police worsened against peasant activities. In August 1946, Juan Feleo, a PKM leader was killed, resulting in the rebellion of the Huks in central Luzon. The People's Liber- ation Army *(Hukbong Mapagpalaya ng Bayan)* became the new name of the People's Anti-Japanese Army.

VI. FROM PHILIPPINE INDEPENDENCE TO RAMOS REGIME

The United States, as provided in the Jones-McDuffie Law of 1934, granted independence to the Philippines on July 4, 1946.

The Roxas Administration (1946-1948). Inaugurated as first president of the new republic was Manuel A. Roxas, who defeated then-President Sergio Osmeña, Sr., in the April 1946 national election. (Osmeña was elected vice president in 1935 and succeeded Quezon to the presidency after the latter died while in exile in the United States.)

President Roxas, a native of Capiz (now Roxas City) had to deal with the rehabilitation of the Philippines, tremendously ravaged by World War II.

Various agreements with conditions, in favor of the United States, were discussed and approved by the authorities. One such condition was that American investors be given "parity" rights. That is, the U.S. investors had the right to be treated as equals of Philippine nationals, not as investors from any other foreign country.

At the same time, there were absolute quotas of Philippine exports to the United States. On the contrary, there were no quotas for American exports to the Philippines. Moreover, the U.S. military obtained military bases in the Philippines without any rent for 99 years. The duration was later reduced. The lease was to end in 1991.

In February 1948, President Roxas pardoned those who had cooperated with the Japanese during the war. Those who had served the Japanese were called "collaborators." Roxas himself had played a part in the Japanese-sponsored wartime "puppet government."

It was during the Roxas administration that the Philippine Constabulary and landlord private armies had their days fighting the Huks and their farmer supporters over tenancy problems. The Huks had earlier fought the Japanese along with U.S-supported Filipino guerillas. But later, they supported the peasants in their fight with the landlords to improve the economic conditions of the land tenants.

At first, President Roxas held negotiations with the Huks. As a matter of fact, his administration created an Agrarian Commission that passed a law giving 70 percent of the harvest to the tenants. However, there were difficulties in implementing the law.

On the other hand, the Huks demanded the winning congressmen of the Democratic Alliance be reinstated, among whom was Luis Taruc. They likewise demanded that the military police be disbanded and a general amnesty be given to those involved in the movement. Instead, President Roxas in March 1948 declared the People's Liberation Army as a subversive organization.

Quirino Comes to Power (1948-1953). In April 1948, Roxas died of a heart attack. He was succeeded by Elpidio Quirino, his vice president. Quirino, a native of Vigan, Ilocos Sur won as president in the 1949 election against Jose P. Laurel, who was president in the Second Puppet Republic during the Japanese Occupation of the Philippines.

Quirino's main goals in his administration were to obtain peace and order and minimize graft and corruption in the government. He believed that mass corruption existed during the Roxas administration. But Quirino also was severely criticized by the press and the public for alleged corruption.

It was during his administration that the Huks increased to a greater number. In the 1949-51 period, there were between 11,000 and 15,000 armed Huks. Although they were mostly in central Luzon, there were regional committees of the People's Liberation Army in provinces now known as Southern Tagalog region, in northern Luzon, Visayan Islands, and Mindanao. Quirino appointed Ramon Magsaysay, a former guerrilla and a congressman from Zambales Province, as secretary of defense to fight the Huks. With the efforts of Magsaysay, the backbone of the Huk movement in central Luzon was broken.

The Magsaysay Era (1953-1957). In 1953, because of his popularity and his success in fighting the Huks, the Nacionalista Party lured Magsaysay to be its presidential candidate. He was then called as "Man of the People." They also said, "Magsaysay Is My Guy."

Born in Iba, Zambales, Magsaysay defeated Quirino of the Liberal Party in the November 1953 election. As a man of the people, he opened the Malacañang Palace, the White House of the Philippines, to the people. He also established special courts for landlord-tenant disputes and built roads, bridges, irrigation canals, and "liberty wells" in the rural areas. The Huk movement further weakened with the surrender of Luis Taruc in May 1954.

In 1955, Magsaysay worked for the redistribution of land. In that same year, Congress passed the so-called Land Reform Act. The law created the Land Tenure Administration that had the power to acquire private lands through either purchase or expropriation. Such lands would be sold by the government to farmers at reasonable prices.

However, the law was hampered by a lack of funds. Hence, Magsaysay, was not able to push through in Congress his full program for land reform. He died in March 1957 in a plane crash at Mt. Pinatubo.

The Garcia Regime (1957-1961). Carlos P. Garcia, Magsaysay's vice president, succeeded him to the presidency. Garcia, a native of Talibon, Bohol Province, was himself elected president in the 1957 election. Diosdado Macapagal, of the opposing Liberal Party, won the vice presidency.

President Garcia immediately imposed import controls on manufactured goods from abroad. His objective was to jump-start the Philippine economy. His administration was known for its program of austerity and its "Filipino First" policy, with a view to creating economic independence for the Philippines. This led to a kind of industrialization. However, as in the time of President Quirino, Garcia's government was plagued with graft and corruption.

The Macapagal Administration (1961-1965). With graft and corruption as the election issue for the 1961 election, Garcia was defeated by the Liberal Party's Diosdado Macapagal. Calling himself the "Poor Boy" from Lubao, Pampanga, Macapagal lifted the import controls imposed by Garcia.

In 1963, Macapagal signed the Agrarian Land Reform Code into law. The code abolished tenancy by the institution of an agricultural leasehold system, which was intended to lead toward the eventual goal of ownership of the land by the farmers. However, when Macapagal's term ended in 1966, the extent of the land area affected was not significant. Only about 29,150 hectares of the 405,000 hectares of rice and corn, were cultivated by tenants.

Macapagal was also known for his changing the Independence Day of the Philippines from July 4, 1946 (given by the United States) to June 12, 1898. It was on the latter date that President Emilio Aguinaldo had declared the Philippine independence in his hometown in Cavite from Spain.

Besides launching his version of Agrarian Reform, Macapagal promoted the stability of the peso and initiated a socio-economic program for the betterment of the poor.

The Era of Marcos: A President Who Became a Dictator (1965-1986). In the 1965 presidential election, Macapagal was defeated by Ferdinand E. Marcos, a former Liberal, who became the Nacionalista Party's presidential candidate. In 1969, Marcos, a native son of Sarrat, Ilocos Norte, won his reelection.

However, during the Marcos regime, corruption in the government reached unparalleled proportions. Thus, opposition to Marcos's administration grew stronger and stronger. On September 21, 1972, President Marcos imposed martial law. He abolished Congress, clamped opposition print and broadcast media, and jailed thousands of his critics. He became an absolute dictator. His presidential proclamations became the laws of the land.

In 1973, his second and final term as president should have ended. However, with martial law, Marcos continued to rule as the absolute dictator in the Philippines. Plebiscites were held during the years 1973, 1975, and 1978. However, the will of the Filipino

people didn't prevail. All the plebiscites of disputable legitimacy gave approval to the extension of martial law.

In 1978, the Philippines held elections for the legislature (the National Assembly had replaced the former Congress). Marcos' party, the *Kilusang Bagong Lipunan* (KBL), or New Society Movement obtained three quarters of the seats in the national assembly. In 1981, Marcos formally ended martial law. However, as president, he had emergency powers. In June 1981, in an election during which many people didn't vote, Marcos won another six-year term as president.

During the martial law era, both the administrations of U.S. Presidents Ronald Reagan and Jimmy Carter continued to give military and other economic aid to the Marcos administration.

In August 1983, Senator Benigno Aquino, Jr., a staunch Marcos critic, went home to the Philippines from his exile in the United States. He was murdered at the Manila International Airport upon his arrival.

In February 1985, General Fabian Ver and 24 other soldiers were tried by a special court composed of what the opposition groups called "Marcos loyalists." Ver and his soldiers were acquitted.

A so-called "snap" presidential election, proposed by President Marcos himself, was held in February 1986. Corazon Aquino, wife of the late Senator Aquino who was murdered, became Marcos' rival candidate. Aquino, with the backing of the people, won a clear majority of the votes. However, Marcos had the National Assembly declare himself winner in the election.

A section of the military, led by Juan Ponce Enrile, Marcos' secretary of defense, and Fidel Ramos, chief of staff of the armed forces of the Philippines, rebelled against the dictator. Due to the mass demonstrations in Manila, called "people power," Marcos was forced to escape aboard a U.S. Air Force plane to the United States. That ended the Marcos regime and started the rule of President Aquino. Marcos died in exile in the United States.

The Aquino Regime (1986-1992). Upon taking over the presidency, President Aquino, freed all political prisoners jailed by President Marcos. In the same year, all presidential decrees by Marcos were revoked, and the constitution, the fundamental law of the land, was adopted by a nationwide plebiscite in 1987.

During her administration, Aquino attempted to alleviate the economic conditions of the people. However, she was not successful. In fact, some criticized the weakness of her administration in dealing with economic problems. Furthermore, during her term, some elements of the armed forces, along with Marcos loyalists, revolted seven times against the Aquino government. The coup attempts were thwarted by loyal sectors of the military, led by Fidel V. Ramos, chief of staff of the armed forces and secretary of defense.

It was during the Aquino administration that the issue of extending the expiring leases of U.S. military bases in the Philippines came about. In September 1991, as Aquino objected to it, the Senate disapproved the extension of the leases of the bases. (Earlier, in June 1991, the nearby Mount Pinatubo damaged the Clark Air Force Base in Pampanga rendering it unusable.)

Former Executive Secretary Joker Arroyo said of Aquino, "Cory Aquino's greatest legacy is the fact that we are all here today, talking freely."

In the next presidential election, President Aquino didn't seek reelection. She chose Fidel V. Ramos, as her candidate for president.

The Ramos Administration (1992-1998). Fidel V. Ramos won in the 1992 presidential election against six other candidates. In the last five years of his administration, he has changed the Philippines from being "the Sick Man of Asia" into "The Next Tiger of Asia."

In September 1992, he lifted the ban on the Communist Party. Likewise, he eliminated foreign-currency restrictions to attract foreign investment to the Philippines. Ramos, besides courting foreign investment, has liberalized the Philippine economy to move toward industrialization.

He negotiated with the Moro National Liberation Front (MNLF), headed by Nur Misuari, to bring peace in Mindanao, the southern part of the Philippines.

A peace agreement between the Philippine government and the Muslim group was signed on September 2, 1996, that ended the 24-year-old war in Mindanao. The agreement was signed by the government chief negotiator Manuel Yan, Nur Misuari, Indonesian Foreign Minister Ali Alatas, and Secretary General Hamid Algabid of the Organization of Islamic Conference (OIC).

Later, Misuari ran for and won the governorship of the Autonomous Region for Muslim Mindanao (ARM) in the September 9, 1996, elections.

Due to his economic programs and accomplishments, *Newsweek Magazine*, cited the Philippines as the "The Next Tiger of Asia." The Ramos term ends this year, 1998. (See Ramos' economic program as envisioned in Philippines 2000.)

VII. THE MODERN PHILIPPINES

Today, the Philippines, an independent nation of about 70 million people, is becoming

The well-known Shoe Mart Mall in Metro Manila, Philippines.

one of the most progressive countries in Asia. The Philippines has rebounded from the economic debacle that former dictator Ferdinand Marcos had put her into. Investors from the United States, Japan, Malaysia, and other nations in Asia are bringing in millions of dollars as investment in factories, recreation establishments, and other businesses.

The "States" of the Philippines. A "state" in the Philippines is called a province. The Philippines has 72 provinces and 61 chartered cities.

Manila and Its Satellites. Metro Manila is the political, economic, social, educational, cultural and recreational hub of the Philippines. It comprises the city of Manila, Quezon City, Makati, and other suburban cities.

Malls, boutiques, flea markets, and other shops abound in Manila and its environs. You'll be amazed at beautiful attractions in Manila itself, like the Intramuros, the old walled city, and Chinatown. Here you'll see a number of McDonald's, Burger King, Wendy's, and Kentucky Fried Chicken. When you're inside the malls and you don't concentrate on the crowd, you'd think that you were somewhere in America.

Manila: Where Admiral Dewey Met His Destiny. A long time ago, Manila was a small tribal settlement on the banks of the Pasig River near Manila Bay. On May 1, 1898,

The inside of a mall in Makati, Metro Manila.

Dewey's naval fleet destroyed the Spanish Fleet on Manila Bay.

It was on May 24, 1570, when Spanish Marshall Martin de Goiti's expedition reached Soliman's settlement. On June 24 of the following year, Adelantado Miguel Lopez de Legazpi founded the city of Manila, which he called the "distinguished and ever loyal city" of Manila. He proclaimed it as the capital of the islands.

During the old times, in the suburbs or *arabales,* such as Quiapo, Tondo, Santa Cruz, and Malate, the Filipinos, then known as *indios,* lived and worked together with the so-called *mestizos* (of mixed Filipino and foreign descent). The Chinese merchants called *Sangleys,* lived in a district called *parian,* which now comprises an area known as Binondo. Intramuros, which means within the walls, was the original Walled City. It was the site of the native settlement called *Maynilad,* ruled over by Rajah Soliman. It was at that time the center for the trade of goods from Asia. It was in this walled city where the Spaniards sought refuge when the American troops came during the

A MacDonald's restaurant in Manila.

Old Intramuros Gate. Puerta Real, one of the original gates. In the foreground is a carabao or water buffalo, the principal beast of burden at that time in Manila (1899).

New Intramuros Gate. One of the modernized gates.

Spanish-American war. It was also here that the so-called "mock battle" took place between the Spanish and American forces, where Filipino troops were excluded from participating.

Intramuros is now a tourist attraction. Local and foreign tourists have the option of enjoying walking tours from 30-minute to 2 hours. Among the attractions in Intramuros are Fort Santiago, Rizal Shrine, Casa Manila Museum, San Agustin Church, Intramuros Walls Museum, and San Agustin Museum.

Moreover, performances such as *Serenata sa Fort Santiago* and the Marian Procession are held in Intramuros. The Serenata sa Fort Santiago is performed as an open-air band concert in the tradition of the outdoor concerts in the *paseo* of the Old Luneta. It is held every Sunday from April to mid-May. On the other hand, the Marian Procession is held annually in December. This procession is in commemoration of the 400-year-old celebration of the Feast of the Immaculate Concepcion. The activity is a grand display of various images of the Virgin Mary.

There are also other activities in Intramuros.

Where to Go. What to See. There are a lot of tourist attractions in the Philippines. Here are some suggested destinations by the Philippine Department of Tourism:

Boracay. Made up of three little communities, Boracay, a "paradise island," is at the northwestern tip of Panay Island in the West Visayas region. The communities are Yapak in the north, Balabag in the middle, and Manocmanoc in the south. About a dozen beaches dot the island. Bamboo outriggers ferry visitors. There are also horses and bicycles for riding.

Night life is fun. Avail yourself of bars and discos up to the wee hours of the night.

Or take a stroll in the beach by the moonlight. At Yapak, with an experienced guide, you may wish to explore the bat caves.

Windsurfing and parasailing gear are readily available in the 2,000-hectare area of Boracay. You can enjoy sailing with the help of local sailors to make your stay enjoyable and memorable.

Boracay is an international place. When you're there, you'll hear different languages: English, Pilipino, German, etc. Foreign cuisine such as French, Belgian, German, Thai, Spanish, and Australian are available, together with native cuisine. What a wonderful life!

If you're going there from Manila, you can go to Boracay by taking a 50-minute Philippine Airlines flight to Kalibo, Aklan Province. From there, you'll take another 2-hour inland ride via bus or jeepney to Caticlan. (Or you may take a flight straight to Caticlan). At Caticlan, you may be asked to complete forms with regard to travel information. From there, you you'll reach Boracay via outrigger boats.

Banaue/Mt. Data, Saga-da. The natives of Banaue are called Ifugaos or rice eaters. The attractions there are the Banaue Rice Terraces, which were carved out of the mountain about 2,000 years ago. These rice terraces are called the "magnificent stairway to the god's domain." They rise up to 1,500 meters high and extend to over 20,000 kilometers. The ideal visiting time to see them is between March and June, when the terraces are green with shoots or golden with ripe rice seeds.

VIII. THE PHILIPPINES 2000

The Philippines 2000, is a strategy and a movement; it is the Filipino people's vision of development by the year 2000. As envisioned, the Philippines by the year 2000 will have the decent minimum of food, clothing, shelter, and dignity. The major goal of Philippines 2000 is to make the Philippines the next investment, trade, and tourism center in Asia and the Pacific.

The Birth of Philippines 2000. The Philippines 2000, as a movement, started to gather momentum in the form of multi-sectorial consultations. These consultations were geared to pave the way for the Philippines' entry into the 21st century. Today, involved in these endeavors are people from government, business and private sectors, labor, and other sectors forming a "strategic alliance" under the leadership of President Ramos.

IX. RESULTS OF THE PANIC IN ASIA

In July 1997, as a result of the Hongkong stock market crash, all the currencies in Southeast Asia, including the Philippine peso, suffered steep falls in value against the U.S. dollar. The collapse of the stock market there was triggered by the jacking up of interest rates initiated by Hong Kong to protect its currency against any speculative attack.

Philippine Department of Tourism

The Banaue Rice Terraces, a few hours' drive from Baguio City. They were carved from mountain ranges centuries ago by the Ifugaos. They rise to 4,921.26 feet (1,500 meters) high and expand to over 7,720 miles (20,000 kilometers).

THE SPANISH COLONIZATION OF THE PHILIPPINES (1565-1898)

The conquest and colonization of the Philippines by Spain began with the great demand of Europe for spices, which were abundant in Asia. Asia was also a good source of such Oriental goods as silk, jewelry, precious stones, fine textiles, and medicinal herbs. The spices were pepper, ginger, cloves, nutmeg, cinnamon, and other similar food flavorings. They were needed not only to enhance the taste of food, but also to help keep meat from spoiling. Spices and these other Oriental products commanded very high prices in Europe. So the cry was: "On to Asia!" And they went adventuring—to seek new route to the continent of spices.

How that happened is a long story.

In the 15th century, the Muslim Turks came into power in a big portion of what is now known as the Middle East. In 1453, they captured Constantinople, now Istanbul, in Turkey. A Christian city, it was then the capital of the Byzantine Empire and an important stopover of those using the traditional trade routes. After its capture, the Turks closed these sea routes and gave control of the only route that remained to Venice, a city state on the Italian peninsula and which had been one of their allies and supporters. Taking advantage of this control, the Venetians raised their prices. Thus, they made the cost of goods from the Orient, especially spices, exorbitant. This started the quest for alternate trade routes.

The Role of Spanish and Portuguese. For the Spanish and the Portuguese, their location gave them better chances than the rest of Western Europe for finding new routes. Moreover, they were determined to control the Muslim power by introducing Christianity.

The missionary spirit was to be the guiding light in the preservation of the Spanish Empire. The search paved the way for the historic discoveries of new lands in the 15th and 16th centuries. The Portuguese and Spanish navigators claimed these discoveries for their respective kings.

Actually, the Portuguese started sending expeditions a few years ahead of the Spaniards. They explored the non-European World in search of new trade routes. In 1487, they circumvented the Cape of Good Hope. Later, Vasco de Gama found a route to India by moving eastward from the cape, opening another sea route.

Then the Portuguese reached Goa, Malacca, Moluccas, Japan, and China (Macao, Amoy, and Ningpo). They captured some of the places and turned them into trading centers. These signified the start of Portugal's empire in Asia. Refusing to be outdone, Spain sent her own expeditions. They searched for another sea route to Asia, and, like her rival, her navigators found new lands.

"This Is Ours, That is Yours!" The rivalry continued. It turned bitter by the last decade of the 15th century and steps were taken to prevent conflict between these two Catholic nations. Finally in July 1494, Spain and Portugal signed the Treaty of Tordesillas. This agreement moved an earlier demarcation set by the Papal Bull *Inter Caetera*, issued by Pope Alexander IV on May 4, 1493, to about 502.96 miles (1,303 kilometers) further west of the Azores and the Cape Verde Islands. It was agreed that all islands west of this line would belong to Spain and east of it to Portugal. In other words, one party told the other party, "This is Ours, That is Yours!"

I. SPAIN'S EARLY ADVENTURES

It seems that a mistake on the part of the Spaniards was an important factor in their going to the Philippines. They wrongfully believed that the Spice Island lay west of the demarcation line. Such a belief sealed the fate of an Asian people!

The Magellan Expedition. A Portuguese, Ferdinand Magellan renounced his allegiance to his king because the king had not rewarded his services as officer and soldier in the Portuguese possessions in India and Malacca. Magellan sought his own destiny. He became a Spanish subject, and might have said to himself, "See what might happen."

Therefore, he convinced King Charles I that the Moluccas could be reached from a westwardly direction and said that he could do it. He was granted a royal commission to head an expedition of five ships with a fleet of 237 men and set out to sea on September 20, 1519. He found what is now known as the Straight of Magellan.

On November 20, 1520, he reached the Pacific Ocean minus two ships and after quelling the mutiny of the captains. The three remaining ships crossed the Pacific Ocean after four gruelling months. He had miscalculated the great distance of the ocean and the end of his journey was a considerable distance farther north of the Moluccas. In other words, he got lost.

II. DISCOVERY OF THE PHILIPPINES

On March 6, 1521, Magellan's expedition reached what is now the Marianas Island group in the Western Pacific, about 1,499.09 miles east of the Philippines. Magellan landed on the island, now known as Guam, where natives gave him and his men enough food and water. He named the island "Islands of Sails" because he saw many sailboats there.

Some natives stole one of his boats. He had his revenge, however. He later changed the name to "Ladrones" or Island of Thieves. To resume its westward voyage, the expedition left on March 9, 1521.

On March 17, 1521, they saw the mountains of what is now known the island of Samar, part of a group of islands they named the Archipelago of St. Lazarus. They called that a discovery. This sighting is referred to by Europeans and other Western historians as the discovery of the Philippines. (The official chronicler of the expedition noted the date as March 16 because, not being aware of the International Dateline, had not added one day upon crossing it. It was in 1845 that the Spaniards corrected the calendar.)

Magellan weighed anchor on the islet of Homonhon and was welcomed by some natives from the nearby island of Suluan. This was the first meeting between the Spaniards and the Filipinos, who were used to seeing strangers going to the islands. The Filipinos didn't know that would be the start of the campaign for their colonization by Spain.

Agreement Penned with Blood. Magellan subsequently entered into a blood compact with Raja Kulambu, chief of the island of Limasawa. It was there where he had the first Catholic mass celebrated and where he claimed the islands in the name of the King of Spain. If they tossed drinks for the king, nobody knew. He also had a blood compact with Rajah Humabon of the island of Cebu, where the expedition planted the first seeds of Christianity by conducting a mass baptism. (The blood compact was the ancient Filipino method of sealing blood brotherhood and friendship.)

While in Cebu, two rival chieftains of the nearby Mactan Island, Sula and Lapu-Lapu, had a quarrel. Sula, with the hope of enlisting Magellan's help in the fight, told the latter that Lapu-Lapu had refused to recognize Spain's sovereignty. So during that time, intrigued worked, too.

The Battle of Mactan: Magellan Versus Lapu-Lapu. On April 27, 1521, Magellan set out for Mactan with about 1,000 Cebuano warriors and 60 Spaniards to intervene in the power struggle. So the Spaniards had the Cebuanos fight their own people. Magellan demanded that Lapu-Lapu acknowledge Spain's sovereignty and pay tribute or else be attacked. Lapu-Lapu refused—probably saying, "No Way!" Magellan then persuaded Humabon not to have his men join the battle, but to let the Spaniards do the fighting to show off their ability in war. They had the edge because of their superior weaponry and fighting skill. "Here's how we fight," the Spaniards might have uttered. The Filipinos, in turn, might have countered, "Let's see!"

Magellan and several Spaniards were killed and Lapu-Lapu became victorious. This event marked the first successful defense by the Filipinos against a European nation.

The Retreat to Cebu. The Spanish survivors returned to Cebu. In the meantime, several of Magellan's men had abused the hospitality bestowed on them by robbing the Cebuanos and raping some of their women.

Revenge Is Sweet. Rajah Humabon gave a party for some of the Spaniards. Afterwards they massacred them to avenge the indignities on the natives. The surviving members of the expedition left on the ships *Victoria* and *Trinidad*. The third, *Concepcion*, was destroyed off the coast of Bohol because there were insufficient men to sail it. The *Victoria*, captained by Juan Sebastian de Elcano, made it back to Spain on September 6, 1522, with only 22 crew members. *Trinidad* and its crew had been captured by the Portuguese; some were able to return to Spain, among whom was Antonio Pigafetta.

The so-called discovery of the Philippines led to its conquest and colonization by Spain. In addition, Magellan's expedition blazed a new sea route to Asia, and, most important, the surviving men of the expedition were responsible for completing the first circumnavigation of the world. What a way to seek new routes just to obtain those Asian spices!

III. SUBSEQUENT EXPEDITIONS

King Charles of Spain decided to send several expeditions to the East. The first was headed by Garcia Joffree de Loaisa in 1525, with orders to establish a colony in the Moluccas. It failed although it was able to reach Mindanao (in the Philippines) and the Moluccas. In 1526, the expedition of Sebastian Cabot left, but reached only Brazil. A third expedition, headed by Alvaro de Saavedra, likewise failed. They were captured by the Portuguese, although they were able also to reach Mindanao and the Moluccas.

In 1542, the Ruy Lopez de Villalobos expedition formed in Mexico was ordered to colonize the Philippines, probably hearing the words, "Go ye and spread Catholicism to the natives." He was also to look for a new sea route back to Mexico. Although he failed, Villalobos played an important role in Philippine history because he was the one who gave Philippines, the name "Filipinas" in honor of Prince Philip, son of King Charles. Later, he became king of Spain himself as Philip II.

Another Super Powers' Dispute. Several other expeditions were later sent to the Moluccas. However, a dispute eventually developed between Spain and Portugal, two of the superpowers of that time, about who owned the land. It was another way of saying, "This land is mine!" Both claimed that the Moluccas lay on their respective sides of the demarcation line although, in reality, the island was rightfully on the side of Portugal.

The dispute was settled through peaceful negotiations, and on April 22, 1529, they signed the Treaty of Zaragoza, under whose terms the demarcation line was extended to 297-1/2 leagues east of the Moluccas. Although the Moluccas and the Philippines belonged on the side of the Portuguese, both powers were unaware of this, having insufficient knowledge of the exact position of the demarcation line. Thus Spain ironically sold its rights over the Moluccas to Portugal, which rightfully should have been Portugal's in the first place. It claimed ownership over the Philippines, which was still on the Portuguese side of the line.

IV. THE START OF COLONIZATION

The Spanish adventures were considered as expeditions only. The actual colonization of the Philippines started in 1565. When Prince Philip became king of Spain upon the death of King Charles, he decided to establish an indisputable Spanish rule over the Philippines.

The viceroy of Mexico (then the Spanish colony called New Spain, was ordered to prepare an expedition to install a permanent settlement in the Philippines. From there, they were to look for a return route to Mexico. The expedition was headed by Miguel Lopez de Legazpi, a sailor-missionary. Father Andres de Urdaneta was the chief navigator and spir-

itual leader. Aside from commercial gains, King Philip wanted to expand his empire and spread Catholicism. Among King Philip's sealed orders to Legazpi, which were opened upon instructions when he would be already on the high seas, was to colonize the Philippines.

Fr. Urdaneta had been a survivor of an earlier expedition. He was aware that both the Philippines and the Moluccas were within the Portuguese domain. Thus, he suggested to King Philip and the viceroy that they drop any intentions on these two but instead colonize New Guinea, which was on the Spanish side. The expedition set out thinking that New Guinea was their objective. Later, they learned upon opening the sealed orders that it was the Philippines they were going after. Legazpi had no choice but to obey his orders.

The expedition passed by the island of Bohol (Philippines) and was met with hostility by the natives. It turned out that two years earlier, the Portuguese had committed atrocities in the coastal villages in the guise of Spaniards. After several peace-making attempts on the part of Legazpi, he and Sikatuna, chief of Bohol, had a blood compact.

The Conquest of the Philippines. On April 27, 1565, the expedition arrived in Cebu. His initial efforts to land peacefully were unsuccessful so they attacked the Cebuanos, who fled to the hills. He then sought to befriend them by allowing the natives to return to their homes unpunished.

As a result, he and Rajah Tupas, chieftain of the island, signed a peace agreement. This treaty thus signalled the final conquest of the Philippines. It was actually one-sided because, whereas the Filipinos could be punished for crimes against the Spaniards, there was no punishment for crimes committed by the Spaniards against the Filipinos. This rendered the chieftain powerless and signified the loss of freedom of the Filipinos. The natives also had to pay tribute to the King of Spain to show they recognized him as their sovereign. In return, Legazpi promised them the protection of Spain.

A permanent settlement in Cebu was established by Legazpi. The settlement was named San Miguel. It was later renamed the

City of the Most Holy Name of Jesus. This took place after one of Legazpi's men found the wooden image of the Infant Jesus, which had been given by Magellan as a gift to the wife of Rajah Humabon.

Later, however, after being harassed by the Portuguese and having inadequate food, he decided to move to Panay, where he put up a second settlement. From there, he sent expeditions to other islands that came under Spanish rule.

Meanwhile, on June 1, 1565, after the settlement in Cebu had been established, Fr. Urdaneta and Felipe de Salcedo, Legazpi's grandson, left aboard the *San Pedro* to look for a way back to Mexico. They crossed the Pacific Ocean, sailed down the coast of what is now California and reached the port of Natividad in Mexico on October 1, 1565. This new route was what the Spaniards would use in travelling between the Philippines and Mexico, and enabled Spain to send additional men and supplies needed by Legazpi in firming up Spanish rule in the Philippines. One of the soldiers who eventually went to the Philippines was Captain Juan de Salcedo, Legazpi's youngest grandson.

To Manila They Go. Legazpi heard news from traders about a rich Muslim kingdom in Luzon called Maynila. Thus, he sent an expedition there in May 1570. It was composed of 120 Spanish soldiers and several hundred Visayan warriors, and was headed by Captain Martin de Goiti. His second-in-command was Juan de Salcedo. Maynila or Manila was then jointly ruled by Rajah Soliman and his uncle, Rajah Matanda.

Rajah Matanda was hospitable to the Spaniards but Rajah Soliman was said to be suspicious of the Spaniards' motives. As a result, an armed confrontation between the Spaniards and the natives ensued. The Spaniards defeated Rajah Soliman and his men with their superior weapons and fighting skills. Later, de Goiti returned to Panay to recommend to Legazpi the conquest of Manila.

In May 1571, Legazpi himself headed a second expedition there with more men. He was able to convince Soliman and Matanda, as well as Lakandula, ruler of Tondo, to recognize Spanish sovereignty and the natives

agreed to pay tribute. Thus, Manila's acquiescence to Spanish rule was peacefully achieved. On June 24, 1571, Legazpi moved his headquarters to Manila and made it the capital of the Philippines. In 1574, King Philip II named Manila *Insigne y Siempre Leal Ciudad* or Distinguished and Ever Loyal City.

To Other Parts of Luzon. From Manila, Legazpi sent military expeditions to explore and conquer the different parts of Luzon. It was mandatory that the natives be made to pay tribute to the King of Spain. In central Luzon, Martin de Goiti met little resistance from the natives. In southern Luzon, Juan de Salcedo was met with some kind of hostility but was able to conquer the Laguna de Bay region before moving on towards a region that is now known as the provinces of Quezon, Camarines Sur, and Camarines del Norte.

After his success in southern Luzon, Legazpi sent his grandson to northern Luzon, where Salcedo also conquered several native kingdoms in Zambales and Pangasinan, as well as the Ilocos region. From Ilocos, he moved further north along the Ilocos coast and around the tip of northern Luzon. He then went southward along the shores of Cagayan Province and along the eastern coast of Luzon. Along the way, he was able to explore Polillo Island. He returned to Manila by crossing the rugged Sierra Madre Mountains.

Then to the Bicol Region. In July 1573, Legazpi conquered the whole Bicol region. Because of his successful campaigns, he was given a part of the Ilocos region as his *encomienda* by Governor-General Guido de Lavezares, who succeeded Legazpi. (Legazpi had died a poor man on August 20, 1572). Salcedo made his residence there and named the place Villa Fernandina in honor of Prince Ferdinand, son of King Philip II. It is now known as the town of Vigan, Ilocos Sur Province.

In 1574, Salcedo helped repel the invasion of a Chinese pirate, Limahong. Two years later, on March 11, 1576, Salcedo died at the age of 27. He was well-liked by the natives because he was kind and generous and treated the natives with respect. He had even willed most of his possessions to the natives of his *encomienda* before he died. Salcedo has been hailed by historians as the Hernando Cortes (the greatest Spanish conquistador of Mexico) of the Philippines. Legazpi, did not live to see firm Spanish rule established throughout the Philippines. However, he is considered a great colonizer, having laid the foundations of Spain's colonial rule that lasted for 333 years over the archipelago.

Occupation of the Visayan Islands. By 1576, the Spaniards had succeeded in controlling a great part of the Philippines, i.e. Luzon and Visayas. This was because there was no unity among the *barangays* on these two islands. Other factors were the lack of a cohesive and highly integrative political system, the diversity of languages, and the willingness of many chieftains to cooperate. The Spaniards were able to successfully convert the natives of lowland settlements, which were later to become provinces, to Catholicism.

However, they were unsuccessful in conquering the areas in the mountain regions of Luzon, such as the Cordillera Mountains. Thus, the mountain people were able to retain much of their native culture and tradition.

Mindanao and Sulu Resist. The Spaniards failed to subjugate and proselytize Mindanao and Sulu, in the southern portion of the Philippines. Thus, the Muslim natives of these parts were able to preserve their Islamic faith and culture. The Filipino Muslim resistance to Spanish rule came to be known as the Moro Wars, a long, bloody, and costly conflict.

These Muslims were a constant threat to the islands in the Visayas and Luzon under Spanish subjugation. They harassed many of these islands by raiding the coastal towns, killing or capturing many of the inhabitants.

The Spaniards conducted military operations against them. The first of these operations was an attack on Jolo in June 1578, led by Captain Esteban Rodriguez de Figueroa. He was able to capture the island, but was unable to maintain his hold. Once the Spaniards left, the Muslims returned.

In 1876, after several subsequent failed attempts, the Spaniards were finally able to establish a permanent camp on Jolo, Sulu Province. The Muslims continued to sow terror with their raids from the sea. They used vast vintas that outraced armed Spanish ships.

However, in the middle of the 19th century, the former proved no match for the fast steam-powered warships brought in by the Spaniards. The first three such warships were the *Elcano*, the *Reina Castilla* and the *Magallanes*.

V. SPANISH ABUSES

In 1524, the Spaniards administered the Philippines through the Council of the Indies. It was a very powerful body with legislative, executive, and judicial powers. The council relayed the royal decrees to the Viceroy of Mexico, who, in turn, relayed them to the governor-general in the Philippines. From 1565 to 1821, the Philippines was, in effect, a dependency of Mexico, since Spain ruled the former through the latter.

In 1863, the Overseas Ministry took over the functions of the Council of the Indies and the peninsular laws enacted in the 19th century were extended to the Philippines.

The Governor-General. The governor-general was the only representative of the Spanish crown in the Philippines and the highest colonial official. He was appointed by the Viceroy of Mexico and later by the Spanish king. He had vast executive, military, ecclesiastical, and legislative powers.

Several checks were instituted to prevent the governor-general from abusing his power. One was the *Royal Audiencia,* which was like a Supreme Court. It was established on May 5, 1583 by virtue of a Royal Decree. He used to be the president of the *Royal Audiencia,* but many years later, he was no longer a part of this court.

Another check, ordered by the king, was the *visita,* a secret inquiry into what top colonial officials were doing. However, the governor-general was able to abuse his powers, just the same. For example, he could ignore any royal order if he deemed conditions in the colony did not warrant its implementation.

Complase, as the power was called, was frequently used to advance his selfish interests and that of his cohorts. The big distance between the Philippines and Spain also gave them the courage to commit abuses. Bribery and political influence also played an important part in encouraging abuse of office.

Thus, the governorship was fraught with graft and corruption. Because of the short term of a governor-general, he had to let his greed run wild to be able to amass wealth as much as he could within the term. Taxation and speculations in the galleon trade characterized the administration of most of the governor-generals.

Encomienda System. The Spaniards divided the Philippines into jurisdictions called *encomiendas*. Theoretically, the encomienda was a right vested by the king on the *encomendero*, a Spaniard, who had helped in subjugating a pagan country, thus making it a public office. However, in the Philippines, it was different. The reward of the *encomendero* was not land, but the right to collect taxes in a certain territory.

There were three classes of *encomiendas*. They were royal, ecclesiastical, and private encomiendas. The royal encomiendas were for the king, the ecclesiastical encomiendas were for those assigned to different religious orders, and the private encomiendas were for the Spaniards who had helped in the colonization of the Philippines.

Encomenderos committed abuses. The abuses came in the form of tax collections considerably bigger than that allowed by the king. They seized lands, crops, animals, and farm tools of the natives. They treated the people cruelly. They forced them to work without pay. However, because of the abuses, the encomienda system was abolished little by little. Encomiendas that became vacant were reverted to the Crown and no longer given to others.

Local Governments. The Spaniards divided the Philippines into provinces, cities, and towns. Only Spaniards were chosen to head the provinces and cities.

Provinces. The provinces were known as pacified or unpacified. In the pacified provinces, called *alcaldias*, the inhabitants had accepted Spanish rule and lived peacefully.

In the unpacified provinces or *corregimeintos, the* natives, headed by the *corregidores*, still resisted the Spaniards.

The head of a province was the *alcalde mayor*, who was usually appointed by the governor general. The former had a dual function. As chief executive of a province, he enforced the laws in his province and collected taxes. He also was the provincial judge.

Since he had only a small salary, he was given the privilege of *indulto de commercio* or to engage in trade in his province. This privilege was gravely abused. His position gave him an unfair advantage over the other traders and many of them monopolized trade in their territory. They dictated the prices of commodities in their alcaldias. Some also engaged in usury. No one could question these practices because as alcalde mayor, he was also the judge, the one to act on the complaints and interpret the law. Usually, though, he often lacked the background in law and used his power solely for his own interests.

In 1844, the alcalde mayor's privilege to engage in trade was removed. In 1886, the separation of the executive and judicial functions of the alcalde mayor took effect. He became merely a judge and, for that matter, a person could not become a judge without being a lawyer or knowledgeable about the law. Later, the alcadia became a civil province headed by a civil governor, appointed by the Ministry of Colonies.

Cities and Towns. The government of a city was called the *ayutamiento*. It consisted of a city council or *cabildo*, whose key members were the *alcalde, regidores*, or councilors and an *alguacil mayor* or city chief of police.

In turn, the towns or *pueblos were* subdivided into *barangay* or villages. The town's leader was the *governadorcillo*, who was assisted by several lesser officials such as the *teniente mayor* or town police chief, and the deputies in charge of the cattle and fields in the town. He had to answer for uncollected taxes in the town.

Filipinas Heritage Library

Real Street in Intramuros, Manila, in 1851, with imposing residential houses. At left is San Juan de Dios Hospital. Taken from *Puerta del Parian*.

The *cabeza de barangay* headed the barangay. His main duty was to collect taxes or tributes within his village. At first, the position was inherited from one's father, but later, it became appointive and, subsequently, elective.

The only positions open to Filipinos were municipal offices. The pre-colonial units of government, the *barangays*, were headed by datus and rajahs. The Spaniards chose them and their descendants to hold these offices, thus earning their loyalty. These made Filipinos natural allies and they protected the colonial masters against the wrath of the natives. Aside from this, the Spaniards were able to make sure that the traditional ideas, religious superstitions, and pre-colonial forms of exploration continued. The last became one of the bases of the feudal economy during the Spanish reign.

The Missionaries. Graft, corruption and incompetence continued from the provincial level down to the lowest levels of government. No venue for grievance was open to the Filipinos. Not even with the Church.

One of the principal goals of Spain in colonizing the Philippines was to Christianize the natives. This had been an obligation to the

Pope taken on by both Spain and Portugal under the papal bulls that divided the non-European world between these two Catholic nations in 1493. Spain was able to propagate Catholicism in the Philippines and prevent the spread of Islam throughout the country. Today, the Philippines is the only Christian country in Asia.

The Spanish missionaries who went to the Philippines during the first century of the Spanish rule were patient, selfless, and dedicated. Because of their sincerity and zeal, they were able to spread Christianity. They contributed to the social development of the country. They built roads, bridges, and schools. They, likewise, built hospitals, orphanages, and asylums.

Complaints about the abuses of the colonial officials reached the ears of the king of Spain through the missionaries. (One of the leading defenders of the natives was Father Domingo de Salazar, the first bishop of Manila.)

This was to change later on. Corruption also crept in among the clergy. The union of Church and State gave the archbishop and heads of the religious orders the chance to occupy significant positions in the central government. They controlled the educational system, public works in the municipality, the press, and the entry of printed matter into the Philippines. They supervised collecting taxes, taking census, conscripting natives into the army and police force, and municipal elections. They also certified to the correctness of the residence certificates or *cedulas*. (*Cedulas* were pieces of paper that served as identification papers. These were paid for by every individual. Of course, they also served as

Watercolor drawing of Binondo River in Manila. At the right are some commercial houses. Bancas and cascos are on the river. In the foreground are anchored water vessels.

individual taxes.) The clergy added much to the sufferings of the people because they used their positions to amass wealth.

"Do This!" "Do That!" or "Board the Ships and Ahoy!" Another form of Spanish abuse was the exploitation of human resources. Filipinos were required to render forced labor. "Do this!" "Do that!" the Spaniards said. There was no pay, however. Filipino males between 16 and 60 years old had to render services for 40 days, later to 15 days, each year. They had to work in such projects as construction of bridges, churches, and galleons. The galleons plied the Manila-Acapulco route.

Called *polistas*, these laborers were also drafted to serve in Spanish expeditions to the Moluccas, Indochina, and other parts of Asia to stave off the attempts of the Portuguese, Dutch, and English to gain a foothold in the colony.

VI. THE FILIPINO RESISTANCE

The love for freedom of the native Filipinos was never fully suppressed by Spain. Throughout the years of colonization, Filipinos resisted. Brave men and women groups attacked Spaniards and they might have said, "Come and get us!" Yes, they attacked and later fled to the hills and mountains.

Actually, there occurred more than 100 major revolts against Spain. More than the love of freedom, though, the majority of the revolts were against abuses by both civil officials and the clergy.

There were 13 revolts from 1565-1600, 40 during the 16th century, 35 in the 17th century, 35 in the 18th century and 14 in the 19th century.

Among these were the

- 1574, Lakandula Revolt in Tondo in 1574;
- 1584, Tondo Conspiracy;
- 1596, Magalat Revolt in Cagayan;
- 1622, Bankaw Revolt in Leyte;
- 1649, Sumuroy Uprising in Samar;
- 1660, Maniego Revolt in Pampanga;
- 1660, Malong Revolt in Pangasinan;
- 1744-1828, Dagohoy Revolt in Bohol (the longest revolt);
- 1762, Ilocos Revolt of Diego and Gabriela Silang;
- 1762, Palaris Revolt in Pangasinan;
- 1840, Religious Revolt of Apolinario de la Cruz or Hermano Pule in Tayabas (now Quezon province); and
- 1872, Cavite Mutiny.

However, the reason why not one of these succeeded was the fact that the Filipinos did not consider themselves as one people; hence, they had neither unity nor a political leader.

Moreover, there were Filipinos who became loyal to Spain. However, Spain herself, though not intentionally, helped lay down the foundation of nationalism. It was because she gave the Filipinos a common (although foreign) government, a common religion, a common and a Hispanic cultural heritage. Most of all, Spain gave Filipinos a common grievance in the form of Spanish oppression.

The British occupation of Manila had also opened the eyes of Filipinos to the fact that the Spaniards were not invincible after all.

Representation in the Spanish Cortes. When the colonies were granted "representation" in the Spanish Cortes, the Philippines was given representation in the years 1810-1813, 1820-1823, and 1834-1887. However, in actuality, the delegates were full-blooded Spaniards who could not be expected to work for the interest of the Filipinos. In the first half of the 1890s, when the propaganda movement was in full swing, there were Filipino reformists or propagandists who called for reforms in the Philippines without separating from Spain. They demanded true Philippine representation in the Cortes.

Filipinas Heritage Library

Drawing of street clothes vendors.
From J.A. Karuth Album, September 2, 1858.

Filipinas Heritage Library

A view of the town of Calamba, Laguna Province, Philippines, with the church at right.

From J.A. Karuth Album, September 2, 1858.

VII. FILIPINO NATIONALISM

Before the 19th century, there was no feeling of nationalism among Filipinos, which might have been due to the following factors:

■ Spaniards required Filipinos to travel from one province to another.

■ They used the divide-and-rule policy, whereby Filipinos from one region were sent to quell revolts in another region.

■ The communities had limited opportunities to share experiences due to the lack of transportation and communications facilities.

■ There was the absence of a common language.

■ Geographical factors hindered the Filipinos' social intermingling and communi-

**Drawing of a woman and a man
of the middle class in costume
of the 19th century.**

From J. A. Altum, September 2, 1858.

cations among themselves.

■ There was the absence of leadership to unite the different ethnic groups into one nation.

■ There was no means of long-distance communications.

The people were separated by bodies of water and could not just swim to be on the other side of the shore. (Of course, it's different today, with fast planes, a resident in Luzon can just call by long distance phone a friend in Davao in Mindanao, and say, "I'll be there this afternoon.")

Spanish abuses and exploitation, however, eventually paved the way for a rising sense of nationalism. It was done by giving the different ethnic Filipino groups a common cause for grievance. In the early part of Spanish rule, educational opportunities offered to Filipinos were limited. But later, especially during the last century of Spanish colonization, children of wealthy Filipino families were permitted to enroll in colleges and universi-

ties. Moreover, Spain gave the Filipinos a common religion—the Roman Catholic religion—geographical identity, and the existence of one supreme government ruling over the whole archipelago.

The following events also contributed to the rise of nationalism among Filipinos:

■ The Philippines was opened to world trade in 1834 when a port was established in Manila. Other ports were established in many cities such as in Sual, Iloilo, and Zamboanga in 1855; Cebu, in 1860, and Legazpi and Tacloban in 1873.

■ The new economic prosperity resulted in the emergence of a new social class, the middle class. Such social class status was given to them by some historians. But some scholars said they belonged to the upper class. It's because the real middle class were government employees and other segments of society. The upper class was composed of businessmen and traders, professionals such doctors and lawyers, and planters and landowners. Included were *creoles* or Philippine-

Drawing of a man trying ready-made trousers.

From J.A. Karuth Album, September 2, 1858.

**Drawing of a fisherman
with a bamboo trap.**

From J.A. Karuth Album, September 2, 1858.

born Spaniards, *mestizos* (Spanish and Chinese), and some native Filipinos who had become wealthy and were able to send their children to local and foreign universities. They were known as the *ilustrados* (the enlightened).

■ There was the emergence of the secularization movement initiated by secular priests. (These were priests who were not members of any religious order, but they administered the parishes that were left to them by the regular priests.) In the beginning, it was a struggle between two classes of Spanish priests, i.e. the *peninsulares* or those who came from Spain, and the *creoles* or those who were born in the Philippines. Furthermore, some Filipinos who had gained some degree of affluence chose to have their children become priests. It was because it was then considered a prestigious profession. Since the number of native priests increased, the secularization movement became a campaign for the Filipinization of the parishes. They were supported by the creoles.

■ A liberal Spanish regime was established in Spain under General Francisco Serrano as Regent. In June 1869, the Regency in Madrid brought back Philippine representation in the Spanish Cortes and appointed a new governor-general to the Philippines, General Carlos Maria de la Torre. General de la Torre became the most popular and most loved governor-general among the Filipinos, particularly the native priests and ilustrados, because of his liberal policies. He abolished press censorship and encouraged the open discussion of political issues. He mingled with Spaniards and

**Drawing of a native couple from
the Manila suburbs.**

From J. A. Karuth Album, September 2, 1858.

natives alike, without bodyguards. Thus, Filipinos were able to speak freely about freedom, democracy, and political reforms. The campaign for Filipinization of the parishes gained more momentum. Unfortunately, this liberal administration did not last long. In 1871, another government was established in Spain; monarchy was brought back by the Spanish Cortes. In April 1871, a Spanish governor-general, Rafael de Izquierdo, assumed office in Manila. He informed the people that he was going to reassert Spanish authority on the islands. Nevertheless, the seeds of nationalism had been sown.

CUADRILLEROS

Filipinas Heritage Library

Pen drawing of two *guardrilleros* (municipal policemen), circa 1885.

From *El Globo*, "Exposicion de Filipinas," Madrid 1887.

Mutiny or Revolt? The liberal policies under the de la Torre administration displeased some friars and other Spaniards on the islands. They found a chance for revenge when a group of Filipino soldiers and workers under Sergeant La Madrid at the Spanish arsenal in Cavite Province staged a mutiny on January 22, 1872. The mutiny was the result of Governor-General Izquierdo's having abolished some privileges that arsenal workers had been enjoying since 1740. The privileges included their exemption from the tribute and forced labor.

In less than a day, the mutiny was quelled. But the colonial authorities took advantage of the situation. They claimed it was not only a revolt, but a part of a large conspiracy against Spanish rule. Izquierdo used the incident as an excuse to sow terror and persecution in the country. Many Filipino reformists, especially those who were identified with de la Torre, were arrested and imprisoned. They were accused of involvement in the supposed Cavite revolt. They were either given long prison terms or banished to the Marianas or the Mountain Province, in the northern part of the Philippines, which was very desolate and undeveloped at the time.

The Spanish friars also accused Fathers Jose Burgos, Jacinto Zamora and Mariano Gomez of being the brains behind the mutiny. They were not given the chance to defend themselves. After a trial fraught with fake and manufactured evidence, they were sentenced to death. On February 17, 1872, they were put to death by means of the *garrote* at the Luneta.

The execution of the three priests was witnessed by Filipinos from all parts of Manila and the neighboring provinces of Bulacan, Laguna, and Cavite. The Spaniards allowed the Filipinos to witness the execution as a means of cowing the Filipinos. But the Spaniards sensed that it had merely caused further restiveness among the spectators. It can be said that nationalism among the Filipinos emerged on that tragic morning of February 17, 1872. Furthermore, the natives and the *creoles* came to realize that they had a common grievance, which finally united them.

A typical scene in a barrio on Talim Island,
Binalonan, Rizal Province, Philippines.

From *Vistas de Filipinas*, 1890.

The Battle Cry: There Must Be Reforms!

Shortly after the mutiny, a new generation of ilustrados emerged. They became the spokesmen of the masses. Many of them went to Europe to wage a peaceful campaign calling for reforms in the Philippines. They didn't seek separation of the Philippines from Spain. They just wanted equality between the Filipinos and Spaniards. One of their demands was that the Philippines become a province of Spain. Their grievances centered around Spanish abuses. They didn't advocate the taking up of arms against Spain because they believed in the power of the pen. Hence, the movement was also known as the Propaganda Movement.

Liberal-minded Spanish Filipinos exiled in Spain joined the Filipino ilustrados. Also, they were aided by a number of prominent liberal Spaniards.

The leaders of the movement were Jose Rizal of Laguna, Marcelo H. del Pilar of Bulacan, and Graciano Lopez Jaena of Iloilo. Others in the movement were Juan Luna, a famous painter; his brother Antonio, a pharmacist and writer; Pedro A. Paterno, a writer and lawyer; Mariano Ponce, a writer; Gregorio Sanciango, a lawyer-economist; Jose Ma. Panganiban, a writer-linguist; Antonio Ma. Regidor, a lawyer; and Isabelo de los Reyes, a writer and historian.

They wrote articles and delivered speeches. Their intention was to make the Spanish people and government realize the need to free the Philippines from the deplorable conditions it was under.

They published a newspaper in Barcelona, Spain called *La Solidaridad* (Solidarity) which became the organ of the movement. Its first issue came out on February 15, 1889. Graciano Lopez Jaena was the newspaper's first editor. He was succeeded by Marcelo H. del Pilar. The Filipino intellectuals used different pen names. Marcelo del Pilar used *Plaridel*; Jose Rizal, *Laon-Laan*; Antonio Luna, *Taga-Ilog*; and Jose Ma. Panganiban, *Jomapa*.

The newspaper had to be smuggled into the Philippines and read in secret by the people. Funds for its maintenance came from the colony, the pockets of the propagandists themselves, and contributions from Spanish and other foreign sympathizers. Due to lack of enough funds, however, the newspaper was forced to cease publication after its final edition came out on November 15, 1895.

In the end, the Propaganda Movement did not succeed in obtaining the reforms it demanded for various reasons. The reformists themselves were not united; there were several rival groups, with each group having different ideas on what to do. Within the groups themselves, there were jealousies and intrigues.

There came a time when the propagandists were divided into two camps. One was headed by Jose Rizal and the other by Marcelo H. del Pilar. Rizal left Spain in 1890 so del Pilar could assume the leadership. Another reason of the movement's failure was lack of funds and support. Among the leaders of the propagandists, del Pilar, Panganiban and Lopez Jaena died penniless in Spain.

The Propaganda Movement, despite its failure, contributed to the development of Filipino nationalism and helped pave the way for the Philippine Revolution.

La Liga Filipina. In 1892, Rizal returned to the Philippines to continue the peaceful campaign for reforms. In July of that year, he organized a civic association called *La Liga Filipina* (the Philippine League), one of whose members was Andres Bonifacio, later to establish the Katipunan. The Spaniards felt that the association would pose a threat to Spanish rule. Thus, only four days after its organization, Rizal was arrested and deported to Dapitan, Zamboanga Province. After this, the league became inactive.

Filipinas Heritage Library

Spanish and native guards (*guardia civil*), circa 1892.

From Joaquin V. Fernandez Album, 1892.

Dr. **Jose Rizal.** Considered the most cultured of the reformists, Dr. Jose Rizal was born in Calamba, Laguna, on June 18, 1861. Rizal

first studied under a private tutor in Biñan, Laguna. Then he was sent to Manila to continue his studies at the Ateneo Municipal and later at the University of Santo Tomas.

In 1882, he left for Spain to study medicine. He studied many subjects and mastered several languages. The persecutions of 1872, including the execution of Fathers Gomez, Burgos, and Zamora, made such an impact on his precocious youth at the age of 11 that he became a propagandist.

Rizal was 26 when he completed writing his first novel, *Noli Me Tangere*, in which he depicted prevailing conditions, abuses, and hypocrisy of the Spanish clergy. He finished his second novel, *El Filibusterismo*, in 1891. He always believed that freedom must be attained by peaceful revolution.

In 1892, when Rizal returned to the Philippines, he was arrested and imprisoned in Fort Santiago. Then on July 7, 1892, he was placed in exile in Dapitan. He later was permitted to go to Cuba and enlist as a military doctor. When the ship which took him to Cuba arrived, the revolution there broke out. He returned to Spain.

On reaching Barcelona, Spain, however, he was arrested and returned to the Philippines. He was tried for and found guilty of the baseless charges of treason and involvement with the revolution. He was shot to death on December 30, 1896 at the Luneta in Manila.

VIII. THE KATIPUNAN

In 1893, the Liga Filipina was revived by Domingo Franco, who became its president, and Andres Bonifacio. However, by this time, Bonifacio didn't believe that reforms could be achieved by peaceful means. The Liga became divided, and Bonifacio left the association. Members of the Liga who were behind his idea of reform joined him in the Katipunan.

The Katipunan was organized after Bonifacio and some trusted friends met in the house of Deodato Arellano in Tondo, Manila. There, they organized a secret society called *the Kataastaasan, Kagalang-galang na Katipunan ng mga Anak ng Bayan.* It was later known as the Katipunan or by its initials KKK.

The KKK's political objective was the separation of the Philippines from Spain. Actually, its organization basically followed that of La Liga Filipina, of which Bonifacio had been a leading member. The highest body was called the *Kataastaasang Sanggunian* or Supreme Council. Each province was to have a *sangguniang bayan* or provincial council and each town a *sangguniang balangay* or municipal council.

When the membership of the Katipunan had increased to more than a hundred, Bonifacio divided the members of the Katipunan into three grades. They were *katipon, kawal* (soldier), and *bayani* (patriot). A katipon, whose password was *Anak ng Bayan* (son of the nation), could be upgraded to kawal class if he could recruit several members, and at the same time the kawal could become a bayani.

Later, women joined the society. However, Bonifacio limited them to the wives, daughters, and sisters of the male members. Their duty was to recruit new members, whether male or female, and ensure that the meetings of the men were not disturbed by surprise raids.

Ang Kalayaan. The association didn't have a printing press. However, two *Katipuneros* from the Visayas, Candido Iban and Francisco del Castillo, who returned to the Philippines from Australia and won a thousand pesos in the lottery, bought the small printing press *Bazar El Cisne*. It was transferred to the house of Bonifacio along Oroquieta Street near Zurbaran, but later was moved to Nicolas, Manila. Thus, the publication *Kalayaan* (freedom) was born.

For several weeks, Dr. Pio Valenzuela, who suggested the name Kalayaan; Ulpiano Fernandez, a printer of the daily newspaper *El Comercio*; and Faustino Duque, a student of the Colegio de San Juan de Letran; took turns as they worked day and night to come out with the newspaper. Its maiden and only issue, dated January 18, 1896, actually came out in the middle of March. There were two thousand copies printed. Marcelo H. del Pilar appeared as editor but, in actuality, the editorial was written by Emilio Jacinto. Among its contents were: *Catuiran?* (Is it Right?) describing the cruelties of the Spanish priests and civil guards of San Francisco del Monte (presently in Quezon City); *Manifesto*, where Jacinto (using the alias *Dimas-Ilaw*) urged the Filipinos to win their freedom from the Spaniards by means of revolt; and *Pag-ibig sa Tinubuang Bayan (Love for One's Country)*, a poem by Bonifacio, who wrote under the pseudonym *Agap-ito Bagumbayan*.

Copies of the paper were secretly distributed in Manila, Cavite, Morong (renamed Rizal Province), Kalookan, and other places.

The paper was well received. Jacinto had prepared a second issue, which would contain nothing but his works. However, the Spanish authorities raided the place where printing was to be undertaken, Thus, the *Kalayaan* never had another issue.

Nevertheless, its first and only issue had succeeded in rousing the masses in central Luzon. Membership in the Katipunan increased. The Katipunan reached the provinces of Bulacan, Cavite, Laguna, Batangas, Nueva Ecija, and Pampanga. From the initial 300 members, the Katipunan's numbers rose to around 30,000.

The Katipunan in Cavite. The Katipuneros in Cavite were divided into two factions, the Magdalo and the Magdiwang. The former, led by Baldomero Aguinaldo, had headquarters in Cavite el Viejo (now Kawit) and the latter, led by Mariano Alvarez, an uncle-in-law of Bonifacio, in Noveleta, Cavite.

3

THE PHILIPPINE REVOLUTION (1896-1898)

In Manila, in its suburbs, and in the provinces of Luzon, the *Katipunan* became the talk of the town. This happened after copies of the publication *Kalayaan* were circulated among the people. However, the new members were rash and impatient so nightly meetings had to be held. It was, thus, inevitable that the suspicions of the authorities were aroused. Rumors about the meetings circulated in Manila and caused worry particularly among the Spanish friars.

In fact, the friars blew the rumors out of proportion to force Spanish Governor-General Blanco, who was unsympathetic to them, to act on the matter. He, however, did not.

The discovery of the Katipunan was the result of a misunderstanding between two Katipuneros. The Katipuneros were Teodoro Patiño and Apolonio de la Cruz. Both of them were working at the Spanish-owned *Diario de Manila*. As an action against de la Cruz, Patiño revealed the secrets of the society to his sister, Honoria, an inmate at the orphanage in Mandaluyong in the suburbs of Manila. She was shocked about the revelation and she cried. A *madre portera*, Sor Teresa saw her

cry. Then the sister asked Patiño to tell all he knew to Father Mariano Gil, the parish priest of Guadalupe and one of those trying to convince Governor-General Blanco to act quickly.

In the afternoon of August 19, 1896, Patiño disclosed the secrets he knew to Father Gil. The friar rushed to the printing shop of *Diario de Manila* and, with its owner, conducted a search of the premises. The friar sought hidden evidence of the existence of the secret society. They found the lithographic stone used to print Katipunan receipts, which was confirmed by Patiño. "So here they are," Father Gil might have whispered. A locker was forced open. There he found a dagger and other documents.

"Arrest Them!" A series of arrests of prominent Filipinos, took place. Even the innocent ones, were thrown in jail or imprisoned at Fort Santiago in Manila. The implication of some was the offset of a quirk of fate. The wealthy Filipinos had refused to join the Katipunan. So Andres Bonifacio, head of the Katipunan, thought that drawing up a list to make it appear that numerous wealthy Filipinos were contributing to the cause would force them to join.

Instead of being coerced to join, however, these wealthy Filipinos denounced or denied any knowledge of the existence of the Katipunan. The authorities did not believe them. One of the prominent men, Francisco L. Roxas, was executed.

Emergency Assembly. The news of the discovery of the Katipunan spread rapidly. Upon learning of this, Bonifacio told his runners to call all the leaders for an emergency general assembly to be held on August 24, in Balintawak, Caloocan. On the night of August 19, he, his brother Procopio, Emilio Jacinto, Teodoro Plata, and Aguedo del Rosario were able to slip past the Spanish sentries in the area. Before midnight, they were in Balintawak.

On August 21, Bonifacio changed their code as the original one had been broken by the Spaniards. Afterwards, about 500 of the rebels went to Kangkong from Balintawak—then, to Pugadlawin. On August 23, Bonifacio met his men in the yard of Juan A. Ramos, son of Melchora Aquino, who later became known as the "Mother of the Katipunan." Bonifacio asked his men if they were committed to carry on the fight. Against the objections of Teodoro Plata, all agreed to fight until the last drop of blood.

To symbolize the commitment for an armed struggle, Bonifacio led his men in tearing up their *cedulas*, (residence certificate),

shouting: "*Mabuhay ang Filipinas*!" ("Long live the Philippines"). For some time, the event was commemorated in the Philippines as the "Cry of Balintawak." Later, it was corrected to the "Cry of Pugadlawin."

I. START OF THE REVOLUTION

Bang! Bang! Bang!. The first shots of the Philippine Revolution were fired the next day between several Katipuneros and a patrol of Spanish civil guards. That happened in the *sitio* of Pasong Tamo in Kalookan.

However, the first real battle of the revolution took place on August 30, 1896. Bonifacio, with about 800 Katipuneros, attacked the Spanish arsenal in San Juan del Monte, which is now the municipality of San Juan in Metro Manila. The Spaniards were outnumbered and weak. But reinforcements turned the tide in their favor. The Katipuneros were forced to retreat. They left more than 150 Katipuneros dead and many more captured.

The revolution spread to several Luzon provinces nearby. This prompted Governor-General Ramon Blanco to place the first eight provinces to revolt against Spanish sovereignty under martial law. They were Manila, Laguna, Bulacan, Batangas, Cavite, Pampanga, Tarlac, and Nueva Ecija.

Governor-General Blanco also included in the decree the condition that anyone who would surrender within 48 hours after its publication would not be tried in military courts. Some Katipuneros were duped into surrendering, only to be subjected to torture. Due to torture, some Katipuneros revealed the names of some of the other Katipuneros.

Hundreds of suspects were arrested and imprisoned. Those from the provinces were brought to Manila. Fort Santiago became so crowded that many Filipinos who were thrown there for suspicion of involvement in the revolution were suffocated to death. Hundreds of

Dr. Jose Rizal's execution at the Luneta on December 30, 1896.

heads of families were transported to the Carolines or to the Spanish penal colony in faraway Africa.

A great number of Filipinos were executed at the Luneta, most notable of whom was Jose Rizal. He was shot at the old Bagumbayan Field on December 30, 1896. This was ironic as Rizal was innocent of the charge of rebellion. He was recognized by the Katipuneros for his intellectual accomplishments. However, he rejected their invitations for him to join the Katipunan. To his death, Rizal had remained a reformist.

All the tortures and executions, however, embittered the Filipinos more and fanned the fires of revolution in their hearts. The revolu-

tion continued to spread throughout the archipelago.

Revolution in Cavite. There, the rebels stormed the municipal building of San Francisco de Malabon on August 31, 1896. The Magdiwang group also attacked the Spaniards in Noveleta. In Cavite el Viejo, the Magdalo group, under Candido Tirona (a bosom friend of Emilio Aguinaldo), captured the Spanish garrison while Emilio Aguinaldo and his men tried but failed to intercept Spanish reinforcements from Manila.

Aguinaldo retreated to Imus, Cavite Province. There on September 5, 1896, he defeated the Spanish command of General Aguirre. Thus, Aguinaldo returned to Imus the hero of the hour, no longer *Kapitan* (Captain) Miong but *Heneral* (General) Miong.

Emilio Aguinaldo. An *ilustrado*, Emilio Aguinaldo studied at San Juan de Letran College. However, he quit his studies when his father died so that he could take care of the family farm and could engage in business. When the revolution broke out, he was the mayor of Cavite el Viejo (now Kawit), where he was born on March 22, 1869. A cousin of Baldomero Aguinaldo, leader of the Magdalo faction, Emilio joined the Katipunan when he was 25.

Betrayal. There were early signs that the rebels in Cavite were leaning towards the establishment of a new leadership and government. On October 31, 1896, General Aguinaldo issued two decrees. They both stated that the aim of the Revolution was the independence of the Philippines. Therefore, he urged Filipinos to fight for freedom, following the example of civilized European and American nations. He also proclaimed "Liberty, Equality, and Fraternity" as watchwords of the revolution.

Although the Magdalo was only one of the two factions of the Katipunan in Cavite, Aguinaldo, who belonged to this faction, made no mention of the parent organization. The letter K appeared on the seal of both documents, though. One manifesto announced that they (implying the Magdalo faction) had formed a provisional government in the towns that had been "pacified." It was the government's task to pursue the war until all of the archipelago was free.

According to author Renato Constantino, one was forced to conclude that Aguinaldo and the other leaders of the Magdalo had decided at this early stage to withdraw recognition of the Katipunan and install themselves as leaders of the revolution.

Cavite. The Spaniards decided to concentrate on Cavite, after they had been defeated in other places. Governor-General Blanco ordered attacks on rebel troops in early November. But they suffered heavy losses in Binakayan and Noveleta, Cavite. (Aguinaldo led the Filipinos. Many died, including Carlos Tirona.)

As a result of the defeats of the Spaniards, Governor-General Blanco was relieved upon the instigation of the friars. He was replaced by General Camilo de Polavieja on December 13, 1896. Little by little, de Polavieja was able to recapture about a third of Cavite.

Divided They Fall. The disunity between the rival Magdalo and Magdiwang factions of the Katipunan in Cavite fought independently of each other. This was a major factor for the success of General Polavieja in his victories in Cavite. Realizing this, the Magdiwang faction asked Bonifacio, who had refused because he was needed in Morong (now Rizal Province), to mediate. Later, he finally accepted the invitation.

In the latter part of December 1896, Bonifacio went to Cavite with his wife and brothers Procopio and Ciriaco. They were personally met in Zapote by Aguinaldo and other leaders. Bonifacio was received enthusiastically by the Caviteños.

However, in his memoirs, General Artemio Ricarte recounted that a few days after Bonifacio's arrival, black propaganda against Bonifacio in the form of anonymous letters circulated all over Cavite. The letters described him as unworthy of being idolized. The letter writers called him a mason, an atheist, an uneducated man, and a mere employee of a German firm.

On December 31, the Imus assembly was convened to determine the leadership in the province. The purpose was to end the rivalry between the two factions. The Magdalo group wanted a revolutionary government to supplant the Katipunan. Such an idea was objected to by the Magdiwang faction that maintained that the Katipunan already had a constitution and by-laws recognized by all. The meeting ended without a resolution of the conflict.

First Meeting at Tejeros: The End of the Katipunan. With the continuing successes of Spanish campaigns against them, the Katipuneros decided to have another meeting on March 22, 1897, to discuss how Cavite should be defended. This was not even touched on. Instead, it was decided that an election of officers of the revolutionary government be held. That meant that the Supreme Council of the Katipunan was being discarded, and that would be the end of the Katipunan.

Bonifacio reluctantly agreed to chair the assembly. Before the voting was started, he admonished everyone that whoever was elected to any position should be respected. Ironically, after the elections, Bonifacio, founder of the Katipunan and initiator of the revolutionary struggle in the country, lost the leadership to Emilio Aguinaldo, who was voted president. Bonifacio was merely elected to the minor post of director of the interior. None of the other leaders of the Katipunan, not even Emilio Jacinto, were considered for positions at Tejeros.

When Bonifacio was being proclaimed, Daniel Tirona, a Magdalo, had even questioned this on the grounds that the position should not be held by someone without a lawyer's diploma. The angry Bonifacio demanded a retraction from Tirona, who, instead, turned to leave. Bonifacio was about to shoot Tirona when Artemio Ricarte intervened.

As the people began to leave the hall, Bonifacio shouted that he, in his capacity as chairman of the assembly and president of the Supreme Council of the Katipunan,

declared the assembly dissolved and annulled all that had been approved and resolved. Then he left with his men.

Second Meeting at Tejeros: A Confrontation. Aguinaldo, engaged in a battle in Pasong Santol, a barrio in Cavite, was not present during the elections. He was notified of his election to presidency in Pasong Santol the following day. He was later convinced by his elder brother, Crispulo, to leave his men and take his oath of office. Thus, he and the others who had been elected the day before, except Bonifacio, took their oath of office in Santa Cruz de Malabon (now Tanza), Cavite.

Among those who were installed in office were Emilio Aguinaldo, president; Mariano Trias, vice president; Artemio Ricarte, captain-general; Emiliano Riego de Dios, director of war; Pascual Alvarez, director of the interior; and Severino de las Alas, director of justice.

In the meantime, Bonifacio and his remaining men of about 45 met at the estate house in Tejeros on March 23, 1897. They drew up a document, now called the *Acta de Tejeros*, where they cited their reasons for not accepting the results of the first Tejeros convention. From there, they went to Naic to get away from the Magdalo faction, which they held responsible for the anomalies during the election. Aguinaldo sent a delegation to Bonifacio to try to convince him to cooperate with the new revolutionary government, which the latter rebuffed.

Rival Government. In Naic, Bonifacio and his men prepared another document. The agreement specified the establishment of a government independent from Aguinaldo's revolutionary government. Called the Naic Military Agreement, it also rejected the first Tejeros convention and reasserted Bonifacio as leader of the revolution. To be organized was an army whose members were to be recruited by persuasive or coercive means.

Among the 41 signatories were Bonifacio, Artemio Ricarte, Pio del Pilar as commander-in-chief and Emilio Jacinto as general of the North Military Area (provinces of Morong, Bulacan, Nueva Ecija, and Manila).

Emilio Jacinto. The so-called "Brains of the Katipunan," Emilio Jacinto, was born in Tondo, Manila on December 15, 1875. Her parents were Mariano Jacinto and Josefa Dizon. At a young age, he learned how to speak a kind of Spanish, sort of pidgin Spanish, on the streets. Although the family was poor, his parents managed to send him to school. He first studied at San Juan de Letran College and later at the University of Santo Tomas. However, as a member of the Katipunan, he was forced to speak Tagalog, the language of the Katipuneros.

He painstakingly mastered Tagalog and wrote most of his articles in this language. Because of his honesty and intelligence, he became the trusted friend and adviser of Bonifacio. The two were almost inseparable until late December 1896, when Bonifacio went to Cavite to sort out the differences between two rival factions of the Katipunan and Jacinto went to Laguna as commander-in-chief. However, they kept in constant communication. Jacinto died of a fever on April 16, 1899 in Mahayhay, Laguna.

Besides the *Kartilla*, which became the primer for the Katipuneros, he wrote *Pahayag* or *Manifesto* (which had appeared in the only issue of *Kalayaan*), *Liwanag at Dilim (Light and Darkness)*, *Sa mga Kababayan Ko (To My Countrymen)*, *Ang Kasalanan ni Cain (Cain's Sin)*, *Pagkatatag ng Pamahalaan sa Hukuman ng Silangan (Establishment of the Provincial Government of Laguna)*, and *Samahan ng Bayan sa Pangangalakal (Commercial Association of the People)*.

Death of Bonifacio. Bonifacio moved from Naic to the barrio of Limbon in Indang, Cavite. He was accompanied by his wife, two brothers, and a few loyal soldiers. By then, Aguinaldo had learned of the Naic Military Agreement. He immediately ordered Colonel Agapito Bonzon and a group of soldiers to arrest the Bonifacio brothers. *"Dakpin sila!"* ("Arrest them!") he might have said.

In the ensuing confrontation, Bonifacio was stabbed in the larynx but taken alive. His brother Ciriaco was killed, while his brother Procopio was wounded. Bonifacio was transported in a hammock to Naic, the capital of the revolutionary government.

General Mascardo
Jim Zwick Collection

From April 29 to May 4, Bonifacio was placed on trial, together with Procopio, by the Council of War. General Tomas Mascardo was one of the members of the Council of War that tried the Bonifacio brothers.

Despite the lack of evidence, the Bonifacio brothers were found guilty of treason and sedition and recommended to be executed. Aguinaldo commuted the sentence to deportation on May 8, 1897, but Generals Mariano Noriel and Pio del Pilar, both former supporters of Bonifacio, upon learning of this, immediately asked General Aguinaldo to withdraw his order. Their reason was that there would be no unity among the revolutionaries as long as Bonifacio was alive. They were supported by other leaders.

Aguinaldo withdrew his order for reversal of the death sentence. As for Severino de las Alas, it was he who had made the false accusations against Bonifacio.

On May 10, General Noriel ordered Major Lazaro Makapagal to bring the Bonifacio brothers to Mount Tala near Maragondon. He was also given a sealed letter to be opened and read upon reaching their destination. The letter contained orders to execute Andres and Procopio Bonifacio. He was warned that severe punishment would follow if he failed to comply with the order. Hence, Makapagal made no hesitation to carry out the execution. Bonifacio and his brother were buried in shallow graves marked only by a few twigs.

Andres Bonifacio. The founder and organizer of the Katipunan, Andres Bonifacio was born on November 30, 1863, in Tondo (then a province of Manila), a son of Santiago Bonifacio and Catalina de Castro. He learned the alphabet in a school. When his parents died, he was forced to quit school as he had to become the breadwinner for his three brothers and two sisters.

As a livelihood, Bonifacio made canes and paper fans to sell. He loved books and was able to do some self-studying. In his late teens, he landed a job as clerk-messenger at Fleming and Company, where he was promoted to agent. He sold rattan, tar and other products of the firm. Later, he moved to Fressel and Company, also as an agent.

He read *Noli Me Tangere* and *El Filibusterismo*, *The Ruins of Palmyra*, *Les Miserables*, *The Wandering Jew*, and read about the presidents of the United States, international law, the penal and civil codes, a book on the French Revolution and some novels.

At a young age, he married a certain Monica. The marriage did not last long as she died of leprosy. In 1892, he met Gregoria de Jesus of Kalookan, who became his second wife. Gregoria later joined the women's chapter of the Katipunan.

Bonifacio adopted Emilio Jacinto's *Kartilla* as the official teachings of the society. Although its founder, he didn't intend to become president of the Katipunan. However, he became president when the first two presidents did not come up to expectations.

II. THE BIAK-NA-BATO REPUBLIC

Maragondon, Cavite, became the new rebel capital after the Spanish forces had captured Naic. However, many of the Spanish soldiers had just arrived from Spain and they suffered greatly from the tropical climate.

General Camilo de Polavieja requested that he be relieved as governor-general. On April 23, 1897, he was replaced by former governor-general of the Philippines, Fernando Primo de Rivera. Against Primo de Rivera, Aguinaldo and his men were forced to retreat to Batangas Province by Spanish forces.

The Spaniards gained control of practically the whole of Cavite. Thus, Primo de Rivera extended a decree granting pardon for those Filipinos surrendering beyond the initial deadline of May 17. There were some Filipinos who took advantage, but the others continued their fight.

Aguinaldo, who had established his headquarters in Talisay, Batangas Province, managed to escape the Spaniards who had surrounded the place. Then he proceeded with his men to the hilly province of Morong (now Metro Manila). From there, he and about 500 handpicked men went to Biyak-na-Bato, San Miguel de Mayumo, in Bulacan. There, Aguinaldo established a new government, which is now known as the Biak-na-Bato Republic.

He also issued a proclamation in July entitled "To the Brave Sons of the Philippines." The proclamation enumerated the revolutionary demands as:

1. Expulsion of the friars and the return to the Filipinos of the lands they appropriated for themselves.

2. Representation in the Spanish Cortes, freedom of press, and tolerance of all religious sects.

3. Equal treatment and pay for peninsular and insular civil servants and abolition of the power of the government to banish citizens.

4. Legal equality for all persons.

This proclamation showed that Aguinaldo was still willing to return to the Spanish fold if these demands were met. That was in spite of the fact that he and his men had already established the Biak-na-Bato Republic.

The constitution of the new republic was prepared by Felix Ferrer and Isabelo Artacho. They copied it almost verbatim from the Cuban Constitution of Jimaguayu. It was signed on November 1, 1897. In accordance with Article I, a Supreme Council was created on November. Aguinaldo was elected president.

Peace! Peace! Peace! Governor-General Primo de Rivera realized that he might not be able to quell the rebellion. Hence, he tried to end it by peaceful negotiations.

The chance came when Pedro A. Paterno, a *mestizo* who had spent some years in Spain, offered to act as a peace negotiator. On August 9, 1897, Paterno brought Primo de Tavera's offer of peace to Aguinaldo's headquarters. It took four months before Paterno was able to come up with a peace agreement, now called the Pact of Biak-na-Bato, signed by Paterno as representative of the revolutionists and Primo de Rivera for the Spanish government.

Made up of three separate documents, the peace pact was signed on December 14 and 15, 1897. The pact provided for an end to the revolution by the laying down of arms by the revolutionary forces of Aguinaldo. They would then be granted amnesty and allowed to return to their homes. Aguinaldo and the other leaders would go on voluntary exile to Hong Kong. They would be given P800,000 by the Spanish government in three installments:

1. P400,000 upon leaving the Philippines.
2. P200,000 when at least 700 arms have been surrendered.
3. the balance upon declaration of a general amnesty.

Spain also promised to pay P900,000 to Filipino civilians who suffered losses because of the revolution. (Renato Constantino: *The Philippines: A Past Revisited*).

To be sure that the Spaniards were to make good their promises, Aguinaldo's camp demanded that two Spanish generals remain at Biyak-na-Bato as hostages. Also, Colonel Miguel Primo de Rivera, the governor's nephew, was also required by the Aguinaldo camp to accompany the exiles to Hong Kong.

On December 27, 1897, Aguinaldo, with a check for P400,000, left for Hong Kong with 25 revolutionary leaders. Those left behind asked Primo de Rivera to give them the balance of P400,000, supposedly to be given to the needy ones among them. Instead, they were given P200,000, which they then divided among themselves.

Continuation of Hostilities. There was celebration in Manila the following month. However, although some of the Filipino generals left behind did all they could to surrender the arms from the rebels, some of them were suspicious of the Spaniards. Thus, they declined to give up their arms. One of them, General Francisco Makabulos of Tarlac Province, established the Central Executive Committee, which would exist until a general government of the republic would again be established. For their part, the lower-ranking Spanish authorities continued to arrest and imprison many Filipinos suspected of having been involved in the rebellion.

Thus, the rebellion spread further to the different provinces of the archipelago. including Zambales, Pampanga, Laguna, Pangasinan, Nueva Ecija, Tarlac, La Union, Ilocos Sur, Cebu, Bulacan, Caloocan, and Camarines Norte. Far from mere banditry, as the Spaniards termed these acts of resistance, they were, on the contrary, attempts to achieve the objectives of the old Katipunan. The Pact of Biak-na-Bato was thus a cessation of hostilities only for the compromisers, Aguinaldo and his group. For the people, the struggle continued.

Filipino soldiers during the revolution.

III. SPANISH-AMERICAN RELATIONS

In 1817, the United States established a consulate in Manila. After the Philippines was opened to world trade in 1834, several American companies established businesses in Manila.

Even before 1898, American ships already had been sailing to Manila to trade with the Philippines. The first American ship to reach Manila was the *Astrea* in the later part of the 18th century.

In the meantime, in February 1895, Cuba, which Christopher Columbus had discovered for Spain in 1492 to become a colony, revolted against the Spaniards. In answer, Spanish General Valeriano Weyler, commander of all Spanish forces in Cuba, established concentration camps for the rebels and sympathizers. Being close to the United States, many American businessmen had large investments in Cuba, especially in the sugar industry. Thus, it was not difficult to obtain American support for the Cuban cause.

In January 1898, President William McKinley sent the U.S. Navy battleship *Maine* to Cuba in case American citizens needed to be evacuated. However, on February 15, 1898, an explosion sank the ship in the Havana harbor. This resulted in the loss of 260 of the crewmen and in a huge outcry from the American public.

Earlier, on February 9, 1898, a private letter from Enrique Dupuy de Lome, the Spanish minister to the United States, which had been stolen from a post office in Havana was published in the *New York Journal*. It described President McKinley as a "would-be politician" and a weak president.

The sinking of the *USS Maine* added fuel to an American public already enraged against the Spaniards because of the letter, although an investigation had failed to establish who was responsible for the explosion.

On February 25, 1898, Commodore George Dewey in Hong Kong received a directive from the United States. He was ordered to take his Asiatic squadron to Manila and attack Spanish forces in the Philippines should war break out between Spain and the United States.

Although President McKinley wished to avoid war with Spain, which also wanted to avoid a war with the United States, he ultimately had to give in to pressure from his own Republican Party. On April 11, 1898, he recommended direct American intervention in Cuba to the United States Congress, which voted for war with Spain.

Meanwhile, Spanish Governor-General Primo de Rivera was relieved of his position after the Conservative Party in Spain, to which he belonged, was replaced by the Liberal Party. His replacement, Governor-General Basilio Augustin, knew nothing about conditions in the Philippines. Primo de Rivera had wanted to stay there for a while in the event that Spanish-American relations might turn into a shooting war, in which case it would not have been practical to have a new governor-general in the Philippines.

Governor General Augustin arrived on April 9, 1898. He announced he would continue his predecessor's work of pacification and then assumed a wait-and-see position.

The Battle of Manila Bay. On April 25, 1898, Commodore George Dewey, upon orders, proceeded at once to the Philippines with a squadron of four armored cruisers, two gunboats, and a revenue cutter. It was led by the flagship *Olympia*. They entered Manila Bay in the early morning of May 1, 1898, and engaged the Spanish fleet of 12 ships, headed by Admiral Patricio Montojo, in a battle that lasted for only a few hours.

The more-modern American warships, although fewer in number, proved to be superior to the old and weaker Spanish vessels. The not-so-hard-fought Battle of Manila Bay was one of the most significant battles in American history because it established the United States as a world power.

For the Philippines, it signalled the end of more than 300 years of Spanish colonial rule. It also signalled the start of a new colonial rule, this time under the Americans. Dewey requested for army reinforcements because he had no troops to capture Manila. All he could do while waiting was blockade Manila Bay.

Admiral Patricio Montojo's flagship *Reina Cristina* destroyed by Admiral Dewey's
fleet at the Battle of Manila Bay on May 1, 1898.

Spanish prisoners of war captured by Americans in Manila (1898).

IV. THE EXILES IN HONG KONG

In Hong Kong, the Filipino exiles followed closely the developments in the Philippines and the conflict between Spain and the United States. They thought of seeking American assistance in their revolutionary cause against the Spaniards. In the meantime, there was a problem regarding disposal of the P400,000 from Governor-General Primo de Rivera, under the terms of the Pact of Biak-na-Bato.

Isabelo Artacho wanted the money to be divided among themselves. When Aguinaldo refused, Artacho sued him in the Hong Kong Supreme Court. To escape the inconvenience of having to go to court, Aguinaldo, with Gregorio del Pilar and J. Leyba, secretly went to Singapore and arrived there on April 23,

General Pio del Pilar, Aguinaldo's body-guard.

1898. In the afternoon, Howard Bray, an Englishman who had been living in Singapore, gave Aguinaldo the message that E. Spencer Pratt, the American consul, wanted to talk with him.

It turned out that the Americans were thinking of winning the Filipinos over to their side should hostilities between the U.S. and Spain take a turn for the worst.

Pratt gave the impression to Aguinaldo that the Americans would not colonize the Philippines. He said that if they were going to leave Cuba ("which is just at our door") alone after driving the Spaniards away, why would they want the Philippines, which was 10,000 miles away. Aguinaldo then consented to return with Commodore Dewey to the Philippines to once more lead the revolution against Spain, fighting alongside the Americans.

Dewey had already sailed for Manila when Aguinaldo returned to Hong Kong. But Rounseville Wildman, American consul in Hong Kong, told him that Dewey had left instructions that Aguinaldo's return to the Philippines be arranged. He and Wildman met several times after this. He later suggested that Aguinaldo establish a dictatorial government, which was needed in the prosecution of the war against Spain, but it had to be replaced with a government similar to that of the United States once the war was over and peace was restored. Wildman and Pratt assured Aguinaldo that their government sympathized with the Filipinos' aspirations for independence, but they did not make any formal commitment.

"What Shall We Do?" On May 4, Filipinos comprising what was called the Hong Kong *Junta* met to discuss what to do in the light of the new developments.

Those present were Felipe Agoncillo, temporary president; Doroteo Lopez, temporary secretary; and Teodoro Sandico, Anastacio Francisco, Mariano Llanera, Miguel Malvar, Andres Garchitorena, Severo Buenaventura,

Maximo Kabigting, Faustino Lichauco, Antonio Montenegro, and Galicano Apacible. Aguinaldo apprised them of what transpired in his meetings with Pratt and Wildman, and asked for their advice on what to do. After discussions, the *Junta* unanimously decided that Aguinaldo should return to the Philippines to lead the struggle against the Spaniards.

Have Guns, Will Fight. In preparation for his return to the Philippines, Aguinaldo gave Wildman P117,000 to be used in buying guns and ammunition. The first shipment for P50,000 arrived promptly, but Aguinaldo never learned from the consul where the rest of the money went.

Aguinaldo's Return to the Philippines. Consul Wildman arranged Aguinaldo's return on the revenue cutter *McCulloch,* which he and his companions boarded at night to avoid rousing the suspicion of the Spanish consul in Hong Kong.

On May 17, 1898, the ship left and arrived in Cavite two days later. Aguinaldo was then taken to the *Olympia,* where he was accorded honors due a general. Aguinaldo reportedly said that in their conference Dewey had given him assurance that the United States would recognize Philippine independence, which Dewey, however, denied. It is suggested that, there being no sufficient evidence to prove Aguinaldo's statement, he had mistakenly thought that Dewey was speaking for the American government.

Renato Constantino *(The Philippines: A Past Revisited)* points out that historians have treated the time when Aguinaldo was in Hong Kong as a period when the revolution was put on hold. That was during a time when he and others in Hong Kong were planning its resumption and, with this view, the acts of resistance in the country while Aguinaldo was away were "dismissed as if they were not part of the revolutionary stream.... Actually, the different manifestations of resistance which Aguinaldo so cavalierly branded as banditry just because he had chosen to surrender were the continuing expression of the people's determination to fight for the goals of the Katipunan."

Then, Aguinaldo was again in the Philippines, ready to lead the very ones he had branded bandits.

With Aguinaldo's return to the Philippines, Constantino saw "four major forces on the historical stage":

1. Spanish colonialism, which was trying to ward off its impending end.

2. American imperialism, which was waiting for such time when it had gathered sufficient military strength in the Philippines before showing its real motives.

3. The Filipino ilustrados, whose main concern was to place themselves in a jockeying position whatever political setup was to emerge. (However, their ultimate objective was supposedly independence, but they were ready to accept becoming an American protectorate or even annexation, just as they readily accepted continuing Spanish rule after the Pact of Biak-na-Bato).

4. And the masses, who still believed in and fought for the revolutionary objectives of the Katipunan.

The people showed that they could continue the struggle without the leadership of those who entered into the Pact of Biak-na-Bato. However, they were unaware of the "dangers that its (leadership) inherently compromising nature posed for the goal of independence."

On May 21, 1898, two days after he arrived, Aguinaldo in a letter advised the people to "respect foreigners and their properties, also enemies who surrender...if we do not conduct ourselves thus the Americans will decide to sell us or else divide up our territory as they will hold us incapable of governing our land, we shall not secure our liberty; rather the contrary; our own soil will be delivered over to other hands."

When news of Aguinaldo's arrival spread, a number of Filipino volunteers in the Spanish army defected to the Filipino side. They were assigned to occupy Dalahikan, the Cavite shipyard, to prevent it from falling into the hands of the Spaniards. Munitions were obtained from the captain of the American warship *Petrel*.

By the end of May, with the growing number of revolutionary supporters, 5,000 Spaniards had been captured. Within a week, Imus and Bacood, in Cavite, and Parañaque and Las Piñas in Morong, were seized from Spanish control, so with San Fernando and Macabebe in Pampanga. Joining the fight for freedom were the provinces of Laguna, Batangas, Bulacan, Nueva Ecija, Bataan, Tayabas (Quezon), and Camarines.

Spanish Last-Ditch Attempts. Governor-General Augustin was demoralized by the defection of the Filipinos from the Spanish army to Aguinaldo's side and Dewey's victory over the Spanish fleet on Manila Bay. Nevertheless, he desperately tried to save the situation.

In May, he issued two decrees creating a Filipino Volunteer Militia and a Consultative Assembly. His purpose was to win over the ilustrados, whom he appointed to both bodies. However, this backfired because all of those appointed in the militia instead joined Aguinaldo. On the other hand, the Consultative Assembly, which was headed by Pedro Paterno, the negotiator of the Pact of Biak-na-Bato and who appealed to the Filipinos to stand by Spain, accomplished nothing.

Cavite Falls. The renewed revolution after Aguinaldo's arrival from Hongkong immediately became a success. By June 2, 1898, General Artemio Ricarte accepted the surrender of the Spanish commanding general in Cavite.

The Filipinos gained victory after victory. Within the month of June 1898, almost the whole of Luzon (except for the port of Cavite and Manila) had fallen into rebel hands. It was these victories by the people that "gave substance to the legal institutions the ilustrados were establishing.

American Duplicity. All the while, the Americans waited for reinforcements. Aguinaldo was treated with the courtesies befitting a head of state. Playing safe, the Americans took care not to make any commitments at the same time, continuing to let the Filipinos think they meant well. Their motive was to use the Filipinos to fight the Spaniards until reinforcements arrived.

The Siege of Manila. The Walled City (Intramuros) was then known as the City of Manila. (The outlying districts were the *arrabales* or suburbs.)

When the Spanish navy was destroyed, many Spaniards had taken refuge there. When Dewey did not bombard the city after winning the Battle of Manila Bay, the Spanish became optimistic. They didn't know that he was just waiting for reinforcements. However, Aguinaldo seized the opportunity to besiege the city and cut off its food and water supply to force the Spaniards out. Aguinaldo offered the option of surrender three times, with generous terms, to Governor-General Augustin but these were rebuffed.

V. DICTATORIAL GOVERNMENT

When Aguinaldo had arrived from Hong Kong, he had with him a draft of a plan drawn up by Mariano Ponce. The plan was for the establishment of a revolutionary government. However, he was prevailed upon by his adviser, Ambrosio Rianzares Bautista, to form a dictatorial government instead. On May 24, 1898, Aguinaldo issued a decree formally establishing such form of government, albeit temporary in nature. The decree also nullified the orders issued under the Biak-na-Bato Republic.

Having a government in operation, Aguinaldo then deemed it necessary to declare the independence of the Philippines against the objections of Apolinario Mabini, who had become his unofficial adviser.

Mabini considered it more important before declaring independence to first reorganize the government into one that could prove to the foreign powers its competence and stability. It was Aguinaldo who won.

Apolinario Mabini: The Brains of the Katipunan. Born in Talaga, Tanauan, Batangas Province, Apolinario Mabini played an important role in the Aguinaldo government. Born of poor parents, his poverty did not deter him from pursuing high studies. His mother wanted him to become a priest. However, he opted to study law, and he received his degree in 1894 from the University of Santo Tomas.

In 1896, he contracted an illness that left him paralyzed in the lower limbs. He had been arrested on suspicion of involvement in the revolution, but he was released when the Spaniards saw he was paralyzed. However, in truth, he did have some involvement, having been a member of Rizal's reformist *La Liga Filipina*.

While taking his vacation in Los Baños, Laguna, in 1898, he was fetched by Aguinaldo's men. The men alternated in carrying him in his hammock. Afterwards, he was made Aguinaldo's adviser. Those envious of his position regarded him the "Dark Chamber of the President," but he is better known in history as the "Brains of the Revolution" and the "Sublime Paralytic.""

VI. PROCLAMATION OF PHILIPPINE INDEPENDENCE

On June 12, 1898, Philippine independence was proclaimed in Kawit, Cavite. The Philippine flag, which had been hand-sewn by Marcela Agoncillo in Hong Kong, was first offi-

Muzzle-loading cannons mounted on the walls of Intramuros in the area of Fort Santiago, Manila.

cially raised. Also, the *Marcha Nacional Filipina*, the Philippine national anthem composed by Julian Felipe, was first played in public. The declaration of independence was patterned after the American Declaration of Independence. It was signed by 98 persons.

Revolutionary Government. For his part, Apolinario Mabini considered the declaration of independence premature and inadequate, due to the lack of participation of the people. Thus, he urged Aguinaldo to change the form of government from dictatorial to revolutionary. That was done on June 23, 1898. The decree also provided for the creation of Congress.

VII. BACK TO THE WALLED CITY

While the Walled City was under naval blockade from the Manila Bay, in June and July, 1898, Aguinaldo had already accomplished a complete tight land siege around the city. For the fourth time, on July 7 (since August 1896) Aguinaldo made another demand from the Spanish general to surrender.

The Spanish official, however, refused to do so upon instruction from Madrid. He was ordered that if it was inevitable to surrender, he should surrender to the Americans, not to the Filipinos.

American troops on sailing ship in the Philippine Islands, 1898.

(In another development, on July 15, 1898, the first cabinet appointments were made. Aguinaldo's cabinet was composed of ilustrados, most of whom had been on the Spanish side. It is also noteworthy that Cayetano Arellano, who was held in high regard even by the Spaniards, was offered the post of secretary of foreign affairs. However, he declined, pretending to be ill because his loyalties lay with the Americans. Mabini later accepted the position.)

Provinces Recovered One by One. By the time the Battle of Manila was to be held, other parts of the country were already in complete control of Aguinaldo's forces. In July, the provinces of La Union, Pangasinan, and Mindoro were taken. Generals Manuel and Casimiro Tinio went to Ilocos from Nueva Ecija to Ilocus Sur. Other forces were sent to Antique and Capiz.

Surrender Negotiations. After fresh American troops arrived on June 30, July 17, and July 31, 1898, Dewey started negotiating with Governor-General Augustin and with Belgian Consul, Andre, acting as go-between for the surrender of the Spaniards. Word about this reached the Peninsular Government, which immediately replaced Augustin with General Fermin Jaudenes. The two powers then very secretly agreed to stage a mock battle between them on one condition—that no Filipino troops would be allowed to enter Manila, clearly an act of betrayal of the Filipinos on the part of the Americans.

American troops standing at attention in the Philippine Islands (1898).

Mock Battle of Manila. All along, Aguinaldo and his forces guarded the city, and waited for the Spaniards to give in to hunger and thirst and surrender. After the secret deal between the Americans and the Spaniards, General Merritt, who had overall command of the American forces, decided to conduct the "offensive" against Manila from the side of Manila Bay.

General Francis Greene, who headed the second reinforcements, was instructed to tell Aguinaldo and his troops to show their cooperation with the Americans by leaving the area free for the foreigners to occupy. Although Aguinaldo showed caution by demanding that this request be made in writing, he gullibly withdrew his troops when Greene promised to grant that request after the evacuation. But Greene reneged on his promise.

Aguinaldo started to get suspicious about the continuous arrival of American reinforcements. He considered them unnecessary because the Filipinos had the situation well in hand. His sentiments were shared by his generals. They did not, however, do anything about this. Therefore, the American troops were able to be installed in place.

On the eve of the mock battle, General Anderson, commander of the first reinforcements, even telegraphed Aguinaldo not to let his troops enter Manila without permission from the American commander or else they would be fired upon.

However, the Filipinos were not to be left out of the assault. On the dark and rainy morning of August 13, 1898, they amassed on the right side of General Arthur MacArthur, who had led the third American reinforcements, ready for battle.

The Americans started their mock attack, with the Filipinos unsuspectingly fighting with all their might. There was token resistance from the Spaniards.

At about 11:20 a.m., the Spaniards raised a flag of surrender, but it was only noticed at noon. By 5:00 p.m., the surrender negotiations were completed. The Spanish authorities agreed to surrender the Spaniards and the Filipino volunteers in the city on the condition that the Americans would safeguard the city and its inhabitants, churches, and religious worship.

The next day, August 14, the document stating the terms of surrender was formally signed by representatives of both parties. General Merritt then announced the establishment of the Military Government.

It turned out that the mock battle need not have been staged, as the two powers had already been negotiating to end hostilities.

Thus, on August 12, Washington, D.C. time, American President McKinley issued a proclamation directing the suspension of all military operations against the Spaniards. However, this did not reach Dewey as he had cut the cable between Manila and the outside world after winning the Battle of Manila Bay. By the time he received it, on August 16, the surrender agreement had been signed.

VIII. REVOLUTIONARY CONGRESS

President Aguinaldo convoked the Revolutionary Congress in Barasoain, Malolos, Bulacan Province. Those officers elected on September 15, 1898, were Pedro A. Paterno (the very same man who had brokered the betrayal of the revolution at Biak-na-Bato) as its president; Benito Legarda, vice president; Gregorio Araneta, first secretary; and Pablo Ocampo, second secretary.

The leadership of the revolution had been seized by the Cavite elite when Aguinaldo came into power in Tejeros, Cavite. He then reasserted his (and thus ilustrado) leadership after surrendering in the Pact of Biak-na-Bato and returning from exile in Hong Kong, both with the help of the Americans.

Constitution. The Congress, which Mabini had envisioned to be a mere advisory, not legislative, body of the president, proposed that a constitution be drafted, overruling Mabini's objections. He had meritoriously argued that the constitution had to be framed under peaceful conditions, but he was outvoted by the majority under Paterno. He proposed a constitution, which was rejected. Instead, one planned by Filipino lawyer Felipe Calderon was considered.

More Provinces Recovered. In September, 1898, the provinces of Isabela and Nueva Vizcaya were recovered. General Vicente Lukban also rushed to Samar and Leyte where he met little opposition. On September 15, 1898, in Malolos, Bulacan, President Aguinaldo formally declared the conclusion of the liberation of the Philippines. By October, General Lukban was in control of the situation Camarines.

On November 29, 1898, the Malolos Congress approved the constitution. However, Aguinaldo refused to sign it due to Mabini's objections.

Meanwhile, there were still Spanish garrisons in Cebu and Iloilo under General Montero and General de los Rios respectively. (Montero and his forces later surrendered on December 24, 1898. General de los Rios was to evacuate to Iloilo on December 26 and leave for Zamboanga on the way home to Spain.)

When Mabini's objections were satisfied the Malolos Constitution was promulgated on January 21, 1899. On January 23, 1899, the Philippine Republic was inaugurated in Malolos, with Aguinaldo as its first president.

Despite the proclamation of the Philippine independence and the establishment of the First Philippine Republic, the Philippines did not become a member of the family of nations. Among others, the United States and Spain did not recognize it. The U.S. had by then decided to annex the Philippines as its territory in the Pacific.

4

THE PHILIPPINE-
AMERICAN WAR
(1899-1902)

On July 1, 1898, American forces engaged in a fierce battle with the Spaniards at El Caney and San Juan Hill in Cuba. After the skirmishes, they occupied the high ground overlooking Santiago. On July 3, Admiral Pascual Cervera y Topete ordered his squadron to leave the harbor. The Spaniards attempted to escape toward the west along the coast. Then a running battle took place. All the Spanish ships either burned or sank. From there, American troops invaded and captured Puerto Rico, another Spanish possession.

As a result of these defeats, Spain sued for peace. On August 12, 1898, the day before the fall of Manila, Spain and the United States signed a peace agreement. Spain agreed to evacuate all her troops from and give up control over Cuba, cede Guam and Puerto Rico to the United States, which was also allowed to occupy Manila. The last condition was temporary while what was to be done with the Philippines was being determined.

In October 1898, representatives of Spain and the United States met in Paris to draft a peace treaty. One of the vital issues to be discussed was the status of the Philippines. Spain wanted the United States to return the Philippines to Spain because Manila had been occupied by the Americans only after the armistice had been signed on August 12, 1898, but to no avail. The United States insisted on obtaining the Philippines.

Treaty of Paris. On December 10. 1898, the Treaty of Paris, was signed in Paris, France, by both Spain and the United States. It formally ended the war between them. Under this treaty, Spain recognized the independence of Cuba; ceded Guam, Puerto Rico and the Philippines to the United States; and received a $20 million payment from the United States for giving up the Philippines.

The treaty had to be ratified by the U.S. Senate before it could take effect. It, however, met opposition, mainly against the annexation of the Philippines. An Anti-Imperialist League was formed to rally American public opinion against the annexation. Some prominent Americans, such as former President Grover Cleveland, Andrew Carnegie, and Mark Twain, also opposed the ratification.

One of the reasons why the United States should not acquire the Philippines was that the Filipinos themselves were fighting the Americans in the Philippines. Such an act, they said, showed that the Filipinos did not want to be under American rule. They also reasoned that it was inconsistent for the United States to disclaim—through the so-called Teller Amendment—any intention of annexing Cuba and then annex the other Spanish colonies, such as the Philippines.

Annexation Fever. There were also many in the United States who saw the advantages of taking over the Philippines. Many missionaries, for instance, favored annexation. So did people who feared that Germany might get the Philippines if the United States did not. Some favored annexation to give America a "foothold" in the populous markets of Asia.

On February 6, 1899, the U.S. Senate, by a vote of 57 to 27, ratified the Treaty of Paris. The American people, in effect, also endorsed the treaty when they reelected President McKinley in the 1900 U.S. presidential elections. Thus, the Philippines formally came under the rule of the United States.

I. THE PHILIPPINE-AMERICAN WAR

The Filipinos had become suspicious of the true motives of the United States in going to the Philippines. In fact, they were prevented by the Americans from entering Manila after its fall. Their suspicions were confirmed by the Treaty of Paris under which Spain ceded the Philippines to the United States. Neither Spain nor the United States gave Felipe Agoncillo, Aguinaldo's special envoy, a chance to present the wishes of the Filipinos in the Paris peace talks. Suspicion turned to hostility, and war between the two sides became inevitable. The Filipinos were outraged when they learned that Spain, which no longer controlled the Philippines, had ceded the country to the United States.

Benevolent Assimilation Proclamation. On December 21, 1898, President William Mckinley announced his decision to keep the Philippines as an American colonial possession.

Entitled "Benevolent Assimilation Proclamation," the McKinley proclamation was announced in the Philippines on January 4, 1899. It stated clearly the intention of the United States to stay permanently in the Philippines. The mission of the United States was described by McKinley as one of "benevolent assimilation." In the same proclamation, General Elwell Otis was named the commander of American ground forces in the Philippines, which was to "extend by force American sovereignty over this country."

On January 5, 1899, Aguinaldo issued a counter-proclamation. He warned that his government was prepared to fight any American attempt to forcibly take over the country. This sounded like a declaration of war to the American military although Aguinaldo had no wish to get into a war with the United States. He knew that war would only cause untold suffering to the Filipino people. He was still hopeful that the situation could be saved by peaceful negotiations between him and the American military leaders in the Philippines. Aguinaldo wrote General Elwell S. Otis calling for peaceful negotiations.

On January 9, 1899, Otis appointed three American officers to meet with three Filipino military officials appointed by Aguinaldo. However, they didn't accomplish anything.

"Halt!" Then Bang! Bang! Bang! The tension between the Americans and the Filipinos was so great that it was easy to precipitate a war. On the night of February 4, 1899, as described in *Aguinaldo: A Narrative of Filipino Ambitions*, (E. Wildman 1901, Norwood Press, Norwood, MA) an American sentry, Private William W. Grayson, with another soldier, encountered three armed Filipinos on a bridge in San Juan del Monte near Manila.

Recalling the incident, Grayson said:

> About eight o'clock, Miller and I were cautiously pacing our district. We came to a fence and were trying to see what the Filipinos were up to. Suddenly, near at hand, on our left, there was a low but unmistakable Filipino outpost signal whistle. It was immediately answered by a similar whistle about twenty-five yards to the right. Then a red lantern flashed a signal from blockhouse number 7. We had never seen such a sign used before. In a moment, something rose up slowly in front of us. It was a Filipino. I yelled "Halt!" and made it pretty loud, for I was accustomed to challenging the officer of the guard in approved military style. I challenged him with another loud "halt!" Then he shouted "halto!" to me. Well, I thought the best thing to do was to shoot him. He dropped. If I didn't kill him, I guess he died of fright. Two Filipinos sprang out of the gateway about 15 feet from us. I called "halt!" and Miller fired and dropped one. I saw that another was left. Well, I think I got my second Filipino that time....

The Filipino troops fired back at the American lines and before the night was over, fighting had broken out between Filipino and American forces. Most of the Filipino commanders at that time were attending a dance in Malolos, Bulacan Province. When told of the outbreak of hostilities, they rushed back to their units, which were already shooting it out with American troops.

When war finally came, Aguinaldo still tried to stop it by sending an emissary to General Otis to appeal for an end to the fighting. But Otis responded, "fighting, having begun, must go on to the grim end."

II. IN THE UNITED STATES

The American people, however, received a different version of how the war started. Newspaper reports made it appear that the Filipinos had started the fighting. This was the time when the Treaty of Paris was pending ratification in the U.S. Senate. Previously, because of strong public opinion against the U.S. annexation of the Philippines, ratification of the treaty was uncertain. But the distorted news that reached the United States, specifically that the Filipinos were the ones who started hostilities, changed the minds of several U.S. senators to vote for ratification. On February 6, 1899, the U.S. Senate ratified the Treaty of Paris.

Philippine Insurrection? Ouuucccch. The Americans viewed the fighting as an insurrection, not a war. Hence, Americans refer to this episode as the Philippine Insurrection, not the Philippine-American War. The Spanish-American conflict that lasted only three months, is referred to as the Spanish-American War. But the Philippine-American conflict officially lasted three years and is known only as the Philippine Insurrection by America. Actually the fighting between American and the remaining armed groups of Filipinos, whom Americans branded as "bandits," lasted 16 years (1899-1914).

James Loewen, a Washington, D.C.,-based scholar and author of a forthcoming book titled *Lies Across the Landscape: What Our Historical Markers and Monuments Get Wrong*, said, "What we call the Philippine Insurrection should be called the Philippine War. We had never conquered the Philippines, so you can't call it a revolt."

Loewen's comment was mentioned in an article published in the *Star Tribune* in Minnesota, in its issue of November 15, 1997.

A battalion of Filipino soldiers.

III. THE WAR GOES ON

After the refusal of General Otis to end hostilities following the San Juan bridge incident, General Arthur MacArthur ordered the advance of American troops toward Filipino positions in Manila and the suburbs. Regiments from Kansas and California captured Santa Ana and Makati. Troops from Nebraska and Utah occupied the San Juan Bridge. On the other hand, volunteers from Idaho and Washington massacred hundreds of Filipinos who were then trying to cross the Pasig River. The coastlines were pounded continuously by Admiral Dewey's naval guns.

Capturing Manila and the Suburbs. Several American soldiers who took part in the battles in Manila and the suburbs wrote letters telling about those battles to their relatives in the United States. These letters were published in local and national press in the United States by the Anti-Imperialist League in 1899 in the United States.

Source: *Soldiers' Letters: Being Materials for the History of a War of Criminal Aggression.* (N. p.: Anti-Imperialist League, 1899). http://www.accinet.net/ ~fjzwick/ailtexts/soldiers.html In Jim Zwick, ed., *Anti-Imperialism in the United States, 1898-1935.* http://www.accinet.net/~fjzwick/ail98-35.html (December 12, 1996.)

From Manila, wrote Private Fred B. Hinchman, Company A, United States Engineers:

At 1:30 o'clock, the general gave me a memorandum with regard to sending out a Tennessee battalion to the line. He tersely put it that "they were looking for a fight." At Puente Colgante (suspension bridge) I met one of our company, who told me that the Fourteenth and Washingtons were driving all before them, and taking no prisoners. This is now our rule of procedure for cause. After delivering my message I had not walked a block when I heard shots down the street. Hurrying forward, I found a group of four men taking pot-shots across the river, into a bamboo thicket, at about 1,200 yards....

Narrating his exploits in Santa Ana, Manila, Captain Albert Otis, wrote:

I have six horses and three carriages in my yard, and enough small plunger for a family of six. The house I had at Santa Ana had five pianos. I couldn't take them, so I put a big grand piano out of a second-story window. You can guess its finish. Everything is pretty quiet about here now. I expect we will not be kept here very long now. Give my love to all.

On to Marikina. The Americans pushed towards the suburbs, including Marikina.

National Archives

**American sentries on duty
in Santa Ana district.**

Filipinos died as they fell in Santa Ana, Manila. The trench was circular in form and the photograph shows only a small portion.

Thinking of the impending Marikina fight, James A. Reid, a Colorado volunteer, had this to say:

> Maybe you think this isn't a fine country—to keep away from. In fact, all of the country around here is just "lousy" with "niggers." To the right of us is the lake. About seven miles away, to the north and east, is the little town of Marquina, which will soon have to be taken. As it is the birthplace of Pio del Pilar, one of "Aggie's" great generals, we expect quite a fight. Malabon and Malolos have not as yet been taken. Don't know about Malolos, but Malabon can be taken any time, as it is next to the bay....We are not nearly as anxious to fight these people as some of people may think we are, and we do not enter any of the fights with the same spirit we did when fighting the Spaniards. If a vote was taken to take us home now or wait six months and discharge us here with our travel pay and finals, which would amount to nearly five hundred dollars, I do not believe that ten percent would be willing to stay, so you see how the men look at this addition to the United States....There have been about one hundred and twenty-five killed and three hundred wounded all together, and, when you consider that these beastly islands are not worth one American life, you can see what they are costing.

National Archives

American breastworks in old Camp Dewey in Manila.

La Loma Fight. Major Jose Torres Bugallon, one of the bravest Filipino officers, was killed in the battle of La Loma, near the Chinese cemetery. After capturing La Loma, General MacArthur pushed toward Caloocan. General Antonio Luna and his brave troops were there to fight the Americans.

Caloocan Battle. Describing the Caloocan battle, Charles Bremer, of Minneapolis, Kansas, wrote:

> Company I had taken a few prisoners, and stopped. The colonel ordered them up in to line time after time, and finally sent Captain Bishop back to start them. There occurred the hardest sight I ever saw. They had four prisoners, and didn't know what to do with them. They asked Captain Bishop what to do, and he said: "You know the orders, and four natives fell dead."

Writing his own version of the Caloocan fight, Captain Elliot, of the Kansas Regiment said:

> Talk about war being "hell," this war beats the hottest estimate ever made of that locality. Caloocan was supposed to contain seventeen thousand inhabitants. The Twentieth Kansas swept through it, and now Caloocan contains not one living

native. Of the buildings, the battered walls of the great church and dismal prison alone remain. The village of Maypaja, where our first fight occurred on the night of the fourth, had five thousand people on that day—now not one stone remains upon top of another. You can only faintly imagine this terrible scene of desolation. War is worse than hell.

Due to the Americans' superiority in arms, Caloocan fell. But General Luna didn't give up.

On February 22, Luna marched towards Manila to try to capture it. He even ordered the burning of houses in the suburbs to create confusion to the American troops. Afterwards he fought the enemy on Azcarraga. General Luna and his troops suffered heavy losses so he then retreated to Polo, Bulacan.

Malabon, Here we Come! The Americans advanced towards Malabon (near Caloocan), as if saying, "Here we come!"

Describing their adventures in Malabon, Anthony Michea of the Third Artillery wrote:

> We bombarded a place called Malabon, and then we went in and killed every native we met, men, women, and children. It was a dreadful sight, the killing of the poor creatures. The natives captured some of the Americans and literally hacked them to pieces, so we got orders to spare no one."

Cavite Fight. Burr Ellis, of Frazier, Valley, California, narrated what he did in Cavite. He wrote:

> They did not commence fighting over here (Cavite) for several days after the war commenced. Dewey gave them till nine o'clock one day to surrender, and that night they all left but a few out to their trenches, and those that they left burned up the town, and when the town com-

National Archives

Filipino prisoners taking a Sunday morning bath, 1901.

General L. L. Hines' Collection.

menced burning, the troops were ordered in as far as possible and said, "Kill all we could find." I ran off from the hospital and went ahead with the scouts. And you bet, I did not cross the ocean for the fun there was in it, so the first one I found, he was in a house, down on his knees fanning a fire, trying to burn the house, and I pulled my old Long Tom to my shoulder and left him to burn with the fire, which he did. I got his knife, and another jumped out of the window and ran, and I brought him to the ground like a jack-rabbit. I killed seven that I know of, and one more, I am almost sure of: I shot ten shots at him running and knocked him down, and that evening the boys out in front of our trenches now found one with his arm shot off at the shoulder and dead as h____. I had lots of fun that morning....

From Fred D. Sweet, of the Utah Light Battery, came these words:

The scene reminded me of the shooting of jack-rabbits in Utah, only the rabbits sometimes got away, but the insurgents did not.

Help! Help! Help! Reinforcements from the U.S. American reinforces arrived from the United States in late February and early March 1899. Then Americans advanced towards Polo, Bulacan, capturing other towns along the Manila-Dagupan Railway.

Battles in the Visayas. The Americans then decided to invade the Visayan provinces. In particular, General Otis directed General Miller to invade and capture Iloilo Province. The Filipinos, headed by General Martin Delgado, did not surrender as demanded by Miller. Instead, he decided to fight the Americans. The Filipino soldiers burned Iloilo City to prevent the Americans from making it as the enemy's base of operations.

Describing their invasion of Iloilo City, D.M. Mickle, of the Tennessee Regiment, wrote:

The building had been taken possession of by a United States officer, and he looted it to a finish. I suspected something and followed one of his men to the place. I expected to be jumped on by the officer as soon as I found him there, as I was away from my post, but it seems he was afraid I would give him away; in fact, we were both afraid of each other. He was half drunk, and every time he saw me looking at anything he would say, "Tennessee, do you like that? Well put it in your pocket."...The house was a fine one, and richly furnished, but had been looted to a finish. The contents of every drawer had been emptied on the floor. You have no idea what a mania for destruction the average man has when the fear of the law is removed. I have seen them—old sober business men too—knock chandeliers and plate-glass mirrors to pieces just because they couldn't carry it off. It is such a pity.

On February 14, 1899, the town of Santa Barbara was captured by the Americans. Next they captured Oton, Mandurriao, and Jaro, Iloilo. On February 22, Cebu was surrendered to the Americans by the Filipinos.

On to Malolos. In central Luzon, by March 30, the Americans were already near Malolos, Bulacan, where the Philippine government was headquartered. General Aguinaldo evacuated Malolos and moved his headquarters to San Isidro, Nueva Ecija.

At that time, General Otis ordered General MacArthur not to pursue Aguinaldo, but to temporarily stay in Malolos.

Meanwhile, the Americans immediately captured Bacoor, Zapote, and Dasmarinas, all in Cavite; Paranaque and Las Pinas, in Morong, and Paete, Santa Cruz, and other towns in Laguna.

On April 23, the same year, General Gregorio del Pilar, known as the "boy general," defeated the American cavalry under Major Bell in a stiff battle in Quinqua (now Plaridel), Bulacan. The enemy suffered heavy losses, including Colonel Stotsenberg who was killed in action. On the other hand, General Licerio Geronimo overpowered the Americans under General Lawton in San Mateo, Morong, in which battle Lawton was killed.

General MacArthur moved towards Kalumpit, Bulacan, where General Luna was waiting for him. According to Teodoro Agoncillo (*History of the Filipino People,*) when the Americans were about to attack, Luna, together with his foot soldiers, cavalry, and artillery left Kalumpit to punish General Tomas Mascardo for his insubordination. Mascardo was then in Pampanga Province. General del Pilar was left to fight and repulse the enemy, which the "boy general" was not able to do. It was too late when Luna and his soldiers came back at nightfall. The Americans had already broken through the Filipino defensive lines. Thus they lost the fight, The Filipinos sustained other battle losses.

IV. THE WRITINGS OF MARK TWAIN

The Anti-Imperialist League was formed in the United States against the annexation of the Philippines. Among the writers of that time was Mark Twain, vice president of the League from 1901 until his death in 1910.

Mark Twain wrote an essay entitled *To the Person Sitting in Darkness.* published by the *North American Review* in February 1901. This essay sparked a nationwide controversy and Mark Twain as one newspaper said "has suddenly become the most influential anti-imperialist and the most dreaded critic of the sacrosanct person in the White House...."

Source: Twain, Mark. *To the Person Sitting in Darkness. North American Review* 172 (Feb 1901). http://www.accinet.net/~fjzwick/twain/persit.html In Jim Zwick, ed., *Anti-Imperialism in the United States, 1898-1935.* http://www.accinet net/~fjzwick/ail98-35.html (December 12, 1996).

Here's an excerpt from Twain's essay, *To the Person Sitting in Darkness*:

Our case is simple. On the 1st of May, Dewey destroyed the Spanish fleet. This left the Archipelago in the hands of its proper and rightful owners, the Filipino nation. Their army numbered 30,000 men, and they were competent to whip out or starve out the little Spanish garrison; then the people could set up a government of their own devising. Our traditions required that Dewey should now set up his warning sign, and go away. But the Master of the Game happened to think of another plan—the European plan. He acted upon it. This was, to send out an army—ostensibly to help the native patriots put the finishing touch upon their long and plucky struggle for independence, but really to take their land away from them and keep it. That is, in the interest of Progress and Civilization. The plan developed, stage by stage, and quite satisfactorily. We entered into a military alliance with the trusting Filipinos, and they hemmed in Manila on the land side, and by their valuable help the place, with its garrison of 8,000 or 10,000 Spaniards, was captured—a thing which we could not have accomplished unaided at that time. We got their help—by ingenuity. We knew they were fighting for their independence, and that they had been at it for two years. We knew they supposed that we also were fighting in their worthy cause—just as we had helped the Cubans fight for Cuban independence—and we allowed them to go on thinking so. *Until Manila was ours and we could get along without them.* Then we showed our hand. Of course, they were surprised—that was natural; surprised and disappointed; disappointed and grieved. To them it looked un-American; uncharacteristic; foreign to our established traditions. And this was natural, too; for we were only playing the American Game in public—in private it was European. It was neatly done, very neatly, and it bewildered them. They could not understand it; for we had been so friendly—so affectionate, even—with those simple-minded patriots! We, our own selves, had brought back out of exile their leader, their hero, their hope, their Washington — Aguinaldo; brought him in a warship, in high honor, under the sacred shelter and hospitality of the flag; brought him back and restored him to his people, and got their moving and eloquent gratitude for it. Yes, we had been so friendly to them, and had heartened them up so many ways! We had lent them guns and ammunition; advised with them; exchanged pleasant courtesies with them; placed our sick and wounded in their kindly care; entrusted our Spanish prisoners to their humane and honest hands; fought shoulder to shoulder with them against "the common enemy" (our own phrase); praised their courage, praised their gallantry, praised their mercifulness, praised their fine and honorable conduct; borrowed their trenches, borrowed strong positions which they had previously captured from the Spaniards; petted them, lied to them—officially proclaiming that our land and naval forces came to give them their freedom and displace the bad Spanish Government—fooled them, used them until we needed them no longer; then derided the sucked orange and threw it away. We kept the positions which we had beguiled

them of; by and by, we moved a force forward and overlapped patriot ground—a clever thought, for we needed trouble, and this would produce it. A Filipino soldier, crossing the ground, where no one had a right to forbid him, was shot by our sentry. The badgered patriots resented this with arms, without waiting to know whether Aguinaldo, who was absent, would approve or not. Aguinaldo did not approve; but that availed nothing. What we wanted, in the interest of Progress and Civilization, was the Archipelago, unencumbered by patriots struggling for independence; and War was what we needed. We clinched our opportunity. It is Mr. Chamberlain's case over again—at least in its motive and intention; and we played the game as adroitly as he played it himself.

V. OTHER HAPPENINGS

As early as March 6, 1899, Apolinario Mabini, in his capacity as premier and minister of foreign affairs, met with the Schurman Commission. The commission had offered the Filipinos some form of autonomous government. Mabini's request for time to consult the people on the offer and a ceasefire in the meantime was refused. Mabini made another attempt, which turned to be futile, to seek an armistice on April 28. He later issued a manifesto criticizing the Americans, whom he described as a free people trying to rob others of their liberty. He then rallied the Filipino people to go on with the fight against the Americans.

When Mabini resigned from his post on May 7, 1899, President Aguinaldo named Pedro A. Paterno to head a new cabinet. It was Biak-na-Bato all over again. Notified of his replacement by Paterno, Mabini scoffed at the negotiations of the new cabinet on the basis of autonomy, calling it a desire for "independence without any struggle." As expected, nothing came out of the Paterno peace efforts because the U.S. insisted that the Filipinos lay down their arms first.

Disunity Among the Filipinos. Among the military and political leaders, disunity again caused divisions. Although they were in a war against a common enemy, many of their leaders in the government and in the army sadly still found time to engage in personal, and often bitter quarrels, with disastrous and tragic consequences to the First Philippine Republic. The power struggle served to weaken Filipino unity at a time of great peril to the nation.

Apolinario Mabini was considered an obstacle who was put out of the way with his resignation on May 7, 1899, by those who were later named to the Paterno cabinet. But a more formidable obstacle was General Antonio Luna, who was recognized as the ablest general of the revolution. Earlier, he was one of those who had revealed the existence of the Katipunan to the Spaniards.

A well-off ilustrado, Luna had joined Aguinaldo in 1898 and proved his worth as an officer. As a result, he was appointed commander-in-chief for central Luzon when the Filipino-American hostilities erupted.

However, he had a volatile temper and sharp tongue. He was very vocal against entering into any deal with the Americans; he opposed autonomy and strongly advocated a fight for independence. He even arrested members of the Paterno cabinet after he learned that they were planning to negotiate with the Americans, calling them traitors. Turned over to Aguinaldo, the Cabinet members were turned loose as soon as Luna left. These men then poisoned the mind of Aguinaldo against Luna, saying the hot-headed general was eyeing the presidency. In reality, Luna was only trying to get popular support for his arrest of the Paterno cabinet and to drum up opposition to autonomy.

As he fell on the convent yard, all Luna could say was "Cow....ards! As..sas...sins!"

Here's how Luna was killed as narrated in the book *History of the Filipino People* by Teodoro Agoncillo and Milagros C. Guerrero:

Upon Aguinaldo's invitation, General Luna on June 5, 1899, went to a convent in Cabanatuan, Nueva Ecija, which served as Aguinaldo's headquarters. When he arrived, Aguinaldo had already left for San Isidro, Nueva Ecija. Luna slapped the sentry at the convent as he went upstairs. There, he saw Felipe Buencamino, whom he despised, and they exchanged heated words. A rifle shot was heard from downstairs. He rushed downstairs, and there, members of the Kawit Company, one of whom he had recommended for punishment, mobbed him. Several stabbed him with daggers; others shot at him. He was able to run to the street. He fired his pistol, but he didn't hit anybody. Colonel Francisco Roman, his aide-de-camp, came to his defense, but he was shot to death. As he fell on the convent yard, all Luna could say was, "Cow....ards! As...sas...sins!" The next day, he was buried with military honors. However, no soldiers were investigated for the killing.

The killing of Luna was a big blow to the cause of the Filipinos. It was, as Constantino puts it, "Bonifacio's fate repeated." His death deprived the nation of an able militarist. After Luna's death, Aguinaldo ordered all chiefs of brigades under Luna arrested. He also ordered the disarming of two companies suspected of being pro-Luna. Such acts, especially the slaying of Luna, led to the demoralization of the army, as he had had a wide following.

VI. BACK TO THE BATTLEFIELDS

The Filipino army gradually broke up with one defeat after another on the battlefields. By the closing months of 1899, the army of the Philippine Republic was no longer a regular fighting force, and on November 12, 1899, the army was dissolved by Aguinaldo. It was formed into guerrilla units that would carry on the war.

One by one, towns and provinces throughout the archipelago fell to the U.S. forces. Many of his civilian and military officials surrendered to or were captured by the Americans. Many of them, including Mabini, who was captured in December 1899, were deported to Guam in January 1901.

The Capture of Aguinaldo. The capture of Aguinaldo was placed by the Americans as one of their priorities. He was able to avoid capture for quite sometime, though. That was due to the loyalty of many townspeople in the different provinces, who warned his party whenever American troops were closing in.

He was also able to win some more time because of the heroic sacrifice of General Gregorio del Pilar, the "boy general" in the famous Battle of Tirad Pass on December 2, 1900, in Mountain Province. In this narrow 2,800-meter-high pass, General del Pilar, with a handpicked force of only 60 men, held off for more than five hours a battalion of Texans of the U.S. 33rd Volunteers led by Major Peyton C. March. They had been pursuing Aguinaldo and his party. Of the 60, 52 were killed

National Archives

Emilio Aguinaldo, Philippine leader, after he was captured in Palanan, Isabela Province, Philippines. Photo was taken in Manila, 1901.

General G. del Pilar

Jim Zwick Collection

and wounded; one of the last to be killed was General del Pilar.

Aguinaldo was finally captured on March 23, 1901, in Palanan, Isabela Province, by means of a trick planned by Brigadier General Frederick Funston. A party of pro-American Macabebe scouts marched into Palanan pretending to be the reinforcements that Aguinaldo was waiting for. With the Macabebes were two former Filipino army officers, Tal Placido and Lazaro Segovia, who had surrendered to the Americans, and five Americans, including General Funston, who pretended to be captives. Caught by surprise, Aguinaldo's guards were easily overpowered by the Macabebes after a brief exchange of shots. Aguinaldo was seized by Tal Placido and placed under arrest by General Funston.

He was brought to Manila to be kept a prisoner at Malacañang. There he was treated by General MacArthur more as a guest than as a prisoner. On April 1, 1901, convinced of the futility of continuing the war, the ambivalent Aguinaldo swore allegiance to the United States.

On April 19,1901, Aguinaldo issued a proclamation calling on the Filipino people to lay down their arms and accept American rule. His capture signalled the death of the First Philippine Republic. But the war continued.

Dragged by Galloping Horses. During the war, torture was resorted to by American troops to obtain information and confessions. The water cure was given to those merely suspected of being rebels. Some were hanged by the thumbs, others were dragged by galloping horses, or fires lit beneath others while they were hanging.

Another form of torture was tying to a tree and then shooting the suspect through the legs. If a confession was not obtained, he was again shot, the day after. This went on until he confessed or eventually died.

Villages were burned, townfolks massacred and their possessions looted. In Samar and Batangas, Brigadier General Jacob H. Smith and General Franklin Bell, respectively, ordered the mass murders in answer to the mass resistance.

On the other hand, Filipino guerrillas chopped off the noses and ears of captured Americans in violation of Aguinaldo's orders. There were reports that some Americans were

National Archives

Macabebe scouts who captured President Emilio Aguinaldo on March 23, 1901, in Palanan, Isabela Province.

buried alive by angry Filipino guerrillas. In other words, brutalities were perpetrated by both sides.

The Balangiga, Samar, Massacre. The so-called Balangiga Massacre happened in 1901, a few weeks after a company of American soldiers arrived in Balangiga, Samar, upon the request of the town mayor to protect the inhabitants from the raids of Muslims and rebels. How the massacre took place is best described in Joseph Schott's book, *The Ordeal of Samar* (The Bobbs-Merrill Company, Inc./ Howard W. Sams & Co., Inc., Publishers, Indianapolis, Indiana, Copyright 1964). Here's an excerpt from the book:

On the night of September 27, the sentries on the guard posts about the plaza were surprised by the unusual number of women hurrying to church. They were all heavily clothed, which was unusual, and many carried small coffins. Sergeant Scharer, sergeant of the guard vaguely suspicious, stopped one woman and pried open her coffin with his bayonet. Inside he found the body of a dead child.

"El calenturon! El colera!" the woman said.

The sergeant, slightly abashed by the sight of the dead child, nailed down the coffin lid again with the butt of his revolver and let the woman pass on. He concluded that cholera and fever were in epidemic stage and carrying off children in great numbers. But it was strange that no news of any such epidemic had reached the garrison.

If the guard sergeant had been less abashed and had searched beneath the child's body, he would have found the keen blades of cane-cutting knives. All the coffins were loaded with them.

The night passed and morning came. At about 6:20 a.m. a sergeant was in the door of his squad hut. At that time, the unarmed Americans were going to breakfast. Some of them, of course, had finished their breakfast.

The sergeant saw Pedro Sanchez, chief of police of the town, line up prisoners for work. Then Sanchez sent all the workers to work in the plaza and in the streets. After that, Sanchez went to a hut and even talked with a corporal who knew pidgin Spanish and Visayan.

After speaking with the corporal, Sanchez walked behind Private Adolph Gamlin, the sentry on the area. All of a sudden, Sanchez grabbed the Gamlin's rifle, and he smashed the rifle's butt on the American soldier's head. The Filipino fired a shot and shouted a signal. Then pandemonium broke loose.

Joseph L. Schott, describes what happened next:

The church bell ding-donged crazily and conch shell whistles blew shrilly from the edge of the jungle. The doors of the church burst open and out streamed the mob of bolomen who had been waiting inside. The native laborers working about

the plaza suddenly turned on the soldiers and began chopping at them with bolos, picks and shovels.

As the church bells were being rung, Sanchez fired upon the Americans at the breakfast table. He then led the Filipinos in attacking the American soldiers.

Schott continues:

The mess tents, filled with unarmed soldiers peacefully at breakfast, had been one of the first prime targets for the attackers. They burst in screaming and slashing....

Then, as the soldiers rose up and began fighting with chairs and kitchen utensils, the attackers outside cut the tent ropes, causing the tents to collapse on the struggling men. The natives ran in from all directions to slash with bolos and axes at the forms struggling under the canvas.

Members of C Company were almost all massacred during the first few minutes of

One of the bells seized from the Balangiga Catholic Church in Samar by the Americans after the massacre. Filipino officials are seeking the return of one of the bells to the Philippines. The bells are housed at the Francis E. Warren Base, in Cheyenne, Wyoming.

attack. The main action took place around the plaza and tribunal building. There, Filipino bolomen attacked the soldiers. They boloed to death the Americans who tried to escape; other soldiers were hacked from nose to throat.

About 250 Filipinos were reported to have been killed by a number of American troops who were able to get rifles from the rack and shoot at the bolomen. (However, first-hand Filipino accounts put the dead at less than 40.) On the other hand, the Americans suffered 78 casualties: 48 killed and 22 wounded. Only 4 were not injured. (Gamlin survived the massacre. He died at age 92 in the U.S. in 1969.)

(In 1995, Philippine President Fidel V. Ramos, issued Proclamation No. 674 declaring November 15, as "Don Eugenio Daza Day" in eastern Samar. November 15, 1995, marked the 125th birthday anniversary of Daza. Daza, being the overall commander of the revolutionary forces in the east coast of Samar during the Philippine Revolution, was reported to be one of those who have masterminded the Balangiga massacre. Daza, besides being a revolutionary leader, was also a member of the First Philippine Assembly in 1907.)

The Pacification of Samar. Due to the public demand in the U.S. for retaliation, President Theodore Roosevelt ordered the pacification of Samar. And in six months, General "Jake" Smith transformed Balangiga into a "howling wilderness." He ordered his men to kill anybody capable of carrying arms, including ten-year old boys.

Smith particularly ordered Major Littleton Waller to punish the people of Samar for the deaths of the American troops. His exact orders were: "I want no prisoners. I wish you to kill and burn, the more you kill and burn, the better you will please me."

'**The Americans Are Coming! The Americans Are Coming!**' Maybe these shouts were heard while the Americans were chasing and shooting the guerrillas and their sympathizers. And maybe, too, some U.S. troops might have uttered: "So there you are! You've no where to go!" And the shots were heard as burning houses lighted the night.

When the campaign was over, the U. S. army court-martialed and retired General Smith from the service. There were reports that about one third of the entire population of Samar was annihilated during the campaign.

Moreover, when members of the U.S. Army 11th Infantry Regiment left Balangiga, Samar, they took with them two church bells from the Balangiga Catholic Church. They were placed in a brick display museum in their home base Fort Russell, Wyoming, where they still remain today.

> "I wish you to kill and burn, the more you kill and burn, the better you will please me."
>
> —General "Jake" Smith

Concentration Camps. General Miguel Malvar of Batangas, who took over the leadership of the fallen Aguinaldo, continued the fight. He was the commanding general of all forces south of the Pasig River. The Americans committed barbaric acts because of the population's support to the guerrillas.

For instance, by December 25, 1901, all men, women, and children of the towns of Batangas and Laguna, were herded into small areas within the *poblacion* of their respective towns. The American troops burned their houses, carts, poultry, animals, etc. The people were prisoners for months.

National Archives

About 3,000 Filipino soldiers taking the oath to the United States on the plaza in a town in Luzon in 1901.

Those acts were considered by many as an early version of the concentration camps used by American soldiers in the Vietnam War.

The same tactics were perpetrated by the American army against non-combatants from March to October 1903 in the province of Albay and in 1905 in the provinces of Cavite and Batangas.

Enough Is Enough. Many Filipino soldiers and military officers surrendered to the Americans, but there were some who refused to give up. On February 27, 1902, General Vicente Lukban, who resorted to ambushing American troops in Samar, was captured in Samar. General Malvar surrendered to General J. Franklin Bell in Lipa, Batangas, on April 16, 1902.

"Official" End of the Philippine-American War. On July 4, 1902, President Theodore Roosevelt declared that the Philippine-American War, which Americans called the Philippine Insurrection, was over. He made the declaration after the Philippine Commission reported to Roosevelt that the recent "insur-rection" in the Philippines was over and a general and complete state of peace existed.

Sporadic Fighting Continues. Official history proclaims Filipino struggle against the Americans as a short one and honors those who connived with the Americans. But little importance has been given to those who stood by the original goals of the Katipunan.

However, according to author Constantino, peace in the Philippines was merely propaganda. He said, in reality, the reports of the American commanding general and several governors showed that numerous towns and villages remained in a state of constant rebellion. They themselves recognized that this could not have continued without the people's support. Many collaborators were killed by resistance forces.

The civil government, composed of 6,000 men, was established. It was, however, led by American officers and former members of the Spanish civil guards.

Civil Guards. Initially, the highest rank a Filipino could hold was only second lieutenant. (Americans continued to head the constabulary until 1917.) The constabulary was used to quell local resistance. Constantino terms these suppressive efforts of using a native force "the original Vietnamization." He adds that some military techniques employed against Philippine resistance groups "strikingly similar to those that have more recently shocked the world."

The Katipunan Becomes Alive. Many resistance groups under different leaders had emerged during the war years. Luciano San Miguel, who joined the Katipunan in 1886 revived the Katipunan in his command in Zambales Province. He was a colonel when the Philippine-American War broke out. As a commander, he participated in the battles of 1899 in central and western Luzon, including Morong and Bulacan.

In 1902, he was elected national head of the revived Katipunan. He continued the guerrilla war. He died in a battle with Philippine Constabulary and Philippine Scouts in the district of Pugad-Baboy, in Morong, now Metro Manila.

Faustino Guillermo, assumed the leadership of the new Katipunan movement when San Miguel was killed. Others who took part in the guerrilla warfare were Macario Sakay, who had been with Bonifacio and Jacinto during the initial struggles of the Katipunan, and Julian Montalan and Cornelio Felizardo.

The Philippine Constabulary, Philippine Scouts, and elements of the United States Army combined to go after the guerrillas.

In the province of Albay, General Simeon Ola launched guerrilla raids on U.S.-occupied towns until his surrender on September 25, 1903. He was the last Filipino general to surrender to the Americans.

Sakay, leader of a band of patriotic Filipinos and whom the Americans branded as a bandit, continued to fight. He even established the Tagalog "Republic." He surrendered on July 14, 1906. Sakay and his men were tried and convicted as bandits. Sakay was hanged on September 13, 1907.

VII. FLASHBACK: THE ESTABLISHMENT OF AMERICAN RULE

The first government established by the Americans in the Philippines followed the surrender of Manila in August 1898. It was a military government. During the duration of the war, the Philippines was ruled by the president of the United States in his capacity as commander-in-chief of the United States Armed Forces. In its brief existence, from 1898 to 1901, the military government established a supreme court composed of six Filipinos and three Americans. The first chief justice was Cayetano Arellano.

Towns and provincial governments were organized and elections for local officials held. Also introduced was the public school system in the Philippines, with English being taught for the first time; American soldiers acted as the first English teachers.

On March 2, 1901, the military government in the Philippines ceased to exist when the United States Congress enacted the Army Appropriations Act. This law carried the Spooner Amendment, which removed from the United States president the final authority to govern the Philippines. This power was to be exercised by the United States Congress through the president.

As a result, a civil government was established in the Philippines and inaugurated on July 4, 1901. Judge William H. Taft was the first civil governor. (In 1905, the title was changed to governor general).

Taft's Role. History schoolbooks portray Taft as a well-loved governor who did his best to promote the welfare of the Filipinos. He adopted a "Philippines for the Filipinos" policy, thereby even earning him the ire of Americans who wanted to exploit the country for their own selfish interests. It was said to be during his administration that many of the "foundations of a stable and democratic government" were laid. One of his greatest achievements was supposedly the purchase of 410,000 acres of friar lands. He resold them to landless Filipino tenants on easy installment terms.

On the other hand, Constantino says that, if taken in the correct context, Taft's "Philippines for the Filipinos" was "not an endorsement of Philippine independence" but "good business." As he saw it, an improvement in the standard of living and education for the Filipinos create a taste for American products, resulting in a potential market for American products.

Philippine Bill of 1902. The next stage in the development of civil government in the Philippines was the passing of the Cooper Act on July 1, 1902, or the Philippine Bill of 1902. It was the first organic law for the Philippines enacted by the United States Congress and named after its sponsor, U.S. Representative Henry A. Cooper of Wisconsin.

Among its key provisions were

1) a bill of rights for the Filipinos;

2) the appointment of two Filipino resident commissioners to represent the Philippines in the United States Congress but without voting rights;

3) the establishment of a Philippine Assembly to be elected by the Filipinos two years after the publication of a census and only after peace had been completely restored in the country.

VIII. EPILOGUE

It took the United States more than three years to defeat the army of the first Philippine Republic. However, the outcome of the war was never in doubt, mainly because the United States enjoyed tremendous military advantages.

In numbers alone, the U.S. was superior. Although there were only 20,032 enlisted men and 819 officers in the U.S. Expeditionary Force in the Philippines as of January 31, 1899, more troops arrived in subsequent months. By April 16, 1902, more than 120,000 American soldiers had fought or served in the Philippines. Even more superior were the arms used by the Americans, who were well-equipped. U.S. warships were on the coast, ready to fire their big guns when needed.

In contrast, the Filipino arms were a motley of rifles. Some had been supplied by the Americans during the Spanish-American War, others smuggled in by Filipino patriots, seized from the Spanish army, or taken from American soldiers. Artillery was likewise limited. Most of their cannons were captured from the Spaniards. Many Filipino soldiers did not even have guns, but used spears, lances and *bolos* (big knives) in fighting. Filipino soldiers also lacked military training. They did manage to win some small battlefield encounters, but these only delayed the ultimate victory for the Americans. Their resistance did not arouse public opinion in America against the U.S. military campaigns in the Philippines to the same degree that American public opinion forced the United States to withdraw from the Vietnam War more than 70 years later.

Nevertheless, the United States had to pay a very high price, more than 4,000 American soldiers' lives. One of them was Major General Henry C. Lawton, who was killed in the Battle of San Mateo on December 23, 1899. He was the highest-ranking U.S. military officer to be killed in action in the Philippine-American War. The U.S. government also spent about $600 million in all.

THE AMERICAN RULE
AFTER THE 1899-1902 WAR

5

After the 1899-1902 Philippine-American War, the U.S. authorities adopted a regime of "democratic partnership" with the Filipinos. This paved the way for the beginning of Philippine economic, political, and social development. The Americans introduced a new system of public education; improved public health and sanitation; developed the means of transportation and communications to promote trade, commerce, and industry; and introduced political consciousness to the people. As a result, the Filipinos also learned self-government.

I. EDUCATIONAL SYSTEM

In August 1898, almost right after Admiral George Dewey demolished the Spanish fleet at Manila Bay, the U.S. opened American schools in Manila.

At that time, General MacArthur assigned chaplains and on-commissioned officers as teachers. Actually, the Americans established the first American school in the Philippines on the island of Corregidor.

It was on January 21, 1901, that the Philippine Commission enacted a law that established a centralized public schools system. The law provided free public primary education. Therefore, free books and other school supplies were furnished to the children. Compulsory enrollment of children was enforced. First to be established were the public schools in Manila and in its suburbs. At that time, the law also called for the establishment of the Philippine Normal School in Manila, where Filipinos could study and be trained as teachers.

Later, American teachers who were known as the "Thomasites" replaced the soldiers.

Filipinas Heritage Library

An American teacher helps his wife get on a *calesa* in the photograph taken by their co-Thomasite Luther Parker.

From the Luther Parker Collection, National Library.

They were called "Thomasites" simply because they went there on board the ship S.S. *Thomas*. Thus, the Filipino school children were compelled to learn English. American textbooks were used in class, a contradiction to the Spanish policy of discouraging the Filipinos from learning Spanish. Instead, they used the Philippine dialects in teaching the Catholic religion. The American system of education emphasized democratic ideals and adherence to the compliance of law.

In 1902, the Philippine Commission passed a law that established a high school system throughout the country. In 1903, the commission enacted a law for the sending of pensionados (scholars) to study in U.S. colleges and universities. (From 1903-1914, Filipino pensionados were sent to the United States. They later returned home to become leaders in their own fields of endeavor.)

Songs. During flag ceremonies, before entering their classes, school children sang *The Star-Spangled Banner* and *God Bless America*. They also sang *Philippines, My Philippines* that had the tune of *Maryland, My Maryland*.

100,000 Pupils. By 1899-1900, there were already 100,000 Filipino pupils enrolled in public schools throughout the country. In 1908, the University of the Philippines was established to provide higher education. Other private institutions, such as the University of Santo Tomas (the oldest university in the Philippines established in 1611), the Escuela de Derecho (School of Law), and others established by private persons and corporations continued to use the Spanish language as the medium of instruction. Later, they switched to English.

Then more schools, colleges, and universities were opened. During the U.S. occupation of the Philippines, the Americans introduced an adult educational campaign that reached even the rural areas.

To sum it up, education has been considered as America's most important contribution to the Filipino civilization.

II. PUBLIC HEALTH AND SANITATION

The Americans gave priority to the health and sanitation of the Filipino people by adopting a scientific program of public health and sanitation.

Health and Sanitation During the Spanish Regime. During the Spanish regime, the Spaniards established the Bureau of Health in 1806 and the Central Council of Vaccination in 1851. The purpose was to prevent the spread of such diseases as smallpox, cholera, malaria, tuberculosis, and other diseases. But their efforts were not enough and their services were not satisfactory. So when the

III. TRADE, COMMERCE, & INDUSTRY

The U.S. Congress in 1909 passed the Payne-Aldrich Tariff Act. That law authorized the partial free-trade relations between the United States and the Philippines, thereby improving trade, commerce, and industry.

Less to the U.S.; More to the Philippines. Philippine exports, except rice, were permitted to enter the U.S. markets free of duty within some quota limits. The United States, in turn, had unlimited duty-free exports to the Philippines. Because of the huge American export trade to the Philippines, the Filipinos became used to buying U.S.-made goods. In 1913, the Simmons-Underwood Tariff Act was approved by the U.S. Congress; it removed the quota limitations on Philippine exports. As a result of this act, the Philippine foreign trade increased tremendously. Years before the Payne-Aldrich Tariff Act was passed into law, the average Philippine exports amounted only to P60,900,000. In 1925-1930, the figure rose to P297,900,000.

Local trade, likewise, was developed. The gross merchant sales in 1917 totalled only P400,197,966. By 1935, the sales had increased to P631,614,000.

Cigarette, Anyone? More factories were built, including textile and cigar and cigarette factories. Sugar manufacturing centrals, coconut-oil mills, sawmills, and fish-canning factories, among others, were widely established. By 1929, the gold-mining industry had produced P6,740,781 worth of gold. In 1935, household industries had hiked their capital investment, which were only P16,500,000 (pesos) in 1918.

To U.S. Yes; To Foreign Markets, No. At that time, the Philippine exports went to U.S. markets only due to the free-trade relations between the two countries. In view of this, the

Filipinos in the Philippines, circa 1900.

Americans took over, they saw to it that proper health measures were undertaken. To prevent the immigration of epidemics from abroad, they established the Quarantine Service managed by U.S. physicians and other public health officials.

Oh Cholera! As a result, infant mortality and the occurrence of cholera and other deadly diseases decreased. By 1901, the Board of Public Health, which became a bureau later, was already established. Medical teams were also sent to Philippine towns and barrios to explain the significance of modern health sanitation and hygiene. The Americans also opened asylums for the insane, orphans, and others.

As a result of the measures taken by American authorities, mortality rates declined and the Filipinos improved their standard of living.

Filipinos could not find any foreign markets for their surplus products.

IV. TRANSPORTATION AND COMMUNICATIONS

Without good transportation and communications, trade and commerce would be hard to develop. Hence, the Americans, during their administration of the Philippines, built roads and bridges and improved transportation and communications.

Have Trains, Will Travel. The Philippines at the end of the Spanish occupation had only less than 1,000 miles of road. By 1935, the country's mileage rose to less than 13,000 miles. In 1898, there were only 2,600 bridges and culverts; by 1935, they had increased to 8,100. Trucks, cars, and railway cars were introduced, making the speedy transportation of commercial goods. There were only 121.10 miles of railway in 1903; the figures rose to 866.30 miles in 1935. The government acquired the Manila-Dagupan Railway Company, which later became the Manila Railroad Company. They later added more railroad lines to the northern and to the southern part of Luzon. Thus, trains were widely used in the Philippines.

They Still Love The Bull Carts. Of course, today they still love the bull carts (*karitons*) used by farmers in the rural areas, in spite of the presence of trucks. They still use them for transportation of goods. But the *calesas*, and the *karetelas*, which were still common during the American regime until the recent years, have been replaced by the U.S. Army vintage jeeps converted into Philippine jeepneys, new vehicles, particularly from Japan, and motorized tricycles. They now clog the traffic in Manila and towns and barrios in the country.

From Island to Island, They Go. Since the Philippines is composed of more than 7,000 islands, water transportation plays a major part in the economic development of the country. During the Spanish time, there was only a small significance of interisland shipping in the country. At that time, all they had were *cascos*, *bancas*, sailboats, and praus. When the Americans occupied the country, they developed interisland shipping. By 1902, they had already more than a hundred ports for domestic shipping. In 1923, a law was passed that allowed locally owned ships to engage in interisland shipping. Today, commercial planes bring people from island to island.

Hello! Hello! How Are You Doing? By 1905, telephone lines were established in Manila. So at that time, they frequently asked, *"Kumusta, anong lagay?"* (How are you doing?) By 1933, radio-telephone service was introduced. Thus, town and provincial capitals were linked together by radio and telephone, and telegraph lines. By 1935, the country's mail offices, more than a hundred of them, handled ordinary mail, telegraphs, money orders, and air mail letters and packages.

V. INDIVIDUAL FREEDOMS

During the first few years of U.S. civil government rule in the Philippines, force was used in suppressing nationalism. Laws were also passed by the Philippine Commission making it a crime for Filipinos to advocate independence. One year before the Philippine-American War or "insurrection" was officially declared over by President Theodore Roosevelt on July 4, 1902, Sedition Law was passed on November 4, 1901. The law was used against journalists, playwrights, and other writers. On November 12, 1902, the Brigandage Act was passed. It classified guerrilla resistance as banditry. Later, there was even a law—the Flag Law—that banned the public display of the Filipino flag from 1907 to 1919. Those conditions made it difficult for any political party that advocated nationalism to survive for long.

More Freedoms. In the later years of American occupation, the Filipinos were allowed to enjoy individual freedoms: freedom of the press, freedom of religious worship, freedom to change residence, and freedom of speech. And hey! Some of them might have said, "I'm free! I'm free!" Yes, democratic ideals were encouraged and practiced.

"Hey, You're Doing Wrong!" Because of the freedoms of speech and of the press, writers and politicians had the chance to complain and protest in their speeches and writings—even against the American administration. (Of course, before the Americans arrived, under the Revolutionary Government and the Republic of Aguinaldo, they had their own freedoms. In fact, they practiced their right to vote when they elected delegates to the Malolos Congress that framed the Malolos Constitution.)

Because of these freedoms, Filipino writers wrote nationalistic plays that were staged, especially in Manila. Some writers, however, were jailed for advocating independence.

VI. INTRODUCTION TO POLITICS

The first political party to be formed in the Philippines in the early years of American rule was pro-American—the Federal Party, which was founded by a group of pro-American Filipinos headed by Trinidad H. Pardo de Tavera.

The Philippines, To Be a State of the U.S.A.? The Federal party wanted the Philippines to be a state of the American union. Naturally, it was from this party that the Americans put men in high government positions during the early days of the U.S. occupation of the Philippines. However, the Federal Party never gained wide acceptance among the Filipinos. To win popular acceptance, the party changed not only its name to Progressive Party but it also abandoned its pro-American ideas. That time, it advocated eventual independence for the Philippines. Despite this change, it won only 16 seats in the 1907 National Assembly elections while the pro-independence Nacionalista Party won 59 seats.

To Be Independent? That's the Question. The Nacionalista Party was formed in March 1907 out of the union of two nationalist parties, the Immediate Independence Party *(Partido Independista Immediata)* and the National Union *(Union Nacionalista).* Both groups were organized soon after Governor-General Henry C. Ide lifted the ban in 1906 on political parties advocating Philippine independence. Sergio Osmena and Manuel Que-

zon were among the leading members of the party favoring immediate independence. Felipe Agoncillo and Rafael Palma were among the prominent leaders of the union that favored early, but not immediate, independence. The two parties merged to better oppose the well-organized Progressives.

VII. SELF-GOVERNMENT

To train the Filipinos in self-government, the United States made it a policy to appoint qualified Filipinos to government positions. As earlier mentioned, a number of prominent Filipinos were named to high positions even during the first few years of the American occupation. Cayetano Arellano was named chief justice of the Philippine Supreme Court. Florentino Torres became the first attorney general.

By 1908, there were already four Filipinos in the Philippine Commission. In the same year, Gregorio Araneta was named secretary of finance and justice. He was the first Filipino to head an executive department.

Americans, 614, Filipinos, 13,240. In the lower levels of government, Filipinos were also appointed to vacant positions, provided they were qualified for the jobs. In 1903, there were more Americans in the government than Filipinos. But by 1921, there were only 614 Americans in the government service compared to 13,240 Filipinos.

In 1912, the Filipinization of the government gained much ground when the Democratic Party won the elections in the United States. President Woodrow Wilson appointed Francis B. Harrison as the new U.S. governor-general. Under his administration, more and more Filipinos were appointed to high government positions. In 1913, five Filipinos were named to the Philippine Commission, thus giving them a majority in this body for the first time.

The Jones Law of 1916. The Jones Law (Philippine Autonomy Act) was signed by President Wilson on August 29, 1916. It was sponsored by U.S. Representative William Atkinson Jones of Virginia.

Filipinos' Bill of Rights. The Jones Law is historically significant to Filipinos. It defined the structure of the government, the powers and duties of the officials, and provided for a bill of rights for Filipinos. It also contained a promise for independence as soon as a stable government had been established.

Under the Jones Law, the executive power was vested in the governor-general (an American). He was appointed by the president of the United States with the advice and consent of the U.S. Senate. The governor-general was assisted by a cabinet composed of department secretaries whom he appointed with the consent of the Philippine Senate. The cabinet was composed of Filipinos except for the secretary of public information who was concurrently the vice governor and had to be an American.

Legislative Power to Filipinos. Legislative power was finally entrusted exclusively to the Filipinos. The law created a Philippine Legislature of two houses—the House of Representatives (lower house) and the Philippine Senate (upper house), in the same manner as the U.S. Congress.

The members of the two houses were elected by the Filipinos. The judicial power was vested in a supreme court to be composed of a Filipino chief justice and associate justices. The Supreme Court members were appointed by the U.S. president with the consent of the U.S. Senate. Filipino and American judges almost equally divided among them the courts of first instance until 1916. After that year, more Filipinos were appointed as judges. Filipinos, as a matter of policy, were appointed as justices of the peace.

VIII. AGITATIONS FOR INDEPENDENCE

In the halls of the Philippine Assembly, the Filipino legislators frequently voiced out calls for independence. So did Filipino resident commissioners in the halls of the U.S. Congress.

Independent Movement Suspended. On April 6, 1917, the United States entered World War I by declaring war on Germany. Thus, the agitations for independence were suspended. The Filipinos supported American's war efforts to show their loyalty to the United States. The Philippine Legislature authorized the construction of a destroyer and a submarine to be given to the U.S. as the Filipinos' contribution to the U.S. war efforts. A Filipino militia was organized and trained for action on the European warfront. Liberty Bonds worth millions of pesos were subscribed by the Filipinos.

Talking About It Again. The campaign for independence resumed once the war ended. In fact, on March 17, 1919, the Philippine legislature passed a resolution expressing the feeling of the Filipinos that the time had come for the U.S. to grant Philippine independence. For his part, Governor-General F. B. Harrison, supposedly sympathetic to the Filipino cause, formally certified that a stable government already existed in the Philippines—a condition provided for by the Jones Law for the granting of Philippine independence.

Plebiscite: What Do You Think? To prove wrong the claims of a number of influential Americans in the Philippines and in the United States that many Filipinos were opposed to independence, the Philippine legislature enacted a bill in 1927. The proposed law called for a plebiscite on the independence question. But this bill was vetoed by President Calvin Coolidge.

In 1930, an independence congress was held in Manila. It was attended by approximately 2,000 delegates representing the various sectors of Filipino society. This congress passed a resolution expressing aspiration for independence of the Filipinos.

The Democratic Party lost in the 1920 U.S. presidential elections. A Republican, Warren G. Harding, became the next U.S. president. Shortly after his inauguration, he sent a special mission to the Philippines to determine the real political situation in the Philippines. The mission was composed of General Leonard Wood and former Governor-General W. Cameron Forbes.

No Independence, They Say. The Wood-Forbes Mission stayed in the Philippines for four months. In October 1921, the mission submitted to the President a report unfavorable to the independence campaign of the Filipinos. Another mission sent to the country also had an unfavorable recommendation to the independence cause.

To support Filipino campaign for independence, special missions were sent to Washington. They were given the task of persuading the U.S. Congress to pass an independence law for the Philippines.

In 1930, the Democratic Party won in the congressional elections. Optimistic, the Philippine Legislature in November 1931 sent another mission to the United States to work for the passage of an independence law. This time, there were more American lawmakers who favored Philippine independence. One of them was U.S. Senator Harry B. Hawes, who came to Manila in 1931 to survey the existing conditions in the country. On his return to Washington, Senator Hawes filed an independence bill in the U.S. Congress, with U.S. Congressman Hare and U.S. Senator Cutting as co-sponsors. It was approved in December 1932. However, President Herbert Hoover, a Republican, vetoed the bill.

At Last! At Last! The U.S. Congress, nevertheless, repassed the bill on January 17, 1933. This law came to be known as the Hare-Hawes-Cutting Act. But before the law could take effect, it had to be approved by the Philippine Legislature.

Sergio Osmeña, as president pro tempore of the Senate and Manuel Roxas, as speaker of the House, headed the independence mission which was in the US when the Hare-Hawes-Cutting Act was passed. Manuel Quezon, at that time the president of the Senate, presumed to be fearful that the success of the two would threaten his leadership, asked them to come home before the bill was finally approved. Probably aware of Quezon's reason for asking them to return home, Osmeña and Roxas refused to do so, even when Quezon stopped further funding for the mission. Thus, when the two finally came home on June 11, 1933, the Nacionalista Party was divided into those who opposed the Hare-Hawes-Cutting Act and those who agreed (the Antis and the Pros, respectively). Quezon headed the Antis and Roxas headed the Pros.

'No!' Says Quezon. The reason Quezon gave why he objected to the Hare-Hawes-Cutting Act was that he believed the law's provisions on trade relations were disadvantageous to the Philippines. He cited the provision that limited the emigration of Filipinos to the U.S. and the retention by the U.S. of military bases in the Philippines. Osmeña and Roxas, on the other hand, claimed that the Hare-Hawes-Cutting Act was the best independence law that the Filipinos could obtain from the U.S.

Something Happens. As Quezon was in control of the Legislature, it was easy to depose Osmeña as president pro-tempore of the Senate and Roxas as speaker of the House. On October 17, 1933, the Philippine Legislature rejected the Hare-Hawes-Cutting Act. Hence, Quezon was instructed to head another independence mission to the U.S.

At Last, Again. The U.S. Congress enacted a new independence bill sponsored by Senator Millard Tydings and Representative John McDuffie. It was signed into law by President Franklin D. Roosevelt on March 24, 1934. This act was almost a word-for-word copy of the Hare-Hawes-Cutting Act which Quezon had opposed so much.

However, Quezon played up the minor differences between the two acts. What was important was that he brought home the Tydings-McDuffie Act. In the elections that followed, the Antis soundly beat the Pros, thus ensuring that Quezon would achieve his lifetime ambition, which was to become the first Filipino Governor General or the First President of the Philippine Commonwealth.

No Independence Yet, Sorry. The Tydings-McDuffie Act provided for the establishment of a Commonwealth of the Philippines which would govern the country for a transition period of ten years. After that period, on July 4, 1946, the United States would proclaim the independence of the Philippines. The Philippine Legislature approved the Tydings-McDuffie Law on May 1, 1934.

IX. THE COMMONWEALTH OF THE PHILIPPINES

In the national elections of September 17, 1935, Manuel L. Quezon was elected as president and Sergio Osmeña as vice president of the Commonwealth of the Philippines.

THE JAPANESE OCCUPATION OF THE PHILIPPINES (1942-1945)

In the second half of the decade of the 1930s, events in Europe and in Asia brought the world into another catastrophic turmoil. Adolf Hitler was determined to expand Germany. In a swift move in 1936, he sent German troops to the Rhineland and annexed Austria two years later. In 1935, Italy invaded the African nation of Ethiopia. In 1938, Hitler controlled half of the Czechoslovakia and took over the rest in 1939. In Asia, Japan attacked and conquered Manchuria in 1931 and by 1938, she had taken over most of the great cities and ports of China.

In 1940, Germany, Italy, and Japan signed the Tripartite Pact to formally become allies. They came to be known as the Axis Powers.

World War II broke out in Europe on September 1, 1939, when Hitler invaded Poland. Great Britain and later, France, who had promised to defend Poland in case of an attack, declared war on Germany.

In Asia, the Japanese attack and invasion of China created some tension between Japan and the United States. In 1939, the United States terminated her trade agreement with Japan after she criticized Japan's aggression in China. As a result, Japan could no longer buy most of the metals, machinery, and other materials she needed for war efforts.

When Japanese forces occupied French Indochina in July 1941, the Americans imposed an oil embargo on Japan, froze all Japanese assets in the United States, and demanded that Japan withdraw her forces from China and Indochina. In the face of these developments, Japan decided to go to war against the United States and Great Britain.

I. OUTBREAK OF WAR

The Japanese, without formally declaring war, attacked by air the U.S. naval base in Pearl Harbor, Hawaii, in the morning of December 7, 1941. Pearl Harbor was the headquarters and main base of the U.S. Pacific Fleet. Caught unaware, the U.S. suffered heavy losses. On December 11, Germany and Italy declared war on the United States. The U.S. Congress immediately responded by declaring war on the two European allies of Japan.

By Air and by Land. On December 8, 1941, Japanese planes bombed Davao, Tuguegarao (Cagayan), Iba (Zambales), Tarlac, and Pampanga where the U.S. had military bases. Thus, the Japanese wiped out American air power in the Philippines. The air raids again caught the Americans by surprise.

At the same time, at dawn of the same day, the first Japanese landing was made at Basco, on Batan Island, north of Luzon. About 4,909 troops captured the airport almost without any opposition. The Japanese made this air strip the base of operations of their fighter planes.

The following day, Manila was bombed. Afterwards, almost daily, there were Japanese air raids in Manila and in other places in the country. Bombed in Manila on December 9 and 10 were Nichols Air Field and the Manila Port Area.

On December 10, about 2,000 men from the Tanaka Detachment occupied Aparri. In Vigan, Ilocos Sur, some 2,000 troops of the Kanno Detachment landed and met little opposition from Philippine Constabulary soldiers.

Some American and Filipino pilots engaged the enemy in the air.

On December 10, Captain Jesus Villamor, a courageous Filipino pilot, flying an obsolete P-26 and in the company of two other pilots, drove off some enemy planes preventing their attack on Zablan Field. Later, with six other planes against 45 enemy planes in two formations over Fort McKinley and Nichols Field in Manila, he shot down one enemy plane. Then they drove off the remaining 44 enemy fight-ers. Villamor was awarded the Distinguished Service Cross.

On December 18, First Lieutenant Boyd, commander of the 17th Pursuit Squadron, shot down four Japanese fighter planes over Aparri. Also, he strafed about 20 planes on the runway at Vigan, Ilocos Sur. He was also given the Distinguished Service Cross award.

The Kimura Detachment of 2,500 men invaded Camarines Norte and Sur provinces on December 12. The airfield at Legaspi was captured. At that time, the airfields at Aparri, Tuguegarao, and at Vigan, Ilocos Sur, were also used by the enemy.

On December 20, the Tanaka Detachment and the Kanno Detachment joined forces in Vigan and proceeded their march to the south. By December 20, enemy landings also took place in Davao City and Jolo, Sulu.

On December 22, landings were made in Agoo, Caba, and Bauang in La Union Province in the Lingayen Gulf area. Almost at the same time, Mauban, Atimonan, and Siain, all in Quezon Province along Lamon Bay, were occupied by the Japanese.

Bataan Is Calling! On December 23, 1941, "WPO-3" took effect; that is, the retreat of Filipino and American soldiers to the Bataan peninsula where they were to make their last stand to await reinforcements from America. President Manuel L. Quezon and his cabinet evacuated to Corregidor Island.

On December 26, Manila was later declared an open city to spare it from further Japanese attacks. However, the bombardments continued. Historic buildings such as The Santo Domingo Church, San Juan de Letran, and Sta. Catalina College were bombed. And on January 2, 1942, Japanese troops entered the city from Lingayen, Pangasinan Province, and from Lamon Bay.

The Filipino and American troops were hard-pressed to prevent the Japanese advance. They, however, were inadequately equipped and didn't have air support.

By January 7, 1942, the United States Armed Forces in the Far East (USAFFE), under the overall command of General Douglas MacArthur, positioned themselves well across the upper part of the Bataan Peninsula. That was part of their strategy. Because they were there and there were forces on Corregidor and its satellite island fortress, the Japanese were not able to use the Manila Bay throughout the siege. (The bay is across the peninsula from Manila.) At the first Japanese offensive, MacArthur's forces gained ground. Fightings stopped by mid-February as the Japanese reorganized and waited for reinforcement. However, the Filipino and American soldiers didn't attack.

Hunger and Diseases. At that time, rations for the USAFFE forces consisted only of about fifteen ounces of food. The diet consisted only of mule, carabao, or monkey meat. Hunger and diseases struck the Filipino and American soldiers. As a result, thousands of them died of malaria, beriberi, amoebic dysentery, and scurvy. Due to the Japanese blockade, food, medicine, and other supplies didn't reach the forces. More troops died of malnutrition and diseases than by the enemy's bullets.

II. BATAAN AND CORREGIDOR

The defense of Bataan and Corregidor played a very important part in the war against Japan in the Far East.

Bataan and Corregidor? Why? Why did the American and Filipino soldiers retreat to Bataan to make their "last ditch stand" against the enemy? And why did General MacArthur and his staff depart for Corregidor?

Here are excerpts from Mariano Villarin's book that may give some answers to the questions. (Reprinted from *We Remember Bataan and Corregidor: The Story of the American and Filipino Defenders of Bataan and Corregidor and Their Captivity* by Mariano Villarin, $21.95 including postage, copyright 1990. Used by permission of Mariano Villarin, 1910 Harding St., Long Beach, CA 90805.)

Bataan is a peninsula jutting out from Luzon between Manila Bay and the South China Sea. To the south, three miles off shore and at the entrance to Manila Bay, lies Corregidor, the so-called impregnable fortress. The province is mostly jungle and is one of the world's worst malarial regions. The situation was aggravated by the presence of 26,000 hungry civilians whose homes along the coastal towns had been obliterated by enemy bombs. Instead of fleeing toward Pampanga or Manila, they preferred to stay on Bataan, believing that they would be safe in a sanctuary protected by the USAFFE. But they were wrong. Into this craggy 28-by-18-mile inescapable trap entered 12,000 American and 66,000 Filipino troops for a "last ditch stand" under WPO-3.

In the chapter entitled *The Defense of Bataan*, Villarin wrote:

While Tokyo was bestowing plaudits on General Tomoyuki Yamashita for his capture of Singapore on February 15, General Homma was having the discomfiture from credentials which didn't impress Premier Hideki Tojo. Homma failed to subdue the USAFFE within the allotted time of fifty days. More than three months had elapsed and the capture of Corregidor did not appear to be imminent, while Bataan was still holding out. Homma's counterparts in Hong Kong, Malaya, and the Dutch East Indies had reaped, or were reaping, productive results and Homma wasn't producing. His 14th Army had sustained heavy non-battle casualties; 13,000 men were in the hospitals between January 1 and March 31. Homma swallowed his pride and asked for reinforcements. The Tokyo warlords sent the 4th Division which reached Luzon on March 15. Other arrivals were a strong air brigade and artillery units.

Here's how Villarin described a part of the final battle of Bataan on April 3, 1942, on Mt. Samat:

The deceptive lull in the front lines took on a sinister note when Homma unleashed the full fury of an all-out air-artillery bombardment. It was April 3, the anniversary of the death of the legendary Emperor Jimmu, the founder of the Empire. Homma wanted to celebrate this religious occasion in a military way by staging the final offensive of the Bataan campaign. It was also Good Friday of Holy Week for the Christian defenders who were observing the anniversary of the Crucifixion. Ironically, it was also the starting day of the crucifixion of Bataan. Dark clouds had been gathering over the peninsula for weeks as we stood there waiting for the zero hour. We knew that the Japanese were in the driver's seat ever since they entered Bataan. We knew we were doomed but the reality was now beginning to sink in.

With an array of 150 pieces of assorted artillery the enemy began his catastrophic devastation of the Mount Samat area. For good measure, the bombers of the 22nd Air Brigade delivered more than 60 tons of lethal steel at will, leaving great balls of fire that lit up the whole blooming sky. Then the lighter planes came swooping down and strafed the area to clear the way for their infantry advance while the defenders lay huddled in their foxholes. As terror rained daily when the planes flew unmolested over the defenders' positions, which were now buckling under pressure, the Japanese directed their five-hour-long artillery barrage at the MLR held by the 21st and 41st Divisions.

No More, We Give Up! It was on April 9, 1942, when General Edward P. King, commander of the forces in Bataan surrendered about 76,000 Filipino and American soldiers to the Japanese. General Jonathan M. Wainwright, overall commander of the USAFFE forces was then in Corregidor. Other figures say 70,000, 78,000, and 80,000 were involved. So those who were surrendered included only the forces on Bataan.

The Death March. The prisoners of war who surrendered in Bataan underwent a horrendous ordeal. Around 2,000 escaped to Corregidor and to the surrounding provinces.

Totally unprepared for the big number of prisoners, the Japanese were under a great deal of pressure as they moved the captives within hostile territory. The prisoners were forced to march from Mariveles on the southern end of Bataan to San Fernando, Pampanga, a distance of about 55 miles. From there, some were taken by rail to Capas, Tarlac, where they walked for 80 more miles to Camp O'Donnell. According to some estimates, only 54,000 of the marchers reached the camp. About 10,000 soldiers died on the way and the others escaped. The prisoners walked under a hot sweltering sun with little or no food or water. Many were also brutally killed by Japanese guards. This came to be known as the infamous "Bataan Death March." (Later, Lieutenant General Masaharu Homma, commander of the Japanese Imperial Forces in the Philippines, was found guilty of war crimes by an allied military tribunal after the war. He was hanged.)

Here are excerpts from a book describing the Bataan Death March. (Reprinted from *Under The Rising Sun: Memories of a Japanese Prisoner of War*, by Mario Machi, copyright 1994, Used by permission of Wolfenden, P.O. Box 789, Miranda, CA 95553-0789.)

The days dragged into weeks. The air was foul with the odor of death. At night we fell asleep where we dropped, and in the mornings we were awakened by outbursts of yelling and screeching. The Japanese guards charged in among us, kicking us to our feet. They then herded us back to the road and started us marching. Walking was torture. Now and again we passed the huddled forms of men who had collapsed from fatigue or had been bayoneted.

Our thirst had become almost unbearable by now. Sometimes one of us was permitted to collect canteens from our comrades and fill them at a stagnant carabao wallows. We held our noses and we drank whatever water we could get.

Prisoners continued to drop, and guards continued their brutal display. There was little we could do for the fallen, except encourage them on. We had learned soon enough that efforts to assist them served only to hasten their deaths and perhaps our own as well. All we could do was encourage them with words. "Don't give up; we're almost there," became our bywords.

The days dragged by, and many prisoners reached the end of their endurance. They went down not singly but by twos and threes. I shall never forget their groans as they tried desperately to get up again, and always with a beaming Japanese guard standing over them with a fixed bayonet. Those who lay lifeless where they had fallen were the only ones free of sinister Japanese brutality.

Bodies were left where they lay, and the stench grew worse and worse with each mile. Occasionally we heard thumping shots from the rifles of guards bringing up the rear, and each shot meant another straggler was dead.

Here are excerpts from chapter 5, "The Death March" in Villarin's book *We Remember Bataan and Corregidor:*

On two occasions I saw the enemy drive his truck deliberately into our marching columns, killing one or two POWs and injuring several others. Invariably, the driver would streak out of sight in order not to be seen by any humane Japanese officer, and the soldiers riding in the rear would laugh at us in sadistic fashion. One of them pointed an accusing finger at me and made a motion with his other hand across the front of his neck as if to say he'd be glad to chop my head off too. We had to be alert at all times because the Japanese soldiers in passing trucks had the annoying habit of reaching out and jabbing at us with bamboo poles. As each truck sped off, the raucous laughter among the Japanese soldiers in the rear would echo in its wake.

At Balanga (Bataan), the Japanese were doling out ladles of steamed rice

U.S. Department of Defense
(Captured photo)

American prisoners of war who died on the Bataan Death March, in April 1942.

from caldrons placed in the rear of a truck. Not all prisoners had mess gear, some were using tin cans, and many were eating voraciously from their bare hands. Then they would go down on their knees to retrieve some of the rice. And that's what the Japanese wanted to see, and derived pleasure from watching.

I saw American and Filipino prisoners crawling on all fours, patiently picking through dirt for grains of rice. A white man and a brown man were now the yellow man's prey, and they were stooping so low that they were relegated to the category of ants looking for crumbs. Those vanquished captives who were tasting a few precious grains of rice picked up from the ground were actually tasting the bitterness of defeat.

During the four days that it took us to cross Bataan Province, it was like living on death row, watching the other captives march with a death-warmed-over appearance. Entering Pampanga Province was like being given a stay of execution. Now we were getting food from our own people. The fistful of rice that each prisoner had received from the Japanese at the last barrio in Bataan was a mere pittance, and not every prisoner was fed. The people thronged the road to see us and, with tears streaming down their faces, they asked for names of their loved ones. Others were flashing the victory sign.

They constantly risked their lives by throwing all kinds of food to us. These included *panocha* (hard brown sugar), *bucayo* (coconut candy), *bibingka* (rice cakes), hard boiled eggs and fruit. The Japanese didn't believe in charity to the captives, so they showed no compunction about swinging their rifles at the women, old men, and children, and kicking over containers with water that had been placed by the residents at the site of the road for us to pick up.

At Balanga (Bataan), they put us into a field, and somebody got to digging around for *camotes* (sweet potatoes). We did find some and a Filipino soldier had a can and filled it with water and he was boiling the camotes. The guard told him to put out the fire, but the Filipino didn't understand what he was saying. The Japanese bayoneted him right under the right shoulder blade and the bayonet came out the front, and this guy screamed and started coughing, and dropped over the fire, putting the fire out with his body. The Japanese put his foot on his back and pulled the bayonet out, wiped it off on the dead man's clothing and moved on.

Ah, Corregidor! After the fall of Bataan, the Japanese intensified their attack on Corregidor. Night and day, the enemy bombings continued. And the USAFFE forces fired back with their guns and mortars. At that time, according to author Villarin, their guns included 56 coastal guns and mortars, 76 3-inch AA guns and ten 60-inch searchlights. The units trapped on the island-fortress were the 59th CA, 60th CA(AA), 91st CA(PS), 92d CA(PS), 4th Marines, 1st CA(PA), and 16th Naval District.

From the chapter titled *The Rock That Crumbled*, Author Villarin *(We Remember Bataan and Corregidor)* has this to say:

After the fall of Bataan, the island-fortress of Corregidor, known as the "Rock," seemed like a burning, derelict ship helplessly adrift upon a sea of distress. Without air or naval support to sustain its strength, the embattled island was left to fend for itself as the intense Japanese bombardment from the mainland and the air raged unabated.

Corregidor is a pollywog-shaped island with its head pointing west toward the China Sea and its long tail curving southeastward into Manila Bay. It is three and a half miles long and narrows down to a width of 600 yards in the middle, the total area being roughly three square miles. The Spanish word *corregidor* (corrector) originated when the Spanish customs inspectors required incoming and outgoing ships to stop at the island to have their papers checked and corrected.

Although the Battle of Manila Bay was won by Commodore George Dewey in 1898, it was not until 1908 that a regular army post was established on Corregidor and it was named Fort Mills, after an artillery general. The three fortified islands around the Rock were also given names: Caballo became known as Fort Hughes, El Fraile as Fort Drum, and Carabao as Fort Frank.

Above the bulbous head of the pollywog was a plateau called Topside, on which were located the headquarters, officers quarters, barracks, the parade grounds and the bulk of the batteries. On

Middleside, a small plateau, were located a hospital, NCO quarters, schoolhouses for dependent children, and a three-story mile-long barracks, reputed to be the longest in the world. Bottomside was just above sea level where the docks, power plant and Barrio San Jose were located.

Construction of additional concrete emplacements and bomb-proof shelters ceased in 1922 when the Washington Peace Treaty imposed restrictions on further military construction. The total cost of the defense installations on the Rock alone amounted to $150 million. The Rock was known as the "Gibraltar of the East" because Malinta Tunnel was considered as one of the most famous underground fortifications in the world. The tunnel was 912 feet long and 24 feet wide and was honeycombed with 24 laterals. During the war, it contained the USAFFE headquarters, the Commonwealth Government, a 1,000-bed hospital, shops and vast quantities of supplies.

In another part of the chapter, Villarin said:

The worst bombardment of the Rock occurred at noon of December 29 (1941) when 18 bombers escorted by 19 fighters dropped some 50 tons of bombs. Half an hour later, a second wave of 22 light bombers dropped 66 bombs on Bottomside and Topside, followed by a wave of 18 dive bombers which dropped bombs from a low altitude. After the dive bombers left at 1300 hours, the last wave of 60 navy planes swooped in to finish the job. The entire raid succeeded in pulverizing 60 percent of the wooden structures on Corregidor while the major installations remained intact. At least 36 were killed and 140 wounded. Japanese losses were 17 bombers.

The next day, President Manuel L. Quezon and Vice President Sergio Osmena were inaugurated into their second term in a simple ceremony at the west entrance of Malinta Tunnel. Fortunately, there were no air raids on that day, which was also Rizal Day.

Goodbye, Corregidor. The Japanese predicted that they could completely capture Corregidor within a matter of hours after the fall of Bataan. However, the siege of Corregidor lasted twenty-seven days.

On the night of February 20, 1942, President Quezon, his family and members of his Cabinet left Corregidor aboard the submarine *Swordfish* for the United States, where, later, a commonwealth government-in-exile was established. With Quezon in Washington were Vice President Sergio Osmeña and some of the members of the Commonwealth War Cabinet. Earlier, U.S. President Roosevelt urged Quezon and other Filipino leaders to escape to the U.S.

Later, on March 11, 1942, General MacArthur, his family, and the USAFFE staff were sneaked off the Rock by a flotilla of four PT boats bound for Australia upon orders from President Roosevelt. MacArthur left the command of the United States forces in the Philippines to Lieutenant General Jonathan M. Wainwright. MacArthur arrived in Australia safely, where he promised the Filipinos, "I came through and I shall return!"

The Rock Crumbles. By May 4, 1942, Corregidor had already absorbed 16,000 hits in a single day. It was at this time, that Japanese forces were already prepared for invasion of the Rock. The invading transports were on 100 boats and barges and 11 gunboats. The attack forces included 5,000 Japanese troops who attacked the Rock in two waves. The defenders fought the invaders gallantly.

It was on May 6, 1942, when General Wainwright sent a message to President Roosevelt, informing the president of his desire to surrender. After that, he sent a message to General Homma through the "Voice of Freedom," offering to surrender, along with his men. Then in the afternoon of the same day, they met at a conference table. That ended the defense of the Rock.

It took the Japanese four months to capture Bataan. Next, the enemy failed to use Manila Bay because courageous American and Filipino soldiers gallantly defended Corregidor for twenty-seven days.

But Bataan and Corregidor fell to the Japanese because of the help that never came. At that time, the United States and Britain agreed on the "Europe-First Policy," which gave priority to the war in Europe.

However, the stubborn defense of Bataan and Corregidor by American and Filipino soldiers disrupted the Japanese timetable for the conquest of Southeast Asia. As a result, General Homma of the Japanese forces was relieved of his position.

III. ESTABLISHMENT OF JAPANESE RULE

After the fall of Manila to the Japanese forces, they began to establish their authority in areas already under their control. As early as January 3, 1942, Lieutenant General Masaharu Homma issued a proclamation declaring that U.S. sovereign over the Philippines no longer existed. He also announced the establishment of martial law under a Japanese military administration.

The Japanese invited a group of prominent Filipino leaders to form a new government of the Philippines. Such government was to be under the supervision and control of Japanese military authorities. He announced the formation of the Philippine Executive Commission to act as a temporary Philippine government. Prominent Filipinos who had served in the Philippine Commonwealth government were named to head each department, to which Japanese advisers were also assigned.

There were, however, some Filipino leaders who chose not to collaborate with the Japanese. One such leader was Jose Abad Santos, the Chief Justice of the Supreme Court of the Philippines. Captured in Cebu, Abad Santos was asked by the Japanese to collaborate with them. He refused and was executed by the Japanese in Malabang, Lanao Province in Mindanao on May 2, 1943.

The failure of the Japanese to win Filipino loyalty was mainly because of their cruelty. Brutally oppressive, they issued many rules, which they enforced with inhumanity. Violations meant a slapping from Japanese sol-

Filipinas Heritage Library

Japanese shouting "Banzai" beside a big gun in one of Corregidor's batteries. The photo was widely circulated by the Japanese, May 1942.

diers, arrest, torture, or, worse, death. The Japanese Army took from the Filipinos whatever it needed, especially food, which was already getting scarce. People suspected of being guerillas were arrested, tortured, and executed. Suspected guerrillas were beheaded and their severed heads paraded in the town to show the people that they meant business.

Many Filipino women, some still in the teens, were forced into being "comfort women" to serve the sexual needs of Japanese soldiers.

Massacres of Civilians. Most of the Filipinos who served in the Japanese-controlled government tried to ease the harsh rule of the

Japanese. However, their efforts were largely in vain. The Japanese became more merciless as the tide of war turned against them and the Americans neared the Philippines. The Japanese were desperate and did barbaric and inhuman acts. They massacred innocent men, women, and children, by bayoneting them to death.

The Second Philippine Republic. The Japanese authorities in the Philippines ordered the creation of the Preparatory Commission for Philippine Independence, headed by Jose P. Laurel. Its task was to frame a constitution for an "independent" Philippines. The Constitution was finished and signed by the members of the commission on September 4, 1943. It was ratified three days later by the members of the Kalibapi (*Kapisanan sa Paglilingkod sa Bagong Pilipinas*). It was not truly a Filipino constitution, as compared to the 1935 Constitution. It established a supposedly independent Republic of the Philippines. The Kalibapi elected the members of the legislature. The National Assembly then elected Jose P. Laurel to be president of the Philippine Republic and Benigno S. Aquino, the Kalibapi director-general, as the National Assembly's speaker.

Japanese-Style Philippine Independence. On October 14, 1943, the "independence" of the Philippines was proclaimed as the Philippine Republic, the second republic in the nation's history, inaugurated. With its inauguration, the Philippine Executive Commission ceased to exist. The Japanese Military Administration was withdrawn.

The new republic, however, was ignored by most countries. Only Japan, her Axis allies (Italy and Germany), Spain, and a handful of other states, mostly Axis satellite nations, recognized the Philippines. The Allied Powers and the rest of the world at war against the Axis did not recognize the new republic. Even the majority of Filipinos did not recognize the new republic, as they considered Quezon their leader and the commonwealth as their legitimate government. They felt that the new republic was merely a puppet government, still subject to the control of Japan.

Dried Papaya Leaf Cigarettes. During the Japanese occupation, the cost of cigarettes was too much—even faked cigarettes such as *Camel, Lucky Strike,* and *Chesterfield*. No problem. The Filipinos manufactured their own cigarettes out of dried Papaya leaves. They used newspapers and even books to wrap the leaves. For tea, they dried used grains of coffee in the sun and then boiled them again for drinking. Also, toasted rice and corn, as well as mango leaves, were boiled as substitutes for tea.

How about rice? Suppose they didn't have rice, especially those Manila residents who suffered most economically during the Japanese regime? Well, they practiced the old way of bartering: they exchanged "something" they had for a sack of rice from farmers and other people.

> On some street corners, there were Japanese sentries. When you passed by one of them, you had to bow properly. If you didn't do it the way it should be done, you would probably be slapped.

Since rice was insufficient, the Filipinos cooked it with corn; sometimes the corn was more than the rice. Filipinos called that mixture *may kisa*.

The Japanese manufactured money—the Mickey Mouse. But they were almost worthless. For example, a few *gantas* of rice could be had with a small sack of Japanese money. In other words, many Filipinos became "rich" in terms of money they possessed, especially those who engaged in buy-and-sell business. Almost everyone in Manila became "buyers and sellers" of just about everything—even gold teeth extracted by thieves from the teeth of the dead at cemeteries.

Because of the lack of food, many Filipinos died of malnutrition, tuberculosis, and other diseases.

Laughter in the Midst of Danger and Uncertainties. During the war, the people had not forgotten to laugh and entertain themselves. They saw slapstick comedies on stage and pre-war films in movie theaters. Also, popular English plays, adapted into Tagalog, were held at the old Metropolitan Theater in Manila.

"Bow to Me!" Bowing was the Japanese soldiers' way of humiliating the Filipino people, whether they didn't know it or not. On some street corners, there were Japanese sentries. When you passed by one of them, you had to bow properly. If you didn't do it the way it should be done, you'd most probably be slapped. The same thing would happen, if you made any mistake in answering his question. Yes, they're still fresh in this author's mind—those years, while as a young boy, I used to bow to a Japanese sentry while on my way to school. How afraid I was then. Of course, not anymore. Now, we pass by Osaka or Narita airports in Japan when we go home for a visit to the Philippines. There are now many Filipinos working in Japan. They are called *Japayukis*.

The Fighting Guerillas. Resistance to the Japanese continued in the form of guerrilla warfare waged by former Filipino soldiers and a few Americans who did not surrender to the Japanese. They were later joined by released Filipino prisoners of war, Filipino civilians who wanted to take revenge on the Japanese for their cruelty, and other patriotic young men and women. The guerrilla movement also included many high-ranking officials of the Japanese-sponsored government who passed on vital information to the guerrillas about Japanese military plans and activities. U.S. submarines supplied the guerrillas with arms and ammunition, communications equipment, food, and medical supplies.

The guerrillas contributed tremendously to the liberation of the Philippines. They gave General MacArthur military information about presence and movements of the Japanese. They carried out acts of sabotage against the Japanese and ambushed Japanese patrols or attacked Japanese garrisons. However, the various guerilla units were not always united. Because of jealousy and intrigue, some guerrillas fought not only the Japanese, but also each other.

IV. LIBERATION OF THE PHILIPPINES

The Philippines was the last major conquest of Japan in the Pacific. The tide of war turned against Japan after the famous Battle of Midway in 1942, with the United States foiling the planned Japanese invasion of Midway Island in the mid-Pacific. This victory ended Japan's naval superiority in the Pacific and was the turning point of the war against Japan. From then on, the Japanese didn't win any major victories against the Americans.

Filipino Regiments. Many Filipinos in America were denied enlistment in the Armed Forces of the United States at the beginning of the Second World War. Since they were then alien; they were not eligible to become U.S. citizens. President Franklin D. Roosevelt signed an executive order in 1942, to permit Filipinos to enlist. The First and Second Filipino Infantry Regiments, consisted of more than 7,000 Filipinos and Filipino Americans.

The First Filipino Infantry Regiment, consisting of Filipinos only, was activated on July 13, 1942 at Salinas, California with 143 officers, 6 warrant officers, and 3,019 enlisted men. On the other hand, the Second Filipino Infantry Regiment was activated at Camp Cooke in California on November 21, 1942. They were trained in several camps, including Camp San Luis Obispo in California. About 1,000 of them were sneaked into the Philippines by submarines for secret missions. Thus, they and other members of the regiments helped in the liberation of the Philippines from the Japanese.

Many of those soldiers found wives in the Philippines and they and their families composed the third wave of Filipinos to the United

> Some guerrillas fought not only the Japanese, but also with each other.

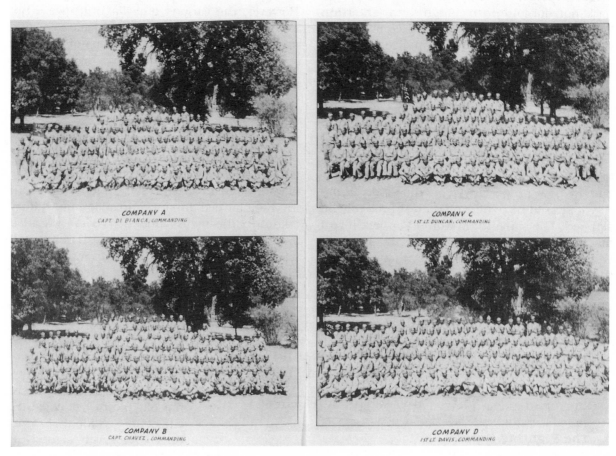

COMPANY A
CAPT. DI BIANCA, COMMANDING

COMPANY C
1ST LT. DUNCAN, COMMANDING

COMPANY B
CAPT. CHAVEZ, COMMANDING

COMPANY D
1ST LT. DAVIS, COMMANDING

Washington State Archives

**Photo shows a part of the thousands of Filipino soldiers
in the U.S. belonging to the Philippine infantry regiments formed
and trained in California to participate in World War II.**

States. Among the war veterans who later served in the U.S. government were former Associate Justice Ben Menor, the first Filipino American Supreme Court Justice, and Chief Justice William S. Richardson, both of whom served in the Hawaii Supreme Court. They both belonged to the First Filipino Battalion.

Filipino Americans. Other Filipino Americans wanted to serve their native country. They joined other branches of the U.S. Armed Forces, including the Army and the Navy.

Guadalcanal Invasion. On August 7, 1942, U.S. troops invaded and wrestled Guad-

alcanal in the Solomons from the Japanese as the first major American offensive in the Pacific. One Japanese-held Pacific island or outpost after another fell to the advancing Americans.

Among America's top military leaders, opinion was divided on the shortest and least costly road to the Japanese homeland. The majority was in favor of a landing in Mindanao, followed by a major assault on Leyte. From Leyte, the Americans would then go to Formosa, bypassing all the other islands in the Philippines. General Douglas MacArthur opposed this plan. He wanted all of the Philippines to be liberated from the Japanese first before invading Formosa.

Leyte Invasion Is Just the Beginning. Under the plans finally approved by the American military leaders, General MacArthur began the liberation of the Philippines with a landing at Leyte. Before the invasion, U.S. carrier-based planes attacked Mindanao on September 9 and 10, 1944. This was the first American raid in the Philippines. Japanese bases in other parts of the country were also bombed. On September 21, American planes raided Manila for the first time, with more raids in the next few days. These air strikes destroyed Japanese air power in the Philippines.

On October 20, 1944, the main invasion of Leyte began. After a bombardment by U.S. warships, troops of four U.S. divisions landed on the eastern beaches of Leyte. In the afternoon of the same date, General MacArthur, together with President Osmeña of the Philippine Commonwealth, Brigadier General Carlos P. Romulo, and a few other American and Filipino officials went ashore at Leyte. A call for the Filipinos to cooperate in the liberation of the country was made. In public ceremonies in Tacloban, Leyte, on October 23, General MacArthur formally announced the restoration of the Commonwealth of the Philippines. Pending the liberation of Manila, Tacloban became the temporary seat of the civil government.

The American invasion of Leyte precipitated serious furious engagements between American and Japanese warships that came to be known as the Battle of Leyte Gulf. Japan assembled most of her remaining fighting ships—7 battleships, 6 aircraft carriers, 19 cruisers and scores of destroyers—and threw them against the U.S. ships protecting the invasion. The battle was a decisive victory for the Americans, who were able to virtually wipe out the Japanese armada. This battle, described by naval historians as the greatest naval battle of the war, led to the destruction of the Japanese navy and gave the United States complete mastery of the sea. it also spelled the success of the Leyte invasion.

With only a few planes and ships left to oppose the American advances to their homeland, the Japanese decided to adopt a new military tactic—suicide attacks by planes on U.S. warships, particularly American aircraft carriers. A Japanese suicide air group, named *kamikaze* or divine wind, was organized in Mabalacat, Pampanga Province, on October 19, 1944. The kamikaze pilots would deliberately crash their planes onto American warships. In the battle for the liberation of the Philippines, 424 Japanese kamikaze pilots flew suicide missions.

After Leyte, U.S. troops invaded Mindoro in Luzon on December 15, 1944. On January 9, 1945, a U.S. flotilla of more than 800 ships arrived in Lingayen Gulf in Luzon from Leyte. In the morning of that day, some 68,000 American troops hit the beaches of Lingayen and quickly advanced inland. Joined by Filipino guerrillas, the Americans advanced southward towards Manila, capturing the coastal towns against light to moderate Japanese resistance. Stiffer resistance was encountered only when they attacked Clark Field, later known as Clark Air Force Base, in Angeles, Pampanga Province.

Nasugbu, Batangas Landing. On January 31, 1945, elements of the U.S. 8th Army landed in Nasugbu, Batangas. Three days later, paratroopers of the U.S. 11th Airborne Division dropped on Tagaytay (Cavite) and headed northward for Manila. Meanwhile, General MacArthur, fearing the fate of 4,000 American and Allied prisoners of war and civilian internees held by the Japanese inside the University of Santo Tomas, ordered the U.S. 1st Cavalry Division in Guimba, Nueva Ecija, to head straight for Manila and free the Americans and Allies.

Manila, Here We Come! Fighting off Japanese resistance along the way, two armored columns of the First Cavalry dashed towards Manila. By dusk of February 3, 1945, the Americans entered Manila. Guided by Filipino guerrillas, cavalrymen in tanks crashed through the gates of the University of Santo Tomas and freed the American prisoners. However, it took the Americans more than a month to rout the last Japanese defender.

Jubilant "Angels" of Bataan and Corregidor on their way home
after they were liberated by American troops from the
University of Santo Tomas in Manila, February 1945.

With the liberation of Manila, the Philippine Commonwealth was reestablished in the nation's capital.

On February 27, 1945, General MacArthur, who had been the Philippines' Military Administrator, turned over the reigns of the civil government to President Osmeña on behalf of the United States government. Osmeña succeeded President Manuel L. Quezon, who died in exile in New York in 1944.

One by one, all the major islands in the Philippines occupied by Japanese troops were liberated by General MacArthur's forces. On July 4, 1945, General MacArthur announced that the whole country had been liberated and the Philippine campaign could be considered virtually closed, although fighting was still going on in Northern Luzon.

End of War. World War II came to an end on August 15, 1945, with Japan surrendering unconditionally to the Allies. The formal surrender documents were signed by the Japanese and the Allies aboard the battleship USS *Missouri* in Tokyo Bay on September 2, 1945.

General MacArthur, who was the Supreme Commander of the Allied Powers in Japan, signed in behalf of the triumphant Allied nations.

V. THE THIRD PHILIPPINE REPUBLIC

As provided for by the Tydings-McDuffie Act, Philippine independence was to be granted at the end of a 10-year transition period. During this time, the Philippines would be governed by a Philippine Commonwealth that would become the government of the Republic of the Philippines once independence was proclaimed. The transition period ended in 1945, the same year that World War II, the biggest and most destructive war in history, came to an end.

The Last Commonwealth. After the liberation of the Philippines, the First Congress of the Philippines, which was not able to meet in its first session because of the outbreak of

World War II, was able to convene. The Congress met for the first time on June 6, 1945. Brigadier General Manuel A. Roxas was elected as Senate president while Representative Jose C. Zulueta was chosen speaker of the House of Representatives. The lawmaking body passed a law calling for national elections on April 23, 1946.

The Collaboration Issue. One of the most controversial issues that arose with the restoration of the Philippine Commonwealth was the collaboration issue. The issue was what to do with the Filipinos who served under the Japanese-sponsored government. It affected or involved many government officials of the commonwealth government whom Quezon had left behind in Manila in December 1941 when he evacuated to Corregidor and, later, to the United States. They became high officials, too, of the Philippine Executive Commission set up by the Japanese and of the Japanese-sponsored Second Republic of the Philippines. They included Jose P. Laurel, Claro M. Recto, Jose Yulo, Benigno S. Aquino, Teofilo Sison, Rafael Alunan, Jorge B. Vargas, Camilo Osias, and Manuel A. Roxas. For serving under the Japanese, they were called "collaborators" and were accused of being disloyal to the United States and the Philippine Commonwealth.

Those accused of collaboration with the enemy justified their actions on the grounds that they served under the Japanese with great reluctance. They reasoned that they had no voice but to obey the Japanese. Some felt that it was their patriotic duty to collaborate with the Japanese to protect the people from a worse fate. However, the U.S. government was most insistent in punishing those who helped the Japanese and even exerted pressure on Osmeña to take action against the collaborators.

Collaboration Issue Divides Nation. The collaboration issue sharply divided the nation. Just the same, Osmeña could not ignore the clamor and pressure to punish the collaborators. On September 25, 1945, he ordered the creation of the People's Court to try collaboration cases. The collaboration issue also became a top issue in the 1946 elections. Many of the candidates had served under the Japanese. (It came to an end when President Roxas proclaimed amnesty to all political collaborators on January 28, 1948.)

Before the elections were held, the Nacionalista Party split into two camps—one led by Manuel Roxas and the other headed by President Sergio Osmeña. The Roxas camp became the Liberal Party. The two political parties were the major contenders in the 1946 elections. The Liberal Party emerged victorious. Roxas defeated Osmeña. Senator Elpidio Quirino won the vice presidency. Of 16 senatorial seats at stake, the Liberals won 9 to give them a 13-11 edge in the upper house. In the House of Representatives, they won 60 out of 98 seats. Roxas was inaugurated as the last President of the Philippine Commonwealth on May 28, 1946.

Third Republic of the Philippines. On July 4, 1946, an independent Republic of the Philippines was inaugurated at the Luneta in Manila. It was called the third Philippine Republic. The American flag was lowered and the Philippine flag was raised. After the flag ceremony, Roxas, and Quirino again took their oath of office, this time as president and vice president, respectively of the newly independent Republic of the Philippines. Thus, Roxas went down in Philippine history as the last president of the Philippine Commonwealth and the first President of the Republic of the Philippines.

7

MANILAMEN: FILIPINO ROOTS IN AMERICA

About 235 years ago, a settlement was established by Filipino deserters from Spanish ships at Saint Malo in the bayous of Louisiana, near the city of New Orleans, Louisiana. The people who settled

there were called *Manilamen*, who jumped ship during the galleon trade era off New Orleans, Louisiana, and Acapulco, Mexico, to escape Spanish brutalities. Known as *Tagalas*,* they spoke Spanish and a Malay dialect.** They lived together—governing themselves and living in peace and harmony—without the world knowing about their swamp existence.

Lafcadio Hearn

Thus, they became the roots of Filipinos in America.

It was only after a journalist by the name of Lafcadio Hearn published an article in 1883 when their marshland existence was exposed to the American people. It was the first known written article about the Filipinos in the U.S.A.

(Note: This write-up was adapted from Hearn's article entitled *Saint Malo: A Lacustrine Village in Louisiana,* published in the *Harper's Weekly,* March 31, 1883.)

Tagalas probably refers to Tagalogs, an ethnic group in Luzon, Philippines. **This dialect is called *Tagalog*.

The *Times-Democrat* of New Orleans chartered an Italian lugger—a small ship lug-rigged on two or three masts—with Hearn and an artist of the *Harper Weekly* on board. The journey began from the Spanish fort across Lake Ponchartrain. After several miles of their trip, Hearn and the artist saw a change in scenery. There were many kinds of grasses, everywhere along the long route. As Hearn described it, "The shore itself sinks, the lowland bristles with rushes and marsh grasses waving in the wind. A little further on and the water becomes deeply clouded with sap green—the myriad floating seeds of swamp vegetation. Banks dwindle away into thin lines; the greenish, yellow of the reeds changes into misty blue."

Then later, all they could see was the blue sky and blue water. They passed several miles of unhampered isolation. They found a cemetery in the swamp where dead light-keepers were believed buried. They passed Fort Pike and a United States customs house, the eastern part of the Regolets; later, they reached Lake Borgne.

I. THE DESTINATION

And then the mouth of a bayou—Saint Malo Pass appeared. Afterwards, they finally reached their destination: Saint Malo! The

sight that first attracted their attention was the dwellings of the Manilamen. The houses were poised upon supports above the marsh. Then they saw the wharf, where unusual dwellings were grouped together beside it. Fishnets were hung everywhere. Almost everything was colored green: the water, the fungi, the banks, and "every beam and plank and board and shingle of the houses upon stilts."

Manila-style Houses. Hearn described the houses:

All are built in true Manila style, with immense hat-shaped eaves and balconies, but in wood; for it had been found that palmetto and woven cane could not withstand the violence of the climate. Nevertheless, all of this wood had to be shipped to the bayou from a considerable distance, for large trees do not grow in the salty swamp.

Below the houses are patches of grass and pools of water and stretches of gray mud, pitted with the hoof-print of hogs. Sometimes these hoof-prints are crossed with the tracks of the alligator, and, a pig is missing. Chickens there are too—sorry-looking creatures; many have but one leg, others have but one foot: the crabs have bitten them off. All these domestic creatures of the place live upon fish.

—Nestor Palugod Enriquez Collection

**Bayou St. Malo. A drawing
by T. de Thulstrup from
a sketch by O.J. Davidson.)**

There were about thirteen or fourteen large dwellings standing upon wooden piles. Considered as the "most picturesque" of these houses was perhaps that of Padre Carpio, the oldest Manilaman in the village.

Carpio was like a judge in the settlement. All quarrels among the inhabitants were submitted to him for arbitration and decisions. Carpio's house consisted of three wooden edifices; the two outer edifices looked as if

Oldest House in St. Malo

**Oldest House in St. Malo. A drawing
by T. de Thulstrup from
a sketch by O.J. Davidson.)**

**What Do They
Looked Like?** Hearn
described the dwellers:

Most of them
are cinnamon-col-
ored men; a few
are glossily yel-
low, like that
bronze into which
a small proportion
of gold is worked
by the moulder.
Their features are
irregular without
being actually
repulsive; some
have the cheek-
bones very promi-
nent, and the eyes
of several are set

they were wings. The wharf was built in front
of the central edifice probably for conve-
nience.

To protect themselves from bites of mos-
quitoes and other insects, the dwellers had
every window closed with wire netting. During
warm weather, sandflies attacked the fishermen, and, at all times, fleas attacked them.
Reptiles, insects, and other animals abounded
in the swamps.

slightly aslant. The hair is generally
intensely black and straight, but with
some individuals it is curly and
browner....None of them appeared tall; the
great number were under-sized, but all
well-knit, and supple as fresh-water eels.
Their hands and feet were small: their
movements quick and easy, but sailorly
likewise, as of men accustomed to walking
upon rocking decks in rough weather.

In the fishing village, there was one white
man called the *Maestro* (the Tagalog word for

El Maestro's House

**El Maestro's House. A drawing
by T. de Thulstrup from
a sketch by O.J. Davidson.)**

teacher) who had been the ship's carpenter. There was one black man, a Portuguese Negro, who was believed to be a Brazilian castaway.

The Maestro spoke the Manilamen's dialect (probably Tagalog, the dialect in Manila). There were times that he acted as a "priest" or man of God by conferring upon some non-Christian dwellers the sacrament of the Catholic faith.

According to the Maestro, the Manilamen often sent money to friends in Manila to help them emigrate. Usually, the Filipino seamen continued to desert at every chance from

—Nestor Enriquez Palugod Collection

Gambling at St. Malo. A drawing by T. de Thulstrup from a sketch by O.J. Davidson.)

Manila galleons when they docked in New Orleans, Louisiana, or in Acapulco, Mexico. They settled in the marshlands of Louisiana where no Spaniards could reach them.

Living there, they had their contacts with inhabitants of Louisiana, particularly with residents of New Orleans, only a few miles away from the swamplands.

II. THEIR WAY OF LIFE

The Filipino fishermen seldom got sick, although they lived mostly on raw fish that was seasoned with oil and vinegar. (There was no mention of rice, even though rice was and still is the staple food of Filipinos.) There was no liquor found in any of the houses.

Those Manilamen were polite. In fact, every man in the settlement greeted Hearn and the artist with *buenas noches* when they met them at night.

For Men Only. No woman lived in the settlement during Hearn's visit. The fishermen with families had their wives and children in New Orleans and in other localities.

There were two occasions in the past, however, during which two women dwelled in the village. The first woman left after her husband died. The second woman departed after an attempted murder was made on her husband.

One night a man attacked her husband, but the woman and her little son helped subdue the culprit. The villagers tied his hands and feet with fishlines. Then the man was fastened to a stake driven into the muddy land. The next day he was dead. The Maestro buried him in the gray mud. A rude wooden cross was placed on the grave.

No Tax Man, No Policeman. In the settlement, the Manilamen promulgated their own rules and laws. This was done even though they had no sheriff, police, or prison. The settlement was never visited by any Louisiana official, even though it was within the jurisdiction of the parish of St. Bernard. No tax man ever attempted to go there, either.

During busy fishing seasons, the settlement usually had about a hundred men. In case of disputes, the problem was usually submitted to the oldest man in the settlement, Padre Carpio. Usually, Padre Carpio's decisions were final; no one contested them. If a man refused a verdict or became a problem, he was jailed within a "fish-car." Naturally, due to hunger and the harsh weather conditions, coupled sometimes with rising tides, he would usually change his mind and obey any rule or decision. Even if the settlers were all Catholics, a priest rarely went to the village.

No Furniture. There was no furniture in any of the dwellings: no table, no chair, and no bed. What could be considered as mattresses were filled with what Hearn called "dry Spanish-beard." These were laid upon "tiers" of shelves faced against the walls. The fishermen slept at night "among barrels of flour and folded sails and smoked fish."

Art Treasures. What could be considered art treasures preserved at the village were a circus poster and two photographs placed in the Maestro's sea-chest. One was a photo of a robust young woman with "creole eyes" and a bearded Frenchman. They were the wife and father of the Maestro, the ship's carpenter.

Saint Malo-New Orleans Connection. The swamp dwellers had contacts with the city of New Orleans as it was in New Orleans where some of their families lived. It was also the headquarters of an association they formed, *La Union Philipina.* Furthermore, when a fisherman died, he was usually buried temporarily under the reeds in the village. A wooden cross was planted on his grave. Later, the bones were transported to New Orleans by other "luggers" where they were permanently buried.

At the Restaurant They Eat. There was a restaurant in the locality of Lake Borgne. Formerly owned by a Manilaman and his wife, but owned by some Chinese during Hearn's visit, the eatery was mostly patronized by Spanish West Indian sailors. Even businessmen of New Orleans frequented it. The cost of food was cheap and the menu was printed in English and Spanish.

Father and Son. A half-breed Malay, Valentine, was considered as the most intelligent among the fishermen. Educated in New Orleans, Valentine left his job in the city to be with his father, Thomas de los Santos, in the settlement. His father, married to a white woman, had two children, Valentine and a daughter named Winnie. Valentine became the best "pirogue oarsman" among the swamp dwellers.

Latin Names for Men and Boats. Some Latin names (many of which are still today's Filipino names with different spellings) of the swamp dwellers were Marcellino, Francesco, Serafino, Florenzo, Victorio, Paosto, Hilario, Marcetto, Manrico, and Maravilla. Some had names of martyrs. Boats were also named after men and women.

"Let's Play Monte." It was at Hilario's *casa* (house) where dwellers entertained themselves at night after a hard fishing day's work. They played *monte* or a species of Spanish keno. The games were played with a *cantador* (the caller) who would sing out the numbers. Such singings were accompanied by "the annunciation with some rude poetry characteristics of fisher life or Catholic faith:"

Paraja de uno;
Dos picquetes de rivero—

a pair of one (1); the two stakes to which the fish-car is fastened.

Farewell, Manilamen! After Hearn and his group said goodbye, they departed. Hearn described his farewell:

Somebody fired a farewell shot as we reached the mouth of the bayou; there was a waving of picturesque hands and hats; and far in our wake an alligator splashed, his scaly body, making for the whispering line of reeds upon the opposite bank.

III. MANY YEARS AFTER

In 1988, Marina Espina, then a librarian in the University of New Orleans, published a book entitled *Filipinos in Louisiana* (A. F. Laborde & Sons, New Orleans, Louisiana, 1988). Included in the book's front matter is an excerpt from Larry Bartlett (*Dixie*, July 31, 1977):

> The year was 1763, and the schooner had unloaded its cargo at the Spanish provincial capital of New Orleans. Then its crew of Filipino sailors jumped ship and fled into the nearby cypress swamp....

1763 was thus recognized by the Filipino American National Historical Society (FANHS) as the year that the Manilamen arrived and settled in the marshlands of Louisiana. In fact, in 1988, it marked the 225th anniversary of the first Filipino settlement in Louisiana. The association that was organized in 1982 by Frederic and Dorothy Cordova has branches in different parts of the country.

Espina published her book after an extensive research on the first Manilamen who settled in the United States.

According to Espina's findings, every year, during those early years of American history, some of the Filipino sailors jumped ship off Acapulco, Mexico. Afterwards, many of them migrated to the bayous of Louisiana and other gulf ports. Since they spoke Spanish, others married Mexicans, and they assimilated easily with the population there.

Saint Malo, Etc. According to Espina's accounts, Saint Malo was only one of the Filipino settlements. The other settlements were the Manila Village on Barataria Bay in the Mississippi Delta by the Gulf of Mexico; Alombro Canal and Camp Dewey in Plaquemines Parish; and Leon Rojas, Bayou Cholas, and Bassa Bassa in Jefferson Parish, all in Louisiana. The oldest of these settlements was Saint Malo. But Manila Village on Barataria Bay was considered as the largest and the most popular of them all. Houses were built on stilts on a fifty-acre marshland.

Because there were no Filipino women, the Manilamen courted and married Cajun women, Indians, and others. Some of them enrolled their children in schools in New Orleans.

Filipinos in the Battle of New Orleans in 1815. According to oral history passed from generation to generation and later cited by Filipino historians, Filipinos took part in the Battle of New Orleans in 1815 as part of the War of 1812. Those were the men who signed up with the famed French buccaneer, Jean Baptiste Lafitte to join the army of Major-General Andrew Jackson.

—Courtesy: The Historic New Orleans Collection
Acct. No. 1974-25.4.128

Filipino fishermen are shown standing in front of the general merchandise store at the Manila Village.

On January 8, 1815, a British army numbering about 8,000 men prepared to capture New Orleans, Louisiana. Under the command of Major-General Sir Edward M. Pakenham, the British soldiers were pitted against the American army composed of only 1,500 under the command of Major-General Jackson. The American Army consisted of "regular army troops, state militia, western sharpshooters, two regiments and pirates from the Delta Swamps." (Could the Manilamen have been mistakenly identified as pirates having come from the swamps?)

The British moved directly into New Orleans. The English soldiers attacked the American entrenchments. The Americans had fortified their positions behind the earthworks and the barricades of cotton. The battle lasted only half an hour. The British suffered 2,000 casualties, with 289 killed. On the other hand, the Americans had only 71 casualties with 31 killed.

Actually, the battle was meaningless. It occurred before news of the Treaty of Ghent arrived on December 24, 1814, ending the so-called 1812 War.

The Filipinos participation in the war, however, was not recognized in American history.

Here's an excerpt from the book *The Baratarians and the Battle of New Orleans* by Jane Lucas de Grumond. ((Louisiana State University Press, Baton Rouge, Louisiana.)

Cochrane (Admiral Cochrane of the invading British fleet) had sent two officers in a boat to reconnoiter the area below New Orleans via Bayou Bienvenu. They were disguised as fishermen and some of the Spanish fishermen were their guides. They reached the bayou and ascended to the village of the fishermen.

Perhaps the fishermen had something to do with the situation. They were accustomed to fish in Lake Borgne and then to take their fish in pirogues to the canals of De Laronde's and Villere's plantation...

In the above quote, the author mentioned "Spanish fishermen" and the fact that they were used to fishing in Lake Borgne. The only known fishermen in the Lake Borgne area, who spoke Spanish, were the Manilamen. Could there be other Spanish fishermen in the area? Or could they be the Filipinos who were not known as Filipinos but might be known as Spaniards because they spoke Spanish? Could some of the Filipinos from the fishing village have been signed by Lafitte to join the American soldiers? It is indeed a great possibility.

Shrimp Drying. It was at the Manila Village that they started their shrimp-drying industry. The Filipinos built platforms for drying shrimp in an area southeast of New Orleans in the early 1800s. The Manilamen were considered to have introduced in the state and in America the drying of shrimps. The Saint Malo settlement was destroyed by a strong hurricane in 1915 and the Manila Village was washed away by Hurricane Betsy in 1965.

Filipino fishermen trampling on sun-dried shrimp on a platform to take away the hulls and heads.

Courtesy: The Historic New Orleans Collection
Acct. No. 1974-25.4.131

THE FILIPINO IMMIGRATION TO THE UNITED STATES

The Filipinos began to settle in the United States in 1763 when Filipino seamen, called *Manilamen*, jumped ship off New Orleans, Louisiana, and Acapulco, Mexico, during the Manila-Acapulco galleon trade era (1565-1815). Most of the seamen who escaped the brutalities of the Spaniards lived in the bayous of Louisiana, while some settled in Mexico.

Then came students and workers who arrived from 1903 to the early 1930s. However, it was only after the passage on October 3, 1965, of the amendment to the Immigration Nationality Act of 1924 that the Filipinos came to America in significant numbers. The 1965 amendment removed the 1924 "national origins quota system." All of them came to seek economic opportunities and to obtain good education for themselves and their children.

Although the *Manilamen* began to settle in the bayous of Louisiana in 1763, Filipinos arrived in the United States as early as 1587. The galleon *Nuestra Senora de Buena Esperanza*, captained by Pedro de Unamuno, anchored at Morro Bay on October 18,

Washington State Archives

Before departure for the U.S.

1587, off the coast of what is now known as California.

According to de Unamuno's journal cited in Henry R. Wagner's book *Spanish Voyages to the Northwest Coast of America* (San Francisco: California Historical Society, 1929) the landing party, including eight Filipinos disembarked to survey the area.

The captain noted, "Monday, the 19th, about two hours before dawn, I set out on the expedition, with Father Francisco de Noguera and 12 soldiers and eight Luzon Indians with their swords and shields."

On October 20, members of the landing party were attacked by the local Indians. One Filipino was killed in the attack. The landing group retreated to the safety of their ship. They left the dead and wounded behind.

However, the Filipinos' first presence in the United States was considered as a visit, not a settlement.

Periods of Migration. The periods of immigration may be divided into the following:

■ 1763-1903 — Manilamen, mariners, and others;

■ 1903-1934 — *pensionados*, nonsponsored students, and workers;

■ 1945-1965 — military personnel and their families, students and exchange workers; and

■ 1965-to the present — professionals (composed of doctors, nurses, medical technologists, engineers), entrepreneurs, and others.

■ 1903-1992 (overlapped by certain periods above) — thousands of Filipino navy men brought their families to the United States.

I. THE MANILAMEN

The Manilamen jumped ship off New Orleans, Louisiana, and Acapulco, Mexico, during the Manila-Acapulco galleon trade era. They started to settle in 1763 in the bayous and marshes of Louisiana after they escaped from the brutalities of the Spaniards who treated them as slaves aboard ship.

They lived in at least four settlements in the marshland of Louisiana. Most famous of the settlements were the Manila Village and the Saint Malo settlement, about 31 miles from New Orleans. The Manilamen were considered as the first Filipino immigrants of the 1763-1903 period of immigration.

In 1970, Marina Espina, then a librarian in the University of New Orleans undertook an extensive research on the history of the Manilamen. (See the chapter, *Manilamen: Filipino Roots in America.)*

This period of immigration from 1763 to 1903 covered Manilamen, stowaways, seamen, and others.

II. THE *PENSIONADOS* AND THE NON-SPONSORED STUDENTS

The pensionados and the nonsponsored students were part of the 1903-1934 era of immigration to the United States.

In October 1903, the first group of pensionados, composing of 100 students, selected from 20,000 applicants, left the Philippines for America. That was part of an educational program that started in August 1903 following the enactment of the Pensionado Act. They were called pensionados simply because their education in the U.S. was pensioned or supported by the colonial government. They arrived in San Francisco, California, on November 3, 1903.

The pensionados, predominantly males, were most often children of well-to-do families who had connections with the colonial government. Their purpose in coming to America was to obtain degrees or training so that they could become leaders in the private sectors or in the government in their native country.

Of course, these pensionados, mostly men, didn't suffer much difficulty in money, as they had scholarship money from the government. They, however, took part-time jobs, including summer jobs. And they also received support from their families, relatives, and friends.

In 1907, the scholars numbered 183 in colleges and universities. The largest number of students were at the University of Illinois, vator boys, etc., They also worked on farms on the West Coast and in Alaska.

Between 1910 and 1938, there were about 14,000 nonsponsored students. Actually, they came as laborers to make money to attend U.S. schools. Some of them worked in Hawaii and then moved to the mainland. From the mainland, they went to Alaska during the summer months to work in canneries. Some of the successful students were able to save enough money for school and to finish their two-year course in four years. However, many of them, because of lack of money, lack of academic preparation and lack of English efficiency, were unsuccessful in their endeavor. They just worked as laborers on the farms or in hotels, restaurants, homes, and other services.

However, toward the end of the 1920s, the large number of nonsponsored students had a hard time in becoming self-supporting. Among the nonsponsored students were graduates of a normal school in the Philippine Islands who wanted to complete their studies in America

By 1940, there were only few students enrolled in college institutions. Those who

Two Filipina immigrants on a ship.

nine; followed by Purdue University, where eleven were enrolled. The government expense was estimated at $479,940. The total number of pensionados who entered the United States reached 500 by the end of the program. By 1910, almost all of them had returned to the Philippines.

The Nonsponsored Students. Inspired by the accomplishments of these pensionados, other students came to the United States on their own. Being nonsponsored, they sold property to be able to raise the fare for transportation and pocket money. The ship fare to the U.S. was about $70 at that time. Most of these students worked in hotels and restaurants as dishwashers, bellboys, janitors, ele-

Broadway High School students at the Volunteer Park in Seattle, Washington, circa 1927.

completed their college courses became leaders in their own fields in both private and government employment in the Philippine Islands.

III. THE WORKERS

From 1906 to 1934, the bulk of Filipino migration to the U.S. consisted of young males under the age of 30. Most of them had only grade school education. Their destination was either Hawaii, the mainland, or Alaska.

Immigrants on arrival in Seattle, Washington, circa 1927.

But although the initial groups of immigrant workers started in 1906, the majority of Filipinos came after the passage of the 1924 Exclusion Act. The law stipulated that aliens were subject to limitations, restrictions, or exclusions from the United States at its discretion. At that time, those considered aliens were the Japanese, Chinese, and Koreans. The law opened the doors for the Filipinos' migration to America because, at that time, they were nationals of the U.S. In other words, they were not aliens but nationals, so they could emigrate from the Philippines to America at any time. They didn't need passports; they only needed cedulas or residence certificates from their native towns or cities.

The first group was composed of 15 Ilocanos who arrived in Hawaii in 1906, followed by other groups in 1907 and beyond. They were part of the *second period of immigration, 1903-1934.* (See the chapter, *The Workers in Hawaii* and *The Mainland Journeys.*)

IV. THE NAVY MEN: 1903-1992

Not long after the United States bought the Philippines from Spain for $20 million in 1898, the U.S. Navy started to enlist Filipinos as stewards and mess boys.

Ahoy! Ahoy! Ahoy! It was during that time that the United States established its first three military bases in the Philippines. The enlistment of Filipinos in the U. S. Navy covered the years 1903 to 1992.

In 1903, there were only nine Filipinos in the Navy. By World War I, the Filipinos' number in the Navy rose to 6,000. Many of them secured their discharge in continental ports. Many worked in Navy yards while others served in the merchant marine. Still others worked in a variety of occupations. By 1930, there were about 25,000 Filipinos in United States Navy, according to the statement of Brigadier General F. Lej Parker, chief of the Bureau of Insular Affairs, who appeared during a hearing in Congress before the House Committee on Immigration and Naturalization on April 11, 1930.

Most of the Filipinos who worked in the Navy yards had completed their primary education in the Philippine Islands. Those who had ambitions attended evening classes so that they could prepare for other jobs. Some even took civil service examinations. For instance, at the Chicago Post Office, there were about 300 Filipinos working there in 1930. In the San Francisco Post Office, about 18 were employed in May 1930.

In the beginning, the recruitment was done in the U.S. Naval Base in Cavite. Then in the 1960s, the recruitment was held at the U.S. Naval Station at Subic Bay in Olongapo, Zambales Province. As to be expected, many of the enlistees were from Manila, Cavite Province, and neighboring provinces.

The Recruitment Continues. After the Philippine Islands gained independence from the United States on July 4, 1946, the U.S. Navy could no longer recruit Filipinos because they were no longer U.S. nationals; they had become citizens of the Philippines. However, in its 1947 Military Bases Agreement with the Philippines, it was able to insert a provision in the agreement that permitted the U.S. Navy to continue recruiting Filipino citizens. In the early 1950s, the U.S. Navy allowed the recruitment of about 4,000 a year for a term of four or six years. In the 1960s, about 100,000 applied for enlistment in the Navy. But only few were accepted. In 1969 for example, 1,284 were admitted by the Navy; in 1970, only 420 new recruits were accepted. However, by 1970, there were more than 14,000 Filipinos serving in the U.S. Navy. The majority of them worked as cabin boys, personal valets, and stewards of admirals and captains. Ashore, some had duties at the White House, the Naval Academy, the Pentagon, the U.S. Naval Academy, and other naval installations. In 1973, the Navy reduced the number of Filipino recruits from 2,000 to 400 a year.

The main attraction of the Filipinos' desire to be in the U.S. Navy was the high pay as compared to salaries in the Philippines. Moreover, they wanted to be American citizens. The Filipino navy men were granted U.S. citizenship by serving for a number of years. Earlier, in 1925, the U.S. Congress had passed a law that required them to serve the Navy at least three years to be eligible for U.S. citizenship.

Because of their citizenship, the Filipino navy men furthered their education and got jobs. Many of them retired after serving at least 20 years in the Navy. Many retirees stayed in major seaport cities, such as San Diego, where they worked in shipyards.

The Way It Used to Be. Before World War I, Filipinos were allowed to become petty officers, seamen, machinists, firemen, commissionary stewards, officers' stewards, band masters, musicians, mess attendants, and other positions. But after the war, the Navy issued a new ruling, which stipulated that Filipinos, even if they were college graduates, were restricted to the ratings of officers' stewards and mess attendants. The stewards were assigned to the ships' galleys and officers' quarters.

Change of Heart. In the early 1970s, the U.S. Navy changed its policies and granted Filipino enlistees the right to enter any occupational rating. For instance, in 1973 alone, Filipinos served in 56 of 87 ratings. In that same year, 40 percent of Filipinos were still stewards. The other 60 percent represented those who worked as commissary men, storekeepers, disbursing clerks, and others. Lately, Filipino American sons of ex-navy men have become officers in the U.S. Navy.

By the end of 1992, the U.S. Navy stopped recruiting Filipinos. By that year, there were about 12,600 Filipino sailors. Now, many of navy veterans and their families live in coastal regions of the United States, such as San Diego and San Francisco, California; Norfolk, Virginia; Charleston, North Carolina; Jacksonville, Florida; and other military cities. Of course, some of the retirees went home to the Philippines to spend the rest of their lives there.

Navymen and their families, indeed, have added to the Filipino presence in the United States.

Merchant Marine. Filipinos, many of them after their service in the U.S. Navy, worked as seamen in U.S. commercial ships. From 1925 to 1932, the total number of Filipinos in the U.S. Merchant Marine was estimated to be between 5,500 and 6,000. By June 30, 1929, there were 7,305 Filipinos signed on by shipping commissioners. Most of them were signed on for one voyage only, with a smaller number for a period of time, seldom exceeding six months. In addition to the 7,305 enlisted by shipping commissioners, 498 more were signed on by collectors of customs and 87 by American consuls, increasing the total number of Filipinos who had worked for commercial ships.

Shipowners found Filipinos to be excellent seamen. However, Andrew Furuseth, president of the International Seamen's Union, who was opposed to the hiring of Filipinos because they were threatening American jobs, was critical of Filipinos. He claimed that the Filipinos were not good sailors.

On to Unemployment. The enactment of the 1936 Merchant Marine Act wiped out the Filipino Merchant Marine employment. A provision of the law stipulated that 90 percent of the crews on American flagships must be U.S. citizens. By 1938, large numbers of Filipinos, U.S. nationals but not citizens, were dismissed from the service.

Men in the U.S. Armed Forces. Thousands of Filipinos served as volunteers in the U.S. Armed Forces during World War I. They included several thousand Filipinos who worked in the Navy yards of Manila.

V. THE MILITARY PERSONNEL

The *third period of immigration (1945-1965)* involved American citizens, military personnel who took part in the World War II, and their families.

World War II Army Men. During the Second World War, about 80,000 Filipinos volunteered for enlistment in the Armed Forces of the United States. However, most of them were rejected because they were not American citizens. They were also not allowed to work in defense factories.

In view of this, President Roosevelt issued a proclamation allowing the Filipinos to enlist in the U.S. Armed Forces. In fact, the proclamation changed the draft law to include Filipinos. Also, the First and Second Filipino Infantry Regiments were formed.

Many of these draftees became citizens through mass naturalization held before their induction into service during the war.

Washington State Archives

About 1,000 Filipino soldiers being sworn in as American citizens in Camp Beale, California, in 1943, before their departure for the Pacific to participate in World War II.

The immigrants from 1945-1965 also included descendants of veterans of the Spanish-American War and of the government personnel who had settled in the Philippines after the Philippine-American War of 1898-1902 ended. Also included in this immigration were members of the Philippine Scouts and their families. The Scouts, part of the U.S. Army, participated in the war against the Japanese in the Philippines.

Many of the military men were members of the First Filipino Infantry Regiment and the Second Filipino Infantry Regiment of the U.S. Army that were sent to the Philippines for secret missions. They were trained in military bases in the U.S. Some of them participated in the war in the Pacific.

The immigration of the military men and their dependents was not covered by the migration quota system.

More Students and Workers. During the *third period of immigration*, more students and exchange workers immigrated to the U.S.

talents. Thus, they were permitted to immigrate to the U.S. without regard for national quotas. Many foreign medical graduates already in training in U.S. hospital availed themselves of the opportunity to get this kind of visa. A lot of doctors in the Philippines received such visas.

Foreign Medical Graduates. The first groups of doctors arrived here by virtue of the terms of the McCarran-Walter Act and by the Foreign Exchange Visitor Program.

Then came the Immigration Act of 1965 that permitted the migration of 170,000 people from the Eastern hemisphere. However, no more than 20,000 could be allocated to any particular country. The Filipino medical graduates applied for an immigrant visa under the third preference category, competing with other professionals who fell under the same third preference classification on a first-come-first-served basis.

Thus, many Filipino immigrants headed for America. Later, the 1976 Immigration Act required, among others, that foreign medical

VI. THE PROFESSIONALS

Shortly after the amendment to the Nationality Act of 1924 in 1965, the professionals, mostly doctors, nurses, lawyers, engineers, medical technologists, pharmacists, and lately, physical therapists, arrived in the United States as immigrants. They covered the *fourth period of immigration* (1965 to the present).

Actually, it was the liberalized immigration policy of 1962 that paved the way for the foreign medical graduates (FMGs) to attain their postgraduate medical education in the United States. Foreign medical graduates, under the 1962 immigration guidelines, could apply for permanent resident visas before April 1, 1962. However, they should have had specialized skills and

Dr. Lilia S. Mangulabnan, carrying a small child, with her husband, Celestino (at right), father, Pedro Serrano (back), her children, and other relatives before she left the Philippines for the United States in 1974.

graduates pass the Visa Qualifying Examination (VQE) before they could migrate to the U.S. to take up postgraduate medical training.

In general, the 1965 Immigration Act brought in thousands of Filipinos to the U.S. In the 1970s, the Philippines became the number one Asian country to send new immigrants to the U.S. By 1981, the Filipinos became the number one Asian group in California, with a population of 357,514, an increase of 158 percent since 1970. The Filipinos beat other Asian groups, including the Chinese, which had a population of 322,340. The Japanese population had 261,817, and the Koreans, 103,891. However, the Chinese

Cenon Abes with several members of his family before he left for the United States in the 1960s. He settled in southern California.

were and still are the number one Asian ethnic group in the country, and the Filipinos are second.

By 1970, great numbers of Filipino professionals had become part of what is known as "brain drain" from the Philippines. The medical working forces were led by physicians and nurses. Pharmacists, dentists, engineers, teachers, and accountants were in significant numbers.

In 1970, the Philippines sent the largest number of foreign medical graduates which comprised 17.8 percent of the physicians coming from Asia. The Philippines was followed by India with 15.0 percent, and Thailand with 4.8 percent

(In 1950, there were only 722 foreign medical interns and residents from several countries, undergoing training in U.S. hospitals.) From 1970 to 1971, the number increased to 3,339. In 1974, about 7,000 Filipino physicians worked in the United States.

These medical doctors, however, suffered difficulties in their training. The physicians' visas said that they were doctors. Yet, although the majority of them were licensed and practiced their profession in the Philippines, they were not allowed to practice medicine by state boards of medicine. They had first to take the ECFMG, which later was changed to the VQE (Visa Qualifying Examination) to be able to take their residency training and to pass the FLEX (Professional Licensing Examination) to practice their profession.

At first, if they had not passed the necessary examination, these FMGs served as historians or physician assistants with very low pay. Then after they passed the qualifying test, they had to take their training. But some doctors found it hard to get residency training because there were not enough positions in training hospitals. Some doctors did not pass or could not pass the exams that up to now are still doing the jobs of physician assistants in some hospitals or clinics.

Some doctors found it difficult to pass the qualifying tests because they had to support their family while temporarily working as physician's assistant or laboratory assistants.

Filipino doctors who passed the state board examinations and specialty exams engaged in private practice. Others worked in hospitals in cities of the United States.

Other Immigrants. According to estimates, during the 1970s, about one-fifth of the 20,000 nursing graduates from Philippine schools migrated to the United States.

Like physicians and nurses, other professionals such as lawyers, optometrists, and others, were not recognized by state governments to be licensed to practice their professions. For instance, some of these professionals from he Philippines were not even allowed to take state exams.

Many lawyers, teachers, accountants, pharmacists, also licensed in the Philippines, still work as clerks in hospitals and public and private institutions. Some engineers work as draftsmen or as laborers in factories.

These professionals, like those before them— students and workers—suffered much discrimination and prejudice in the work force.

Many professionals and entrepreneurs, however, have excelled in the fields of their endeavor, whether they are doctors, lawyers, engineers, etc. Some of these achievers grace the pages of this book, particularly in Part IV: *Profiles of Notable Filipino-Americans.*

VII. THE POPULATION

In 1910, the U.S. Census counted 160 Filipinos in 16 mainland states. The top state in population was Louisiana where the U.S. census listed 84. (However, Louisiana Filipinos disputed this figure, because they said that during that time, there were already several hundred Filipinos, excluding the 2,000 descendants of the Manilamen in New

Dr. Genoveva Abes Bautista, (second from left), who came to the United States in March 1976, is shown with her five children, (l to r), Lester, Melvin, Ronald, Janet, and Hubert (at her left), when she picked them up at the Detroit International Airport upon their arrival from the Philippines in July 1977. Others in photo are their relatives, Dr. Lilia S. Mangulabnan, her son Melvin (second from right standing), and Ruben Abesamis (at extreme right at the back).

Orleans. In Washington, several Filipinos were counted. Also, some Filipinos were listed in the District of Columbia, Texas, Montana, Wyoming, Oregon, California, Nebraska, Florida, Alabama, Illinois, and Mississippi.

From 1920 to 1930. In 1920, the U.S. Census counted 5,603 Filipinos in the United States. From 1920 to 1930, 44,404 Filipinos entered the United States through Honolulu, Hawaii and 21,123 through California ports.

The 1930 U.S. Census counted 45,208 Filipinos in the 48 states on the mainland. Again, this figure was disputed by Filipinos because the descendants of the Manilamen in Louisiana were not counted as Filipinos. The Filipino sex ratio was determined as 14.4 male to 1 female.

The 1930 census revealed the following population: California, 30,470; Washington,

3,480; Illinois, 2,011; New York, 1,982; Oregon, 1,066; Michigan, 787; Pennsylvania, 416; Louisiana, 518; and Arizona, 472. In several other states, more than 200 Filipinos were found in each state.

In 1960, the U.S. Census counted 176,310 Filipino Americans living in Hawaii and California.

Amnesty to Illegal Immigrants. The U.S. Congress, in 1986, passed an immigration law that gave amnesty to undocumented immigrants living at the time in the United States. The illegal aliens were told to produce documents to prove that they had been living in the United States continuously for a specified number of years to be able to take advantage of the new act. In view of this, thousands of undocumented Filipinos became permanent residents.

The 1990 Act. Furthermore, the Immigration Act of 1990 provided that families of those who were given amnesty in 1986 were allowed to reunite with them. In spite of this law, however, the flow of illegal aliens has not stopped. Some have come here through arranged marriages. That is, they arrange the marriage of an American citizen to a Filipino man or woman. They get married in the Philippines and the Filipino native is petitioned by the husband or wife to come to the U.S. After two years or so, they divorce here in the United States, as earlier agreed upon. Then they can marry again to have families of their own.

Another provision of the 1990 Immigration Act stipulated a provision that allowed Filipino veterans of World War II to migrate to the United States. These were the veterans who missed the opportunity to be U.S. citizens from 1942 to 1946. They charged that they were not able to apply for citizenship immediately after the war because President Harry Truman recalled officials of the Immigration and Naturalization Service in 1945, who had been processing papers in Manila.

However, it took them years to migrate to the United States after winning in court cases. In the end, the U.S. Supreme Court ruled that those Filipino war veterans were still eligible to come here as immigrants on one condition; that is, they had to prove that they had tried

to make application for citizenship before the 1946 deadline. There are estimates that about 150,000 Filipino World War II veterans can benefit from the 1990 Act. However, this is a very large number as many of the veterans have already died.

Also, Congress stipulated in the law that these veterans, in spite of their being citizens, are not eligible to any veteran benefits, such as retirement, health insurance, or death pay to families.

However, many veterans don't care about the non-eligibility to veteran benefits. Their only intention to come here was to petition their families. Indeed, the coming of the veterans and their families have added to the Filipino American population.

To Become a Citizen. Filipino immigrants, as well as other immigrants, are given visas to come here. Then the immigrants with visas apply for a green card. Green cards are given shortly upon their arrival in the United States. After five years of living here, if they so desire, they can apply for American citizenship.

Current Population. The latest official figure by the U.S. Census has placed the Filipino population at 1.4 million. However, according to the National Filipino American Council, a coalition of community associations, the most realistic figure is about 2.2 million.

Of the estimated 2.2 million Filipinos, approximately 1 million are in California and 200,000 are in Hawaii. Other states with large numbers of Filipino Americans are New York, Illinois, New Jersey, Washington, and Texas. According to some estimates, the population of the Filipinos in the United States may reach 3 million, if the number of Filipinos classified as illegal aliens or TNTs (tago nang tago or "always hiding"), is to be considered, the Filipinos may be considered, although not officially, as the second largest immigrant group next to the Hispanics (Mexican, Puerto Rican, Colombian, etc.)

Officially, according to estimates based on INS statistics, the Filipino Americans are expected to be the largest Asian ethnic group, beating the Chinese, by the year 2000.

The Workers in Hawaii: The Life They Lived

The first workers on sugarcane plantations in Hawaii were Germans, Scotsmen, Scandinavians, and Russians. They were followed by Spaniards and Portuguese. Next came Chinese and Japanese, Puerto Ricans, Koreans, and other foreigners.

The annexation of Alaska to the United States brought two significant events: The 1885 Foran Act abolished the "contract labor system" and sugarcane growers opened up new lands for cultivation.

The abolition of the old contract labor system providing five or ten-year terms of employment displaced several hundred Chinese, Japanese and Portuguese workers. They left Halekoa, Hawaii, in 1898.

The Japanese, however, continued to dominate the labor force. By 1907, there were 100,000 Japanese workers with their dependents in Hawaii.

A sakada with a goggle and a knife.

I. THE VOYAGE TO HAWAII

When did the Filipinos first go to Hawaii? The Filipinos came into the picture after the Japanese workers staged a strike in 1906. In that same year, the Hawaii Sugar Planters Association (HSPA) recruited 15 workers from Ilocos Sur Province, Philippines, that resulted in the movement of more Filipinos to Hawaii. They became known as *sakadas*, a term that identified them as "laborer-recruit." In 1907, about 210 men, women, and children came from the Philippine Islands, then a territory of the United States. By 1919, 23,418 men, accompanied by 3,009 women, and 2,022 children arrived in Hawaii to seek economic opportunities.

One-Way Trip. The Philippine Commission, then the U.S. government body in the Philippines, demanded that the HSPA provide a model individual labor agreement. Under the provisions of the agreement, the recruit, his wife, and minor children were to be given free passage to Hawaii. Furthermore, the agreement provided that the recruits would work for three years. However, the recruits, 81 percent of whom were adult males, would work for 10 actual hours in the field every day. The laborers in the sugar mills would work up to 12 hours. If they agreed, they were given free passage to Hawaii.

However, one thing that was not included in the contract was the provision for free passage to return home. The starting wage then was $16.00 a month. (In 1912, it was raised to $18.00 a month.)

The Philippine Assembly forced the HSPA to include in the labor agreement the guarantee of free return passage to each worker. Such free transportation back home was for those who completed 720 days of work in three consecutive years. Those who came before 1915 were not covered by the law. (But later on, in 1921, the HSPA gave free return

Hawaii State Archives

Four sakadas ready for work.

fare to sakadas who came before 1915 and completed 720 days of work in three years.)

Have *Cedulas*, We'll Migrate. All a man needed to go to Hawaii was to get a *cedula* (residence certificate) at the municipal hall to be recruited by a sub-agent in his locality. "Just get a cedula!" was the instruction of a sub-agent. They didn't need passports because at that time, the Filipinos were nationals of the United States. Therefore, they were not considered as aliens. These recruits—farmers, tailors, laborers, whatever—came from remote barrios of Luzon, particularly from the Ilocos Region. The others were from different parts of the Visayas and Mindanao. They were shipped to Hawaii from Manila and Cebu City. The recruits from the Visayas and Mindanao were workers from sugarcane and other plantations on the Island of Negros and in other provinces. They were assembled at a designated area in the province and then taken to Manila and Cebu by trucks or cars.

How's Your Body? The recruits underwent physical examinations by a physician to determine if they had any disease. Those who passed the physical exam were given new clothing, a pair of shoes, two pairs of socks, and some underwear. Of course, the women and children were also furnished with clothing. The Filipinos were placed below the deck as steerage passengers. It took the ship one month to reach Hawaii.

Fifteen male Ilocanos were hired during a six-month campaign in 1906. The workers, the first arrivals in Hawaii, disembarked from the *S.S. Doric* on November 18, 1906.

After 1907, during which more than 150 laborers were sent to Hawaii, the president of the sugar association halted the recruitment.

In 1909, Chinese, Japanese, and Koreans were barred from immigrating to Hawaii. Therefore, at that time, there were no available workers, except the Filipinos.

Hence, in April 1909, the sugar association commenced large-scale recruiting in the Philippine Islands, especially in Manila and Cebu. The first batch of these new recruits arrived in Hawaii on July 20, 1909. In September of the same year, 500 Filipinos from the Visayan Islands migrated to Hawaii. By December 31, other groups had arrived In 1910, 4,173 new workers were shipped to Hawaii.

In 1915, a Philippine law regulated the emigration of workers. The law also set up a licensing system in which the Bureau of Labor supervised the contracts. The law stipulated that the Manila office of the sugar association give each laborer a written contract before leaving for Hawaii. The HSPA paid P6,000 for a license to recruit sakadas in the provinces of Ilocos Sur, Ilocos Norte, La Union, Tarlac, Abra, Zambales, and in Manila in Luzon and in Capiz on Panay Island. The Ilocanos comprised the bulk of workers.

However, after 1925, the HSPA stopped their recruitment in the provinces. Those Filipinos who wanted to go to Hawaii just went to the HSPA office in Manila where they applied for work. Then several thousand Filipinos migrated to Hawaii each year. A number of them were recruited by private agencies who promised them jobs upon arrival in Hawaii.

Why Emigrate? The workers emigrated for various reasons, but the major causes of their going abroad were poverty, lack of economic opportunities, and worsening farm tenancy problems. The farmers who worked for landlords had nothing left for themselves for subsistence at the end of each year's harvest. Then they had to borrow money from their landlords even if the planting season had not yet started.

According to Ruben R. Alcantara, author of the book *Sakada: Filipino Adaptation in Hawaii*, most of the *sakadas* were illiterate or

had little schooling who could not read, write, and speak in English. It was because they were recruited from remote barrios where public schools were not yet been established. It was reported that the recruiters preferred those who could not read and write because they were not likely to leave the plantation for other work in other cities. They agreed to "signing" a supposed contract by affirming their thumb marks on the papers.

Periods of Recruitment. The recruitment of Filipino workers to Hawaii may be divided into five periods:

■ *The First Period, 1906 to 1919.* This period brought in 28,464 Filipinos: 23,433 men, 3,009 women, and 2,022 children.

■ *The Second Period, 1920-1924.* This period drew 29,226: 23,187 men, 4,178 women, and 1,861 children.

■ *The Third Period, 1925-1929.* This period brought in 44,404: 42,186 men, 1,468, women, and 750 children.

■ *The Fourth Period, 1930 to 1934.* This period drew 14,760: 13,488 men, 610 women, and 662 children

■ *The Fifth Period, 1946.* This period, drew 7,361: 6,000 men, 446 women and 915 children.

The 23,433 men during the first period included the 15 who came to Hawaii in 1906, the only arrivals in that year.

Pineapple Plantations. In 1903, pineapples were packed in a primitive cannery, James Dole who began growing pineapple in 1900 improved the canning of pineapple. In the 1930s, the Filipinos became the largest ethnic group who worked in the pineapple fields.

After the War. When the Tydings-McDuffie Act was passed, only 50 Filipinos were permitted to emigrate from the Philippines to the United States every year. But a provision in the act gave authority to the U.S. Secretary of the Interior to authorize the state of Hawaii to import Filipinos without obtaining passports or visas if a labor shortage existed. After World War II, this provision was used by the sugar growers. Thus in 1946, the HSPA imported Filipinos, both for sugarcane and pineapple growers. In that year alone, 6,000 Filipino workers were recruited. They were not allowed to have free passage to Hawaii, nor were even given wages based on prevailing rates in the sugar industry. Also, an amount was deducted monthly from their wages to pay back their $100 ship fare. However, they were given free return passage upon completion of 250 days of work per year for three consecutive years.

From Hawaii to the Mainland. From the Mainland to Hawaii. There were exchanges of Filipino workers between Hawaii and the continental United States. From 1907 to 1919, some 2,382 Filipinos (including 2,309 men, 37, women, and 36 children), moved from Hawaii to the mainland. Meanwhile, in that year, only 47 Filipinos (including 39 men, 5 women, and 3 children), moved from the mainland to Hawaii.

Between 1920 and 1924, 3,654 Filipinos (including 3,438 men, 125 women, and 91 children), moved from Hawaii to the mainland and 83 (including 72 men, 9 women, and 2 children), moved from the mainland to Hawaii.

From 1925 to 1929, 9,786 Filipinos (including 8,807 men, 529, women, and 450 children), emigrated from Hawaii to the mainland. Emigration from the mainland to Hawaii involved 689 Filipinos (including 560 men, 86 women, and 43 children).

In 1932, 232 Filipinos migrated to Hawaii. From 1932-1936, the workers consisted only of 462 persons. When contracts expired, about 19,618 Filipinos returned to the Philippines. In 1940, there were 52,659 Filipinos in Hawaii. Most of them lived in rural areas; others lived in Honolulu.

As you can clearly see, more Filipinos moved from Hawaii to the mainland, than from the mainland to Hawaii.

When they arrived in the Philippines, those who had been able to save money were able to buy a piece of land of their own. They were seen in the barrios in their best clothes.

They became "somebody" in their locality, so other people became inclined to go to Hawaii.

Of course, those who had worked for three years, went home to the Philippines. As veterans of the Hawaii plantation system, some of these workers returned to Hawaii later.

From 1907 to 1919, about 4,336 left Hawaii for the Philippines after finishing their time as sakadas. From 1920 to 1924, 8,177 went home, and from 1925 to 1929, 17,972 said, "I'm going home!"

Many of these returnees, with their newly bought clothes and accessories might have said to their friends and relatives: "We made it in America."

II. SO THIS IS WORK?

As soon as the workers arrived in Hawaii, they were given plantation identification tags and assigned to different sugar plantations based on requests previously submitted to the HSPA by the sugar manufacturers. They were transported to one of the forty-four plantations on the four major islands: Big Island of Hawaii had 29 plantations, Kauai had 9, Oahu had 9 and Maui had 6.

Hawaii State Archives

Laborers working on a farm.

Three Sakadas on lunch break.

Hawaii State Archives

At that time, too, the Hawaiian Sugar Planters Association recruited Filipino workers to work for its sister association, the Pineapple Growers Association of Hawaii.

Gangs, Gangs, Gangs. There were two kinds of workers: the short-term contract workers and the long-term contract workers.

Short-Term Contract Workers. These workers plowed and irrigated the field, and cut and loaded the cane. Workers were divided into crews, with each crew member sharing equally in the total wages. In 1925, they were paid $2.25 to $2.50 a day, with bonus, to those who met or exceeded the monthly minimum number of days worked. During the depression the average wages fell to $1.39 per day.

Long-Term Contract Workers. These workers were divided into gangs supervised by a *luna*, or foreman, who had a contract with the sugar company to do the cultivation and irrigation and to take care of the plants until they were harvested. In 1925, the average wage for a long-term contract worker was $2.40 per day. In 1933, it was reduced to $1.88 per day.

The average wages of the sugar mill workers ranged from $2.20 to $3.27 a day. They moved the cane to the crushing mills and operated the mills or the centrifugals. They also worked inside the warehouses.

However, the minimum pay for those on daily pay was $1.00. The plantation workers usually worked 10 hours a day, six days a week. Harvesting and planting were done simultaneously.

There, They Go. Let's relive those days on the screen of our imagination:

You see an open field. You hear the luna say many times: "Let's go, men!" You see a gang burn the field to rid the stalks of dead leaves. Then another gang with long knives cuts each stalk at the base and chops off the top leafy part. Then comes another gang who collects the stalks, as if saying, "It's our turn

Sakadas with their harvest.

Hawaii State Archives

now, men!" Another gang follows to load them on can cars.

After everything is collected, other gangs follow in succession. They do the laying out of furrows and irrigation lines. Afterwards, they seed and fertilize the soil.

Time passes by. The laborers have to wait for some time in their cultivation work. Later, they are divided again into different gangs. They care for and irrigate the growing cane, hoe the weeds, and dig irrigation ditches. Then after some time, the cane is ready for harvest.

The job cycle is done.

Their Days in the Fields. The lunas scolded the workers for slight mistakes they made in their work. And some of them felt the pain as they were whipped by several abusive Portuguese lunas. In short, the luna, the "king" in the fields, wrought havoc on the physical and mental being of the Filipinos. They were shouted at and harassed. The luna fined, suspended, and fired workers. The luna set workers' earnings and assigned them to other jobs. But sometimes the workers slowed down when the luna was nowhere to be seen.

There were instances probably when their supervisor might have scolded them, "You're so slow!" "Hurry up! We're late in our schedule!" or whatever. Yes, the lunas scared and intimidated the workers. And one more thing, the Filipinos were dealt with differently: they were considered inferior to other ethnic groups.

The different ethnic groups were assigned into different types of work. Usually, the whites, called "haoles," took management positions and the Spanish and Portuguese were appointed as lunas, plantation overseers. Technical and mechanical jobs were held by the Japanese. The Filipinos got the lowest jobs—of being the ordinary laborers in the field—doing the dirtiest jobs.

Discrimination was rampant against the Filipinos. For instance, they were seldom appointed as a luna. Abuses and discrimination against Filipino workers were complained to Philippine officials, but they had done little to solve the workers' problems.

The Women Do Other Chores. Some women on plantations also worked in the field. Others earned money by washing clothes of workers and they cared for their children who went to school on the plantation.

The Son of a Worker. Benjamin "Ben" Cayetano, the son of a laborer from Urdaneta, Pangasinan Province, Philippines, who worked in the plantations of Hawaii up to 12 hours a day, six days a week, became the first Filipino American to be elected governor of a state when he won in the Hawaii November 1994 gubernatorial race. In his campaign speeches, he said, "For all these years, we Filipinos have  helped so many others realize their dreams. Now it is our turn. Our chance. We collectively have within our grasp the potential to break the barrier and open the door for a better life for our children and grandchildren. I want to be their role model. I want to help encourage them to set higher goals, dream bigger dreams and to not only reach for the stars but to touch them. It is our turn, our chance. Let us reach our goal together. We can do it." (See his profile in Part IV: *Profiles of Notable Filipino Americans.* in this book.)

III. LIFE ON THE PLANTATION

The workers' settlements were like little towns. The manager of the plantation acted as the "mayor," solving disputes among workers, Filipinos, and other ethnic groups. Some kind of policemen preserved peace and order.

The Place They Call Home. Let's travel again with our imagination.

You see barracks or cottages which serve as the homes for single workers. Each of those cottages houses seven to ten laborers, depending on which plantation they are. You also see separate houses where various families live. People living in plantation villages are segregated. Management people, Japanese, Koreans, Filipinos, and others live in separate cottages.

You see Hawaiian plantation settlements in isolated places. However, people living in the community are considered self-sufficient. There are hospitals where medical services are rendered. The hospitals provide facilities at the rate of one bed to each hundred plantation population. There are also recreational facilities, such as athletic fields and billiard halls.

The hospitals provided free medical and surgical treatment. However, every family was limited to a hospital expenditure of $100 each. Those workers who earned more than $100 a month were charged modest fees. However, those with large families were exempted from the rule. In the early 1940s, running water, electricity, kitchen, and bathrooms were installed in most homes.

What Shall We Eat? Early in the morning, the workers who had no families prepared their breakfast and their lunch to be taken to the fields for their long workdays. Usually, they took turns in buying food and doing household chores.

"Where's My Wife?" "Where's My Wife?" Several times some workers might have asked, "Where's my wife?" or they might have shouted, "My wife is missing!" The dreaded thing on the Hawaiian plantation is what they called *coboy-coboy*, which simply means the abduction of someone's wife by a fellow laborer or laborers. It might have been blamed on the dearth of women on the plantations. Because of this, many workers didn't bring their wives to Hawaii. First, a man infatuated with someone's wife might shower her with gifts and words of love, while the husband was away at work or gambling somewhere. So there were instances, when a woman ran away with another man. There were also cases of married women being abducted by men—for a friend. As a result, fights and murders took place.

Days of Fun After Days of Work. It was not all work on the plantations. Filipinos in their own community practiced the Filipino way of life. On the plantations, boxing, baseball, volleyball, and weightlifting competitions were held, sponsored by the sugarcane owners. On Sundays, Filipinos usually went to cockfighting games, where they could see fighting cocks killing each other. with *taris* (knives) tied to their legs. Some sakadas played card games. The children played with each other.

They held dances and picnics and attended baptismal and birthday parties. They formed their own clubs and associations and socialized with each other. They were one big family.

Of course, one of the happiest days for a worker was Saturday, twice a month; it was payday.

Manong, Tata. The sakadas, as Filipinos always do, respected their elders. They called them *manong* (older brother) and *tata* (father). Afterwards, the sakadas were known as *manongs*, an Ilocano word.

During the Depression. During the Depression, many sakadas left the sugarcane fields for better pay and jobs in hotels and hospitals, on the docks, and in canneries. About one-third of the workers in Hawaii went home to the Philippines during the Depression Era. About 7,000 sakadas left in 1932 for their home

Hawaii State Archives

Sakadas on a picnic on the beach.

country. Besides the money they sent home while they were working, they brought home some saved money.

IV. WHEN ACTION IS NEEDED

In 1909, the first major strike was staged by plantation workers in Hawaii. At that time, several unions were already organized to ask for increased wages and better living conditions. Although not a total success, the workers obtained some concessions. Besides furnishing better housing, the sugar plantation owners set up water and sewage systems. Moreover, they expanded their medical services. In addition, a 10 percent monthly bonus incentive system was adopted. But the plantation owners hiked the minimum days of work from 20 to 23 days.

By 1919, Filipino and Japanese unions pressed for a minimum daily wage of $2.50 and an eight-hour workday. They also demanded improvements of living and working conditions.

After no solution to the labor problems was in sight, Pablo Manlapit, a licensed lawyer and head of the Filipino Federation of Labor, issued a notice for strike on January 3, 1920. Over 3,000 Filipino workers struck on four Oahu plantations. However, the Japanese Association of Hawaii (union) was reluctant to follow, as if saying, "Not yet!" Later, on February 1, the Japanese and the Filipinos joined forces. The strike was stopped after 165 days.

In April of 1924, Manlapit ordered another strike involving about 3,000 Filipino workers and 23 sugarcane plantations. The strike ended after eight months. The sugarcane owners put the strike leaders in jail, evicted strikers from their houses, and hired new workers. As a result, a riot took place and

> The sugarcane owners put the strike leaders in jail, evicted strikers from their houses, and hired new workers.

lasted for several days. Four policemen and 16 Filipinos were killed in the riot. Manlapit and 60 of his followers were sentenced to jail.

More Strikes. The Filipinos persisted in their demand for higher pay and increased benefits. In the 1930s, they kept striking. For instance, in 1937, Filipino workers struck in three plantations. The workers were given a 15 percent wage hike, considered as the first direct victory of the strikers. In 1940, a union signed the first contract for sugar plantation workers after bargaining negotiations. From then on, field and mill workers were unionized.

V. NEW ERA

After World War II. In 1946, the year that the Philippines gained its independence from the United States, 7,361 Filipinos migrated to Hawaii to work on sugarcane plantations. The majority of them came to beat the quota of 100 persons a year that would became effective after the Philippine independence was proclaimed because of the Filipinos' loss of the right as nationals of the U.S.

Descendants of Workers. Today, several descendants of those workers have emerged as leaders of the state, including Governor Ben Cayetano and others who have been elected to political offices. Furthermore, many have distinguished themselves in other fields of endeavors.

THE MAINLAND
JOURNEYS

10

The Manilamen settled in the bayous of Louisiana as early as 1763. Many years later, they were followed by the pensionados (scholars), nonsponsored students, and workers. These groups of pioneers crisscrossed the mainland United States.

They sought to work on the farms, in hotels and restaurants, private homes, sawmills, etc. Those who settled on the mainland came either directly from the Philippines—or Hawaii where they had worked on sugarcane and pineapple plantations.

Most of the workers, however, had little schooling, some didn't even reach the seventh grade, and few even reached high school. Of course, particularly the nonsponsored students came to America as high school graduates to pursue higher education.

Many of the workers who completed their stint as laborers on sugarcane and pineapple plantations in Hawaii moved to the mainland. Some of them went to the mainland also to fulfill their dream of studying in high school or in college.

Of course, the others who completed their contract went home to the Philippines with their hard-earned dollars. Those returnees told their friends and relatives of the "nice life"

as workers in the fields of Hawaii. So more Filipinos went to Hawaii.

The Filipino students worked as laborers on farms. And some of them worked in industrial plants and by the railroads. But wherever they worked, they accepted and received less wages than the white Americans. Other nonstudents also worked in the fields.

I. PRIVATE HOME, HOTEL, AND RESTAURANT WORKERS

The immigrants included many students, except those who migrated directly to Hawaii to work on plantations. The Filipino students,

**A photograph of a car attracted many
Filipinos to the United States.**

Other workers who were directly employed were not included in this survey.

It determined that the Filipinos accepted wages much lower than those accepted by white American men and women. According to some estimates, their wages were from 50 cents to $1 a day less than white workers in restaurants.

Why They Liked the Filipinos. Little by little, after some hotels and restaurants started with Filipinos as bus boys, white Americans were replaced by Filipinos in other types of work. And wages depended on where the Filipinos worked. For instance, in the late 1920s in San Francisco, the average wages for Filipino busboys ranged from $30 a month (plus food) in modest restaurants to $65 and $75 in restaurants in first-class hotels. In the Portland, Oregon, area, the average busboy pay for Filipinos was $60 a month.

comprising the nonsponsored ones, worked mostly in private homes, and in hotels and restaurants. In homes, the students were called "school boys" and worked as domestic helpers, cooks, and gardeners. As domestic helpers, the Filipino houseboy earned from $10 to $15 a week, plus his free board and lodging. Usually, the $10 pay (with room and board) for houseboys was in larger cities on the West Coast and $15 for those working in small college cities.

In hotels and restaurants, they worked as busboys, cooks, janitors, etc. In private homes, hotels and restaurant, the Filipinos were said to be in direct competition, not necessarily with white male Americans, but with white female Americans.

Average Monthly Wages. In 1929, Dr. Louis Block of the Department of Industrial Relations surveyed employment agencies and discovered the average monthly wages:

1. For cooks in hotels and restaurants, it was $80 a month with room and board.

2. For dishwashers with room and board, it was $58 a month.

3. For janitors, it was $75 a month, with room only.

II. FARM WORKERS

Filipino students and other migrant workers in the early years of migration had worked the farms of California, Washington, Utah, Minnesota, and other states.

The farm owners favored Asian labor to work in their fields. They specifically liked them, particularly the Filipinos, because they could hire them in organized gangs. Moreover, they didn't provide any amusements for them; the Filipinos provided their own entertainment. That's why Filipinos in the early years took over largely seasonal labor from foreign white workers, especially to the picking of apricots, cherries, and peaches. Also, they replaced Portuguese, Spanish, Italian, and Mexican workers in tomato communities. In the case of the Japanese laborers, the Filipinos displaced them in potato picking and in other stoop labor. However, there was no active competition between Filipinos and white American workers in the vegetable growing and picking business.

Exclusive to Filipinos. In Salinas, California, in the late 1920s, the field work in the lettuce and carrot fields was almost exclusively in the hands of Filipinos under Filipino contractors. However, white American workers exclusively did the packing and refrigerating products for eastern transport.

In 1928, the Division of Housing and Sanitary of the Department of Industrial Relations in California made a survey of the different occupations of the Filipinos in different counties in California.

Filipino Farm Occupations. The survey, as published in *The Filipino Immigration to the Mainland and to Hawaii* by Bruno Lasker, revealed some of the occupations:

Alameda—ranch workers; Butte—rice harvesters and peach pickers; Contra Costa—asparagus cutters and washers, fruit pickers, and sugar beet workers; Glenn—ranch workers; Imperial Valley—grape, melon, and tomato pickers; Kern—farm workers, grape and other fruit pickers;

Monterey—lettuce thinners and harvesters; Sacramento—asparagus cutters and washers, asparagus sorters, and grape and pear pickers; San Joaquin—asparagus cutters, grape pickers, and celery planters.

They Are Everywhere. In the late 1920s, Filipino workers in the White River Valley of Washington worked in large numbers in general farm work. They took over the jobs after they accepted lower pay. From 1925 to 1929, the daily wage had decreased from $6.06 to $3.75.

A report of California Governor Young's Fact-Finding Committee, in October 1930, revealed that the daily pay for Filipino ranch laborers was from 30 to 50 cents an hour. Some fruit pickers were paid less than 40 cents per hour.

However, the majority of the fruit pickers, the survey showed, received $4 and more per day.

As mentioned before, the Filipinos worked as gangs. These gangs, headed by contractors, usually did certain works in a crop sea-

son. Usually, the contractor would talk to a farm owner and ask, "Wanna harvest your crop? I have a gang of 30 to 50 persons. We can do the job quick!"

It must be emphasized that wages were different from year to year in various locations, whether they were in California, Washington, Oregon, or Minnesota.

III. INDUSTRIAL WORKERS

Filipino laborers also worked in sawmills, and box factories, on railroads, and in industrial plants. A case in point, in Oregon, a student reported that Filipinos were paid $3.25 a

Washington State Archives

A Filipino picking apples in Washington State.

**A typical farm dwelling
in Washington State.**

**Workers posing for
a photo during a
breaktime in a hop field,
circa 1929.**

day in contrast to $3.50 a day paid to white Americans.

In Stockton in 1929, a Filipino box factory worker was paid 35 cents an hour when the old pay was 40 cents an hour. The newer Filipinos were paid less, although they did the hardest work.

IV. OTHER OCCUPATIONS

Filipinos also worked as common laborers in the construction industry in California, particularly in the Los Angeles and San Francisco areas. Some Filipinos, however, worked as electricians and painters.

They also worked on the railroads as porters and attendants. It was in 1925 that the Pullman Company hired Filipinos on the Pennsylvania lines and on transcontinental trains. In most cases, the Filipinos, numbering about 500, were provided by Oriental employment agencies. It was said that an additional 500 worked temporarily during the summer.

V. FORMS OF RECREATION

Filipino communities grew around farms and plantations where entrepreneurs established their stores, prostitution centers, dance halls, and gambling joints. Thus, the workers frequented these places. They were addicted to playing cards at night and to going to the dance halls to dance with white girls at 10 cents per dance.

Gambling Their Wages. The *Philippines Free Press* in Manila, in describing the addiction of the Filipinos to gambling said in one of its articles in 1929:

Those Filipinos who send money home are the "blanket boys." These have steady jobs on the farm....The pastime of the "blanket boys" is playing cards. After a day's work, they assemble around the improvised table and play cards till late at night. Poker and black jack are the popular games. Their hard-earned money is easily lost. In the town or city, the *Pinoys* may be found in the billiard rooms and pool-halls from after breakfast till late at night.

There are many gambling houses, mostly managed and controlled by Chinese. They are popularly known as "sikoy-sikoys." The Filipinos who are usually there are called "sikoy-sikoy boys...."

Dance Halls. There were many dance halls, particularly in Stockton, Sacramento, Los Angeles, and San Francisco, California; Seattle, Washington; and Portland, Oregon.

The dance halls lured the Filipinos. From the outside, these dance halls seemed to say to them, "Have a good time! You may come in!" Inside they went, as often as they could. Of course, as they danced, they might have thought of hardships in working in the fields. But what could they do? They were lonely; there were no loved ones to be with. The Filipinos, well-dressed with their best suits, danced and danced, until their pockets were empty of money. Most of the women were white, but there were also blacks, Mexicans, and Italians.

Because of rivalry over women, Filipinos sometimes fought with other Filipinos. There were times when altercations led to stabbings or shootings.

Cockfights. As a form of recreation, the Filipinos also held cockfights in secluded places where they could not be seen by authorities because cockfighting was illegal. In the cockfights, the cocks fought to death with sharp slashing "knives," called *tari*, tied to one of their legs. And the spectators enjoyed watching their chosen cocks win to bring money for them.

Usually these games were held during the weekend. Also, some workers engaged in prostitution.

VI. EMPLOYMENT DISCRIMINATION

Filipinos in the 1920s and 1930s were discriminated against at work, in public places, and in social functions. Many white Americans considered Filipinos as uneducated, job grabbers, and menaces to society. Some of them even called them "brown monkeys" or just plain "monkeys." Some even tagged them as "knife-wielding savages."

Flagrant discrimination and prejudice were experienced by Filipinos in all parts of the U.S. where they lived. But it was on the West Coast that they suffered most, where they experienced the most humiliating and embarrassing moments of their lives.

It was on the West Coast, particularly in California, that the majority of Filipinos chose to live and to work. That happened because they usually wanted to be with their friends and relatives. Also, it was the weather in these states that attracted them—it's similar to the Philippine weather.

During the early years, when the pensionados and a few nonsponsored students came to the United States, they were treated well. In the East, there were those Filipinos who had the opportunity to hold skilled, clerical, or technical work. But when hundreds, and afterwards thousands began to immigrate to America, white Americans' attitude towards them changed.

Skilled Jobs, No; Laborers, Yes. In the West, it was rare that you would find Filipinos working as nurses, mechanical engineers, tailors, librarians, store clerks or salesmen, electricians, etc. These jobs, however, were available to a few Filipinos in the East. On the Pacific Coast, the Filipinos worked as laborers on farms and as houseboys in private homes.

Being a College Graduate Doesn't Make a Difference. Later on, even in the East, graduates from technical schools and colleges were refused jobs in their chosen professions. They wanted the training and experience, yet they were denied the chance of obtaining them. It was due to this fact, that many of them continued their graduate studies, if their financial situation allowed them. There was the case of a journalism graduate who went back to the farms and then went back to college again to further his studies. In other words, he alternated working and studying.

As the negative reports in the West against Filipinos reached the East, more and more establishments decreased the number of Filipino workers. For instance, in 1930, there was only a bare dozen of Filipino workers in one plant that previously had employed a few hundred three years prior to that year.

Their greater number on the West Coast worked against the Filipinos' chances to enter semi-skilled and skilled jobs. They competed with each other and with whites for a few jobs available in business establishments and public institutions.

The Color of Their Skin. The color of their skin, being brown and not white, worked against them. They were considered as not dependable employees because they had dark skin. In those years, too, there were sentiments against Asians in general. Racists considered Filipinos as belonging to the "third wave" of Asians in America—the other two "races" were the Chinese and the Japanese.

On the Pacific Coast farms, particularly in California and Washington, the Filipinos were given lower wages than the whites, although they did the hardest and the dirtiest jobs.

The negative comments by racists and the press against Filipinos further aggravated the discrimination against Filipinos.

VI. SOCIAL DISCRIMINATION

Discrimination against Filipinos was not limited to the West, where Filipinos were refused admittance to hotels, restaurants, swimming pools, and other public places.

There were signs on hotel doors and on entrances to restaurants, swimming pools, etc. that said, "Absolutely No Admittance to Filipinos." There were signs that said, "No Dogs or Filipinos Allowed."

In Their Own Place. Filipino workers, who had been denied admittance to other social clubs, formed their own groups and clubs. They went to Oriental-owned dance halls, gambling dens, etc., where they sought their recreation. There were rumors that Filipinos were dangerous to white women, so some women avoided them. Even in the Middle West and in the East, students who had been respected in the early 1920s were unwelcome at dances. Their presence was resented when they were seen on campuses with coeds. Moreover, their coed companions were criticized and harassed. Whether in the West or in the East, Filipino students were prevented from taking part in some campus activities.

"Here He Comes, Let's Go!" In a state university, a student had the most embarrassing experience of his life. When he entered a cafe where students congregated, white American students instantly left upon seeing him, without finishing their meal. They seemed to have said, "Here he comes, let's go!" That incident was the Filipino student's most humiliating experience of his life as a Filipino in America—whites resenting his presence in a public place.

Filipinos with Books? There were white Americans who were surprised at seeing Filipinos with books and brief cases. They thought that all of them belonged only to the farms.

The pensionados, in order to be recognized as educated foreigners, spoke in Spanish in the presence of other people, the whites. *muy bien* or *buenas noches*, they might have said. (Most of the pensionados were sons and daughters of rich and influential families during the American regime in the Philippines.)

Absolutely No Filipinos Allowed! The hostile propaganda against Filipinos conducted in the West reached the East.

In the East, too, Filipinos had the experience of being refused services in restaurants. In those days, Filipino waiters were considered as a novelty, though. Even students, who could not find decent jobs, worked as servants in fraternity houses.

In movie theaters, Filipinos were admitted. However, they were to be seated only in the gallery. When they entered business establishments, they got "dirty looks" from the owners or employees. In short, they wanted only white customers. In San Francisco, a professional photographer placed an ad in a publication saying that he didn't want to have Filipinos as customers.

Filipinos were refused jobs because they were not white. They were not allowed to rent a room or a house in a decent neighborhood where the whites lived. That's why the Filipinos lived among themselves, in the crowded and secluded districts of San Francisco, Los Angeles, and Stockton, California; and Seattle, Washington. On farms, they were accused of having too many people in a room and of living in unsanitary conditions.

But the Filipinos, in spite of their failures to get decent jobs and wages, would not go home. What would their families, relatives, and friends say? They could not tell at home that life was hard and that money was not easy them to come by. So they remained— working on farms, in private homes, in hotels, restaurants, and so on.

VII. INTERRACIAL MARRIAGES

Generally, the Filipino workers were intending to go home to the Philippine Islands after saving some money. That's why many of them didn't want to start a family in America. For those few who decided to have a family, they had difficulties in finding a mate. There was no choice. Their choices were limited by state laws in California, Arizona, Nevada, Oregon, and Idaho. Therefore, they went to other states that didn't have legal restrictions against mixed marriages.

Filipinos: Malays or Mongolians? In California, marriage between whites and Mongolians were not permitted in accordance with section 69 of the California Civil Code, which was passed into law in 1884. The law specifically stipulated that no marriage between a white person and a Mongolian or a Negro would be performed in the state of California. This law was amended in 1901 to stipulate: "All marriages of white persons with Negroes, Mongolians, or mulattoes are illegal and void." The interpretation of this law brought trouble to Filipino bachelors.

In February 1930, the mother of a white girl filed a case in the Superior Court at Los Angeles against the county clerk of Los Angeles to prohibit him from issuing a marriage license for a Filipino and her daughter. The county's counsel argued that the Malays were not Mongolians, while the mother's attorney claimed that all brown races were Mongolians. The county's counsel further cited an opinion rendered in 1921 saying that the 1884 Civil code didn't intend to prohibit the marriage of people of the Malay race with whites.

Judge Renders the Decision. Judge Smith finally decided the case in favor of the American mother, thus prohibiting the marriage of her daughter to a Filipino. He based his decision on an opinion rendered by California Attorney General U.S. Webb who said that Filipinos were Mongolians, not Malays.

For this reason, all marriage applications between Filipinos and whites were denied in the county of Los Angeles.

Filipinos Declared as Malays. On March 30, 1933, Salvador Roldan by a court decision, was allowed to marry to a white woman because he was a Malay and not a Mongolian.

Malays Banned from Marrying Whites. On April 21, 1933, the California State Assembly amended the Civil Code again. The new law excluded Malays among those who could marry white women. A number of states, 12 of them, also passed laws prohibiting Filipinos from marrying white women. Wyoming and South Dakota, in particular, used the term "Malay" to prohibit interracial marriages.

Some Filipinos married Mexican women. It was reported that some of the most successful marriages turned out to be those between these two races; there were, however, some divorces, too.

Miscegenation Law Ruled Unconstitutional. In 1948, the California Supreme Court ruled the state's miscegenation law as unconstitutional. In hearing the case *Perez v. Sharp*, the state supreme court said that the law limiting the rights of a race to marry those of another race was a violation of civil rights. After the Perez decision was rendered, about a hundred interracial marriage license applications were issued in Los Angeles County alone. Filipinos comprised most of the applicants, 40 males and 2 females.

VIII. VIOLENCE AGAINST FILIPINOS

In the late 1920s until the late 1930s, Filipinos were chased, harassed, beaten, and wounded. Some were even killed. For example, 22 Filipino workers were harassed by a group of 200 white workers in Wenatchee, Washington. The white workers raided the Filipinos' camp and warned the workers to leave town.

Riot in Exeter. In the last week of October 1929, angry white American workers staged a riot in Exeter in the San Joaquin Valley of California. Consisting of a few hundred of them, they raided every ranch that employed Filipinos and demanded they be dismissed. The white Americans destroyed the Filipinos' property.

There were three different accounts on how the trouble started. One account said that some Filipinos threw stones at an Italian truck driver who they thought insulted one of them. Some white workers joined the melee, in which the driver was wounded with a knife. One version said the whites resented a Filipino's behavior toward a white girl. The third account said that the confrontation was the result of jealousy over a Mexican girl.

Whatever reason, in the succeeding weeks, Filipinos were harassed in the street of Exeter by a few hundred white men. The whites burned the barn where the Filipinos lived. From thereon, the general movement to drive out the Filipinos began.

The Watsonville Incident. The most well-known of the riots took place in Watsonville, California, where resident youths, instead of workers, were involved. The Watsonville riot was said to have been precipitated by rivalry over the attention of Filipinos to white girls and the bringing of white female entertainers to the community.

Watsonville was a progressive town in Santa Cruz County, California, in the Pajaro Valley. The population then was about 10,000. Neighboring this town was the town of Pajaro. A bridge over the Pajaro River connected Watsonville and Pajaro.

When the demand for a new crop, the lettuce, increased, many land owners in Watsonville decided to transform their lands into lettuce fields. Generally, many white Americans didn't like hard work on crop farms. Mexican workers were, therefore, hired to work in the fields. But their work was not satisfactory; hence, the land owners turned to Filipinos, who were then in great number in California. However, very few workers were hired directly by the lettuce growers. The crop growers availed themselves of the Filipino contractors who brought their own men to work on the farms. The contractors established camps, in or near the town. The contractors were paid a fixed amount by the owners. Then the contractors paid their workers 30 to 45 cents per hour,

Nevertheless, the Filipinos, had competition with a number of local white residents, including women and girls, who had worked in the fields for seasonal crops.

On January 7, 1930, Justice of the Peace D.W. Rohrback of Pajaro township, worried about the increasing presence of the Filipinos there, denounced the Filipinos as a race in a resolution proposed to the Chamber of Commerce of Northern Monterey County. The chamber of commerce met and adopted the resolution. He specifically denounced the Filipinos were landing along the California coast by the shipload. He then charged that these Filipinos were taking over the jobs of white Americans. Rohrback thus demanded the Filipinos be given freedom and be sent home so white people could live in peace. Afterwards, he gave his views in an interview in the *Evening Pajaronian*. He claimed that Filipinos were "little brown men about ten years removed from a bolo and breechcloth...strutting about like peacocks, endeavoring to attract the eyes of young American and Mexican girls." He also said that "fifteen of them will live in one room and content themselves with squatting on the floor eating rice and fish." A Filipino organization got hold of the article and flooded the valley with leaflets denouncing the judge.

On January 11, 1930, two Filipino brothers rented their resort home in Palm Beach, about two miles from Watsonville. It was rented by the Monterey Bay Filipino Club.

White women were brought to the club, where dancing was held.

On January 19, 1930, local white youths riding in cars tried to enter the club but they were refused by the security guards. But each night, the white thugs tried to enter the club. The Filipino operators of the club requested local authorities for protection against the intruders. However, the local sheriff and other authorities took no action.

White gangs began attacking Filipinos in the streets of Watsonville and Pajaro. Then the white mobs attacked Filipinos in their camps. On January 22, 1930, several carloads of white youths fired shots into a bunkhouse where Filipino workers, including Fermin Tobera, 22, and his brothers, were sleeping. The bunkhouse was at a camp at the Murphy Ranch, four miles east of Pajaro. When the shooting ended, Tobera, 22, was found dead in his bed.

The incident gained international prominence. When Tobera's body arrived in the Philippines, it was given a state funeral.

Other Cases of Violence. Other cases of confrontations and violence between white Americans and young Filipinos followed.

In January 1930, after the Watsonville, California, riots and killings, the following incidents happened:

■ The clubhouse of the Filipino Federation of America in Stockton, California, was bombed by Americans, who threw a bomb from a passing car. It landed and exploded under the porch of the wooden building. However, only the porch and part of the front wall were destroyed. No Filipino was wounded or killed.

■ In San Francisco, two Filipino boys were confronted by a group of white hooligans who resented the Filipino youths' escorting two white women. The American youths were able to escape. Two Filipinos were arrested by the police for public disturbance.

■ In the White River Valley, south of Seattle, Washington, 40 or 50 armed white farm workers, raided camps where about 200 Filipinos lived in May 1930. They kidnapped some of them; others escaped. Those white workers were replaced by Filipino workers in their jobs as peas and lettuce packers.

On December 22, 1930, several carloads of white youths fired shots into a bunkhouse where Filipinos lived.

■ In the West Wapato District in Washington, on October 25, 1930, white workers raided the ranches where Filipinos worked. Armed with clubs and other weapons, they threatened to hang white ranch owners if they didn't dismissed their Filipino laborers.

■ In Imperial Valley, California, on December 8, 1930, a Filipino rooming house was bombed by white Americans. The bomb was thrown from a speeding car. Among the 65 Filipinos sleeping in the building, 1 was killed and 3 others were wounded.

■ Near Canal Point, Florida, on July 23, 1932, about 58 Filipinos were harassed and warned to leave town by about 200 white workers.

Night raids by white American mobs harassed, beat, and chased Filipinos everywhere. These raids took place from January 1930 up to 1941.

Filipinos Go Home! Starting in the late 1920s, more and more people took action to limit the immigration of Filipinos to the U.S. The battle cry in many parts of the West was "Filipinos, go home!"

IX. ASSOCIATIONS TAKE CHARGE

From 1928 to 1932, The A.F. of L., had conducted its anti-Filipino campaign in its five national conventions. This association was the strongest of the exclusionist groups that launched smear campaigns against Filipinos. Belonging to these groups were influential white Americans, such as two U.S. senators. There were also two congressional representatives from California and South Carolina in the A.F. of L.

Other organizations, such as the Commonwealth Club of California, the American

Legion, and the Native Sons of the Golden West, led the Filipino exclusion movement.

Some of the actions taken by U.S. legislators against Filipinos follow:

■ In 1928, Representative Richard Joseph Welch of California proposed House Resolution 13900. His purpose was to place the Filipinos in the category of "alien peoples," not "nationals" of the United States. This resolution never passed the committee.

■ In 1929, Representative Albert Johnson of Washington filed a bill that would exclude Filipinos from becoming eligible for U.S. citizenship. The bill didn't pass the committee.

■ In 1929, Representative Richard Joseph Welch of California filed the resolution that would categorize Filipinos as "aliens." It followed the exclusions of the Japanese and Chinese at an earlier date.

The Hostile Campaign Continues. The white Americans, especially those who charged Filipinos with getting their jobs, resented the presence of Filipinos everywhere. To express their anger, they held disorderly demonstrations against Filipinos.

For instance, in the summer of 1930, the demand for Filipino exclusion became a major issue in the Congressional elections campaign in the Santa Clara Valley of California. Minor outbreaks of anti-Filipino feelings occurred. In addition, pear growers in a certain part of the valley were all warned by the exclusionists not to hire Filipinos. If they did, their trees would be destroyed.

Nationals, Yes; Benefits, No. During that time, the Filipinos were in a precarious situation: they were considered as nationals of the United States and yet they were not entitled to government fringe benefits or other welfare programs. Unlike the Japanese and the Chinese, Filipinos were not considered as aliens.

The United States had two options to solve the "Filipino problem": (1) to retain the status of Filipinos as nationals, without government benefit programs, or 2) to declare Filipinos as aliens.

Finally, the U.S. government decided to declare them as aliens.

Thus, on March 24, 1934, President Franklin D. Roosevelt signed into law the so-called Tydings-McDuffie Act that was passed by the U.S. Congress. The law, also known as The Philippine Independence Act, stipulated that the U.S. government promised political independence to the Commonwealth of the Philippine Islands. Thus, the law categorized the people of the Philippine Islands as aliens. Immigration of Filipinos to the U.S. was limited to 50 persons per year.

How about the Filipinos Already in the U.S.? The law didn't mention anything about the situation of the Filipinos already in the U.S. who were considered as nationals. Although they were nationals in the U.S. before the act was passed into law, they were categorized as aliens.

Wanna Go Home? The majority of Filipinos who were on the West Coast and in other parts of the country suffered much misery during those years. However, they could not get any government help because they were discriminated against. Many decided to go home. But they didn't have money for transportation.

Therefore, the Filipinos sent a petition to President Roosevelt and expressed their desire to be repatriated.

It was only on June 25, 1935, that the U.S. Senate sent to President Roosevelt a bill granting permission to the government to give free transportation to Filipinos who wanted to be repatriated, to return to the Philippine Islands.

President Roosevelt signed the law on July 10, 1935. The Filipinos asked each other: "Wanna go home?" But only 2,190 Filipinos took advantage of the Repatriation Act, although the offer of free fare was addressed to about 45,000 Filipinos. The U.S. spent an average of $116 per person to send the Filipinos home.

Benefits to Japanese, Chinese...But Not to Filipinos. In 1937, the U.S. government approved the Relief Appropriation Act. The law provided that its purpose was to give some relief to aliens because of the hard times of that era. However, instead of relief, the law caused the Filipinos to despair and shout "Unfair!" The law specifically stipulated that it was not for immigrants who did not officially intend, from the beginning, that they would apply for naturalization or citizenship before the law was approved. Although entering legally as nationals, the Filipinos had not applied for naturalization or citizenship. So with the passage of the law, the Filipinos, although declared as aliens after the passage of the Philippine Independence Act, didn't qualify for government benefits. However, such benefits were given to other aliens: Japanese, Chinese, Koreans, etc.

During World War II, however, many Filipinos who had enlisted in the Armed Forces of the United States, became U.S. citizens

It was only in 1946 that Filipinos, in general, became eligible to be citizens of the United States.

X. Filipino Workers Strike

As early as 1930, Filipinos and Mexican workers struck against farm owners in the Imperial Valley of California. The growers had the workers arrested to break the strike.

Because of low wages, on August 28, 1934, Luis Agudo and another Filipino from Chicago, Illinois, formed the Filipino Labor Union. In September 1936, the union struck against lettuce growers and shippers in Salinas, California. This strike, which lasted one month, was unsuccessful. It only resulted in a small token wage increase of five cents.

On April 7, 1939, the Filipino Agricultural Laborers Association, headed by Dr. Macario Bautista, president, and Juan C. (Johnny) Dionisio, vice president, struck against asparagus growers in the San Joaquin delta. The strike involved about 6,000 workers. The union, 36 hours after it staged a strike, gained the wage hike for asparagus cutters.

Larry Itliong, Labor Leader. In 1956, Larry Itliong organized the Filipino Labor Union. In September 1965, the union mem-

bers struck for better wages against 31 grape growers in the Coachella Valley, east of Los Angeles, California. The strike was successful. Inspired by that strike, Itliong's union, affiliated with the AFL Congress of Industrial Organizations, went on strike in Delano, California, on September 8, 1965, against 33 grape growers. But the union's demand was promptly rejected by the grape growers. A week later, the Mexican-dominated National Farm Workers Organization (NFWO), headed by Cesar Chavez, joined the Filipino strikers. In support of the strike, millions of Americans boycotted California grapes and wine. After seven months of strike, Schenley Industries, owner of the largest vineyards, recognized Chavez's union as the sole bargaining agent. In August 1966, to avoid any conflict of interests, the Filipino and Mexican unions merged. The name of the new union was United Farm Workers Organizing Committee (UFWOC)

Later, the union was renamed the United Farm Workers of America, AFL-CIO. Soon the UFWOC became the bargaining group for workers at the Di Giorgio Corporation, a large Kern County, California, vineyard owner. Thus, the Filipinos and the Mexicans improved the wages and working conditions in California. In July 1970, the Delano strike finally ended, obtaining wage increases and a medical plan for the workers. (See Itliong's profile in Part IV: *Brief Profiles of Notable Filipino Americans* in this book.)

Philip Vera Cruz, Labor Leader. Another Filipino labor leader involved in the Filipino and Mexican labor union activities was Philip Vera Cruz. He became involved in the labor movement in September 1965, after he learned about the Filipino farm workers' strike just a few miles from where he was working.

Vera Cruz helped in the merging of the Filipino and Mexican unions. (See his profile in Part IV: *Profiles of Notable Filipino Americans* in this book.)

THE ALASKA PIONEERS

11

L ong before the *Alaskeros* started to work in Alaskan canneries, some other Filipino pioneers visited and interacted with native Alaskans. According to Thelma Buchholdt, author of *Filipinos in Alaska: 1788-1958* (Aborigines Press, Copyright 1996), the first Filipino to step on Alaskan soil was a native of Zamboanga, Philippines, who arrived at the Cook Inlet, Alaska, on June 17, 1788, aboard the *Iphigenia Nubiana*. That ship left Zamboanga on February 22, 1788. William Douglas, captain of the *Iphigenia Nubiana*, identified this Filipino in his journal as follows:

"My servant, who was a Manilla (sic) man, and spoke the language very well, was not permitted to come near me, for fear of discovering some of the...[Spanish] proceedings...."

The Filipino spoke his native language, Spanish, a native American language, and, presumably, English. He was also heard "bargaining with the natives for some fish they had in their boat...."

I. SMALL FILIPINO GROUPS

Buchholdt also said the second and third groups of Filipinos to go to Alaska were 29 "Manilla men": 24 of the 55 crew of the *Eleanora*, and five "Manilla men" assigned to the *Fair American*. That was in 1789. Both ships, *Eleanora*, commanded by Captain Simon Metcalfe, an American fur trader and the *Fair American*, commanded by his son, Thomas Metcalfe, came from Manila where the Filipino crew members were hired.

The Lone Arrival. Another Filipino, known again as a "Minilia (sic) man" who arrived aboard the *Gustavus III* in Alaska in 1789 and again in 1791 was identified as

John Mando, according to the journal of John Bartlett of Boston, also a crew member of that ship. In 1791, Filipinos were also included in a Spanish expedition to Alaska.

Ship Crew Members. In the 1850s, Filipinos were crew members on whaling ships that operated off Alaska. At the New Bedford Whaling Museum, there was a listing, with full names, of Filipino crew members, identified as "Manilla men." Some of them came from the Sulu Islands, Philippines.

80 Filipinos. After them came the 80 Filipinos who did the laying of underwater communications cables that linked Juneau, Alaska, and other Alaskan areas with Seattle, Washington. The Filipinos were on board the cableship *Burnside*.

Miners. In the early 1920s until the late 1930s, Filipinos also worked in Alaska gold mines. They worked mostly as ore sorters at the Alaska-Juneau (A-J Mine) Gold Mining Company, the largest of the gold mining companies, at Mount Roberts, south of Juneau, at the Treadwell Mine and Mills, Ready Bullion Mine and Mill, and at other mines. Most of the men who worked there met and married Indian natives.

II. ALASKEROS

In 1864, the first salmon-canning venture was launched on the Sacramento River in Alaska. Aggressive entrepreneurs built canned salmon factories to take advantage of the rich supply of salmon that abounded from the Monterey Peninsula to the Alaska coast along the Bering Sea. For instance, in 1910, the Columbia River Packers Association (CRPA) constructed a cannery at Chignik, Alaska. European Americans, Native Americans and Chinese worked in the cannery during the early part of the Pacific Coast canned-salmon industry.

By the late 1920s and early 1930s, Filipino laborers on West Coast farms and college and university students, known as "schoolboys," worked in the canneries, from two to four months in Alaska during the spring and summer. During the canning season, these men, later to be known as *Alaskeros* arrived

there. Indeed, they went there every canning season of the year.

"Want to Go to Alaska?" The laborers usually took their time off from their work on the farms on the West Coast to earn money in canneries. On the other hand, the schoolboys would go there to raise money for their tuition, board, lodging, and other expenses in pursuing their education. During the school year, they studied in high school, colleges, and universities.

In 1921, nearly 1,000 Filipinos were recruited by Chinese and Japanese contractors to work in Alaskan canneries. By 1928, there were 3,916 Filipinos in Alaska, comprising the majority of the work force. In comparison, there were 1,445 Japanese, 1,269 Mexicans, and 1,065 Chinese. By 1930, of the 45,280 Filipinos in the United States, about nine percent or 4,200 worked in Alaska. However, there were only a few Filipino contractors. Moreover, all the Filipinos could only work as unskilled laborers. The highest position Filipinos could hold was that of a foreman. In 1930, about 500 of the 4,200 Filipino workers who worked in Alaska were college students. Of the others, about 800 came from trade schools.

The workers came from ports in San Francisco and Seattle. The canning season was from April to August. But some of the workers, particularly the students who worked during their vacation, had to leave when classes started.

Right on the Dock. Some cannery job seekers gathered in Seattle, the converging point for workers bound for Alaska. Workers came from different states who temporarily left their farm or domestic work to work in canneries. There were those who left San Francisco, directly to Alaska.

The trip from Seattle to Alaska usually took one week. Per trip, a few hundred workers (for example 200 to 400) usually were shipped in steerage down at the bottom or "basement" of steamboats going to Alaska. Many became seasick during their voyage to the Last Frontier. Alaska-bound men squeezed themselves into bunks with their suitcases, sea bags, and blankets. Meals in steamships would usually include rice, pig's

Filipinos on a ship bound for Alaska.

Washington State Archives

boxes and other things.

The Filipinos held unskilled jobs in fish-houses and warehouses, such as box maker, butcher, slimer, egg puller, slicer, and others. They used the jitney, a small tractor-like vehicle, to pull flatbed gurneys of canned salmon. The jitney was later replaced by the forklift. Filipino laborers also worked in the summertime as temporary crew members of fishing boats.

In the late 1920s mechanization was introduced in canneries. In 1930, closing machines operated 120 to 125 cans per minute, whereas they previously could operate only 60 cans

feet and tails, and fried fish. But in the boats, workers played cards, played music, and even danced with some first-class women passengers to while away the time. In later years, the workers were transported to Alaska by commercial aircraft.

III. THE CANNING SEASON

Usually, the canning season was from April to August. But a number of people worked only for two months. Some of the workers, particularly the students, were there during their vacation. But some workers arrived there earlier to make fish

Alaska cannery workers, circa 1928.

Washington State Archives

per minute. At that time, all "filling" previously were done by hand was already being done by machine. In three or four years, the speed of this operation was hiked from 60 to 125 cans a minute. A new rapid cutting machine was also used to replace two older types.

Under Contract. The Alaska workers were hired by Chinese, Japanese, and Filipino contractors. In the early years of cannery operations, all hiring was done by contractors. It was a common practice that Filipino crews were headed by Filipino foremen. However, there were also Filipino laborers who worked

Washington State Archives

Filipinos aboard a U.S. surveying ship in Alaska, circa 1929.

Washington State Archives

Workers in the mess hall in Sunny Point, Alaska.

with Chinese, Japanese, Mexicans, and natives.

Flat Rate. In the contract system, a contractor would make a deal with the cannery owner to form his crew of workers at a flat rate. He would then figure out his profit and then set the wages for the workers.

The Filipinos, as well as other workers such as Japanese and Chinese, lived in bunkhouses. The Filipinos who predominated the work force in Alaska worked in canneries such as those in Alitak, Kodiak Island, Ward's Cove, Petersburg, Unalaska in Dutch Harbor, Naknek, Red Salmon, Ketchikan, Bumble Bee, Cook Inlet, Georgetown, Cordova, Egegik, Yakutak, Anchorage, and Moser Bay.

IV. Contractors

The Filipinos were usually taken advantage of by contractors. Even before the salmon canning season, some contractors forced workers to buy food, clothes, and other things at high prices from their stores. At that time, all loud complainers were fired the next day. Work was hard and life was boring in canneries.

V. THEIR WAYS OF LIFE

Their ways of life in Seattle and Alaska were different.

In Seattle. Usually, Alaskeros lived in Seattle and waited for the can-

Washington State Archives

An inspector estimating the volume of a scowload of salmon.

ning season. Most of them stayed in hotels and boarding houses. Those workers were dependent on their contractors for advances; that's why they accumulated a large amount of debt even before the canning season started.

Life in Alaska. The Alaskeros lived in bunkhouses, where workers provided their own bedding for the bunks. The bunks were made of planks nailed together. They had no springs and mattresses. Actually, the bunkhouse was just a big empty room, according to one Alaskero. If you were an Alaskero, you had to make your own partition to have privacy.

Washington State Archives

Culinary Crew, Red Salmon Company, Alaska, circa 1946.

Since life was boring in canneries, Filipino workers engaged in card games, ping-pong, volleyball, and other games.

Early in the morning, the workers ate their breakfast, which was no good. Others were served biscuits, with no jelly or butter, and black coffee. Others ate rice and eggs.

The early average wage was $25.00 a month. It reached $35.00 by the year 1910. Eventually it increased to $45 a month. There was a time that the pay increased to $47 and then to over $50.00 a month.

In some canneries, work started early in the morning, about 4 a.m. In others, the schedule might be from 6 a.m. to 6 p.m. In general, they worked up to 12 or 18 hours a day. Some worked until midnight.

Have Music, We'll Dance. The Filipinos solicited prostitutes. Some of them returned to the mainland empty-handed.

The Filipinos were lovers of music. The workers brought their guitars and other musical instruments. Then sometimes first-class women passengers would go to the laborers' quarters and dance with them.

Alaskeros display fish.

VI. THE ALASKEROS' UNION AND THE FILIPINO COMMUNITY

Due to the Great Depression, wages for unskilled jobs dropped by 40 percent from 1929 to 1933. Working and living conditions were so poor that Filipinos started to unions in the 1930s. In June 1933, they formed the Cannery Workers and Farm Laborers Union (CWFLU). The union was headquartered in Seattle's Colonial Cafe. Union organizers were harassed and threatened. Violence took place between union organizers and people hired by contractors to harass them.

Working and Living Conditions. The unions succeeded in uplifting the working and living conditions of the Alaskeros. But on December 1, 1936, union president Virgil Duyungan and his secretary, Aurelio Simon, were shot to death by a contractor's nephew during a meeting in a Japanese restaurant in Seattle. Union members continued their struggle but extended their negotiations with the contractors. In the end, they were able to get a monthly wage of $60.00. Two years after the union president's death, the union had from 6,000 to 7,000 members.

Finally, in 1938, the contractor system in canneries was abolished. The Filipinos and other workers had their bargaining negotiations and agreements with the management. They had better working conditions and higher pay.

Population. In 1910, 246 Filipinos lived in Alaska. At the height of the salmon and canning industry, they were about 9,000 Filipino workers there. Today. the Filipino community, numbers more than 8,000.

12

THE FILIPINO AMERICANS: YESTERDAY AND TODAY

The Filipino Americans today are an emerging Asian ethnic group. In fact, they are expected to become the fastest-growing Asian American group by the year 2000. Although they are currently number two only in total Asian American group population, next to the Chinese, they are expected to become the largest Asian American group after three years more, based on current statistics.

Records from the U.S. Immigration and Naturalization Service (INS) show that the Philippines has become the second biggest source of immigrants to the United States for the second year in a row (1995 and 1996), surpassing India, Vietnam, and China, which ranked third, fourth, and fifth, respectively.

Total Population. Although the official 1990 Census shows that there are only 1.4 million Filipinos in the United States, they number about 2.2 million, according to the National Filipino American Council.

According to a report in the *Filipino Reporter* the INS admitted a total of 53,876 legal immigrants from the Philippines in fiscal year 1996.

Mexico, up to 1996, remains the top country of origin of all immigrants to the United States, with a total of 163,572 arrivals in 1996.

Increase of Arrivals. According to INS statistics, the number of Filipino immigrants to the U.S. increased by 2,892 from 1995's total of 50,984 arrivals. In 1993 and 1994, the Filipinos ranked third, with 63,457 and 53,535, respectively. China then was ranked second during both fiscal years, with 53,985 in 1994 and 65,578 in 1993. China placed fourth in 1995 (35,463) and fifth in 1996 (41,728).

The state of California has been the first choice among Filipino immigrants. For 1996, 23,438 out of the 53,876 new immigrants from the Philippines chose to settle in California, mostly in San Francisco and Los Angeles. Hawaii was the second choice with a total of

5,208 arrivals, followed by New York, 3,719; New Jersey, 3,544, Illinois; 2,516; Guam, 2,220; Texas, 2,064; Florida, 1,796; Washington 1,688; and Virginia, 1,446.

Filipino American Contributions. The Filipino Americans are making a difference in government and private sectors—making their own contributions to the social, political, and economic development of the United States.

The Word *Filipino*. The name "Philippines" which was then known as the Philippine Islands originated from the name King Philip of Spain. The word *Filipino* (not Philipino) originally referred to Spaniards and Spanish mestizos (half-Spaniards) born in the Philippines. They were then called Españoles-Filipinos. Later, the natives were called *Indios*. Many years later, Filipinos in the United States were also called *Pinoys*. The term Pinoy became popular during the early 1900s when *pensionados* (scholars), nonsponsored students, and laborers came to America as nationals.

At that time, the Philippines, formerly called The Philippine Islands, was a colony of the United States.

In the 1980s, young Filipino Americans began to use the term Flip, which may mean "funny little island people" or "flippin' little island people." Since the word is derogatory which may also mean *chink* or *gook*, many Filipinos are opposed to using it.

Generally, the term Filipino is used for both male and female. However, *Filipina* is used only for a woman.

I. THE VOYAGE TO AMERICA

In the early 1900s, Filipinos came to the United States by ship, whether through Honolulu, Hawaii, or the California ports of Seattle and San Francisco. The immigrants were on the bottom part of the boat. Usually, the trip took one month.

First, the Trip to Hawaii. Let's see in our imagination how the immigrants managed to reach Hawaii.

About two hundred or so, Filipino emigrants are brought to the very bottom of the ship. See how recruits and several families, with their bedding and new clothing for the trip, sleep on the floor on mats in one big room.

The workers and their families talk with each other: retelling rumors and tales about Hawaii and how laborers work in the fields. They also wonder if the stories in letters from their townmates working in Hawaii, telling about the good life, are true or not. Almost all of them are excited and they are somewhat nervous. They don't know what their life will be on the islands of Hawaii. Many of them become seasick for lack of pure air on the ship. But they can't go upstairs on the deck; it's prohibited.

As they are about to reach Honolulu, the boat people are a little bit apprehensive; they are wondering about the outcome of going to Hawaii. Upon disembarking from their ship, you see them being assigned to plantations in Hawaii. A new life begins.

The Trip to the Mainland. The early Filipinos reached the continental United States by ships. The ships had laborers, pensionados, and nonsponsored workers. Usually, it took the ships one month to reach the Seattle or San Francisco ports.

How Does It Feel to Be Going to America? Here's a typical reaction or feeling of a Filipino going to America in the years past.

(Excerpts from *America Is In the Heart: A Personal History* by Carlos Bulosan, reprinted by permission of Harcourt Brace & Company. Copyright 1943, 1946):

I found the dark hole of the steerage and lay on my bunk for days without food, seasick and lonely. I was restless at night and many disturbing thoughts came to my mind. Why had I left home? What would I do in America? I looked into the faces of my companions for a comforting answer, but they were as young and bewildered as I, and my only consolation was their proximity and the familiarity of their dialects. It was not until we had left Japan that I began to feel better.

One day in mid-ocean, I climbed through the narrow passageway to the deck where other steerage passengers were sunning themselves. Most of them were Ilocanos, who were fishermen in the northern coastal regions of Luzon. They were talking easily and eating rice with salted fish with their bare hands, and some of them were walking, barefoot and unconcerned, in their homemade cotton shorts. The first-class passengers were annoyed, and an official of the boat came down and drove us back into the dark haven below. The small opening at the top of the iron ladder was shut tight, and we did not see the sun again until we had passed Hawaii.

Airports, Not Seaports. Today, Filipino Americans enter the United States through airports. In 1976, when my wife and I arrived here, we disembarked from a Pan Am plane in Honolulu, Hawaii. I was quite surprised to see several American women driving buses. Moreover, I had the opportunity to see American workingmen doing street repairs. My first impulse was that I saw in my imagination images of American soldiers during the war, when we used to greet them, "Hello Joe!" "Hello Joe!" "Victory Joe!"

Moreover, I felt we were like herds of cattle to be branded when we were in line to be documented as immigrants to America. It was really a strange feeling in a strange new land.

II. THEIR WAY OF LIFE

In the 1920s and 1930s, the Filipinos were a mobile people. They were always on the go. Like birds, they moved according to seasons. They moved from city to city, state to state, in search of jobs, when certain crops were grown to be picked up or harvested.

In the 1930s, Filipinos concentrated in large West Coast cities, including Los Angeles, San Francisco, and Seattle, where they had large "Little Manilas." Most of them lived in the San Francisco and Seattle areas because it was there where the ships brought them from Manila. While some worked in California and Washington cities, many worked as stoop laborers in agricultural fields: planting, culti-

vating, and harvesting seasonal crops, from California to Washington to Minnesota.

Little Manilas. The population in the "Little Manilas" increased and dwindled according to seasons. For instance, in the summer of 1931, the population in Seattle was only a few hundred. In the winter, it usually would increase to 3,500, living in almost ghetto areas near centers of vice and entertainment.

In the San Francisco winter, they were on the Kearney Street area, along the northern part of Chinatown. In Stockton, during the summer months, the Filipino population numbered over 6,000, but in the winter it had only 1,000 Filipinos. In Los Angeles, they first created a Little Manila next to "Little Tokyo." Later, however, they moved Little Manila to the neighborhood of Figueroa and Temple Streets, where they had Filipino barbershops, restaurants, grocery stores, pool and dance halls, and other centers of vice and entertainment.

There were also Little Manilas in New York City and Washington, D.C. Some of the Filipinos in New York City were described as well-to-do while others were considered as bums. The early immigrants to New York City were the Tagalogs. They settled on 6th Street, where there were pool halls, a barbershop, and small restaurants. Those who lived in Washington, D.C., were said to have a more organized social life.

There were also Filipinos in the Detroit, Michigan, area. Some of them worked at the Ford plants in Dearborn and River Rouge, Michigan.

In the 1960s, California's agriculture continued to attract Filipino workers. In the 1960s in Hawaii, Filipinos were the majority of workers on plantations, about 40 percent of the employed males.

In the early 1970s, the Los Angeles and the San Francisco Bay areas continued to attract large numbers of Filipinos. Other Filipino immigrants then moved towards Illinois, (most of them in the Chicago area), New York, Texas, New Jersey, Pennsylvania, Michigan, and other states.

Where Do They Live Today? Today, Filipinos live all over the United States. But the majority of Filipino Americans, who came in large groups since 1965 after the approval of the amendment to the 1924 Immigration Act, live mostly in metropolitan areas, such as Honolulu, Chicago, New York, Jersey City, and Seattle, and in the suburbs of other large cities of America. Of course, some Filipinos stay in the confines of a major city, such as Detroit.

When the Filipino immigrant and his family arrive, they first rent an apartment. When they are able to save enough money for down payment on a house, they buy it, being their first house. When they make more money, then they move to the suburbs.

Normally, when a Filipino immigrant or naturalized U.S. citizen is already in the suburbs, he invites his relatives or friends whose families are still in a metropolitan city, such as Detroit, to come to the suburbs.

For instance, when we first arrived in the United States in 1976, my family and I rented an apartment in the western part of Detroit, Michigan. In that apartment, when it rained, it poured. When the children of my wife's brother came to Detroit for a visit in the 1980s, one of them asked, "You lived here?" He was shocked.

When my wife became a medical resident of a hospital in Harperwoods, Michigan, we moved to another apartment in that city. When we had some money saved, we bought a three-bedroom bungalow in East Detroit (now Eastpointe), Michigan.

After living there for eight years, our relatives in the suburbs always said, "Come over here in the suburbs. You've been left behind there!"

"Here' we come!" my wife and I answered in 1990. We decided to construct a detached condominium home here in Farmington Hills, Michigan.

This always happens to Filipino families: They move and move to a better place if the financial situation warrants it. By the time they reach retirement age, when all the children are grown and gone and on their own, some couples sell their house and live in an apartment again. Those who have enough money buy a small house. Those doing this are mostly in winter states who move to the sunbelt areas, particularly Florida, Nevada, Washington State, Texas, or where their savings or retirement benefits can take them. All they want is the sunshine. Of course, some retirees go back home to the Philippines where they want to spend the rest of their lives.

III. THE FAMILY

The key units of the Philippine social structure are the *elementary* family and the *bilateral extended* family. The elementary family, which serves as the nuclear unity around which social activities are organized, is composed of the father, the mother, and the children. The bilateral extended family includes all the relatives of the father and the mother. However, in the Philippines, the typical family is composed of one elementary family with the

Washington State Archives

An extended family in Seattle, Washington.

addition of one or more close relatives, including grandparents.

The Interests of the Family. In Philippine society, the interests of the family are the priority, not the interests of the individual. Because of the close family ties, even in adolescence, the Filipino's peers do not replace his family. They merely widen his social circle.

The Individual's Rights. In the United States, individualism is priority. Every person has his own rights, obligations, and responsibilities. That's why sometimes Filipino parents and children in America have family conflicts. The children demand their rights as individuals to be respected. On the other hand, the parents demand that their "rights" as parents should prevail. Many a father may say to his son or daughter, "As long as you live in this house I'm the one to be followed because I'm the head of the family. My decisions prevail." Of course, in many instances, they patch up their differences, compromising on certain behaviors or practices.

Compromise. Sometimes, the daughter may have arguments with her mother on how a Filipina should dress or act in public or at social functions. Again, they pursue a compromise. That is, the mother may allow certain actions of her daughter as a Filipina American in the United States.

It is said that the Filipino's family is the source of his emotional and material support. Children are generally seen as blessings from God and a lot of emotion is invested in them. Parents have the tendency to identify with the successes and failures of their children. Thus, it becomes natural that parents require unquestioned obedience, overprotect the child and interfere with his affairs, which the child should accept as an expression of love.

Marian Country. Deeply religious and predominantly Catholic, the Philippines is a Marian country and the Virgin Mary is its patroness. Ritual practices and prayers addressing her are very common and widespread. Many Filipino nuclear households, although multigenerational, are matrifocal, i.e., centered around the mother and her relatives. This position is underlined by the symbol of the Holy Mother, whom Filipinos submit to, honor, and revere. The husbands tend to leave the matters of the home in their wives' hands.

IV. THE FILIPINO HOUSEHOLD

In the United States, a family is typically composed of father, mother, and children. The children may number two or more. (If the children were born in the Philippines, they would usually number from three to six. If they were born here, then there would probably be only two.) In some households, the family may include the parents of either or both husband and wife. These senior citizens, if still capable of physical work, help in household chores. They also help in taking care of the kids, especially if they are still young, when the husband and wife are at work. In others, the family may even include a brother or sister of either husband or wife.

Usually, the children, even if they are over 18, as long as they are still single, may stay with their parents. Of course, they leave their home when they go to out-of-state colleges, or work out of state, and come home only on holidays and vacations.

Income. Today, according to the National Filipino American Council, Filipino Americans consist of more than 511,000 households, with an annual collective income of $12.7 billion. According to the NFAC survey, Filipino Americans generally surpass the U.S. national averages in median household income, educational levels, and home values. The survey also shows that an average Filipino household consists of four members and makes at least $25,000 a year versus the national average of $17,200. The Filipino household generally owns at least an $80,000 house versus the national average of $47,200.

Filipino Names. Filipinos in the Philippines and Filipino Americans have usually one given first name; for instance, Hubert, Lester, Melvin, and Ronald, although there may be some who have names such as Peter John, Mary Joyce, or Steven Michael. But there are Filipino Americans who have names that repeat themselves, such as Bong Bong, Jeng Jeng, Deng Deng, and Ling Ling.

Filipino Americans take their mother's surname or last name as their middle name. When a woman, for instance, Mary Joyce Icban marries a Bautista, Icban becomes her middle name. Her name may be Mary Joyce Icban Bautista or merely Mary Joyce I. Bautista.

Traces of Filipino-ness. As soon as you enter a Filipino American home, you may notice particular objects or sights that reflect the identity of the family and that it came from the Philippines. You may see a shrine of the Santo Niño or the Virgin Mary in the living room. You may notice a Weapons of Moroland shield hanging on a wall. (Those are replicas of weapons used by Muslim tribes in Mindanao—the ethnic groups that were never subjugated by the Spanish or American colonizers.) Or maybe there is a wood carving of *tinikling* dancers on the wall.

In some households, the family may own *capiz* lamps and chandeliers. Of course, when you're already there in the living room, the sofas and chairs may seem to say, "Hey, we're clean!" But the fact is that you may not know it, but that furniture was covered with bedsheets before you came in. On the big coffee table, there may be a small laughing Buddha, as if saying, "Hi, how are you?" placed there for good luck. In the living room or family room, there may be a piano that is seldom played or no one plays. (Our piano is in the basement.) Why is it there? It's because when any of the kids were small, they were taught how to play the piano. But as they grew older, they lost their interest in playing.

In the dining room, you may notice a giant wooden fork and spoon attached to one of the walls. On the table may be seen placemats made of abaca fiber, brought here from the old country.

In the kitchen, there may be a rice dispenser, a rice cooker, and maybe a turbo broiler. These are the most important things that a Filipino American family usually have in the kitchen. On the kitchen table there may be lots of food, including delicacies. The food may have been cooked by the mother or bought from a Filipino restaurant. No matter, they are ready to be eaten.

Outdoors, when you see a car with a hanging rosary on the car's rearview mirror, it's almost 100 percent owned by a Filipino American. When a backing-up car emits a warning chirping bird sound or any other sound, probably that car is owned by a Filipino American.

V. DISCRIMINATION AND PREJUDICE

In the early period of their immigration, the Filipinos were discriminated against at work, on the road, in hotel and restaurants, and in almost any place in the United States.

Here's an excerpt from *America Is In the Heart: A Personal History* by Carlos Bulosan, reprinted by permission of Harcourt Brace & Company. Copyright 1943, 1946:

> I came to know afterward that in many ways it was a crime to be a Filipino in California. I came to know that the public streets were not free to my people: we were stopped each time these vigilant patrolmen saw us driving a car. We were suspect each time we were seen with a white woman. And perhaps it was this narrowing of our life into an island, into a filthy segment of American society, that had driven Filipinos like Doro inward, hating everyone and despising all positive urgencies toward freedom.

(Note: Doro was Bulosan's companion in a car on way to Lompoc, California.)

What Did You Do During the War, Daddy? This question might have been asked by some Filipino Americans. During World War II, about 80,000 Filipinos tried to enlist in the armed forces of the United States. But they were rejected because they at that time were considered as aliens, not nationals of the United States. So President Roosevelt issued a proclamation allowing the Filipinos to be drafted into the armed forces.

In the Philippines, the Filipinos fought side by side with the American soldiers. U.S. officers saw the courage of the Filipinos in battles in the mountains of Bataan and Corregidor. The bravery of the Filipinos was recognized throughout the world. With the help of Filipino soldiers, it took the Japanese forces months to capture Bataan and Corregidor, delaying the time-table of Japan's conquest of Asia.

From that time on, the outlook of Americans towards Filipinos changed for the better. However, today, discrimination and prejudice still exist at work, in school, and at some social functions. In some hospitals, nurses are prohibited from talking in their own national language, Tagalog or Pilipino.

In appointments to any positions, Filipino Americans also experience a kind of discrimination and prejudice. Some of them are barred from attaining higher positions in private and government establishments because of the color of their skin and their accent. Many Americans are critical of the accent of the Filipino Americans, even though some Americans have their own regional accents. This, the Filipinos can't understand.

They usually say, "You have an accent." Or one may say, "I've met a foreigner who has also an accent like you. Maybe he's a Filipino like you," particularly addressed to foreign-born Filipino Americans.

Of course, unlike in the years past, Filipino Americans of today have no problem in being admitted to hotels, restaurants, and other public places. In many ways, they are co-equal with other Americans.

Discrimination in School. Many Filipino American students are also often discriminated against. Here's the story of a Filipino American who complained of discrimination and prejudice in school:

Born and raised in the United States, this student became ashamed of being Asian. He often told his classmates that he was of Spanish descent. In grade school, he said, some kids used "to pull their eyes back, stick out their teeth and chant, ching-chong, ching-chong!'".

When he was in high school, he was called Jap, chink, and other names. He was mistaken for belonging to any Asian ethnic group, but not being a Filipino American. He hated what he experienced.

Fitting in. The Filipinos and the Americans have had close association since the United States sent soldiers to the Philippines in 1889. American soldiers in the beginning served as teachers in Philippine schools. Then the Thomasites went to the Philippines to take over the jobs of American soldiers as teachers. English has been the medium of instruction in public and private schools up to now, although Pilipino is taught in the lower grades, along with English. In the years past, American textbooks were used in schools and Filipino students were exposed to American history, literature, society, and culture. Today only one percent of the Filipino American population can't speak English at all. Very few immigrant groups can claim that statistic.

Yet, Filipino Americans, especially the first-generation immigrants, have difficulties in fitting into American mainstream society. While they speak good English and know good grammar and usage, and spelling, they have a different way of pronouncing some English words. Some of them pronounce "f" as "p" and the "th" such "d" as in "them" (dem). So when they talk in accented English, some Americans, especially those who have not had any acquaintance with Filipino Americans, sometimes find it hard or refuse to understand such words, especially when talking over the telephone.

That's why Filipino Americans hold their own parties and form their own associations. To these parties, however, they invite their white and black American friends who enjoy partaking Filipino food and witnessing Filipino celebrations.

Newly arrived students from the Philippines, in their first years in schools, have difficulty adjusting to the new school environment. At first, some of them can't understand some of the things their teacher and classmates are talking about. Of course, after a year or so, they converse with them in good English and imitate them in pronouncing English words. After that, they excel in class; some of them at the top of their class.

VI. FORMS OF RECREATION

In years past, cockfighting, even if it were illegal, became one of the Filipinos' favorite forms of recreation. They also engaged in gambling: playing cards and dice. They went to dance halls or cabarets. These dance halls were established in cities on the West Coast, such as Los Angeles, Stockton, Sacramento, and San Francisco, California; Seattle, Washington; and Portland, Oregon. There were also dance halls in Honolulu, Hawaii for the sugarcane and pineapple workers.

There were instances in dance halls that rival Filipino gangs, belonging to different ethnic groups, engaged in altercations, fist fights, or stabbings. Such fights resulted from rivalry over women. Of course, there were occasions when Filipinos fought with American laborers over women or job opportunities.

In gambling dens, many workers gambled and lost some or all of a hard day's wage.

Dance Halls Are Gone. Today, those dance halls are gone. But they dance with their wives and friends during wedding and club or association dinner-dance parties. No more houses of prostitution for Filipinos. No more cockfighting games, either. Filipino Americans have their own families, not like the years past when most of them were bachelors. Even husbands who were once playboys in the Philippines are now in their own homes with their wives. However, some of them go to Las Vegas, Nevada, to Atlantic City, New Jersey, or to Windsor, Canada, trying to find their luck in gambling—playing cards or playing slot machines.

Like any other Americans, Filipino Americans watch baseball, basketball, football, and hockey games in the confines of their homes. Like any other sports enthusiasts, some also go to the stadiums to watch these games. When I first saw a football game, I couldn't understand it. I thought that whenever there was a "down," it was a touchdown.

Movie Stars and Singers. There are entrepreneurs who bring to their community movie stars and singers from the Philippines for the Filipinos to be entertained. When the Filipino Americans hear Philippine songs and watch Filipino folk dances, they are always reminded of home, the Philippines, and their relatives and friends.

"Don't Know Where the Ball Goes!" Although no one is considered a Tiger Woods, many Filipino Americans play golf during the weekend or on weekdays in the summer. I have a *kababayan* (townmate) who decided to play golf after he retired from work. He told me once, "Most of the time, I don't know where the ball goes!" When I try to hit a ball towards a certain direction, it goes somewhere else." This author doesn't play golf; I would rather play with my computer.

Have Picnics, We'll Chat! As in the past, today's Filipino Americans go on their annual picnics usually held in the summer in July or August. For instance, there are Nuevo Ecijanos' picnic, Papayeños' picnic, and the Tagalog Association's picnic. In other words, these picnics are held by clubs, associations, or just members of a few families from their native towns or provinces in the Philippines. They have a potluck, wherein each family brings its own food for all to eat. Each Filipino ethnic group, such as Tagalog, Ilocano, Pampangueño, Visayan, goes on its own picnic. On these picnics, they bring home-cooked Filipino foods and delicacies and sometimes photos of a birthday party or wedding. A family who has no time to cook brings a bucket or two of Kentucky Fried Chicken. No problem.

On these gatherings, they reminisce the days past.

One may say, "We are lucky, we were able to come here and accomplished our goals. Just imagine, if we were in the Philippines, how could we have educated our children in good educational institutions."

"Yes," another may say, "After we have had sacrifices and hardships, we were able to make it here. Now, we can look to our retirement, whether here or in the Philippines."

"Where are you going to retire?" one may ask.

"I don't know yet," may be the answer.

Year in and year out, they talk about the same subjects. One may say that he's reluctant to retire in the Philippines because he may always be approached by relatives to ask for money, thinking that he is rich. This concerns many prospective retirees. Sometimes, one says, "I'm retiring in the Philippines just to play golf every day, since I have dollars. At the time this book was being written, the exchange rate was about P40 (40 pesos) to a U.S. dollar. Wow! So some retirees really go home to the Philippines to begin a new life or career as businessmen or businesswomen. ("That's not retirement!" one may say.) In the end, most retire in the state where they live or move to Nevada, Arizona, or Florida or in any Sunbelt state.

"Happy Birthday" or "Congratulations on Your Wedding Day!" Filipino Americans usually invite their relatives or friends to their birthday or wedding

Filipino Americans, who are natives of General Tinio (Papaya), Nueva Ecija, Philippines, hold a picnic on a park every year. They are shown posing for a photograph.

Picnickers from General Tinio, Nueva Ecija, Philippines are shown (l to r): Ester Caraig, Dr. Lilia Mangulabnan, Dr. Genoveva A. Bautista, and Jessie Alviar.

parties. Again, on these occasions, they can talk about any news coming from home or how the kids are doing in school, or when they are visiting their native country.

If the parties are held in a residence, there will be plenty of food. If you've not attended a Filipino American party (especially at home), attend one, and you'll know what I mean. In other words, "all you can eat." Not only that, if there are lots leftovers, the hosts usually put some food in plastic or paper plates and wrap them for attendees to take home. Or they may say, "Wrap your own food, there is so much left." What a way to attend a party!

After partaking of the food, they play cards. Some win, others lose. That's always part of some parties.

Holiday Celebrations. In the years past, the Filipino Americans celebrated Philippine national holidays, particularly Rizal Day, December 30, in celebration of the death of Dr. Jose Rizal, considered as the greatest Filipino hero. Today, some communities hold dramas in celebration of the event.

1996 Celebration of the Centennial of the Philippine Revolution (1896). To observe the 100th anniversary of the Philippine Revolution, the *Pintig* (Pulse), the only professional Filipino American Theater Company in Chicago, Illinois, presented Chris Millado's provocative "Scenes from an Unfinished Country 1905/1995," at CCP's *Tanghalang Huseng Batute* in Chicago and at

The cast of Pintig Cultural Group's "Scenes from an Unfinished Country" that presented shows in the Chicago, Illinois, area in 1996.

other places. The play was adapted from two "seditious" dramas written during the early American occupation of the Philippines: Juan Matapang Cruz's *Hindi Ako Patay (I'm Not Dead)* and Aurelio Tolentino's *Kahapon, Ngayon, at Bukas (Yesterday, Today, and Tomorrow)*.

Philippine Centennial 1998: The Largest Celebration of Them All. In the United States and in the Philippines, the largest celebration is the Philippine Centennial Year 1998. The United States on July 4, 1946, "gave" the Philippines its independence. However, the late President Diosdado Macapagal changed the Philippine Independence Day from July 4, 1946, to June 12, 1898, the date when Aguinaldo declared the Philippine independence from Spain in Kawit, Cavite Prov-

ince, Philippine Islands.)

The Philippine Centennial Commission, for the purpose of celebrating the event, created different chapters in the U.S. Among the states that are actively participating in the event are Arkansas, California, Delaware, Illinois, Maryland, Michigan, Minnesota, Missouri, New Jersey, Ohio, Pennsylvania, Tennessee, Texas, Virginia, West Virginia, as well as the District of Columbia. On the East Coast, one of the chapters is the Philippine Centennial Coordinating Council of Northeastern USA (PCCCNUSA), headed by Luz Sapin Micabalo, the overall chairperson.

Included in the PCCCNUSA's observance of the Philippine Centennial are cultural and trade shows, including a Philippine Food Festival, a Santacruzan, and the traditional trade and festival shows. Fashion shows and dance, music, and theater performances are to be held. The celebration will be highlighted by a Centennial Gala night on June 12, 1998. In addition, the celebration will continue to the end of the year 1998 with a series of presentations dubbed as *Sining Biswal* (Visual Arts). To be featured are works of well-known Filipino American artists at the Philippine Center Gallery in New York City.

In the Philippines, the center of the celebration will be at the Philippine Centennial National Exposition 1998 at the former Clark Air Force Base in Angeles, Pampanga Province, where the Philippines will showcase Filipino trades, arts, environmental displays, and international relations.

VII. INTERRACIAL MARRIAGES

In the 1920s and 1930s, many Americans expressed indignation over the Filipinos' wish to be with or marry white women. The Filipinos had no choice; there were only a few Filipinas at that time.

Little Brown Men. For instance, Judge D.W. Rohrback, proposed a resolution to the Monterey County Board in California. The resolution referred to the Filipinos as "little brown men about 10 years removed from a bolo and breach cloth...strutting about like peacocks, endeavoring to attract the eyes of young American and Mexican girls."

In 1930, speaking before the House Committee on Immigration and Naturalization, a white male said, "The Filipinos are a social menace. They will not leave our white girls alone."

V.S. McClatchy castigated the Filipinos' presence "for the white women and the willingness on the part of some white females to yield to that preference." In his testimony before Congress, he called Congress to limit the entry of Filipinos to the U.S.

In reference to what some Americans charged that Filipinos liked white women, Author Elaine Kim, in *Asian American Literature*, sums up writer Carlos Bulosan's opinion: "The white woman is a dream, an ideal. She symbolizes the contradiction between what is brutal in America and what is kind and beautiful. Concretely, the Filipino man's

Celestino Mangulabnan, Jr., a Filipino American, and Kathleen Kapolnek, a Polish-German American, with their two children: Matthew Pedro and Valerie Lilia.

interest in white women did not stem merely from sexual desire...Marrying a white woman would free him from sexual oppression and emasculation, give the possibility of a stable family life and at least a partial entry into the mainstream of American life."

Marriage Ban. In the 1920s and 1930s, Filipinos or Malays were banned from marrying white women in many states. However, the laws against Filipinos were later declared as unconstitutional.

Brown Men with White Women; Brown Women with White Men. Today, it's seldom that heads turn when they see brown men with white women or brown women with white men. There are now many Filipino American men married to white women and Filipino American women married to American men. There are also a few cases of mixed marriages involving Filipino Americans and other Asian Americans and Filipina Americans and African Americans. Therefore, white women are no longer criticized for being with Filipino men, whether in theaters, malls, or wherever. Their children are exposed to two cultures: American and Filipino. Many American men and women enjoy eating Filipino foods, especially the *pansit* (rice noodles) and fried *lumpia* (meat egg rolls).

A Typical Interracial Couple. Here's the story of a typical interracial marriage between Celestino Mangulabnan, Jr., a Filipino American, and Kathleen "Kathy" Kapolnek, a Polish-German American. Five years after they went steady, they married in 1993. Today, they have two children. The name of the boy is Matthew Pedro (the last name being Filipino) and the girl's name is Valerie Lilia (again the other name is Filipino). What do the kids look like? How are they raised? What food do they eat? How does Kathy prepare the family meal? She is married to a Filipino who has eaten a lot of rice since he was born, so she had to learn how to cook it.

Kathy now knows how to cook rice and prepare Filipino food. She likes to cook fried rice and other meals. On the other hand, her husband has learned how to eat some Polish food. With regard to eating Filipino food, Matthew, the older kid, once requested his grandmother, Dr. Lilia Mangulabnan, "Grandma! Please cook me fried rice." It was a delight for Dr. Mangulabnan to cook fried rice, without garlic, but with butter and Filipino food for her two grandchildren. Indeed, Dr. Mangulabnan and her husband, Celestino, like to babysit the two children. The Filipino American couple has adjusted well to each other's cultures, and they are imparting the beauty of two cultures to their children; for instance, Filipino food and Polish American food and respect for their elders, etc. As Kathy once told Matthew, "Don't talk to grandma, like that, Matthew!" In short, the marriage is working.

New Multicultural Category. Because of interracial marriages, there has been a growing movement undertaken by various interracial groups to determine a name for a new multiracial category, so that people of mixed races should not be forced to choose between the racial make-up of either of parent. For instance, for bureaucratic purposes, what shall we call Tiger Woods, a Master's golf champion and the son of an African American father and a Thai mother)? African American, Thai American, or Asian American?

Why Should I Call You "Dad"? You Aren't My Dad. I know of a Filipino whom we may call Aurelio Reyes. He was shocked when his white son-in-law called him Mr. Reyes for the first time. For this reason, he requested his son-in-law to call him Dad.

"Why should I call you "Dad"? You aren't my Dad." the son-in-law said.

The father-in-law answered, "That's how it is in Filipino traditions. A son-in-law or a daughter-in-law should call his or her father-in-law, 'Dad' or *Tatang* or whatever the Filipino son or daughter calls him. And if you

want me to consider and love you as a son, call me 'Dad.'"

The son-in-law was convinced. And then one day, when the son-in-law was so excited when he saw his father-in-law in a restaurant, he called him, "Dad! Dad!" Some of the people in the eatery looked at the father and son: one white and the other brown.

Yes, in Filipino tradition, the son-in-law or the daughter-in-law, should call the father-in-law and mother-in-law "Dad" and "Mom," respectively.

VIII. CITIZENSHIP

In 1902, the U.S. Congress declared that all residents of the Philippine Islands who were Spanish subjects as of April 11, 1899, were all citizens of the Philippines Islands. Included in the declaration were their children.

The immigration law passed in 1917 stipulated that while most Filipinos could not become citizens, they were not considered as aliens. In other words, they were nationals of the United States. Their being nationals was also continued in the 1924 immigration act that specified that they were not aliens, but nationals free to enter the United States. This provision was effective until the Tydings-McDuffie Act, also known as the Philippine Independence Act, was passed by Congress and approved by President Theodore Roosevelt in 1935. At that time, the quota of Filipino immigration was pegged at 50 immigrants per year.

On June 14, 1946, President Harry Truman signed the Filipino Naturalization Bill, giving eligibility to Filipinos for becoming U.S. citizens.

On July 2, 1946, Congress gave American citizenship to foreign-born Filipino residents in the U.S. who had entered the United States before March 24, 1934. The proclamation set the Filipino immigration to the U.S. at 100 persons a year. This quota was enforced until the passage of the 1965 Nationality Immigration Act.

On October 15, 1948, more Filipinos were granted permission to petition their wives and children under 18 years of age to come to the U.S. as "non-quota immigrants." Those were the Filipinos who had lived in the United States continuously for three years before November 30, 1941.

It should be pointed out that prior to 1946, many Filipinos became naturalized citizens when they enlisted in the armed forces of the United States during World War II. They became American citizens in 1943 before they went to war in the Pacific and in the Philippines.

IX. RAISING THEIR CHILDREN

Filipino American parents, in raising their children, try to implant Filipino values in their children's minds—respect for elders, good education, good values, and good morals and right character. The children are told that they should act like Filipinos and should not forget the good things about being Filipinos and their culture.

In short, Filipino American children are forced to live in two worlds: being Filipinos and being Americans.

Since Filipino American parents teach their children to respect their elders, children in many homes call their brothers and sisters by different terms. For instance, among the Tagalogs, the oldest son is called *kuya* or *kuyang* (by the succeeding children, whether male or female); the second son, *diko*; the third son, *sangko*; and the fourth son (if there is any), *kuya* again, *Kuya* or *Kuyang* Felix, then *diko*, etc. The eldest daughter is called *ate*, the second, *ditse*; the third, *sanse* (then back to *ate* Millie or *kuya* Boy, or etc.). In my family, my youngest child, Janet, calls her brothers *kuyang, diko, sangko*, and *Kuyang* (Ronald).

Speak in English, Then in Pilipino. In Filipino American homes in America, parents usually talk with their children in English when they are little in order that their children won't have any foreign accent in English. Their other purpose is for the parents to improve their English pronunciation and reduce their Filipino accent.

Since the children grow up with American friends, they speak without an accent. When they are grown, the parents talk to them in Pilipino or another Philippine dialect so that they can converse with relatives and other Filipinos when they go home to the Philippines for a visit. The children usually answer in English. In other words, they understand Pilipino (Tagalog), but they can't talk in Pilipino. When they say a few words in Pilipino, they normally have an American accent. That is, Pilipino words are pronounced as if they were English words. I know of a Filipino who has an accent both in English and in Pilipino although he belongs to the Tagalog ethnic group.

Because of the fact that their U.S.-born children can't speak in Pilipino, some parents even send their teenaged sons or daughters to the Philippines for a few weeks or months to learn Pilipino and Filipino culture. Some students attend Pilipino classes in their universities in the U.S. or some Pilipino classes held by Filipino associations.

Life in These United States. In a family household, generally, both husband and wife have jobs. Frequently, when they start a family and have one or two young children, the husband works nights and the wife works days, or vice versa. It depends on many factors. If the husband works at an auto company as an assembly worker, he may work the afternoon shift that starts at 3:30 p.m. and ends at 12:00 midnight. Or if the woman is a nurse, then she is the one who works in that shift.

It is not uncommon that some of them may hold two jobs or sometimes several jobs. There was a time in my wife's work as a doctor that she worked or moonlighted in three hospitals.

Generally, Filipino Americans send their children to public schools. However, some Filipinos, as some well-to-do families in the Philippines, do enroll their children in private schools to have a good education. This is done in view of the fact that Filipinos and Filipino Americans give importance to a good education as the number-one goal of Filipino couples for their children.

It's not unusual that their children excel in class or make the honor roll because Filipino American parents always see to it that their children study well and do their homework every day. However, there's always time for studying—and for playing.

In college, Filipino Americans try to regularly send their children to the best schools as possible, depending on their financial resources. Parents living on the East Coast may send their children to a university on the West Coast and vice versa.

The Joy of Going Home. The first time that when my children went home to the Philippines, the first words they learned were *kakain na* (let's eat) and *kumusta?* (how are you?).

When Filipino American children go to their parents' native country, they are not usually called Filipinos but *mga Amerikano* (the Americans) by their relatives and newly acquired friends. In their dealing with them, the Filipino Americans learn some words and phrases in Pilipino or other Philippine dialects. They usually enjoy their stay in the Philippines, where life is quite different from that in the United States.

When one of my sons went home to the Philippines for the first time in 1987, while still in San Francisco (on his way back to Michigan), he said over the phone with an accent, *Ba-ba-lik uli a-ko sa Pi-li-pi-nas* (I'll be back again to the Philippines).

X. IN SEARCH OF IDENTITY

Second-generation and third-generation Filipinos are usually in search of identity. They are called Fil-Ams or Filipino Americans. Those born here sometimes can't understand why although they were born here and are considered Americans, some Americans don't treat them as equals. And other times, they can't consider themselves as Filipinos, either. They don't know Pilipino language or any other Philippine dialects and they don't know anything about Philippine history or culture.

One of the various reasons why Filipino Americans can't speak their own national language is that their parents don't teach them when they are little. They don't want their kids to have Filipino-accented English.

For example, Tia Carrere, born Althea Dujenio Janairo, a Hollywood movie actress, who describes herself as Filipino/Spanish/Chinese was quoted in *Filipinas* magazine:, "My dad never taught us Pilipino because he didn't want us to have an accent. I understood it was because he was an immigrant and didn't want us to be left out. But I do think it's a shame to leave behind that important part of your heritage, your language. "

(Carrere's father, Alexander, hails from Cebu, Philippines. Her mother Audrey's grandmother was Filipina. A native of Kahili, Hawaii, Carrere has appeared in *High School*, with Jon Lovitz. She also appeared in *Rising Sun*, which also starred Sean Connery and Wesley Snipes. (See her profile in Part IV: *Profiles of Notable Filipino Americans*).

Famous Filipino American singer Jocelyn Enriquez swears she considers herself as Filipino first, American second. Enriquez was born and raised by her first-generation Filipino parents in the San Francisco Bay Area.

Sometimes, some young Filipino Americans hate themselves in the beginning because they are different from other Americans. (See her profile in Part IV: *Profiles of Notable Filipino Americans*).

"Why Is My Hair Not Blond?" I still remember when my only daughter was little, she asked me, "Daddy why is my hair not blond? I'm the only girl in my class whose hair is black. Probably, if I were born here, my hair would have been blond." Later, she seemed to have been searching for her identity. She used to rent tapes of Filipino movies from Filipino American stores. The only thing I didn't like was that I became tired of translating to English the stars' conversation. My daughter has been to the Philippines four times and she enjoyed every minute of her visit to our mother country.

Subconscious Denial of One's Filipino Roots. Frequently, the subconscious denial of one's Filipino roots occurs in the pre-high school or high school period of a student's life. But after that time, the young Filipino American makes efforts to reconnect to his or her parents' culture. In fact, in the past years, there has been a rising movement among them to seek their identity: learning the Pilipino language, seeing Filipino movies, and studying the Filipino culture and history.

For example, the young Josephine Roberto, a rising Filipino American singer known as Banig describes herself as a Filipino American. She says, "I'm still very Filipina in so many ways. Although I have come to assimilate some of the aspects of [American] culture, I still speak the language very fluently, never forget to say my *po's* and my *opo's* when I talk to older folks, still crave Filipino foods, watch Filipino movies, and practice Filipino values."

Being a Filipino American. Here are stories of Filipino Americans in search of their identity.

Physical Appearance. Journalist, Angela Lau wrote a feature story about a 15-year-old Filipino American girl in California:

After seeing herself in the mirror, she had realized that she was brown in color and had black hair, not like her Caucasian classmates in school. She thought her white classmates were beautiful. "I was embarrassed of the fact that I was different," she said.

She tried to change the way she looked and acted. She had her hair cut into a bob, then she dyed it blond. She didn't expose herself to the sun to protect her skin from becoming darker. Later, she confessed, "I tried so hard to fit in, but I just could never be like them." So she then acted like any other Filipino American girls; she admitted to being different from the other Americans—and became proud of it.

Being Invisible. A Filipino American male had a heated argument with about 20 to 30 white male classmates in junior high school. The white boys asked him why he was "trying to be black" because he had his hip-hop style and fashion, as opposed to other Asian kids who were quiet in class. According to this student, his classmates considered him as just another Gook or Spic, or Chink. "They took my whole Filipino identity and stomped it into the ground," he said. A would-be fight didn't materialize when a group of girls intervened. That night, the Filipino boy said, he went home wondering who he was.

We're No Different. Once, a Filipino American boy, who had a Filipino upbringing in his family (but didn't know how to speak Tagalog) joined an all-Filipino cast of a play, "Musikal!" This boy said he felt different and that he didn't feel being Filipino because he didn't speak Tagalog. He listened to many conversations and members of the group thought he could not understand them; but he said he could. At those moments, he felt that there was no difference between them. It didn't make any difference whether they spoke Tagalog and he didn't. Then one day, he talked as much "Tag-lish" (combination of Tagalog and English) with the other boys as he could. That day he regained his Filipino identity.

Two Cultures. There was also the story of a Filipino American who tended to be more Americanized without regard to his old upbringing. But later, he said, "In due time, I came to my senses and submitted myself to the right norms of both ways."

Who Says East and West Shall Never Meet? Dalisay Araneta was an-18-year-old senior with a 4.0 grade point average at Kailua High School in Kaneohe, Hawaii. In 1995, she was a runner-up in the "Being Filipino American" Contest sponsored by *Filipinas* magazine. She said, "Whoever said that East and West shall never meet has not met a Filipino American. I am proud of the fact that you can maintain your roots and combine them beautifully with the American lifestyle. I am respectful of my parents but strong in my convictions. I have strong beliefs but am open to the customs, beliefs, and practices of others."

No Longer Wanted to Be a Barbie Doll. Another runner-up in the same contest, Katherine Ann Bacal, a 17-year-old with a 3.5 grade point average at Moreau Catholic High School in Hayward, California, at that time, says, "It was about this time when I realized who I was. I no longer wanted to be the Barbie doll, the blond-haired, blue-eyed American girl, because I gained a sense of self-pride. I cannot deny it. My blood is stained with rich Filipino heritage. My culture speaks all over my body. My eyes tell a tale of my history. and my pride uplifts my soul."

XI. CUSTOMS AND TRADITIONS

Filipino Americans still observe their customs and traditions.

In some communities, fiestas of their own are held. Some civic-spirited individuals also hold barrio fiestas to show Filipino folk dances, paintings by Filipino American artists, and performances by singers. Some associations teach folk dances to the young generation so that they'll know about the native folk dances to preserve the Filipino culture and traditions. They hold their own festivals, such as *Flores de Mayo*, a religious festivity. They celebrate Philippine Independence on June 12 of every year. They also observe the death anniversary of Dr. Jose Rizal, their national hero, on December 30 of each year. In the past, they held programs and they even had their own queens during the Rizal Day celebration. Now, in observation of the event, some social groups hold dramas depicting the life and times of the national hero.

"Where Shall I Sleep?" Once, when a mother told her U.S.-born 16-year-old daughter to vacate her room so that another person could sleep there, she asked, "Where shall I sleep? This is my room." That's not an unusual question by a person who's not familiar with Filipino customs and traditions. "Well, you may sleep with your sister in the basement. This is our *ugaling Pilipino* (Filipino trait), as part of hospitality," the mother answered.

One of the Filipino traits as part of hospitality is giving by the family of its bedrooms (even the master bedroom) and extra beds, including the living room to visitors to sleep in. Not only that. The table is laden with enough food for the visitors.

I knew of a 12-member Filipino American family who toured the whole United States in a month's time — staying in friends' and relatives' houses, instead of hotels. They were our relatives. We let them occupy all the rooms and the living room. Members of my family all slept in the basement. We really enjoyed the occasion.

From the West Coast to the East Coast, or vice versa, touring families or groups of friends may say, "We're coming!" Of course, "We'll be waiting for you!" will be the answer. The satisfaction when they meet after a long absence is mutual. Hosts and visitors enjoy the visiting occasion, particularly for those people with big dwellings with nice decor and furnishings—it's the time to show off their social status in their own community. Then the visitors are given tours and are dined around the city and other areas. They ride in nice cars, including Mercedes and BMWs, for people who have them. Of course, the visitors' turn as hosts will come. What a way to enjoy Filipino life in America!

Regionalism. The concept of regionalism exists among Filipino Americans. It may be defined as regional groupings of different ethnic groups in different regions or islands of the Philippines. Particular groups, such as the Tagalogs in Manila and neighboring provinces, Kapampangans or Pampangueños in Pampanga, Ilocanos in the Ilocos Region, Ilongos in Iloilo, and others, have their own characteristics, beliefs, and ways of life. That's why in the United States, associations are formed based on which provinces in the old country they came from. For instance, there are associations such as Nuevo Ecijanos of Michigan, the Ilocano Association of Michigan, the Pampangueños Club, etc.

Sometimes, more associations are organized in the United States in this way: After an association's election of officers, the candidate who loses for the position of president forms his own association. There are occasions when Filipino Americans try to place these associations under one umbrella association.

Regionalism benefited the Spaniards during their more than 300 years of occupation of the Philippines. The Spaniards employed natives, coming from a central Luzon province, for example, and used them to augment their army to subjugate inhabitants of other provinces or regions who spoke different dialects. In the Philippines, different regions or ethnic groups speak different dialects. For instance, the Tagalogs speak Tagalog, the Ilocanos speak Ilocano, and the Pampangueños speak Kapampangan, etc.

In a nutshell, regionalism may mean pride in one's heritage or brotherhood, but it promotes disunity, not cooperation, in whatever activities and functions engaged in by different ethnic groups.

Regionalism is one negative Filipino attitude. This has proven detrimental as shown by Philippine history. And until today, it is still one of the forces to be reckoned with, especially in the realm of politics. Time and time again regionalism has divided the people, whether they are in the Philippines or in America or elsewhere.

(See Chapter 13: *Philippine Culture, Customs, and Traditions*).

XII. LITERATURE

The Filipinos, in coming to America, brought not only their customs and traditions, but also their culture. Among Asian nations, the Philippines may be considered as the most-influenced country by Western culture.

Pre-Spanish Era. The Philippines, has for many years, preserved a few of the classic examples of the extensive oral literature of the Pre-Spanish era. The literature featured epical stories and chants. There was also the *corrido*, modelled after the Spanish ballad of chivalry, written in different dialects. An example of those epical stories and chants was the *pasyon* (passion), the story of the Redemption chanted during the Holy Week.

The writing of corrido was led by **Francisco Balagtas** (1788-1862), recognized as the first modern Filipino poet. Writing in Tagalog, his best known work was *Florante at Laura*.

Spanish Era. During the Spanish regime, **Dr. Jose Rizal** (1861-1896), the Philippines' greatest hero, wrote the novels *Noli Me Tangere* and *El Filibusterismo*. They became classic novels and were his major contributions to the Philippine Revolution.

Early Filipino Writers. Filipino writers emerged even in the early years of Filipino immigration to America. There are narratives depicting the immigrant's life in the classic books, *I Have Lived with the American People* by **Manuel Buaken**, and *America Is in the Heart: A Personal History*, by **Carlos Bulosan**.

Contemporary Writers. Among the well-known Filipinos in contemporary Philippine literature in English are fiction writer **N.V.M. Gonzalez**; poet **Jose Garcia Villa**; fiction writer **Bienvenido N. Santos**, known for his novel, *"The Man Who Thought He Looked Like Robert Taylor;* and poet **Manuel Viray**.

Among the other well-known novelists and short story writers are **Ninotchka Rosca**, whose second novel, *Twice Blessed*, won the prestigious National Book Award in 1993; **Cecilia Manguerra Brainard**, another award-winning novelist and short story writer; and **Jessica Tarhata Hagedorn**, novelist and artist. Brainard, the recipient of several writing awards, is the author of *When the Rainbow Goddess Wept*, (her first novel in the U.S.), published by E.P. Dutton in the United States. On the other hand, Hagedorn is the recipient of literary awards that include a National Book Award nomination for her novel *Dogeaters* in 1990. (See their profiles in Part IV: *Profiles of Notable Filipino Americans.*)

Among other Filipino American writers with samples of their work are as follows: **Michelle Cruz Skinner** (*Balikbayan: A Filipino Homecoming*), **Marianne Villanueva** (*Ginseng and Other Tales* from Manila), **Alberto S. Florentino** (*Sabrina*), **Paulino Lim, Jr.** (*Michelle and the Jesuit*), **Luis Cabalquinto** (*Phalaenopsis*), **Nadine R. Sarreal** (*Tuition*), **Nutzka C. Villamar**, (*Falling People*), **Manuel R. Olimpo** (*Images*), **Julia L. Palarca**, (*In America, Restaurants Are Crowded*), **Virginia R. Cerenio** (*Dreams of Manong Frankie*) **Samuel Tagatac** (*Small Talk at Union Square*), **Ligaya Victorio Fruto** (*The Fan*) and **Jean Vengua Gier** (*Dancers*).

XIII. COMMUNICATIONS

In the 1920s and 1930s, there were Filipino publications from which immigrants got their news and read stories about their countrymen. Such was the *Philippine Mail*, published in California. Even college students had their own publications.

Today, there are a number of national and local publications, newspapers. and magazines. In some cities, particularly in Los Angeles, California, there are radio and television programs geared toward the Filipino American audience.

The most popular newspapers are the *Philippine News*, a weekly newspaper with headquarters in California, and the *Filipino Reporter*, a New York City-based weekly newspaper.

The most widely circulated magazines are the *Filipinas*, based in San Francisco, California, and *The Special Edition Press: The Filipino American Quarterly*, with offices in New York City.

The publications and their addresses are as follows:

Philippine News
371 Allerton Avenue
South San Francisco, CA 94080
Phone: (415) 872-3000
Fax: (415) 872-0217

Filipino Reporter
Libertito Pelayo
Editor/Publisher
The Empire State Bldg.
350 Fifth Avenue, Suite 6021
New York, NY 10118
Phone: (212) 967-5784

Filipinas
Mona Lisa Yuchengco
Publisher
655 Sutter Street, Suite 333
San Francisco, CA 94102
Phone; (415) 674-0960
Fax: (415) 292-5993

Special Edition Press
The Philippine American Quarterly
104 East 40th Street
New York, NY 10016

Staff members of the *Filipino Reporter,* one of the two largest weekly Filipino American newspapers in the United States, are shown at work at the publication's editorial office in New York City. At the center (second from left) is Libertito "Bert" Pelayo, publisher and editor-in-chief of the newspaper. (Photo was taken before the advent of MacIntosh.)

Phone: (212) 682-6610
Fax: (212) 682-2038

Heritage Magazine
P. O. Box 11403
Carson, CA 90749-1403
Email: vgendrano@earthlink.net

XIV. PRINT AND BROADCAST MEDIA

Several Filipino Americans have made their names in the competitive field of journalism.

Print Media. Two Filipino Americans, **Alex Tizon** and **Byron Acohido**, both reporters of *The Seattle Times*, were presented the much-coveted Pulitzer Prizes at the luncheon awards ceremonies held at Columbia University in New York City on May 29, 1997. Tizon, together with three other recipients, won his prize for investigative reporting and Acohido, for his beat reporting.

Tita Dioso Gillespie, who has the equivalent of a master's degree in French language and civilization, is a general editor of *Newsweek* magazine; Cielo Buenaventura, former features editor in Manila for *We Forum*, an affiliate publication of *Malaya*, is now the *New York Times*' "Metropolitan" section editor; Howard Chua, formerly a reporter and researcher of *Time* magazine, is now the magazine's senior editor; and Hermenegildo "Hermie" A. Azarcon, formerly on the staff of *The Evening News* and *The Manila Times* in Manila, is a copy editor of *The Detroit News*, in Detroit, Michigan.

Libertito "Bert" Pelayo, formerly with the *Manila Times* in Manila, Philippines, is the publisher and editor-in-chief of *The Filipino Reporter*, a New-York based weekly Filipino-American newspaper; Mona Lisa Yuchengco is the publisher of *Filipinas* magazine; Fernando M. Mendez, who has won more than 30 awards in the fields of art and advertising, is the publisher of the *Special Edition Press: The Filipino American Quarterly*; Gene G. Marcial, formerly with the *Manila Chronicle*, and author of the book *Secrets of the Street: The Dark Side of Making Money*, is a columnist, writing *The Wall Street* in the national publication *Business Week*; Alberto M. Alfaro, also formerly with the *Manila Chronicle*, is the editor-in-chief of the Virginia-based *Manila-US Mail* serving Washington, D.C. and neighboring states; and Veltisezar B. Bautista, formerly with the *Manila Chronicle*, is now a successful author and publisher in the United States. (See their brief profiles in Part IV: *Profiles of Noted Filipino Americans* of this book.)

Broadcast Media. The British-accented Filipino American Veronica Pedrosa, currently based in CNNI's headquarters in Atlanta, Georgia, is the anchor of *CNNI World News* and *CNNI World News Asia;* Denise

Dador, born in Warrensburg, Missouri, and raised in San Francisco, California, is a health reporter and news anchor on television station Channel 7 in Southfield, Michigan; and Emme Tomimbang, who worked for 12 years with KITV Channel 4, and NBC affiliate KHON's *Island Style*, is now the host and producer of the monthly television show *Island Moments* that profiles Hawaiian personalities, and offers a glimpse of the local culture and the aloha spirit. (See their profiles in Part IV: *Profiles of Notable Filipino Americans*.)

XV. PAINTING

During the Spanish regime, several Filipinos became well known artists.

Famous Painters. Among the painters were Juan Luna (1857-1899) and Felix Resurrecion Hidalgo (1855-1913). They won recognition as expatriates in Spain with their paintings in romantic and impressionist style.

Those who made their names in paintings during the American regime were Fernando Amorsolo for his landscape paintings and Fabian de la Rosa for his portraitures. These two artists became directors of the School of Fine Arts of the University of the Philippines. Carlos Francisco and Vicente Manansala have been recognized as most outstanding muralists. In musical compositions, the names of Antonio J. Molina, Antonino Buenaventura, and Eliseo Pajaro are to be mentioned.

U.S.-Based Artists. In painting, among the well-known international Filipino American artists in the United States are New York City-based Pacita Abad, an international artist; Genara Banzon, a nature artist; Manuel Rodriguez, Sr., a New-York-based artist who is the father of Philippine graphic arts; Venancio Igarta, the oldest and most celebrated Filipino American master colorist of the visual art scene; **Jose Romero**, a Michigan-based international acrylic-impressionistic artist; and Chicago-based **Bueno Silva**. (See their profiles in Part IV: *Profiles of Notable Filipino Americans.*)

XVI. FOLK DANCE

Filipino folk dances on stage were popularized by the Bayanihan Folk Arts Center of the Philippine Women's University, which has toured the world.

In the United States, dance troupes have been organized, too. They perform in different parts of the country and the world to showcase the culture of the Filipinos.

Folklorico Filipino Dance Company of New York, a non-profit company, is one of the most well-known dance companies in the United States that specialize in Philippine folk dance. Since 1973, Folklorico Filipino with over 50 members, has been showcasing the "Best of the Philippines" in New York parades, cultural festivals, and socio-civic presentations.

Incorporated as a non-profit corporation, Folklorico Filipino has been receiving a yearly grant from the New York State Council on the Arts. It was in 1973 when Folklorico did its debut performance before members of the United Nations General Assembly.

Operating on a voluntary basis, the company's members participate in an annual program that includes eight required shows before community audiences, particularly in the New York City area. Much of the company's funding comes from private donations, corporate solicitations, and performance fees.

The company has performed in such places as Carnegie Hall and Lincoln Center, in New York. It has also held performances during the Statue of Liberty Centennial and Philippine Independence Day celebrations. The

Dancers of the Folklorico Filipino Dance Company of New York perform the *Pandango sa Ilaw* dance. Shown dancing with glasses of lighted candles are (left to right): Arlene Balubayan, Grace Figueroa, and Kristin Mancenido.

FFDC has toured Florida, Israel, Hong Kong and Mainland China. It represented the Philippine government at the World Exposition in Knoxville, Tennessee, and Sevilla, Spain.

Most dance companies present dances, such as the *pandango sa ilaw, binasuan* (wine dance), *pangalay* (long golden nails), *sayaw sa bangko* (bench dance), and *tinikling* (bamboo dance).

XVII. MOVIES AND TV SHOWS

There are Filipino Americans, or Americans of Filipino descent, who have been making news in movies and on television shows. They are **Tia Carrere,** who tangoed with Arnold Schwarzenegger in *True Lies*; **Lou Diamond Phillips**, who became a rising star in *La Bamba*; **Radmar Agana Jao,** who has been cast as a cook on the popular TV show, *The North Shore*; **Sumi Sevilla Haru**, who was cast by producer Ralph Nelson in 1964 in *Soldiers in the Rain*;; **Nia Peoples,** also a singer, who became a television actress in the 1980s and hosted the musical show *Party Machine;* **Rob Schneider** of the popular NBC's popular show *Men Behaving Crazy* and who has been featured in such films as *"Home Alone 2," "Demolition Man,"* and *"The Beverly Hillbillies";* and **Tamlyn Tomita**, who rose to fame in *Karate Kid II.*

(See their profiles in Part IV: *Profiles of Notable Filipino Americans* of this book.)

XVIII. MUSIC

In the music industry, the following names may be mentioned: **Lea Salonga**, a movie actress, Broadway star and singer, who won the prestigious Tony Award; **Jocelyn Enriquez,** the first Filipino American and Asian American who penetrated the mainstream music industry with her pop-dance hits; **Josephine "Banig" Roberto**, another singer who is threatening to conquer the mainstream music industry; **Neal McCoy**, an up and coming country music star; **Prince,** (The Artist), who is reportedly part Filipino; **Tia Carrere**, a movie actress and singer; and **Nia Peeples**, a television actress and singer; **Jaya,** a former San Jose, California, resident and daughter of Philippine comedienne Elizabeth Ramsey who had the first Filipino single to hit the charts in the U.S. with her song *If You Leave Me Now;* and **Glen Madeiros**, a Filipino American from Hawaii, who, like Jaya, had only one hit song. (See their profiles in Part IV: *Profiles of Notable Filipino Americans* of this book.)

XIX. BUSINESS AND FINANCE

In the field of business and finance, the most well-known Filipino Americans are **Loida Nicolas Lewis,** chair and CEO of a $1.8-B business empire, TLC Beatrice International; **Josie Cruz Natori**, international fashion magnate and head of the $40M-a-year business, of the New York-based The House of Natori; and **Lilia Calderon Clemente,** chair and chief executive officer of Clemente Capital, Inc. and dubbed by *Asiaweek Magazine* as the Wonder Woman of Wall Street. (See their profiles in Part IV of this book.)

XX. POLITICS AND GOVERNMENT

Since 1955, many Filipino Americans have been elected or appointed to public offices in the United States.

Peter Aduja became the first Filipino American elected to public office in the United States. He won in his bid for a seat in the Hawaii House of Representatives. After statehood was achieved, he was elected three times, first in 1966, to the Hawaii House of Representatives.

In 1958, **Bernaldo D. Bicoy** was elected to the Hawaii House of Representatives, where he represented West Oahu.

Bicoy was followed in the Hawaii House of Representatives by Pedro dela Cruz, representing the island of Lanai. He served the House for many years.

From 1962 to 1967, **Alfredo Lareta** was the director of the Department of Labor and Industrial Relations. Lareta was appointed by Hawaii Governor John A. Burns. He became the first Filipino American to hold a state cabinet position in the United States.

In April, 1974, **Benjamin Menor,** became the first Filipino to be appointed to the Hawaii Supreme Court. Menor served with the First Filipino Infantry Regiment during World War II.

Thelma Buchholdt was elected to the Alaska State House of Representatives in the 1974 elections.

In 1975, **Joshua C. Agsalud** was appointed by Hawaii Governor George Ariyoshi in 1975 as director of the Department of Labor and Industrial Relations.

Also in 1975, **Eduardo E. Malapit** of Kauai, Hawaii, became the first elected mayor in the United States. Prior to his being elected mayor, Malapit served as member of the Kauai County Council for several years.

In California, in the 1970s, **Maria Lacadia Obrea** served as a Los Angeles municipal judge.

Glenn Olea became a councilman in the Monterey Bay community of Seaside, California.

In 1983, **Ronald E. Quidachay**, half-Filipino, half-Irish, was appointed as law and motion judge in Municipal Court, Civil Division, in San Francisco, California. Later, he was elected and reelected to the same position.

In 1985, **Irene Natividad,** a political activist who champions women's rights, was elected as president of the influential National Women's Political Caucus (NWPC). Thus, this former waitress became the first Asian American to be elected to the position. She was reelected in 1987.

In Washington State, **Gene Canque Liddell** became the first Filipina American to become mayor of a U.S. city on April 11, 1991. She was elected mayor by members of the city council of Lacey City, a suburb of Seattle, Washington. Earlier, she was elected as a council member in 1988. Liddell served as deputy mayor in 1990.

Eduardo "Eddie" G. Manuel was appointed as a council member in Hercules City, California, in November 1991. He was elected as a council member to the seat he had held the past year. Later, he served from November 23, 1993 to December 4, 1994, as mayor after he was elected to the position by his fellow council members.

Running against 10 Goliaths, a David, **David Mercado Valderrama** became the first Filipino elected to a state legislature on the United States mainland in Maryland's November 1990 General Assembly elections. In November 1994, he was reelected to the same position, representing Prince George's County.

In Washington State, **Velma Veloria** was elected to the Washington State House of Representatives in the 1992 elections. Thus, she became the first Filipino to be elected as a state representative in Washington State and the second Filipina to be a member of a state legislature in the United States. (The other was **Thelma Buckholdt** who was elected to the Alaska State Legislature.) Veloria ran unopposed and won in the November 1994 and November 1996 elections.

Benjamin "Ben" Cayetano, holds the distinction of being the first and only person of Filipino descent to become a governor of a state. He was elected governor of Hawaii in the November 1994 elections.

Judge Mel Red Recana was elected as the presiding judge of the Los Angeles (California) Municipal Court for 1996. Prior to his election, Judge Recana had been an assistant presiding judge since 1994. It was in 1994 when he was appointed as a municipal judge of Los Angeles, California.

Robert Bunda is currently a state senator in Hawaii. He was elected to the State Senate in the 1994 elections. He did not resign from the Senate to run in the second congressional district race in the November 1996 elections. He lost in the last elections but he still is in office to finish his term won in the 1994 elections.

In the November 1996 elections, **Romy Cachola**, a member of the Hawaii State House of Representatives, ran unopposed and was reelected for the seventh time to the State House.

Nestor R. Garcia serves as a member of the majority leadership team in the Hawaii State House, as majority whip for the Democrats. Garcia was first elected to the State House in 1994 and won again for the same seat in the November 1996 elections.

In the November 1996 elections, **Ron Menor** was reelected to the Hawaii State House of Representatives. Menor first served in the House in 1982. He was elected to the State Senate in 1986. He was elected to the House in 1992.

Also in the Hawaii State Legislature, **Reynaldo Graulty** won a seat in the State Senate in 1992. He first entered public service in 1982 when he was elected to the State House of Representatives.

Henry Manayan, a council member, became the mayor of Milpitas, California, after he clinched the top position of that Silicon Valley's city government during the November 1996 elections. Manayan was elected to the Milpitas City Council during the November 1994 elections.

Maria Luisa Mabilangan Haley, a member of the board of the Export Import Bank, is the highest Filipino American official in the Clinton administration. She is considered by Filipino Americans as the "key" to the White House.

In March 1997, **Pete Fajardo** became the first Filipino American to be elected mayor of a progressive city in the United States through a direct vote of the people when he won the mayoralty race in Carson, California. He was a member of the city council of Carson prior to his election as mayor of the city.

(For their profiles, see part IV: *Profiles of Notable Filipino Americans* in this book.)

XXI. SPORTS

In the field of sports, the great Filipino athletes that made their name in the United States were **Pancho Villa**, a flyweight champion of the world; **Ceferino Garcia**, the bolo punch boxer who tried two times to wrest the welterweight title of the world, losing to a controversial fight with Barney Ross in 1937 and Henry Armstrong in 1936; **Roman Gabriel**, the well-known quarterback of the Los Angeles Rams; **Tai Babilonia**, the other half of the famed Babilonia-Radner skating team; **Elizabeth Punsalan,** a fifth-time and current U.S. ice dance champion and a 1994 and 1998 Olympic competitor with her partner and husband, Jerod Swallow; **Vicky Manalo Drakes**, who won two gold medals in swimming in the 1948 Olympics in London; **Salvador (Dado) Marino**, who lost a bantamweight championship of the world fight to Manuel Ortiz in 1949,but wrestled the flyweight world crown from Terry Allen in 1950; **Speedy Dado**, the Pacific Coast bantamweight champion who attempted to be world flyweight and bantamweight champion of the world; **Bernard (Big Duke) Docusen** from New Orleans, Louisiana, who challenged but lost to Sugar Ray Robinson for the welterweight championship of the world in Chicago in 1948; and **Jim Washington**, a six-foot-seven forward, who was drafted in 1965 by the St. Louis Hawks of the National Basketball Association.

(Profiles of some of these outstanding athletes may be read in Part IV of this book.

XXII. MEDICINE

Several Filipino Americans have made names for themselves in the field of medicine and dentistry. Among them are **Jose L. Evangelista, M.D.**, appointed by President Bill Clinton as a member of the National Committee on Foreign Medical Education and Accreditation; **Stella Evangelista, M.D.**, Michigan Hall of Famer and former member of the Michigan State Board of Medicine; **Ernesto M. Espaldon, M.D.**, plastic surgeon and six-term Guam senator; and **Rolando A. De Castro, D.D.M.**, famous dental professor-artist, dubbed as the "Frank H. Netter" of the dental profession.

XXIII. FILIPINO AMERICAN GENERALS IN THE U.S. ARMY

There are only three Asian American generals in the Armed Forces of the United States, and two of them are Filipino American generals in the U.S. Army. They are **Major General Edward Soriano**, currently assigned as the director of operations, readiness, and mobilization in the Office of the Deputy Chief of Staff for Operations and Plans of the U.S. Army in the Pentagon; and **Brigadier General Antonio Taguba**, assigned as a special assistant to the commanding general at Fort McPherson in Atlanta, Georgia. (See their profiles in Part IV: *Profiles of Notable Filipino Americans.*)

XXIV. FILIPINO FOODS

Filipino foods, such as *pansit* (rice noodle) and egg roll *(lumpia)*, are the favorites of non-Filipinos at parties and in Filipino restaurants. These non-Filipinos usually are wives, husbands, or friends of Filipinos. Of course, friends of Filipinos, especially at work, have been exposed to Filipino food. In fact, some of these Americans get recipes and try to cook Filipino foods.

FILIPINO CULTURE, CUSTOMS, AND TRADITIONS

13

The Filipino culture, in general, is a combined system of acquired ways and manners, including personal behavior in social interaction. It also includes the total elements of the Filipino way of life: their customs, traditions, beliefs, values, arts, language, rituals, attitudes, and the total characteristics of the members of Filipino society.

Much of the present Filipino culture is an assimilation of cultural influences from past colonizers. After more than 300 years of Spanish domination, Catholicism, although Filipinized (meaning pre-Hispanic religious beliefs and superstitions were mixed with the foreign religion), emerged and became an integral part of the culture.

I. HARMONY IN RELATIONSHIPS

The Filipinos' skills in personal relationships are explained in many ways:

***Pakikisama* (Companionship or Getting Along with an Individual or Group).** *Pakikisama* involves the efforts to get along with other people. It emphasizes that to belong to a group, you must extend your whole efforts to please other members of the group, particularly among friends. One may comment, *"Marunong siyang makisama"* ("He knows how to get along with us.")

Pakikisama plays an important aspect in the Filipino community. For example, when a person becomes successful in his profession or other endeavor, he usually is very careful in dealing with his friends who are not successful or less successful. Or else, his friends may say *"Iba na siya ngayon."* ("He is different now.")

***Bayanihan* (Cooperation or Cooperative Effort).** The Filipinos have a positive value or attitude known as bayanihan, or cooperative spirit. Bayanihan is a concept by which Filipinos and Filipino Americans help each other for the attainment of a certain task.

For instance, in the Philippines, bayani-han may be shown when a group of people transfer a *nipa* and bamboo house to another place. The barrio men, for instance, put strong bamboo poles under the flooring of a house and rest the bamboo poles on their shoulders. Then step by step, the men walk at the same time. They sometimes stop after a few minutes of carrying the house to take a rest, and then continue to carry the house to its destination. This bayanihan spirit shows the willingness of the Filipino to offer a shoulder or a hand in easing the load or burden of a fellow Filipino in any circumstances.

In the United States, Filipino Americans practice bayanihan in simple ways. For instance, when a family moves to another town or city, some friends and relatives help. They help load and unload household appliances, beddings, etc. for a new home. Now, when anyone who took part in that move moves himself, the person who was helped before is expected to return the favor of helping in the new family's moving. And bayani-han goes on and on.

***Pakikiramay* (Offer Of Sympathy).** *Pak-ikiramay* means offering sympathy to other people. This may be best exemplified by the so-called *damayan*. Damayan is the sympathy for bereavement.

The Filipino "I'll See!" When a Filipino tells you, "I'll see," after you invited him to go to a party in your house or in a restaurant, he may be indicating that he's not going. He just doesn't want to disappoint and hurt your feelings if he refuses you. But of course, if you insist, saying "Please come," he may able to say, "Yes, I'll definitely come." But if he says again that he'll try, that may mean that he's not really coming.

Friendship. As a friend, the Filipino is expected to be trusted. On the other hand, he is also expected to trust a friend. When someone violates that trust, the friends usually part ways and may choose not to be friends any longer. When friends become enemies, they may be enemies for life, if no one intervenes in patching up their misunderstanding.

The Use of a Go-Between. Generally, the Filipino is sensitive. He may recognize when one is angry or not. For example, when

Rolando greets Pedro, and the latter doesn't answer, it may mean that he was angry, for unknown reasons at Rolando. In most instances, Rolando won't confront Pedro. He may ask another friend why Pedro seems to be mad at him. So a friend of either of the two may serve as a "go-between" to determine what the problem is. In that way, there's no direct confrontation.

A go-between is also used in many instances. For example, when one wants an agreement or a request or proposal to be made with a friend or someone on a transaction, he may use a go-between. Fred may want to borrow money from a friend but he won't directly talk with his friend to make the request. Fred may ask another friend to do the talking. In that way, when the friend indicates his willingness to lend money, the go-between then tells Fred about it. Then Fred can talk to him because he already knows that he won't be rejected. This is done, of course, to avoid any embarrassment on his part when his request is not granted.

This practice is extended to other matters, including in courting a girl. I remember that a friend of mine used this procedure not only once but several times. One time he, asked his friend, Lino, to tell one of their women friends that he was in love with her and wanted to court her, but he was too shy to do so. Then Lino told him what the girl told him. "Why is he shy to approach me?" the girl asked. With that question, my friend knew then that he would not be rejected in case he decided to court her. In that way, he would have avoided the rejection and embarrassment if she had to reject his offer of love to her. That's the Filipino way of using a go-between.

II. POSITIVE CULTURAL VALUES

As has been stated, Filipino culture includes values. The Filipinos have positive and negative values.

The Filipino positive values include love of family, respect for elders and strangers, respect for the feelings of other people, willingness to sacrifice for the sake of family, unwillingness to complain too much, good humor, and other positive values.

Respect for Elders. Filipinos hold their elders in high respect. Elders, for their part, demand obedience and impose their authority: parents over their children, older siblings over the younger ones, etc. In addition, they are polite and courteous. The words of *po* (sir or ma'am) or *ho* and *opo* (yes, sir or ma'am) are words of respect used even with strangers. This is still practiced in the United States by Filipinos born and raised in the Philippines.

Philippine-born Filipino Americans usually address their parents *po* or *ho,* as it is done in their native country. They also respect elder Filipinos who are not their relatives, addressing them with po's or ho's. When speaking to their parents, they address them in the second person saying *kayo* (plural) not *ikaw* (singular) for you.

However, Filipino Americans, especially those American-born, usually no longer say *po* or *ho* (sir, ma'am) to their parents. But they call their grandparents *lolo* for grandfather and *lola* for grandmother. But, of course, sometimes grandchildren call them grandpa or grandma.

In the majority of U.S. homes, Filipino Americans still practice their respect for elders among the siblings. (See Chapter 12, *subhead: Raising Their Kids.)*

Utang Na Loob (Reciprocity or Sense of Gratitude). The Filipino is very loyal and sentimental. Moreover, he has a strong sense of gratitude or *utang na loob,* or more accurately, a feeling of indebtedness for favors or service, which he feels has to be reciprocated. Sometimes, he even feels beholden to someone for life even for a little thing given or done.

Filipino Hospitality. As a people, Filipinos and Filipino Americans have their own character traits. One of these better-known traits is their sociability and hospitality. They go out of their way to make one feel at home, comfortable, and honored,

The Filipinos brought this tradition to America. They hold parties in their homes and invite Filipinos and non-Filipinos to partake of foods they prepare for an occasion or celebration.

Hiya **(Shame).** *Hiya* is a Filipino trait with emphasis on fear of losing face. Like *amor propio* (self-esteem), hiya can be both positive and negative. If a person does bad things against society, he and his family will be *mapapahiya* (shamed). A parent may tell his son, *"Kahiyahiya kung gagawin mo iyan."* ("It's shameful if you do that.") That is a positive aspect of hiya.

But hiya has also a negative aspect. If a Filipino employee is scolded by a supervisor in front of other people, he'll be *mapapahiya* (shamed). Two things may happen. Without expressing his anger, he may hate the supervisor in silence and sabotage productivity. Or if the person can't stand the situation, he may just quit the job abruptly to avoid any heated verbal confrontation or violence. But there are instances, that a Filipino will engage his supervisor in a heated argument that may lead to violence. If the supervisor knows the Filipino characteristic as pertaining to hiya, the supervisor naturally will get the Filipino's cooperation towards increasing productivity.

In the 1920s and 1930s, a survey showed that Filipinos were easily humiliated when criticized in front of others. When the management and supervisors knew of the situation, they tried to rectify it. The Filipinos' productivity subsequently increased and good relationships between management and labor existed.

That's the negativity of hiya.

Amor Propio. Amor propio means self-esteem or self-love, Like hiya, amor propio may be considered as both positive and negative values and may be used for such ends. The Filipino values his self-image or prestige very much. He always fears losing social acceptance. In other words, he expects to be respected. Amor proprio is to be maintained or protected because loss of self-esteem causes shame. The Filipino, by nature, desires the acceptance of his group or segment of society.

Hiya and amor propio are two traits that act as social sanctions and are crucial in social acceptability or rejection.

Karangalan **(Honor).** A Filipino values honor very highly. He protects his family's name and reputation at all cost. For this reason, he always tries to avoid doing bad things that may destroy his or his family's honor and prestige. The negative part of this value, is that in the defense of a Filipino's honor, it may lead to violent incidents, including killings.

Many years ago, if a man touched a woman too much, the parents naturally demanded that he marry her. There were cases that when a man, after being rejected by a woman, would embrace her in front of other people so that she would be shamed. She then would be forced by her parents to marry the man. This author, when he was little, witnessed such an event involving a man who embraced a woman while she was washing clothes by the riverside. In other words, the incident culminated in a marriage because the embrace tarnished the woman's honor.

Patience and Perseverance, Etc. Generally, the Filipino has patience, perseverance, hardiness, and foresight, whether at work or in business. These traits were given to the Filipinos by the Chinese who influenced their way of life. At work or in business, Filipino is a hardworker, and is not a loud complainer. He usually does his work even if a supervisor is not around.

The Filipinos in general can handle hardships and sacrifices, and they are courageous in the fight for survival. That's the reason, since the beginning of the Filipino immigration to America, Filipino Americans have survived in the bayous of Louisiana and in crowded conditions on farms. That was in spite of discrimination and prejudice in the midst of a cruel American society.

Palabra de Honor (**Word of Honor**). Adopted from the Spanish words, these words simply mean word of honor. That is, if someone promises something, he is to keep that promise whether there is a written agreement or not.

III. NEGATIVE CULTURAL VALUES

The Filipinos have also negative cultural values that may be applied to both Filipinos in the Philippines and in the United States.

Fatalism. The Filipino is religious and, perhaps, this accounts for his being fatalistic. He accepts misfortunes more easily than those who are not religious. The Filipino phrase *bahala na*, which literally means "come what may," leaving everything to fate, best describes this nature.

Generally, the Filipinos who immigrated to America are not fatalistic, in the strict sense of the word; they came here to upgrade their economic situation. They wanted their children to have a better education and a better future than they had. In other words, they are here to pursue their goals and dreams—for them and their children. That is, they believe that they can make their own destiny.

Many Filipinos in the Philippines, due to their belief that everything depends on fate, succumb to the lure of gambling. The most popular forms of gambling in the Philippines are cockfighting, horse-racing, mahjong, jueteng and card games, and recently the lottery and bingo.

In the Philippines, many Filipinos are fond of gambling. The cockpit is a fixture of every town, where, particularly on Sundays, excited people bet on gamecocks. Playing bingo or card games is also a favorite pastime, even among children, who learn these games at an early age. Other favorite games of chance including mahjong, *sakla*, and *pusoy dos* (a form of poker). A card lotto, a form of lottery, has also gained popular acceptance in the country.

In the United States, Filipino Americans also engage in mahjong, or bingo, and the lottery. The Filipinos do their gambling during parties in homes of friends or relatives. Or some of them just go to Las Vegas, Nevada; Atlantic City, New Jersey; or Windsor, Canada. In the 1920s and 1930s, Filipinos in the U.S. used to see cockfighting games. However, there are no more cockfighting games for Filipino Americans. Some just go to see races and bet horses.

***Ningas-Cogon* Mentality.** An undesirable Filipino character is called the *ningas-cogon* mentality. Literally meaning "grass fire," it is defined as a short-lived drive, which leaves work that started off enthusiastically but not completed at all—just like grass fire that burns brightly at the start but dies out after a short while.

Mañana Habit. *Mañana* habit is a trait attributed to the Filipino. It is his habit of postponing what a person has to do and then cramming to finish it when he or she is pressured by time. This is reflected in everyday life—in school, in the office, or somewhere else.

Gaya-Gaya (Copycat). The tendency to imitate what someone else is doing is typical among Filipinos. Although this may sometimes be considered a positive value, *gaya-gaya* leads to cut-throat competition. For instance, when one sees that there is a thriving Filipino American store in a certain locality, one or two more stores are established. Thus, later, at least one or two of the three will not survive.

Even during the Spanish period, certain Filipinos attempted to imitate the Spanish lifestyle. However, they failed to meet the standard lifestyle because they could not afford it. Thus, it led to Filipinos having an inferiority complex.

In short, gaya-gaya signifies the lack of an adventuresome spirit, to go on one's own initiative, into a new territory. This especially happens in business. When one sees another person successful in a business, he also engages in it. This Filipino practice is prevalent in the Philippines, as well as in the United States.

The Crab Mentality. The bad attitude among Filipinos stems from what we call the crab mentality. This attitude results from being envious of those who become well-known in their field of endeavor or those who get promoted to high positions in the government. Such actions may be compared to crabs fighting for survival. For instance, when live crabs are in a container, they cling to each other—each trying to get to the top. For example, when Jocelyn Enriquez had two songs on the charts (being the only Filipino American and Asian American to make it in the mainstream music industry), as reported in *A. Magazine,* she was the subject of rumors: that she doesn't claim her Filipino heritage and that she is a snob. She just took it all in stride. And her response was, "I think people are entitled to their own opinion and it's up to them to judge me...to take the time to actually get to know me. It really doesn't bother me because I think it makes me a stronger person."

Such things happen to Filipinos and Filipino Americans in business, political, and social circles,

Pasikatan (Keeping Up with the Joneses). This practice involves the Filipino way of life. For example, when a family moves to an affluent neighborhood, some other fellow Filipino families may follow it. If one buys a Mercedes, one may buy a BMW, or other high-cost car. This is one way of competition—to be in the higher echelon of society. This attitude sometimes results in financial difficulties for some families if they can't afford what they're trying to achieve.

Extravagance. Generally, the Filipino has a tendency to be extravagant. Some do not mind spending lavishly for such social occasions as weddings, fiestas, and baptisms, even if they have to fall into debt. In the old country and in the United States, many Filipinos, especially those in the upper echelon of society, have their own Mercedes, BMWs and other high-cost cars. If they are rich, they also live in palatial houses, particularly in the suburbs of Manila and other major cities in the Philippines. The Filipinos during the 1920s and 1930s were accused by Americans as lavish spenders—they were well-dressed and groomed and spent lots of money on women.

The Filipino, by nature, is very particular on how he dresses. Even in the barrio, he always tries to have nice fitting clothes, even if they are highly priced or not.

IV. FILIPINO TRAITS AND MENTALITY

The Filipino is distinct from other races in the world.

The Filipino Identity. The Philippine population is a mixture of many races. The Filipino has a mixture of the features of Malays, Indonesians, Chinese, Arabs, Spanish, and Americans.

In business communities, particularly in Manila and the suburbs, many of the rich and

> # The Filipino has the quality of "bending with fate," as the bamboo has the quality of bending with the wind.

the famous are usually of Spanish and Chinese heritage. Such mixtures in the Filipino population are the result of other peoples who arrived in the Philippines, either to trade with or subjugate the Filipinos.

The first group of Indians to arrive in the Philippines came from the Punjabi and Sindhi communities in northwest India. They came to the Philippines to engage in small businesses. Some went from town to town hawking their wares, such as umbrellas.

The Chinese have had great influence on Filipino culture. In fact, some Filipino values, which were planted in the Philippines by the Chinese, were loyalty to family, hiya (sense of shame) and utang-na-loob (sense of gratitude or reciprocity).

Because of the influences of other races on Filipino ways of life, there is a uniqueness in Philippine language, values, culture, customs, arts, music, and dances. Filipino dialects, particularly Tagalog or Pilipino, include Malay, Indonesian, Spanish, Chinese, and English words. In Tagalog, words of Spanish origin include *silya* (chair), *mesa* (table), and *bintana* (window). The words *diko, sangko, ditse, sanse,* are of Chinese origins. Many Filipino dances are of Malay, Indonesian, Arab, and Spanish origin. Everywhere you can see foreign-culture influences.

In physical appearance, the majority of Filipinos look like Malays, Indonesians, Thais, or Chinese as a result of people of different races intermarrying.

The Filipino woman is known for her beauty. There have been several Filipinas who have been international beauty queens such as Gloria Diaz, "Miss Universe"; Gemma Cruz, "Miss International"; Margie Moran, "Miss Universe"; and Aurora Pijuan, "Miss International." In the case of Filipino men, they are known as lovers of beauty. Debonair Virgilio Hilario married Armi Kuusela of Finland, the first "Miss Universe." A scion of the rich Araneta family married Stella Suarez, a "Miss Universe" from Columbia.

The People. In the slums of Manila and in the suburbs, you may find some of the poorest Filipinos and some of the richest people on Earth. In Makati, Metro Manila, and other exclusive subdivisions in the suburbs of Manila, and other cities outside of the Philippine capital, you can find palatial houses that you may not find even in exclusive communities of the rich in many parts of America.

If you go to megamalls in the Philippines, especially in the suburbs of Manila, Cebu, and other modern cities, you naturally cannot not say that the Philippines is a third world country and that majority of the people are suffering. When you're inside a megamall, you wouldn't think that you're not in America. You'll only realize that "that" is not America, because all you see are Filipinos. Of course, there are a handful of Americans and other foreigners.

The Filipino Characteristics. The Filipino who is able to survive under any circumstances likens himself to the bamboo. The bamboo, the tallest of the grass family, symbolizes durability, flexibility, and harmony with nature. In a storm, the bamboo doesn't just stand still to prepare for the impact of the strong wind. Instead, it bends temporarily and sways with the wind, preventing it from being permanently bent and broken by the force of nature. That's why the migrant Filipinos, while working on farms and in the canneries of Alaska, were able to survive the harsh working and living conditions coupled with discrimination and prejudice. Even during the Depression, those Filipinos were able to eke out a living. Why? Because the Filipino has the quality of "bending with fate," as the bamboo has the quality of bending with the wind.

Mild Manner and Courteous. Generally, the Filipino is mild-manner and courteous. He is not usually assertive as compared to Westerners. But of course, there are many exceptions.

Hospitable. The Filipino is usually hospitable. Moreover, his culture allows him to have a lot of compassion for other people. As a newly acquaintance, once told me, "Filipino Americans have wonderfully warm and caring hearts."

Sensitiveness. By nature, the Filipino is usually very sensitive to slights and criticisms. As has been said, he values his honor too much so when you question his integrity, he is likely to get hurt. If you criticize him, more so in public, you may expect that such criticism may lead to heated arguments that may result in violence. So the giving of any negative comments to him should be handled in a very nice way. That's why even in the United States, the immigrant in his first employment may quit his job because he can't swallow his pride when his supervisor scolds him or criticizes him for any little mistakes he may make.

Usually, the Filipino considers Americans as "too direct." That is, they say what they feel—some things that may hurt the feelings of an individual, although it is not intended. To an American, sometimes there is only one answer to a question: yes or no. But a Filipino, especially if he is not yet adjusted to American way of life, finds it hard to give a direct "no" to a request. He may say, "I'll see," or "I'll think about it." However, afterwards, he learns to say, "No, I can't go" or "I don't want it.'"

Can Be a Good Friend and a Bad Enemy. By nature, the Filipino is honest and kind. Yet, when you wrong him, he'll never trust you again. He can be a good friend, yet he can be a bad enemy. He doesn't easily forget what you have done bad to him and he can be your enemy for life. That is, even if he meets you anywhere, he won't greet you.

Good Manners and Right Conduct. As soon as children are old enough to understand good manners and right conduct, parents instill in their minds the importance of being modest, gentle, polite, friendly, hospitable, loyal, kind, and other traits.

However, there are times that some Filipino parents in the Philippines exert too much discipline on their children. For example, when they have adult guests in the houses,

children are not involved in any conversation with them. More often, the children may go to their room or elsewhere. As a result, children grow up being shy in front of other people.

But Filipino Americans born in the Philippines try to forget about the negative part of discipline. In the United States, they tell their children to be assertive and not to be meek. This is because this is America. According to many of them, when you are too modest and unassertive, especially if you belong to a minority group, your rights may be trampled upon by the majority.

Keeping Silent. The typical Filipino, with exceptions, usually play it safe. They just say, *huwag na lang kumibo,* meaning just keep quiet. This doesn't mean that he doesn't know the answer or the subject matter. Filipino immigrants, however, have made changes in their attitude in dealing with white and black Americans and other ethnic groups. They try to be assertive, and some of them have really adjusted well to how they should act when dealing with people in the American society. Generally, however, many of them just do their own thing among fellow Filipinos.

The Filipino Mind. Although there are many exceptions, generally it's usually hard to know what a Filipino is thinking. It doesn't mean when he is silent, he agrees with you or whether he hates you. If he says "yes," it doesn't mean he agrees with what you say. It's because sometimes, he just doesn't want to argue with you. Of course, there are many exceptions.

V. CUSTOMS AND TRADITIONS

The ancient Filipinos normally married within their own class, although this practice was not rigid. Intermarriage among different social classes was not impossible, either.

Marriage. Many years ago, parents arranged the marriage of their sons and daughters as early as their infancy. Before the marriage, a dowry had to be given by the groom to his bethrothed's family. The dowry could be in the form of gold, land, money, slaves, or anything else valuable. He also had to serve the girl's parents for free. This service could be chopping wood, fetching water or whatever else the parents required. The length of service and worth of the dowry were agreed upon by the parents of the bride and groom. This stage of the courtship, when final marriage arrangements were agreed upon, was called *pamamalae* or *pamumulungan*.

On the day of wedding, a go-between, carrying a spear from the groom, would fetch the bride. He would thrust the spear into the ladder and pray for blessing for the coming marriage. He was then let in, then the bride and her parents followed him to the groom's home, where the wedding ceremony was to be held. There, the bride would pretend to be shy and refuse to go up the ladder until "persuaded" by being presented with a gift from the groom's father. Inside the house, she would also refuse to sit, smile, eat, or drink until more gifts were given to her.

After all this, she and the groom would drink from one cup. An old man then would announce that the marriage ceremony was to begin. A priestess would come forward, join the hands of the bride and the groom over a bowl of uncooked rice, then pronounce them man and wife. With an exclamation, the priestess then would toss the rice to the guests, who would respond by giving a similar shout. The wedding ceremony would be over.

Marriage was supposed to be forever, but sometimes divorce was granted. Some causes of divorce were adultery on the wife's part, desertion by the husband, cruelty, childlessness, and insanity. A divorced man or woman was allowed to remarry. In such cases, the man had to give a new dowry for his wife-to-be as if it were a new marriage.

At present, due to the westernization of the Philippines, the practice of customs and traditions is a lot different, especially in the urban areas. However, in the provinces, some of the old customs are still followed. The *harana* or serenade used to play a big part in the courtship of a woman. A man would either serenade the apple of his eye by himself or, if he did not have a good singing voice, would seek the help of one or a number of friends. It was also understood that he had to woo her parents, too. This he did by doing what they

required, such as the men's chores in her home.

After he won the heart of the girl and the nod of her parents, and the time to ask for her hand in marriage had come, he and his parents would go to the house of the girl bringing gifts and foodstuffs. This is called *pamanhikan*. However, pamamanhikan is no longer practiced today among Christian Filipinos in the Philippines. Other ethnic groups, especially the cultural minorities, have different courtship and marriage practices.

Like the major ethnic groups in the Philippines, the Filipino Americans court their would-be partners and hold wedding ceremonies as any other modern Christian people do.

Burial and Mourning Customs. In the olden times, the Filipinos made a great fuss over how their dead were buried because they believed in life after death and in lasting relationships between the living and the dead. The body was embalmed with herbs and native scents, then placed in a burial jar or wooden coffin. Amidst much wailing and crying, the corpse was buried either under the house, in a cave, or on a cliff overlooking the sea.

For his journey in the afterlife, clothes, food, weapons, and gold were buried with him. This practice is carried over even in present times, with superstitious undertones among some minor ethnic groups of the Philippines. In the provinces, old folks take turns in sitting by the coffin, wailing and reciting the good deeds of the deceased. For some, it is considered taboo to leave the dead person unattended by such mourners. The closeness of family ties is also illustrated in the event of a death in the family.

In this day and age, when many Filipinos have gone abroad to seek greener pastures, even the Filipinos who have been living outside of the country for a long time do not hesitate to try to come home when a close relative passes away. Thus, there are many instances when the burial is postponed while awaiting the return of a relative from abroad. During the wake, different forms of gambling are played to while away the time.

In ancient times during the period of mourning, the family and immediate relatives of the dead wore white and rattan bands around their necks, arms, and legs. To show their deep sorrow, they refrained from eating meat or drinking wine. Today Filipinos in the Philippines bury their dead in municipal cemeteries and memorial parks.

There is also the practice of *damayan. It is* the sympathy for bereavement. According to this Filipino practice, when a person dies in the rural and urban areas in the Philippines, majority of the people in that particular locality—be they be relatives, friends, and neighbors—sympathize with the bereaved family. They usually give *abuloy* or any amount of money to the bereaved family.

In the United States, this practice is also done. When any family member dies, Filipinos in the community usually give their share of abuloy. The abuloy maybe bigger if the dead will be brought home to the Philippines for burial.

Some Filipinos send the dead body to their native town in the Philippines for viewing by the deceased person's relatives and townmates. Some families cremate the bodies for their easy transport to the Philippines.

Religious Beliefs. The Filipinos in the olden days believed in one supreme god called *Bathala*, to whom they attributed the creation of the heaven, the Earth, the entire universe, and the human race. However, they had lesser gods and goddesses, such as for agriculture, death, the rainbow, harvest, war, beauty, thunder and birth, as well as lower spirits they called *anito* or *diwata*.

Food, drink, fruit, animals, and sometimes human beings were sacrificed to please or appease the gods and goddesses. Most of the early Filipinos also believed that there is life after death and the soul, which they knew to be immortal, traveled to the next world to receive their punishment or reward, according to what they did while on Earth. Already with a concept of heaven and hell, they believed that the souls of the brave and good men went to heaven and the evil men to hell.

Present-day Filipinos are members of the Catholic Church and other Christian denominations, such as the United Methodist Church, *Aglipay,* and *Iglesia ni Cristo,* and other religious sects. About 80 percent of the Filipino population are Catholics.

In the United States, Filipino Americans, especially the Catholics are active in their respective parishes. Even during the 1920s and 1930s, priests held masses in their communities, including those on Hawaii plantations. Ministers of other religious denominations also held services there.

Hi Kumpadre! In the Philippines, the *kumpadre system* (adapted from the Spanish word *compadre)* or *padrino* system, is practiced among friends or relatives. However, this kumpadre or padrino system is also used by many people for access to power, influence, or economic gains. For example, a parent would get a high-ranking official as a kumpadre (the godfather of his son or daughter in baptism or in marriage) so that he could ask his help in the future, such as obtaining government jobs for his children. "I'll ask my kumpadre's help in fixing this court case," a man may say. A former colleague of mine, a fellow journalist, had the late President Ferdinand Marcos of the Philippines as the godfather or sponsor of one of his sons in baptism for easy access to power or influence. Friends, however, usually practice this system for closer relationship and brotherhood. This system is also practiced by Filipino Americans.

To further explain it, on baptismal occasions, the parents of the child and the sponsors establish a kinship. The male is called *kumpadre, kumpare,* or *pare,* and the woman is called *kumadre, kumare,* or *mare.* At a wedding occasion, the bride and groom have their sponsors, too. And their parents and their sponsors also establish that kind of relationship. This system had been practiced for the past many years and still is practiced today. But sometimes, though, a man calls his friend *pare,* as if they were brothers.

What Time Is It? In general, Filipino time means it's always late. Or you can be at your appointment at a time later than previously scheduled. Same as in the case of parties. When a party is said to begin at 6 p.m., that means it may begin at 8 because most of those invited have not yet arrived. So when the time for an occasion is to start at 6 p.m, and you realize's that it's already 7 p.m., don't be alarmed; you won't be late because majority of those invited may arrive at 8 p.m. or past 8 p.m. In other words, the time has no fixed starting time and a fixed ending time.

Fiestas, Fiestas, Fiestas. Fiestas in the Philippines are a mixture of Christian commemoration and folk elements that are celebrated with great pomp and pageantry.

Fiestas are held to pay homage to the town or barrio's patron saint, to celebrate a bountiful crop harvest, or to reenact a historical religious event.

Common Fiestas. The common fiestas in many parts of the country are held in barrios and towns in the Philippines any time of the year, but mostly, they are celebrated in the month of May. People from all walks of life take a rest from their endeavors to have a day or two of lots of eating and merrymaking.

The whole year prior to the fiesta day, people usually raise hogs and chickens to prepare for this occasion. During a fiesta, even in a barrio, you must eat lightly each time to be able to eat in many houses as possible because after eating in a certain house, you also eat from house to house. You're invited everywhere!

A fiesta is celebrated with religious fervor. The statue of the patron saint of the Catholic Church is usually on procession with members of the church. On this occasion, several bands parade the streets of the barrio or town to provide music. At night, at least two bands compete in a concert held in the barrio or on the town plaza. Performances of movie stars from Manila and other places are also held at night.

Special Fiestas or Festivals. However, there are special fiestas. Two of the most famous of these fiestas, which are considered as festivals, are the *Santa Cruz de Mayo*, held in the evening, during which a candlelight procession is held, and *Flores de Mayo*, which is a ritual of daily offering of flowers carried by little girls. The Santa Cruz de Mayo is held in commemoration of Saint Helena's finding of the Cross on which Jesus Christ was crucified. During these festivals, you don't have to visit houses; it's just a religious celebration—eating not included.

Other festivals include *Pahiyas* of Lucban and Sariaya, Quezon Province; *Feast of San Clemente* of Angono, Rizal Province; *Moriones Festival* of Marinduque, Mindoro; *Carabao Festival* of Bulacan Province; *Maskara Festival* of Bacolod City; *Ati-Atihan* of Kalibo, Aklan; *Sinulog* of Cebu; and the *Obando Festival* of Obando, Bulacan, an hour's drive from Manila.

Featured in the Obando Festival is the dancing and singing of childless women to ask the help of Mary, Saint Pascual, and Saint Clare so that they may bear children.

In the United States, fiestas are held in some cities. There are the usual eating and observation of rituals or games. Filipino Americans also hold in some cities the *Santa Cruz de Mayo*. In one city in Michigan, a wealthy Filipino American family has held a barrio fiesta twice. On the day of celebration, Philippine folk dances were held and there were also performances by singers. A known Filipino American artist also displayed his paintings together with a collection of works by well-known Filipino artists who lived in the Philippines.

Beliefs and Superstitions. Filipinos have their own beliefs and superstitions. They are related to illnesses, death, and other things.

Some of them are follows:

■ A baby born with a mole on one of his feet will travel a lot in his adulthood.

■ If a person breaks a glass, a relative may die.

■ A person should pay his debts before New Year's Day or he will be in debt throughout the whole year.

■ A person who has a mole below any of the eyes will be widowed early.

■ When a cat crosses a person's path, someone might die.

■ A person who has a wide forehead is intelligent.

■ A person who wears amulets may be protected from illnesses.

■ If a bird perches on the roof-top of a house, someone might die.

Part IV

PROFILES OF NOTABLE FILIPINO AMERICANS

14

For the past several years, Filipino Americans have been elected and appointed to high positions in the government, including a state governor, state senators and representatives, city mayors, judges, municipal councilmen, school board members, and others. At the same time, many Filipino Americans or Americans of Filipino heritage have made their names in the fields of arts, sports, education, entertainment, business, finance, and investment. Featured on the following pages are profiles of 150 of the most outstanding Filipino Americans.

ABAD, PACITA. International Artist. With Pacita Abad, art is commitment; and her work is in all media—oil painting, aquarelle, collage, prints, textiles, and trapunto paintings. All these techniques reflect the imprint of her energetic and colorful personality. Hers is an art of visual extravagances, bold rhythms, and imaginative colors.

Born in the Philippines, Abad holds a bachelor of arts degree from the University of the Philippines, Quezon City, and a Master of Arts degree from the University of San Francisco, California. She studied painting at the Corcoran School of Art, Washington, D.C., and The Art Students League, New York City. She was a recipient of a National Endowment for the Arts Visual

Artist Fellowship, the Washington D.C. Commission on the Arts Award, and the New York State Council on the Arts Visiting Artist Fellowship. In 1995, she was the recipient of the Asian American Excellence 2000 Award for the Arts in Washington, D.C. In 1997, she was invited as a participant for the "Asian Achievers in a Global Setting Forum" held at the Louvre Museum, Paris, France.

Solo and Group Exhibitions. Abad's work has been featured in solo exhibitions, among others at the National Gallery of Indonesia; the Metropolitan Museum of Manila; the National Museum of Women in the Arts, Washington, D.C.; the National Museum, Jakarta, Indonesia; the Hong Kong Arts Center in Hongkong, China; the Museum of Philippine Art, Manila, Philippines; the Bhirasri Institute of Modern Art, Bangkok, Thailand; the Altos de Chavon, Dominican Republic; The Art Museum of Western Virginia; and the National Center of Afro-American Republic; and the National Center of Afro-American Artists, Boston, Massachusetts. She has participated in numerous group exhibitions, including the 1966 National Craft Acquisition Award at the Museum and Art Gallery of Northern Territory, Darwin, Australia; the Seventh International Biennial Print and Drawing Exhibit at the Taipei Fine Arts Museum; the Contemporary Art of the Non-Aligned Countries, at the National Gallery of Indonesia; Beyond the Border: Art by Recent Immigrants, at the Bronx Museum of Arts, New York City; the Olympiad of Art (in conjunction with the 24th Olympics), the National Museum of Contemporary Art in Seoul, South Korea; the Asian Art Show at the Fukuoka Art Museum, Japan; the La Bienal de la Habana at the Museo Nacional de Bellas Artes, Cuba, and many others.

ABELITA, GIL B., M.D. Clinical Associate Professor of Psychiatry. Born and raised in a small town in Masbate, Philippines, Dr. Abelita's parents inculcated in him the importance of discipline, hard work, and humility to press forward for a better

life. He says that with support from his family and God's help, he shaped his own destiny by working very hard to ensure admission to the University of San Carlos in Cebu City, Philippines, where he graduated *cum laude*, thus positioning himself for admission to the College of Medicine at the University of Santo Tomas in Manila, purely on his own merits.

There's Nothing Like Home. Dr. Abelita, after graduation from medicine, returned to his hometown and served his people with unconditional commitment. But in keeping with his lifelong dream of pursuing a different life course, he moved to Cardinal Santos Memorial Hospital in Manila to undergo residency in pediatrics. Later, however, the chance to serve as a medical officer in Nigeria, Africa, was too tempting to pass up, so he packed his bags before finishing his residency and spent a year helping children in the northern Nigerian state of Bauchi, cope with their health problems.

America Keeps Calling. Then, after a brief stay there, he set forth for America, bringing with him what he called "nothing more than his dreams, his credentials, and the blessings of God." His journey eventually took him to Brooklyn, New York. There under the tutelage and guidance of the faculty at Maimonides Medical Center, he trained in psychiatry and internal medicine, thus paving his way for a career in academics and private practice. He continued to pursue his dream. Now, Dr. Abelita is a clinical associate professor of psychiatry at the University of Illinois, the medical director of the Eating Disorder Program of OSF St. Francis Medical center in Peoria, Illinois and vice chairman of the Department of Psychiatry for the same hospital. He is highly respected not only in the medical community but among other mental health professionals, including psychologists.

Short in Stature, He Stands Tall. In spite of his busy practice, he devotes a lot of time teaching medical students and internal medicine and family practice residents. Although known for having a very pleasant and easy approach to patient care, his greatest strength lies in teaching at the Peoria site of the University of Illinois. His record of having won the Raymond B. Allen Golden Apple Award for Excellence in teaching eight consecutive years is unprecedented and so far has not been duplicated. As a fine tribute to his efforts, his picture is displayed in the lobby of the college, eight all in all (and possibly more), one for each year he won that most highly prized award. His name is also listed in the 1996-97 edition of "The Best Doctors in America—Midwest Region."

It has been a long journey for Dr. Abelita and now he has arrived in fulfilling his dream. Although short in stature, he stands tall, side by side with his American counterparts, with a solid contribution to medical education in a style and form that is truly Filipino.

ACADEMIA, ELEANOR. International Recording Artist. Born in Hawaii and raised in San Diego, California, Eleanor Academia holds the distinction of being the first Filipino American to land a major recording contract in Japan and in the U.S. The founder of the World Kulintang Institute in Los Angeles, California, Academia used the indigenous beats of the kulintang from the southern Philippines in her albums, "Jungle Wave" and "Global Conversation."

ACOHIDO, BYRON. Pulitzer Prize Winner. Born in Hawaii in 1955, Byron Acohido, of the *Seattle Times*, received a Pulitzer Prize award at ceremonies held last year at Columbia University in New York City under the category of Beat Reporting. He received the award from George Rupp, president of Columbia University, at the same time that another Filipino American, Alex Tizon, also of the *Seattle Times*, received his own Pulitzer Prize award.

Acohido won the award for his series of articles on certain defects of Boeing's 737 aircraft that resulted in several fatal crashes. His published findings led to the correction of a defect in the tail section of 737 series.

Heritage. Like Acohido, his father, Ben, and his mother, Caroline Flores, who were farm workers, were also born in Hawaii. His grandfather was Filipino and his grandmother was Korean. They were among pioneering immigrants to Hawaii. Acohido and his wife, Robin, have four boys: Blake, 20; Justin, 18; Kyle, 17; and Landon, 14.

Education and Work Experience. Acohido received his journalism degree from the University of Oregon's School of Journalism in 1977. Upon graduation, he was on the staff for eight years of the *Everret Herald*, a local newspaper in Everret, Washington. Then he moved to Dallas, Texas, and worked for two years for the *Dallas Times-Herald*. From there, he moved to Seattle, Washington to join the *Seattle Times* in 1987.

ADUJA, PETER. Member, Hawaii House of Representatives. In 1955, Peter Aduja became the first Filipino American to be elected to the Hawaii House of Representatives.

After a Defeat, One More Chance. After losing in his bid for reelection, Governor Samuel W. King appointed him as a deputy attorney general. After Hawaii gained its statehood, Aduja was elected three times, first in 1966, to the Hawaii House of Representatives, representing Oahu.

Born in the province of Ilocos Sur, Philippines, Aduja came to Hawaii with his parents when he was only eight years old. After graduation from Hilo High School, Hilo, Hawaii, he attended the University of Hawaii in Honolulu, where he obtained his bachelor's degree. He served with the First Filipino Infantry Regiment during World War II. He returned to Hilo to practice law after graduating from the Boston University School of Law after the war.

AGSALUD, JOSHUA C. Hawaii Cabinet Member. The son of Filipino immigrants, Joshua C. Agsalud was appointed as director of the Department of Labor and Industrial Relations by Governor George Ariyoshi in 1975. He became the second Filipino American to hold a state cabinet post in the United States. (The first was Alfred Lareta, who served the same position in 1962.)

Agsalud was a newspaper reporter, a teacher, and a school administrator before he was appointed to a cabinet post by Governor Ariyoshi. He graduated from the University of Hawaii, where he received his bachelor's degree.

AGUILA, DANIEL D'UMUK. Cartoonist, Painter, and Songwriter. A multi-awarded editorial cartoonist-painter-songwriter, Dani D'umuk Aguila, aka *el dani*, is one of a few Filipino cartoonist immigrants in America. "We're a dying breed of graphic journalists being quickly shunted by the cheaper syndication system," notes the first Filipino ethnic member of the Association of American Editorial Cartoonists—as well as its first non-former AAEC president—to receive the prestigious InkBottle Service Award in 1992.

Enjoys Cartooning. Since 1976 Aguila has been the editorial cartoonist of the NYC *Filipino Reporter.* He is regularly included in the "Best (U.S. and Canadian) Cartoons of the Year" anthology, including the gold medalist but controversial "Watergate: Sign of the Times." After winning the Wise Owl of Athena prize, it was banned as anti-U.S. and anti-Nixon; but the *Nashville Tennessean* defended it in two editorials and ran a 9-part series. Likewise, the "BECY: 1975," which ran it, was among 50 books banned in the Moscow cultural exchange that year. Thus "Watergate" earned notoriety: censored by rival superpowers U.S.A. and Russia!

Controversial. The diminutive (5"1') Philippine-born artist is no stranger to controversy and censorship. As president of the now defunct Art Directors Club of Nashville, Tennessee, in 1975, he protested

the removal of a nude male portrait from a local art show until it was re-hung. In 1983, six of his editorial cartoons on Israel were banned from his exhibit at Toronto's Public Library by no less than his host, the Filipino consul-general, "lest the sextet embarrass the Israeli envoy" (an invited guest who failed to show up!). Rather than walk out, el Dani fumed quietly but he wrote the incident in his NY weekly *Filipino Reporter.*

Consistent Award-Winning Artist. Aguila won the 1948 Ramon Roces Art Scholarship as a freshman in the University of the Philippines. Although a fine arts major, editorial cartooning became his forte. Two major gold awardees were his "Cartoonitials: Carlos P. Romulo" (1951) and "FAMOUS MEN-agerie" (1955).

In 1967, *el Dani* immigrated to Nashville, Tennessee (aka "Music City, USA") and established a career in graphic communications: art consultant to *The Upper Room,* the "World's Largest Daily Devotional Guide" in sixty-six editions—including four in Filipino languages (Ilocano, Tagalog, Cebuano, and Pampango); art director for R.G. Fields, 1967-72; public TV-Channel 8, 1972-75; Financial Institution Services, Inc., 1976-1985; and United Methodist Communications, from 1986 until his retirement in 1993. He has won numerous international awards as an editorial cartoonist, illustrator, painter, photo-journalist, TV script writer, essayist, hymn composer, and barbershop singer. He edited/art directed *BANCLUB Digest,* a quarterly magazine (cir. 1.25 M) for FISI's 2,300 U.S.-client banks. His World War II story "Emmanuel," chosen from among 422 entries, appeared in *Life* magazine (December 1989).

Becomes President. He was president of the Art Directors Club of Nashville, 1974-75, and International Association of Business Communicators/Nashville Chapter, 1980-81; and commissioner of UMCOM, 1976-1983. He held one-man and in-group art shows in Southeast Asia, Europe, Canada, Kenya, Brazil, and key US cities. Since his retirement, *el Dani* was named editorial cartoonist for three other Filipino American newspapers: *Filipino Monitor,* San Francisco, California; *Manila Headline,* Houston, Texas; and the *Philippine Asian American Times,* Denver, Colorado. A double heart bypass in 1996 and an angioplasty in October 1997, haven't slowed him down. He turned 69 on September 24, 1997, which also marked his 37th wedding anniversary to the former Norma Alampay (a medical social consultant for the Tennessee Department of Health. They have three grown children: Mrs. Mitchell Petrochka (Normalinda), 36, Nashville, Tennessee; Mrs. Joel Russ (Dina), 33, mother of Kathryn, 15, Andrew, 10, and Autumn, 6, Anchorage, Alaska; and Daniel Bliss, 31, laboratory animal caretaker, Peabody College, Vanderbilt University.

With Wings Like the Eagle's. Their Nashville home, D'Umuk Aguila (meaning "EaglesNest") features the family motto *I Fly High,* while trying to abide by a favorite Bible verse: "They that wait upon the Lord shall renew their strength. They shall mount up with wings like the eagle's. They shall run and not be weary, they shall walk and not faint." -Isaiah 40:31. Dani D'Umuk Aguila keeps faith, both with the land of his birth and his adopted America."

ALBANO, ALFONSO M., Ph.D. Physicist/Teacher. Alfonso M. Albano teaches physics at Bryn Mawr College in Pennsylvania, where he has been the Marion Reilly Professor of Physics since 1985.

He was born in Laoag, Ilocos Norte, Philippines, on August 2, 1939, but grew up in the neighboring town of Dingras, where he received his elementary and high school education. He obtained his bachelor of science in physics from the University of the Philip-

pines in 1959, where he continued his studies and teaching until 1962, when he attended the University of Iowa for graduate work. He received a master's degree in physics from Iowa in 1964.

On to Teaching. Dr. Albano moved to the State University of New York at Stony Brook, New York, where he received a doctorate in physics in 1969. After teaching at Stony Brook for one year, he took an appointment at Bryn Mawr College. Except for two years (1974-1975) and 1978-1979), which he spent at the Lorentz Institute for Theoretical Physics of the University of Leiden in the Netherlands, he has been at Bryn Mawr ever since.

Awards and Honors. Bryn Mawr College awarded him the "Christian R. and Mary F. Lindback Foundation Award for Distinguished Teaching" in 1996. In the same year, the Carnegie Foundation for the Advancement of Teaching and Council for Advancement and Support of Education named him "1996 Pennsylvania Professor of the Year" for "extraordinary dedication to undergraduate teaching."

Research Interests. Albano's research interests have included theoretical high- energy physics, non-equilibrium thermodynamics and nonlinear dynamics and chaos. Current work, supported by a research grant from the National Institutes of Health, involves the use of nonlinear dynamical tools for the analysis of biomedical signals such as those generated by the brain (EEG's) or by muscles (EMGs). He is co-author of an introductory physics textbook, two monographs of curricular materials for teaching technology to liberal arts students, and co-editor of three conference proceedings on nonlinear dynamics and chaos. He has published over 40 research articles, book chapters and contributions to conference proceedings. His articles have appeared in such journals as *The Physical Review,* the *Journal of Mathematical Physics, Physica, Journal of Theoretical Biology,* and *The Journal of Neuroscience.* He is a member of the board of editors of *Physica D,* an international journal of nonlinear science.

Albano has served on the Cognitive Functional Neuroscience Review Committee of the National Institute of Mental Health and has twice served as a consultant for the United Nations Development Programme for projects in the Philippines.

Family. He is married to Concepcion V. San Jose, Ph.D. a native of Manila. They have two daughters, Maria Teresa, an environmental engineer; and Sarah Eliza, an engineering student.

ALCON, EMILIO. Hawaii State Representative. A Democrat, Emilio Alcon, was reelected to the Hawaii House of Representatives in the November 1994 elections. Representing the Kalihi-Kapalama Moanalua district, he was reelected to the position when he obtained 2,769 votes to beat Republican R. Santiago who received only 1,580 votes. Born in Lahaina, Maui, Hawaii,

ALEJANDRO, REYNALDO G. Dancer, Choreographer, Chef, Culinary Historian, Author, and Columnist. Reynaldo ("Ronnie") G. Alejandro is a leading exponent of Philippine dance and cuisine in America. He has written 12 books, including *Sayaw Silangan: The Dance in the Philippines* (1972), *Philip-*

pine Dance: Mainstream and Crosscurrents (1978), *Philippine Cookbook* (1982), *Flavor of Asia* (1984), *Restaurant Design* (1987), *Philippine Hospitality* (1987), *Class Menu Design* (1988), and *Pinoy Guide to the Big Apple* (1992), among others.

His published articles have appeared in the following publications: *The New York Times, Cuisine Magazine, Food and Wine Magazine, Pacific Magazine, Mabuhay Magazine, Dance Magazine, Filipinas Magazine, Migration Today, Filipino Reporter, Philippine Magazine, Lifestyle Asia Magazine, International Encyclopedia of Dance, Taipan Magazine, Food Magazine, Philippine Inquirer,* among others.

Inspired by Martha Graham. His interest in America came about when he was going through books of American modern dance at the U.S.I.S. Library in Escolta, Manila and was mesmerized by the works of modern dance icon Martha Graham. He had performed with the world-renowed Filipinescas Dance Company, which toured the Middle East, Europe, and the Americas and had danced and choreographed for the Hariraya Dance Company. He had been involved with the Philippine Educational Theater Association in Manila and had won several awards in choreography in the Philippine Songfest before coming to the United States to study modern dance at the Martha Graham School of Contemporary Dance.

Reinvents Dance Group. In 1969, he reinvented the Filipino Dance Group in New York into the Philippine Dance Company of New York, where he was the choreographer and artistic director until 1981. In 1972, he founded the Reynaldo Alejandro Dance Theater, the first Filipino American modern dance company in the United States, where he mounted his "Sayaw Silangan Dance Series," "Rizaliana Dance Suites," and "Bagong Salta Dance Series" until 1982.

Alejandro Who? Here's what they say about Alejandro and his books:

"Reynaldo Alejandro is both a professional dancer-choreographer and a talented and professional chef (who) moves gracefully, eloquently...skillfully...as he chops a Ruskin tomato into precise cubes...(and) talks about the cuisine of the Philippines, the interplay and layering of cultures."—Dorothy Chapman, *The Orlando Sentinel*

"Mr. Alejandro's beautifully illustrated survey of Philippine dance is also for the general reader...Mr. Alejandro's insistence on going beyond the usual ethnographic description of tribal dances is highly significant."—*The New York Times*

"The heart of the book is his discussion of the efforts done to research and preserve these dances. *Philippine Dance* is an invaluable reference source, a lively social history, and to Filipino experiences and their American friends, a nostalgic and sunny momento of that now embattled land."—*The Sunday Times Journal*

"*Philippine Dance: Mainstream and Cross-Currents*, is a beautifully produced work with lavish illustrations to visually complement a general survey of Philippine Dance."—*Bridge Magazine*

Shifts Career. In 1982, Alejandro shifted careers and studied at the New York Restaurant School. Since then he has been consistently putting the Philippines on the culinary map of the world through his culinary performances, catering, and writing. He has lectured on Philippine culture, arts, cuisine, and dance in Europe, Asia, and the Americas.

Awards and Honors. Alejandro's awards include Creative Artists Public Service Program (CAPS) Award in Choreography; Jaycees "Outstanding Young Man in Arts Award; Outstanding Filipino Award (1978); Outstanding Filipino Overseas Award in Arts (1978); Outstanding Young Men in America Award (1980); New York State Council on the Arts Grantee (1979-1980); *Parangal ng Lahi* Medal of Excellence Award (1987); and Pride of the Malay Race, *Perlas ng Silangan* Award (1989). He was cited in *Who's Who in America*, and was featured in *Filipino Achievers in the USA and Canada* by Isabelo T. Crisostomo. He has received various grants in the arts.

Embarks on Centennial Book Series. Presently, he has conceived the Centennial Book Series, book projects that will keep him busy until the year 2000. He lives in New York City.

ALFARO, ALBERTO M.
Editor-in-Chief, *Manila-Mail.* A former *Manila Chronicle* staffer, Alberto M. Alfaro, is the editor-in-chief of the *Manila Mail*, a forthnightly Filipino American newspaper in the nation's capital. Alfaro is also a partner on the B&W (Bert and Mari Azarcon) talk show program, produced by the Forex Broadcasting Company and

aired on cable television every weekend on the East Coast and occasionally on the West Coast.

Early Years. Alfaro was born in Tetuan in Zamboanga City, Mindanao, Philippines, on August 11, 1929, to Rufo M. Alfaro and Felisa Marcos. He attended the Ateneo de Zamboanga High School in Zamboanga City and completed his associate in arts degree at the Zamboanga A.E. College.

To Manila. In 1954 he left for Manila, where he joined the *Manila Chronicle* as a proofreader. That same year, he won a scholarship from the National Press Club of the Philippines and completed his bachelor of arts degree, with a major in history at the Far Eastern University in Manila in 1955. At the *Manila Chronicle*, he quickly rose from the ranks to become an assistant features editor, deskman, foreign news editor, and diplomatic reporter.

To Abroad and Back. In 1966, Alfaro went abroad after he was chosen as one of two Filipino journalists to take an advance course in mass communications given by the Berlin Institute for Mass Communications in Germany to journalists from developing countries. Returning to Manila, he became the editor of the *Chronicle Magazine*, the weekly magazine of the *Manila Chronicle*. After three years, he was appointed as a senior political reporter covering the Philippine Senate until martial law in 1972. He also taught journalism at the Lyceum of the Philippines.

During the early years of martial law, Alfaro edited the *Weekly Observer* newsmagazine and another trade publication in Manila. A year later, he joined then Information Minister Francisco Tatad as a special assistant, edited *The Republic*, a weekly publication of the ministry, and then joined *Philippine News Arica*.

America, Here I Come! That same year, he came to the United States to become the first bureau chief of the Philippine News Agency in Washington D.C. During his 10th year stint in the US, he became a member of the National Press Club, Sigma Delta Chi and the Foreign Correspondents Association. He was also accredited to cover the White House, Congress, State and Defense Departments as well as other US government offices in Washington D.C. and the United Nations in New York City.

Back to Manila. Returning to Manila after the People Power ended the martial law regime of President Marcos, Alfaro helped found and edit *Dateline Manila*, a weekly news and features service published by Associated Editors. About 13 of the more than 20 newspapers subscribed to the *Dateline* at that time. At the same time, he also edited *The New Republic*, a weekly newspaper in Makati City.

The Return to the U.S. In 1991, Alfaro decided to return to the United States to rejoin his family. Immediately on arrival, he formed, together with other Filipinos in the Virginia area, the *Manila-U.S. Mail*, (later renamed *Manila Mail*), the forthnightly newspaper that he founded and edited since 1991.

Awards and Honors. He has been conferred the coveted lifetime membership award of the Philippine National News Agency, in recognition of his contribution to Philippine journalism. He has also been the recipient of numerous awards and commendations, including one from Foreign Minister Carlos P. Romulo. In 1978, because of his accreditation and membership in various professional organizations in Washington, D.C., he was included in *Who's Who in America* and in 1996 he was featured in the *Filipino Achievers in the USA & Canada: Profiles in Excellence* by Isabelo T. Crisostomo.

Family. Alfaro and his wife, Milagros G. Reyes, have six grown children: Maria Cristina A. Burgos, Rebecca A. Flores, Teresa A. Lopez, and Luisa, Armando, and Jeff Alfaro.

ALVEAR, DOMINGO T., M.D. Pediatric Surgeon, Speaker, and Prolific Writer.

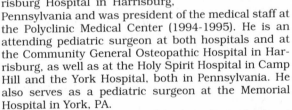

One of the well-known Filipino American pediatric surgeons in the United States, Dr. Domingo T. Alvear, was born in Badoc, Ilocos Norte Province, Philippines, on April 3, 1943.

Dr. Alvear is the chief of the Division of Surgery at the Polyclinic Medical Center and Harrisburg Hospital in Harrisburg, Pennsylvania and was president of the medical staff at the Polyclinic Medical Center (1994-1995). He is an attending pediatric surgeon at both hospitals and at the Community General Osteopathic Hospital in Harrisburg, as well as at the Holy Spirit Hospital in Camp Hill and the York Hospital, both in Pennsylvania. He also serves as a pediatric surgeon at the Memorial Hospital in York, PA.

Boyhood Dream. Dr. Alvear, whose boyhood dream was to be a doctor, graduated *cum laude* and *benemeritus* from the University of Santo Tomas College of Medicine in Manila. He took internship training at the U.S. Air Force Hospital, Clark Air Force Base, in Angeles City, Pampanga Province, Philippines. Later, he was a general surgery resident at the same hospital.

Explaining how he selected pediatric surgery as his specialty, Dr. Alvear says, "At my first year in medical school, I decided to become a surgeon because I liked the anatomy class. At my second year of surgical residency, I decided to become a pediatric surgeon because of the challenge in baby caring."

Surgical Internships. When Dr. Alvear immigrated to the United States in 1966, he undertook rotating surgical internships at the Presbyterian University of Pennsylvania Medical Center; general surgery residency at St. Vincent's Hospital on Staten Island in New York; and general surgery residency at Presbyterian University. From 1971-1973, he was a fellow at St. Christopher's Hospital for Children in Philadelphia, Pennsylvania, and in bronchoesophagology at St. Christopher's Hospital.

Fellowships. He received fellowships from the American Academy of Pediatrics and the American College of Surgeons. He was also awarded an honorary fellowship by The Philippine Society of Pediatric Surgeons in 1994.

Memberships. Dr. Alvear's membership include Dauphin Country Medical Society; Board of Directors, Leukemia Society of America in Harrisburg, Pennsylvania; president of the Society of Philippine Surgeons in America (1995-1996); Central Pennsylvania Business School; and Harrisburg Symphony Association

An Author. Dr. Alvear has written many articles in such prestigious medical publications as the *American Surgeon American, Journal of Surgery, Journal of Pediatric Surgery,* and *American Journal of Childhood Diseases.* He became a diplomate in general surgery of the American Board of Surgery. Next, he became a diplomate in pediatric surgery of the ABS.

To the World He Goes! Dr. Alvear is a world traveler. He has been a participant speaker at medical conferences and conventions in the United States and abroad. He has attended world congresses of surgeons in various parts of the world, such as England, Greece, Mexico, China, Aruba, Russia, and Spain. Describing Dr. Alvear, Michael Paszek, M.D., says, "He's a super pediatric surgeon, the best I've ever seen anywhere. He's also a nice guy."

Family. Married to Dr. Veneranda G. Bruno-Alvear, an anesthesiologist, Dr. Alvear and his wife have two grown children: Domingo, who is a computer engineer, and Jonathan, who is taking a master's degree in international diplomacy.

AMORES, CONSTANTINO, M.D. Presidential Appointee on Arts Committee.

A well-known doctor in West Virginia, Dr. Constantino Amores was appointed last year by President Clinton as a member of the Presidential Advisory Committee on the Arts. He was a founding member of the Charleston Conservatory of Music and Arts in Charleston, West Virginia.

Currently, Dr. Amores is a clinical professor at the department of neurosurgery at West Virginia University in Charleston. He is on active staff at the Charleston Area Medical Center and on the consulting staff at the St. Francis Hospital, Herbert Thomas Medical, and Putnam General Hospital. He is chief of Section of Neurosurgery at the CAMC and is chairman of the Department of Neuroscience in the same hospital. He was chief of Staff of the CAMC from 1986-1987. He was also on the board of trustees of the Charleston Area Medical Center from 1987-90. Since 1971, he has been with the Neurological Associates of Charleston, in Charleston, West Virginia.

Flashback. Born in Cebu City, Philippines, Amores graduated in 1956 as *benemeritus* from the University of Santo Tomas College of Medicine in Manila, Philippines. When he came to the United States in 1971 to take further training, he had his residency in neurosurgery in Pittsburgh, Pennsylvania.

The son of a former medical professor and a full-time housewife mother, Dr. Amores is active in community and professional activities. When asked by a reporter if he had any plans to get further involved in local politics, Amores said, "I'm just a simple neurosurgeon who's very much involved in the community. There are no specific plans."

Memberships. Among others, he is a member of the Congress of Neurological Surgeons, the American Association of Neurosurgical Surgeons, and the American Medical Association.

Awards. Dr. Amores is the recipient of the Distinguished West Virginia Award from Governor Gaston Caperton of West Virginia and a Recognition and Appreciation of Leadership Award from the West Virginia State Medical Association. He has also received several awards from the Charleston Area Medical Center, including the Patient Care Award; Distinguished Service as chief of staff, Distinguished and Devoted Service Award as a member of the board of trustees 1987-90; Outstanding Dedication and Leadership Award as chief of the Department of Neurological Medicine, 1980-1981. He also received a Governor's Commendation, State of West Virginia.

Family. Dr. Amores and his wife have four grown children: Jon, who is an elected member of the West Virginia House of Delegates; a daughter who is a full-time housewife; another daughter who is a journalist; and Christopher, the youngest, who is a stockbroker.

AMORES, JON. West Virginia State Representative.

Jon Amores, 32, is the youngest Asian American elected to public office in the United States. A Democrat member of the West Virginia House of Delegates from Kanawha County's 30th Delegate District, Amores was first elected in 1994. In the House, he serves on the Health and Human Resources Committee, the Banking and Insurance Committee, and the Judiciary Committee. Indeed, after only one term, he has been named vice-chairman of the powerful House Judiciary Committee. Describing his political philosophy as moderate, Amores is progressive on social issues, and emphasizes economic and job growth in his legislative agenda.

Mediation Is His Forte. Amores is an attorney-mediator, and he is the principal of Dispute Resolution Services, which he founded in Charleston, West Virginia in 1993. The group includes eleven former judges from the state of West Virginia, who provide mediation and arbitration services to resolve disputes and avoid lawsuits between businesses, groups, and individuals. Dispute Resolution Services also provides mediation training to schools and businesses throughout the state.

Amores attended the University of Notre Dame for his undergraduate studies, and then he went to the Loyola University of Chicago Law School. He practiced business law at the law firms of Jackson and Kelly, and Vaughan and Withrow before establishing Dispute Resolution Services.

He is a member of the West Virginia and American Bar Associations, as well as the Society of Professionals in Dispute Resolution, the American Arbitration Association, and the Academy of Family Mediators. Amores is also active in community affairs and is on the boards of directors for the Community Council of Kanawha Valley, Keep a Child in School, Inc., Damark, Inc. and Charleston Public Safety Council. He is also on the Fund Distribution Executive Committee for the United Way of Kanawha Valley and a member of the Charleston Rotary Club.

Amores' Dream. Amores' dream, according to him, was "To be directly involved in helping others." His American dream is: to "make a lasting contribution in all areas of my life as Benjamin Franklin said, "Well done is better than well said." His success formula is "to bring enthusiasm and a desire to learn all things; a 'happy warrior': that is, to stay positive and focused when addressing challenges and to see the best in people and situations."

According to him, he has been profoundly influenced by his parents, Drs. Tino and Diana Amores. Dr. Amores, a neurosurgeon, is a man of great achievement, and a former president of the West Virginia State Medical Association. Diana, also a physician, is involved in a number of community activities, and she has helped Jon to develop his commitment to public service.

Awards and Honors. Amores' awards and honors include a Fleming Fellow, a national award granted to a limited number of legislators around the country for participation in a series of leadership-building retreats.

Family. Amores is married to Janet Amores, and they have two boys, Trey, age 5, and Marshal, age 3.

ARTIST, THE. Singer. (See Prince.)

AZARCON, HERMENEGILDO A. Copy Editor, *The Detroit News.*

Formerly on the staff of *The Evening News* and *The Manila Times* in Manila, Philippines, Hermenegildo "Hermie" A. Azarcon is a copy editor of *The Detroit News* in Detroit, Michigan.

Tryout under Time Pressure. Azarcon joined *The News* in 1965 as a copy editor after undergoing a tough tryout, working on the desk for two days under time pressure.

College Experience. Azarcon, after graduating from the Torres High School in Manila, Philippines attended the University of Santo Tomas (UST) in Manila, where he obtained his bachelor of science in journalism in 1958. While in college, he was an assistant and news editor for two years and editor-in-chief of *The Varsitarian,* the official publication of the university. He also obtained a bachelor's degree in public relations in 1960, also from UST.

After graduation from college, Azarcon joined *The Evening News,* where he covered several beats before he was assigned to the copy desk. Later, he moved to *The Manila Times,* then the largest English-language daily newspaper in the Philippines.

To Wisconsin, U.S.A. Born in 1937, Azarcon left Manila in September 1961 for the University of Wisconsin in Madison, Wisconsin, where he later received his master's degree in journalism. Upon graduation from the University of Wisconsin, he joined *The Daily Journal* in Wheaton, Illinois, where he covered the police, the sheriff's office, the city hall, and the board of education. He then transferred to the *Rapid City Daily Journal* in Rapid City, South Dakota, where he covered the police beat and handled special assignments.

Family. A native of Gapan, Nueva Ecija, Philippines, Azarcon is married to the former Felisa P. Timog, a Philippine Women's University graduate with a bachelor of science degree in nutrition. His wife, who has a master's degree in food and institution management from Wayne State University in Detroit, Michigan, works at the Northville Regional Psychiatric Hospital in Northville, Michigan. The Azarcons who live in Troy, Michigan have a daughter, Dawn, who has a bachelor of science degree in marketing from Michigan State University.

BABILONIA, TAI. Former World Ice Skating Champion.

Since the age of 8, Tai Babilonia, the daughter of a Filipino father and an American mother, except for brief hiatuses in 1988 and 1995, has been skating on ice with Randy Gardner, whom she met when he was 10. Babilonia actually started skating at the age of 6.

From 1976 to 1980, the skating partners soared to prominence after they captured five consecutive U.S. amateur pairs titles. It was in 1979 when Babilonia and Gardner won a pairs figure-skating world championship with perfect scores. They are the only American duo to win the title in 74 years of world championship competition. Since then, no American duo has won the title.

Something Happens. The partners were expected to win a gold medal in the Lake Placid Olympics in New York. However, they were forced to withdraw after Gardner suffered a groin injury. The duo then went on a successful professional career. But Babilonia became depressed and drank heavily. A dependence on amphetamines resulted in 1980 in a suicide attempt, when she took an overdose of sleeping pills. With therapy and the support of Gardner, his family, and friends, Babilonia was back on the ice.

"On Thin Ice." In 1990, she went to Toronto, Canada, in connection with the filming of the television movie, "On Thin Ice," which was based on her life story. The movie tells of Babilonia's drug abuse, alcoholism, broken loved affairs, and suicide attempt. Babilonia and Gardner were consultants during the one-month filming of the movie. They performed the skating sequences.

In 1992, the partners were inducted into the U.S. Figure Skating Hall of Fame as a living testimony to their unequalled achievements in American pairs figure skating.

In May 1996, the former world champion skaters, known for their breathtaking maneuvers and innovative routines, were honored, together with past and present Olympians, at the White House.

Friendship Is Forever. Babilonia and Gardner are the best of friends. In a tribute to that friendship, Babilonia has said, "I was lucky to have Randy. He stuck with me when he didn't have to. He's my best friend, and of all the titles we won together, our friendship is what I cherish most." Their friendship, with Babilonia's ups and downs, has survived for the past three decades. They both grew up in Los Angeles, California. Babilonia was then 9 and Radner was 11 when their skating coach in Culver City teamed them together. Four years later, they won the National Junior Pairs Championship.

Future Plans. Babilonia plans to continue skating on ice for many years to make a living. Babilonia and Gardner had exhibition tours, that were televised in the fall of 1996. As members of the Tour of World Figure Skating Champions, the duo also performed in a 25-city tour in 1997. Promoters have said that the "Tai and Randy" headline still draws substantial crowds.

Babilonia, who has a young son, Scout, has moved to her parents' home in Sherman Oaks, California. She is divorced from her husband, Cary Butler, a music producer, who shares custody of their son.

BACHO, E.V. Historian, Seattle Community Leader.

A well-known community leader in Seattle, Washington, E. V. (Vic) Bacho was the author of the book *The Long Road: Memoirs of a Filipino Pioneer*, in which he recalled his

American experience and the happenings of that period.

Bacho arrived in San Francisco, California, in 1926. One of his unforgettable experiences as a Filipino in America was when while aboard a bus, he was ordered to sit in the smoking room at the back of the vehicle because the front seats were for whites.

From San Francisco to Seattle. From San Francisco, he moved to Seattle and attended the University of Washington, as a night student. After earning his bachelor of arts in political science from the university, he participated in civic and political activities in the community and he became a community historian.

As a leader in the community, he headed the Dr. Jose P. Rizal Bridge and Park Preservation Society and established the Jose Rizal Park in Seattle, Washington. The park includes a picnic shelter with an amphitheater, restrooms, tables, children's play area and parking area,

Awards. Bacho's awards and honors include a plaque from the Community of Seattle in reference to his serving as chairman of the Rizal Committee and for his successful efforts in the procurement of funds from the Seattle City Council for construction of the only Rizal Park on the continental United States, 1992; honored by the *Fil-Am* magazine as one of the 20 outstanding Filipino Americans, 1990; honored by

Mayor Charles Royer of Seattle as First Citizen of the City of Seattle, 1984; chosen as one of the Filipino American Achievers by the Filipino Youth Activities in Seattle, Inc.; and a plaque from the Filipino Community of Seattle for the successful publication of the book, *Our Community 1978—Together We Will Succeed*.

Bacho, who died in 1997, was married to Aurelia A. Estacio, a registered nurse.

BALLAO, BERNIE. Alaska Council Member.
Bernie Ballao, a native of Pampanga Province, Philippines, is the first Filipino and Asian council member of Kodiak, Alaska. He was elected to the position for the third time in the October 3, 1994 elections. Ballao, who has lived in Alaska since 1974, was first elected to a three-year position in 1989. He was reelected to the same position in 1991. He is native of Pampanga Province, Philippines. Of the more than 8,000 inhabitants of Kodiak, 1,500 to 2,000 are Filipinos.

BANZON, GENARA. Nature Artist.
Genara Banzon is a Filipina artist whose installation art focuses on natural processes. Her works surround the viewer with organic, often indigenous materials which she hopes will stimulate associations to personal experiences while conveying a sense of her own Philippine roots.

Born in Manila, the fifth of ten children, Banzon received her bachelor of fine arts in visual communications from the University of the Philippines-Diliman in 1974. Since then, she has exhibited her work internationally and has also created several children's books. She has taught art at the high school and university levels, and has conducted field research among various tribal groups in the Philippines.

Influences of Her Life. Banzon cites many influences that have shaped her and her work. Responding to a new aesthetic that was developing in the 1970s, Banzon was urged by Raymundo Albano, the director of the Cultural Center of the Philippines and Roberto Chabet, his art professor from the University of the Philippines School of Fine Arts, to explore artistic boundaries beyond the style of traditional schools. Installation art provided the artistic freedom for her to integrate her skills in printmaking, photography, painting, collage, sculpture, and paper making while encouraging greater audience involvement.

Speaking of her art, Banzon says, "I have stories, dreams, visions that revolve around my experiences in life. I feel deeply about a lot of things, the place I grew up, the places I find myself in, the people I have interacted with. My art reflects such interactions, relations, feelings, attitudes towards these."

Banzon also cites as her influences her fellow Filipino artists, traditions of both East and West, and the diversity of Filipino culture. Her natural processes stem from her interest in and her respect for the cultural environment, her father's role as a nationally honored scientist and chemist, and her mother's work as a general practitioner.

Around the World, Her Works Are Shown. She has shown her works at the Cultural Center of the Philippines; the Museum of Philippine Art; the Fukuoka Art Museum in Japan; the Powerhouse Museum I; the Tin Sheds Gallery; the Performance Space in Australia; and The Black Swan Galley in Frermantle and Perth, Western Australia. She was an invited participant and toured Japan, Korea, and The Hague as part of the "Third Asian Art Show; Symbolic Visions in Contemporary Asian Life" (organized by the Fukuoka Museum of Art, 1989. Locally in Massachusetts, she has shown at the Boston Visual Arts Union (1985; the Cambridge Arts Council (Gallery 57, 1986; the Harvard Neighbors Gallery, 1990; the Cambridge Multicultural Arts Center, Cambridge 1992 and 1995; the Artists Foundation Gallery; the Fuller Museum of Art in Brockton, Massachusetts for the 7th Triennial Art Exhibition 1993; the Habitat Institute for the Environment; Belmont and at the ICA-The Institute of Contemporary Art Boston at the BOSTON (In Dialogue) show, 1994.

More Exhibitions. She has also exhibited in Connecticut: the Atrium Gallery, University of Connecticut at Storrs; The Charter Oak Gallery, Hartford-1992; RAW: Real Artways, Hartford, 1993; New York: DIA Center for the Arts, INTAR Gallery 1994; the Steinbaum Krause Gallery, Abrams Art Center at the Henry Street Settlement 1995; California: The Art Gallery at the University of California at Irvine (UCI) 1996; University of California at Riverside (UCR); and also in Canada. She has been invited to lecture and give side talks in the Philippines, Australia, and in the U.S. at the University of Connecticut of Storrs, the Charter Oak Gallery; The Charter Oak Gallery; Harvard University; Brown University in Providence, Rhode Island; Rutgers University in New Brunswick, New Jersey; the HERA Gallery, Rhode Island; New York University; Steinbaum Krauss Gallery, Soho, New York; and at the Art Gallery University of California at Irvine.

Collaborates With Choreographer. She has developed concepts and artworks for dance collaborations with New York choreographer Kristin Jackson (*Lapis,* 1986,1988; Still Waters, 1990; *Pakiusap* 1992-1993; Fallow Gardens, 1993; and Island/*Pulo,* 1994, which have been performed at the DIA Center for the Arts; the ICA-The Institute of Contemporary Art, Boston, Massachusetts; The Harbor Gallery at the University of Massachusetts, Harbor Campus; The Artists Foundation Gallery, Boston; and also at the Cultural Center of the Philippines, Manila.

Further Education. In 1992, Banzon graduated from the Massachusetts College of Art with a Master of Fine Arts from the Performing and Media Department with a concentration on the Studio for Interrelated Media. Since then, she has continued to exhibit her art locally and internationally as well as give slide talks and lectures regarding her vision in creating art and culture, and also about her art and art processes when she deals with clashes of nature and technology. Through her art/art installations she expresses her views on issues of identity, gender, race, stereotyping, etc. Her narratives on and of women as exiles and migrants, is a spiritual quest and an unending call for equality, development, and peace.

BARREDO, MANIYA. Atlanta and the Philippines' first Prima Ballerina.
Once cast as the Ugly Duckling in a school program, Maniya Barredo became Atlanta and the Philippines' first prima ballerina. Called "the ballerina of your country" by famed Dame Margot Fonteyn, she performed her swan song with partner Tom Mossbrucker in Tom Pazik's *Romeo and Juliet*, at the Atlanta Civic Center, Atlanta, Georgia on February 17, 1995. That performance ended her 18-year illustrious career with the Atlanta Ballet.

"I Love You All!" Commenting on her performance, A. Scott Walton of *The Atlanta Journal-Constitution*, wrote: "Maniya Barredo took her final bow as the Atlanta Ballet's prima ballerina by saying, 'I love you all' and making an embracing gesture toward the audience at the close of Friday night's gala performance of 'Romeo and Juliet."

Co-Hosts Lollipop Party. Born in Manila, Philippines, Barredo was trained in Manila by her aunt Julie Borromeo, at the age of 4. In 1963, she joined Manila's Harinaya Dance Company. After five years, she co-hosted *Lollipop Party*, a children's television show. Barredo is a graduate of St. Paul College in Manila, where she sang and danced children's roles in such musicals as *The Sound of Music* and *Carousel*. At the age of 18, she traveled by herself to the United States to seek training and fame. She auditioned for the American Ballet Center, the Joffrey Ballet School. Later, she won a John D. Rockefeller II scholarship to pursue further training. Then in 1972, she was admitted into the Joffrey Ballet II. She later joined the main Joffrey company, during which she changed her name from Honey to Maniya, to rhyme with Manila.

Walks to the Altar with a Dancer. She married a dancer named Mannie Rowe who was with the Les Grandes Ballets Canadien in Montreal, Canada, which she joined in 1973. Robert Barnett, a former Atlanta Ballet artistic director invited the couple to join the Atlanta Ballet, which they accepted. Thus, she became the Atlanta Ballet's first prima ballerina. However, the marriage ended in divorce. Barredo then married L. Patterson Thompson III, on April 16, 1988.

"A Holiday Should Be Declared!" Writer Will Ryan, in an article in the *Gwinnet Loaf* in Atlanta, made one of the most lavish praises bestowed upon Barredo by any writer. He wrote, "How sad it will be to see her leave! For 18 years, she has given us the marvel of her life and her work. A holiday should be declared; schools and public buildings should be closed. There should be drum rolls and parades, cannon should bellow, and delegations of the distinguished should lay honors upon her. The stage should be carpeted with flowers, men should weep, and the applause should linger until hands grow too sore and arms too tired. She has given us more than we could ever ask, and she deserves no less."

BARRON, PURIFICACION CAPULONG. Registered Nurse.
One of the top ten among nurse examinees on a Philippine board examination years

ago, Purificacion Capulong Barron's nursing career so far has spanned 47 years in the Philippines, Canada, and the United States.

She came to the U.S. and became a hospital staff nurse under the Exchange Visitor's Program. She first worked at St. Anthony's Hospital while she started a B.S. course in nursing at St. Louis University in St. Louis, Missouri. After one year, she continued her education at Columbia University in New York City and worked part-time, first at Mount Sinai, then at St. Claire's Hospital, and then at Women's Hospital.

Educator and Lecturer. As an educator, she was an instructor and lecturer at the Lorrain School of Nursing in Ontario, Canada, where she lived with her husband for five years. She also worked as an assistant professor of nursing at the Indiana State University School of Nursing. She was a director of nursing at the Holiday Home in Indiana and director of nursing at the Pine Knoll Nursing Home in Carrollton, Georgia.

A graduate of the St. Luke's Hospital School of Nursing in Quezon City, Philippines, Barron, a holder of B.S. and M.A. degrees, was included in the *1990-1991* edition of *Who's Who in American Nursing*, published by the Society of Nursing Professionals in Washington D.C., and in the 1992-1993 edition of *Who's Who Among Human Service Professionals*, published in Chicago, Illinois. She is now retired and lives in Carrollton, Georgia, with her husband, Rodrigo Barron and son, Joseph Rodney.

BICOY, BERNALDO D. Member, Hawaii House of Representatives.
Bernaldo D. Bicoy was elected to the Hawaii House of Representatives in 1958 to represent West Oahu, Hawaii. In 1959, Bicoy lost in his bid for a reelection. In 1968, he ran for the same position and he was successful. However, he served only one term.

Bicoy graduated from the Waipahu High School, Oahu, Hawaii. He graduated from the University of Hawaii in Honolulu, Hawaii and the University of Missouri Law School.

BRAINARD, CECILIA MANGUERRA. Award-Winning Writer. As a young girl, Cecilia Manguerra Brainard, saddened by the sudden death of her father, used to write in a lock-and-key journal that evolved into a journal where she poured her feelings of loneliness. Today, that girl of yesteryear has become one of the most well-known Filipino American writers. The recipient of several awards, she is the author and editor of seven books.

Studying Engineering, But Dreaming to Be a Writer. Brainard in recalling her past, says, "I always wrote and stated in my early journals that I wanted to be a writer. However, I started off majoring in civil engineering in college...and didn't know what was going on, then I went back on track by taking up communications arts at Maryknoll College."

Born in Cebu, Philippines, Brainard attended St. Theresa's College in Cebu City and in Manila and graduated from Maryknoll College with a Bachelor of Arts degree in Communications Arts.

Meeting Her Prince Charming. Immigrating in 1969 to the United States, she studied film and creative writing at the University of California at Los Angeles. It was there that she renewed acquaintances with her husband-to-be Lauren Brainard, whom she had first met in the Philippines when he was assigned in Leyte Province as a Peace Corps volunteer. They have three sons.

From 1969-1981, Brainard worked as a documentary scriptwriter and an assistant director of development, including responsibilities in public relations.

Turning Point of Her Life. Revealing the turning point of her life when she became a full-time fiction writer, Brainard says, "When I had my third son, I quit my full-time job. Because I found I had some free time, I started a newspaper column and also took writing classes at UCLA-Extension's Writer's Program. I thoroughly enjoyed taking care of the family and writing. Right about the time my third son went to nursery school, I went job hunting, was offered a job immediately, and discovered I had quite a headache about the matter. I did some soul-searching and realized I couldn't work full-time, take care of my family, and write. I had to choose between that job or my writing; I chose writing."

From then on, there was no turning back. Her writings have been read both in the Philippines and in the United States. Her first novel, *Song of Yvonne,* was published in the Philippines by New Day Publishers. It was published in the U.S. with a new title *When the Rainbow Goddess Wept* by E.P. Dutton and was highly praised by reviewers. *Publishers Weekly,* in its review of the book in its August 1994 issue, says, "In simple yet deeply moving prose, Brainard's first novel presents similar acts of monumental courage: a doctor's sacrifice in the jungle; quiet defiance against terrorist threats...the strengthening of the national spirit; the loss of innocence in two generations—these themes are explored by the author, who was born in the Philippines, with persuasive conviction and stark realism." The novel is about the coming of age of a young girl in the Philippines during World War II.

Mission in Life. Explaining her mission in life, Brainard says, "I have affected many people in a positive way via my writings and my teaching. This gives me great satisfaction. The books I have written and edited have lives of their own and are like children in that way; I am proud of them. I am also touched by the positive feedback I have gotten from people, be it in the form of awards or news coverage or interviews or a simple phone call or note. I am also happy to have served, and continue to serve, my Filipino American community by the forming of PAWWA (Philippine American Women Writers and Artists) and PALH (Philippine American Literary House)."

Brainard has written and edited such Filipiniana titles as *Woman with Horns and Other Stories; Fiction by Filipinos in America; Philippine Woman in America; Acapulco at Sunset and Other Stories;* and *Contemporary Fiction by Filipinos in America.*

Her writings have appeared in several anthologies, among which are *Forbidden Fruit,* published by Anvil Publishing; *The Perimeter of Light: Writing About the Vietnam War; Seven Stories from Seven Sisters; Harvest I,* edited by Lina Espina Moore; *Home to Stay: Making Waves;* and *Songs of Ourselves,* edited by Edna Manlapaz.

Since 1989, this prolific writer also has been an instructor at the Writers' Program, UCLA-Extension. She has also become a lecturer, panelist, presenter, instructor, and coordinator/participant in various lectures, writing workshops, and conferences both in the United States and in the Philippines.

Awards. Her many awards include Literature Award, Filipino Women's Network, 1991; Brody Arts Fund Fellowship, 1991; Special Recognition Award, Los Angeles Board of Education, 1991; City of Los Angeles Cultural Grant, 1990-91; California Arts Council Artists Fellowship in Fiction 1989-90; and several USIS lecture-tour grants.

BUCHHOLDT, THELMA. Alaska State Representative. Thelma Buchholdt was elected to the Alaska State House of Representative in 1974, making her the first Filipino to serve in a U.S. state legislature. Reelected three times, Buchholdt is the author of the book *Filipinos in Alaska: 1788-1958,* published by the Aboriginal Press of Anchorage, Alaska. She is a trustee of the Filipino American National Historical Society (FANHS).

BUENAVENTURA, CIELO. Metropolitan Section Editor, The New York Times. A former features editor in Manila, Philippines, for *We Forum,* a subsidiary of the publication *Malaya,* Cielo Buenaventura is the editor of the "Metropolitan Section" of *The New York Times.*

Background. While serving as an editor at the *We Forum,* Buenaventura obtained a graduate scholarship at Ohio State University. A year later, she received her master's degree in journalism.

The Move to New York. Buenaventura headed for New York City to take an adventure in the heart of publishing. She first worked at a trade publication in Manhattan, New York City. Then she moved to *New York Newsday*, where she became a copy editor at *Newsday's* office on Long Island, working there until 1991. For a while, she worked at *The Advocate* in Stanford, Connecticut, but moved to the *New York Newsday* Manhattan office, where she stayed until 1995. Recommended by one of her former bosses to *The New York Times*, she underwent a series of interviews and tryouts before she joined the publication.

BULOSAN, CARLOS. Outstanding Filipino Writer.

As an exile in America, Carlos Bulosan was a dishwasher, cannery worker, houseboy, and farm worker. He became one of the most outstanding Filipino writers in the United States. The author of the classic book *America Is in the Heart: A Personal Story* (Harcourt, Brace & Company, Inc., Copyright 1943, 1946), Bulosan called it a "personal history of his life." Others have called it an autobiographical fiction or a fictional biography. Bulosan writings stemmed from his call for justice and his anger over the discrimination and prejudice suffered by him and his countrymen in America during his time.

Comments. Here's what they say about Bulosan and his writings:

Saturday Review of Literature:

People (including all Filipinos) interested in driving from America the scourge of intolerance should read Mr. Bulosan's autobiography. They should read it that they may draw from the anger it will arouse in them the determination to bring an end to the vicious nonsense of racism.

Novelist and screen writer John Fante (quoted in the Introduction by Carey McWilliams to the book *America Is in the Heart*):

A tiny person with a limp, with an exquisite face, almost facially beautiful, with gleaming teeth and lovely brown eyes, shy, generous, terribly poor, terribly exiled in California, adoring Caucasian women, sartorially exquisite, always laughing through a face that masked tragedy....

E. San Juan, Jr. (a leading academic and critic, who edited *On Becoming Filipino* and *The Cry and the Dedication*, two newly released books by Bulosan) wrote in 1972:

Of the Filipino writers in English who began their careers before World War II, Bulosan remains the most viable, startling and contemporary."

Tomio Geron (quoted from his article *Filipino Prophet: The Writings of Carlos Bulosan Re-emerge with a Contemporary Relevance, AsianWeek*, August 4, 1995):

One doesn't have to share Bulosan's politics to appreciate his prose, which flows with delicate beauty. His writing sings with an eloquent and polished voice that inspires admiration regardless of political viewpoint.

The Arrival of an Exile. Born in Binalonan, Pangasinan, in Luzon, Philippines, and the son of a farmer, Bulosan arrived in the U.S. on July 22, 1930, at age 17. Truly an exile, he didn't return home to the Philippines nor did he become a U.S. citizen. However, in his book, *The Cry and the Dedication*, he revisits his homeland through his characters.

A school drop-out who spoke only a little English, Bulosan arrived here with only 20 cents in his pocket. All he could raise was the payment for transportation to Seattle, Washington.

He first worked in an Alaskan cannery, where he lived with thousands of Filipinos. When the canning season was over and all itemized charges were deducted from his pay, he received only a take-home pay of $13.00. For sure, he didn't return to Alaska, but he worked later in a cannery in California.

Like a Flying Bird. On the West Coast, like a bird, Bulosan followed the seasons. He picked apples in the valleys of Washington State; he picked peas or oranges in California; he picked peas in Idaho; and he dug beets in Montana. Of course, like other Filipino workers, he also worked as a dishwasher and a houseboy. For recreation, he went to dance halls, with his friends and co-workers.

In 1936, he entered Los Angeles County Hospital, where he underwent three operations for a lesion in his right lung, His two years stay there, mostly in the convalescent ward, gave him a lot of time to think and read. A voracious reader, he read one book a day. After he was out of the hospital and was well enough but could not find a job, he usually went to the Los Angeles Public Library to read more books. At the same time, he tried to write every day. "I'm trying to write every day in the midst of utter misery and starvation," he wrote in 1949, as quoted by San Juan.

"I Can Write! I Can Write!" One day in a hotel in San Luis Obispo, California, when writing to his brother Macario, Bulosan felt the urge to write about the inhuman treatment, prejudice, and discrimination received by him from common whites and the establishment. Thus, he wrote the story of his life. Yes, his rage against society emanated words from his mind. There and then, he realized that he could write in understandable English. With tears in his eyes, he said to himself, "They can't silence me any more! I'll tell the world what they have done to me!"

"I Am Mad!" Some writers encouraged Bulosan to write. And so he did. One of his writing was a story titled *The End of the War*, which was published in the *New Yorker*. He wrote the book *The Laughter of My Father*. Although the stories were serious and even bitter, as he had intended them to be, some critics labelled him as a humorist. Bulosan was angered and said, "I am mad because when my book *The Laughter of My Father* was published by Harcourt, Brace & Company, the critics called me 'the manifestation of the pure comic spirit.'"

Thus, Bulosan kept on writing. He became a writer of essays, short stories, novels, and poetry. He contributed essays and short stories to newspapers and magazines. And later he became a novelist. It was in 1937 that Bulosan contracted tuberculosis; his health declined.

Bulosan and other writers such as Ninotchka Rosca, Jessica Hagedorn, Bienvenido Santos, NVM Gonzales, and Linda Ty-Casper, are contributors to the newly released title *Flippin: Filipinos on America*, a book on Filipino Americans.

Besides being a writer, Bulosan became a radical labor organizer and newspaper editor. Some of the labor groups he worked with were the ones who later organized the United Farm Workers of America.

"Many Laughs Together." Bulosan loved to drink. According to McWilliams, in his introduction to the book *America Is in the Heart*, Stanley P. Garibay, who also knew Bulosan, told him once that he and Bulosan had "many laughters together" and that the Filipino writer's "poetical babbles" occurred when he (Bulosan) had a little drinking. (Garibay used to edit a journal of Filipino poetry.)

His Last Day on Earth. After a night of drinking and strolling on the streets of Seattle, Bulosan was found unconscious on the lawn of the King Country Courthouse in Seattle. He was brought to the Harborview Medical Center, where he died of pneumonia in September 1956. He was 42.

"Here the Tomb of Bulosan Is." On the black granite tombstone in a corner of Mount Pleasant Cemetery on Queen Anne Hill in Seattle, is inscribed an epitaph the Filipino writer had written earlier: "Here, here the tomb of Bulosan is. Here, here are his words, dry as the grass is." On the top part of this epitaph is written:

Carlos Bulosan
1914 - 1956

With the reemergence of his book *America Is in the Heart*, reprinted in 1996, and the releasing of his novels *On Becoming Filipino* and *The Cry and the Dedication* published by Temple University Press), Bulosan may finally reap the respect as an outstanding man of literature and receive the recognition he has long deserved. That is, he was the best Filipino writer of his time and his writings are still relevant to today's political issues and happenings.

BUNDA, ROBERT. Hawaii State Senator.

Robert Bunda is a state senator in the Hawaii State Assembly. Elected in the 1994 elections, he did not resign from the Hawaii Senate to run (and lose) in the second congressional district race in the November 1996 elections. Thus, he remained in the Senate. He represents the Kunia-Wahiawa-Waialua-Sunset Beach district. Wahiawa, which has a 27-percent Filipino population.

First Elected as a State Representative. Bunda first held public office when he was elected to the Hawaii House of Representatives in 1983. He was elected to the Hawaii Senate in the 1994 elections.

Family. Married to the former Gail Shimao, Bunda and his wife have five children.

CABANA, VENERACION G., Ph.D. Research Scientist/Educator.

Dr. Veneracion G. Cabana is a senior research associate in the Department of Pathology of the University of Chicago (Division of Biological Sciences and the Pritzker School of Medicine). Her background includes teaching and research at colleges and universities in the Philippines, Mexico, and the United States.

Child of War: Not Named Bombita. Born in Lopez, Quezon Province, Philippines, on January 9, 1942, a few days after the bombing of Pearl Harbor and the Japanese invasion of the Philippines, Cabana was a child war. She often jokes that with her classmates named Warlita, Warry, and Evacue, she is glad her parents did not name her *Dyanamita* (feminine of dynamite) or *Bombita* (female bomb).

After finishing a bachelor of science degree at the Philippine Union College in Manila and teaching at the same school for four years, she immigrated to the United States on August 8, 1968. She pursued her dream of a higher education, obtaining a Cytotechnology Certificate from the University of Chicago where she worked as a cytotechnologist, becoming a supervisor within a year. She pursued graduate studies under grants and scholarships at the University of Illinois Medical Center in Chicago, and finished both a master of science and a doctor of philosophy degrees.

Likes Investigating Lipids. For the past 20 years, she has been conducting bench-top investigations regarding blood lipids (fats, cholesterol, triglycerides) and their lipoprotein carriers at some of the leading research centers in the United States, including the Northwest Lipid Research Center of the University of Washington in Seattle, and the Specialized Center of Research in Atherosclerosis of the University of Chicago. She has participated in studies that have become the basis for the present public awareness regarding the health risks of high blood cholesterol level. The results of her studies have been presented at national and international scientific conferences.

Author. Dr. Cabana is the leading author in a number of articles published in scientific books and journals. She is a Fellow of the Council in Atherosclerosis of the American Heart Association and a former secretary-treasurer of the Chicago Association of Immunologists. She received a grant award from the American Heart Association as the principal investigator in a project to study lipoprotein/cholesterol alterations precipitated by acute illnesses.

Travels Across U.S.A. Outside the academic setting, Dr. Cabana travels across the USA and abroad conducting lectures and seminars on health maintenance and disease prevention. Her most recent trip abroad (February 2-8, 1997) brought her to a nightly audience of about 3,000 to 4,000 people at the Philippine International Convention Center in Manila. She is also a member of the Seventh-day Adventist denomination whose dietary and lifestyle practices have been widely recognized as models for health.

Awards. In recognition of her contributions to science and health, she received a 1989 Most Outstanding Alumni Award from the Philippine Union College Alumni Association in Silang, Cavite, Philippines, a 1996 Outstanding Alumni Award from the Philippine Union College Alumni Association of Western North America in Palm Springs, California and a 1997 Outstanding Alumni Award from the Adventists University of the Philippines, Silang, Cavite Province, Philippines. She lives with her mother and an older sister in Westmont, Illinois, and is active in the community affairs of Filipino Americans in her area.

CABALQUINTO, LUIS. Writer-Poet. Luis Cabalquinto writes fiction, non-fiction, and poetry in English as well as in two Philippine languages: Pilipino and Bikolano. He has also done translations from Spanish into English and Pilipino. His written work has appeared in many magazines and anthologies published in the United States, France, Australia, the Czech Republic, Hongkong, and in the Philippines. He

has had three books of poetry published: *The Dog-eater and Other Poems,* 1989; *The Ibalon Collection,* 1991; and *Dreamwandere,* 1992.

Fellowships and Awards. Cabalquinto is the recipient of many fellowships and awards, including the Dylan Thomas Poetry Award from the New School for Social Research; an Academy of American Poets prize from New York University;

a Fellowship Award in Poetry from the New York Foundation for the Arts; and a Fulbright-Hays travel grant from the U.S. State Department.

"The Fog": First Fiction Prize. Most recently, his poem "Hometown" was included in three American college textbooks: *New Worlds of Literature,* published by W.W. Norton & Co., New York; *Literature: Reading and Responding to Fiction, Poetry, Drama, and the Essay,* published by HarperCollins College Publishers, New York; and *Literature and Ourselves,* published by HarperCollins College Division, New York. A story, "The Fog," won his first fiction prize from the weekly magazine *Philippine Graphic,* which is published in Manila. His current projects include magazine articles, a new collection of poetry, a book of short stories, plays, and a first novel.

Aside from being a full-time free-lance writer, Cabalquinto is also a part-time lecturer. He has given lectures and readings at the American Museum of Natural History, PEN American Center, Dalton School, Writers' Community, Hunter College, Queens College, Sarah Lawrence College, University of Maryland, St. Mark's Poetry Project, and many others.

To the Philippines and Back. Cabalquinto divides his writing time between his Bicol hometown, Magarao, in the Philippines and New York City, where he

has been a resident for 26 years. He has a bachelor of arts degree in journalism from the University of the Philippines and did graduate work in creative writing at Cornell University and New York University.

CACHOLA, ROMY. Hawaii State Representative. A member of the Hawaii State House of Representatives, Romy Cachola ran unopposed and was reelected for the seventh time to the State House, representing the Kai-Kapalama-Mapunapuna district of Hawaii during the November 1996 elections. He was reelected for the sixth time to the State house in the 1994 November elections. Cachola first sought public office in 1984 and won the 39th District seat in the

Hawaii House of Representatives.

Awards. Born on March 8, 1938, Cachola obtained his law degree from the Quezon University in Manila. Immigrating to Hawaii on February 14, 1971, Cachola has won numerous awards, among which are Public Servant of the Year, 1990, from the *Community Advocate Magazine* and the Distinguished Legislator Award, from the

Democratic State Legislative Leaders Association. The latter award was presented to him at the August 1990 National Conference of State Legislators in Tennessee.

Affiliations. Cachola's affiliations include: member of the board of directors of Kalihi YMCA, Kalihi Business Association, Susannah Wesley Community Center; honorary chairman, Statewide Sakada Committee; past president of the Waipahu Business Association; and member, Ilocos Surian Association of Hawaii.

Family. Married to Dr. Erlinda M. Cachola, M.D., he and his wife have two children: Lyla Marie Cachola Estioco, and Earl Mark Anthony Cachola.

CAGAS, COSME R., M.D. Pediatrician, Pediatric Endocrinologist, and "Father of PEACE." Best known for being the founding president of Philippine Economic and Cultural Endowment (PEACE), Dr. Cosme R. Cagas, is a first-rate physician, a talented academician, and a productive medical researcher. A multi-award-winning doctor, he is the recipient of the Physician of the Year Award in 1989

from the Association of Philippine Physicians in America.

In recognition of his achievements as the founding president of PEACE, Cagas was honored at a gala dinner-dance at the Chicago Hilton Hotel on July 24, 1996 by members of PEACE on the occasion of the 10th PEACE anniversary celebration. (PEACE was founded by Cagas in 1986, soon after the

People Power Revolution in the Philippines that toppled the late President Ferdinand Marcos. PEACE is purely a humanitarian foundation that builds artesian wells and other water systems, especially in rural areas in the Philippines, and raises funds for victims of natural calamities, including typhoons.)

Flashback. Dr. Cagas, an entrance scholar and college scholar, attended the University of the Philippines where he studied pre-medicine. He graduated from the same university with a degree in medicine in 1960.

In 1961, Cagas left for the United States to take up post-graduate education. He interned at the Menorah Medical Center. In 1962, he took his residency in pediatrics at the Children's Mercy Hospital in Kansas City, Missouri. In 1963, he took his residency in pediatrics at the University of Kansas Medical Center in Kansas City, Kansas. From 1964 to 1966, he was a fellow in pediatric endocrinology and metabolism at the National Institute of Health and Human Development at the University of Oklahoma, Oklahoma City, Oklahoma.

Teaching Positions. Dr. Cagas' teaching positions include assistant professor of pediatrics, University of the Philippines, Manila, 1966-1973; assistant professor of pediatrics and adolescent medicine, University of Oklahoma, Oklahoma City, 1973-1976; assistant clinical professor to clinical professor of pediatrics (endocrinology) at St. Louis University in St. Louis, Missouri, 1976-1993; and professor of pediatrics and family practice at Southern Illinois University from 1978-1996.

Association Positions. Dr. Cagas was president of the Philippine Society of Endocrinology and Metabolism, 1970-1971; president of the Bulacan Medical Society, 1971-1972; speaker, House of Delegates, Philippine Medical Association (Philippines), 1971-1973; founder, Association of Filipino Physicians in Southern Illinois, 1977; and founding president of the University of the Philippines Medical Association in America; and president of the Filipino American Historical Society, 1992-1994. He is the president-elect of the Philippine Pediatric Society in America.

Experience in Medical Journalism. Dr. Cagas was the founding editor of *Bulacan Medicine,* 1967-1970; managing editor of the *Philippine Journal of Pediatrics,* 1968-1973; editor of the *Proceedings, Philippine Society of Endocrinology and Metabolism,* 1970-1972; editor, literary editor, etc., of the *Philippine American Medical Bulletin,* 1979-1995; associate editor of *Acta Medica Philippina,* 1970-1972; associate or contributing editor to newsletters, PMA Greater St. Louis and AFPSI, 1978-1990; and founding editor of the *Philippine ILLINI,* 1978-1982.

Awards. Dr. Cagas is the recipient of numerous awards. In addition to the Physician of the Year Award from the APPA, his awards include a presidential award from Dr. Carmelo C. Dichoso, president of the APPA, 1989; "Father of PEACE" award from Dr. Antonio R. Abiog in Atlantic City, New Jersey, in 1991; Special PEACE Humanitarian Award, 1991; two-time awardee as Most Outstanding Physician of Bulacan by the Philippine Medical Association, Philippines. He has been cited in the Marquis *Who's Who in the World*

since 1995. He has also received numerous research awards from different organizations.

Private Practice. Dr. Cagas, who specializes in pediatrics, pediatric endocrinology, and adolescent medicine, operates his medical clinic, the Belleville Pediatric and Adolescent Medicine, in Belleville, Illinois.

CALUD, ANNETTE, *Sesame Street* **Dance Instructor.** Born in Milwaukee, Wisconsin, Annette Calud has played the role of Celina, a Filipina American dance instructor in "Sesame Street." She has also played the lead role in "Miss Saigon," which she quit in 1995 to join the Children's Television Workshop.

CARRERE, TIA. Movie Actress and Singer. About ten years ago, Carrere, born in Hawaii, came to the U.S. mainland to seek her destiny in Hollywood. Today, she's movie star of Filipino descent. Carrere describes her heritage as part Filipino, Spanish, and Chinese. "Yeah, I'm Filipino, Spanish, and Chinese from Hawaii and I eat pork adobo, and I embrace all of this."

Known as a Hollywood Filipino American actress who was cast in the film *Rising Sun,* in which Sean Connery and Wesley Snipes starred, Carrere hasn't forgotten her ambition to be a successful singer. She sang on the *Wayne's World* soundtrack and has also issued her own CD. Her debut CD, *Dream,* is available on Warner Bros.

Her Discovery. The recipient of a Golden Ring Award for her achievements in the film industry, Carrere was discovered by a producer's parents in a Honolulu, Hawaii, grocery store. In 1994, she was awarded the 1994 Show Best Female Star of Tomorrow by the National Association of Theatre Owners. (Juliette Lewis and Wynona Ryder were the past awardees.) She performed in several films, including *True Lies,* where she tangoed with Arnold Schwarzenegger, and in *Wayne's World.* She also appeared in *Kull the Conqueror,* in which she starred with Kevin Sorbo. Carrere, who speaks Ilocano, soared to fame as Cassandra, the Cantonese-speaking rocker woman in *Wayne's World."*

"She Could Look Like Me!" Commenting on the roles she has performed, she says, "From *Wayne's World* to *Rising Sun* to *True Lies* to *High School,* I don't try to choose things that don't really have any bearing on where you're from. Lots of time, when you go in for parts, studios will particularly say 'Oh we weren't thinking of going Asian with that role or exotic with that role.'" And commenting on the girl-next-door, she says, "I think she could look a lot like me."

Breaking Out of Her Asian Roles. Carrere and her husband have established their own film production company called Phoenician Films. Carrere's purpose in doing so was to break out of her Asian roles. So far, the company has produced the following films, in which she stars: *The Immortals, Hollow Point, Natural*

Enemy, Kull the Conqueror with Kevin Sorbo (of *Hercules* fame), and *Top of the World.*

Carrere has also been featured in such commercials as the woman in the Lipton Brisk Tea commercial.

Carrere, born as Althea Dujenio Janairo, is the daughter of Alexander Janairo, from Cebu, Philippines. Her mother Audrey's grandmother was a Filipino.

CAYETANO, BENJAMIN J. Governor, State of Hawaii. As a young boy when he was in the eighth grade, Benjamin Cayetano became interested in law as a career because of a book report on the legendary attorney Clarence Darrow. "But I never thought it could be achieved," he says. "In that society at that time," he says referring to his boyhood years in territorial Hawaii, "it was unthinkable that someone like me could have a shot at it." As a good student, he continued to study hard. However, during his junior year in high school his school work yielded to other teenage interests and he nearly flunked out of high school. "I got too interested in cars and other things," he recalls.

His Story of Hopes and Dreams. Today, Cayetano holds the distinction of being the first and only state governor of Filipino descent. In his inaugural address after he won the election in November 1994, he said, "I

take great pride in becoming our nation's and Hawaii's first governor of Filipino ancestry. My story is one of hopes and dreams, very much like those of many other Asian/Pacific American immigrants who came to America seeking a better life for themselves and their families. I am deeply grateful and honored for being given the opportunity to continue my years as a public servant in Hawaii's highest elective office."

Governor Cayetano is the son of late Bonifacio Cayetano and Eleanor Infante. His father emigrated from Urdaneta, Pangasinan, Philippines, to Hawaii in 1928. There, Bonifacio met and married Eleanor, who was born in Hawaii to parents who were originally from Siquijor, Philippines.

Facing the Hard Facts of Life. Born and raised in Honolulu's Kalihi district, the young Cayetano began facing the hard facts of life at age 7 when his parents were divorced. Raised by his father, he learned quickly how to take care of himself and his younger brother, Kenneth.

After graduating from the Farrington High School in Honolulu, Hawaii, in 1958, he held a number of odd jobs, including one as a rodman on a road survey crew earning $287 a month. Realizing that education was a key to improving himself, he attended Los Angeles Harbor College in Wilmington, California, where he earned an associate of arts degree in 1966. He then attended the University of California at Los Angeles, where he obtained his bachelor of arts in political sci-

ence in 1968, and Loyola Law School in Los Angeles, where he earned a juris doctorate in 1971. He became a prominent attorney in his own right, as a partner in the law firm of Schutter Cayetano Playdon.

Turning Point in Life. The turning point in his life took place in 1972, when his public service career began with an appointment to the Hawaii Housing Authority. In 1974, he sought his first elective office and won. He has held public ever since that first election victory. As a Democrat, Cayetano has served for over two decades in public office. He has won seven elections between 1974 and 1994. He served twelve years in the Hawaii State Legislature—two terms in the State House, from 1975 to 1978 and two terms in the State Senate from 1979 to 1986.

Long List of Awards. As a public servant, Cayetano has received a long list of awards, which have given him national and international recognition for his accomplishments. Among such awards are as follows: 1996 Harvard Foundation Leadership Award from Harvard University for his contributions to American government; 1996 Outstanding Alumni, from the American Association of Community Colleges for his outstanding contributions to his chosen field of endeavor at national or international levels in the public sector; 1995 Distinguished Leadership Award from UCLA's John E. Anderson Graduate School of Management, given to those who "distinguish themselves through their outstanding leadership" and "selfless contributions of time and energy to the public and the community"; 1995 Honorary Doctor of Law Degree from the University of the Philippines, Diliman, Quezon City, Philippines; 1995 Award for Ethics in Government from the Hawaii chapter of the American Society of Public Administration for his contributions to ethics in public administration; 1993 Award for Excellence in Public Service from the UCLA Alumni Association for his work with A+ After-school Program; 1993 Award of Merit, from the University of Hawaii, College of Education, for his contributions to education and for his chairmanship and handling of 1991 Task Force on Educational Governance; 1991 Excellence in Leadership medallion, from the Asia-Pacific Consortium for Public Health, for his work on the A+ After-school Program.

Taking Action. While serving in the Hawaii State Legislature, Cayetano championed legislation in key problem areas. He:

■ chaired the Senate investigative committee that uncovered mismanagement of the 1982 heptachlor crisis;

■ served as primary conferee on the Senate committee that developed the 1985 plan to safeguard and reimburse depositors in the Manoa Finance Company;

■ helped establish the First Hula Mae Loan Program to provide low-interest housing loans;

■ was instrumental in enacting laws that required automobile insurance companies to provide premium rollbacks and to increase no-fault coverage;

■ authored legislation to establish the first program in Hawaii to test Vietnam veterans suffering from the effect of Agent Orange; and

■ authored the law creating the Pacific International Center for High Technology Research at the University of Hawaii.

"The American Dream Is a Never-Ending Journey." Governor Cayetano believes that Filipinos have not yet achieved the American dream. He once said, "The journey toward the American dream is a never-ending journey. You have to try to gain respect for our people. When I'm gone somebody younger must have to pick up the baton and keep on going, whether in politics or in business."

CHAVEZ, REGGIE. City Official, Tacoma Park, Maryland. Reggie Chavez, who immigrated to the United States in 1971, was elected to the six-member city council of Tacoma Park, Maryland, in October 1993. His term expired in 1995. Thus, he became the first Filipino American and Asian member of the council's 103-year. He is a paralegal who specializes in immigration cases. Chavez, 59, is married to Lydia. They have five children: Relyd, Jonathan, Eldred, Jerson, and Lester.

CHUA, FARIDA Q. ISIP, M.D. Accomplished Pediatrician and Mother. Born on July 1st in Macabebe, Pampanga, Philippines, Farida Quiambao Isip, a high school scholar from Centro Escolar University, obtained her Doctor of Medicine degree with honors at the Far Eastern University in Manila, Philippines, in 1961.

She married the president of her class, Philip S. Chua, on June 21, 1959. Two years earlier, Chua who was attracted to Farida, wanted to court her. During a sophomore medical class presidential election, Farida voted for their classmate Romy Taruc, her province-mate and son of the well-known, then HUK Supremo, Luis Taruc. The opponent of Romy Taruc was Chua. The later won the election. Knowing how Farida voted, Chua pursued her with even more vigor. The rest is history.

Together, They Fly. Farida came to the United States together with her husband in 1963 and interned at the Ravenswood Hospital. She obtained her pediatric residency training at the Grant Hospital and Cook County Hospital, both in Chicago, Illinois. While she was in training, she was a busy mother of three. By 1969, she and Philip had five children. While her husband trained as a fellow in cardiovascular surgery under the renowned heart transplant surgeon Denton A. Cooley of the Texas Heart Institute in Houston, Texas, Farida worked as a physician at the Elgin State Hospital and the Chicago Board of Health to help support their family. Philip would fly back home to Chicago each month to be with Farida and their children for a weekend. How Farida juggled her time to be a successful pediatrician and mother of five can be a source of inspiration to many career-women-to-be.

Beds Are Not Made of Roses Without Thorns. In 1980, Farida was elected president of the Women's Auxiliary of the Philippine Medical Association in Chi-

cago and the Midwest. Former U.P. College Dean Andres L. Abejo, Ph.D., in his book *The Philippines Who's Who in America* (1983) wrote: Farida "was very articulate in encouraging colleagues to be really supportive of their physician-husband." In the book *Filipino Physicians in America*, author Pat R. Mamot, Ph.D., was quite touched by the same inaugural speech of Farida, and quoted her in his book: "There are two friends of our association who are missing tonight—Mrs. Joseph Cari, president of the Chicago Medical Auxiliary, and her husband. Last Thursday, I received the sad news from Mrs. Cari about the untimely passing of her husband. I was suddenly jolted into the realization that our husband was not indestructible, and that time with him was short and very precious. So, while we are still able to, while our loved one is still with us, let us appreciate him and let him know that we do. Let us be more tolerant of his temperamental moods...Let us enjoy his company as long as we could. Let us support him all the way. Let us remember that in his profession, the beds are not made of roses without thorns...Let us grow old with him and walk by his side up to the horizon beyond." The speech was honored with a standing ovation.

Dr. Chua is a past board director and secretary of the Asian-American Medical Society of Northwest Indiana, and a recipient of the Circulo Capampangan Recognition Award in 1984.

Farida Isip Chua, M.D., is currently a practicing pediatrician in Merrillville, Indiana, and has two associates. She lives with her husband Philip in Munster, Indiana. Their five children are Sheillah Chua-Gentile, M.D. (Anthony N. Gentile, M.D.); Felipe I. Chua, Jr. M.D.; Portia Chua-Gonzales, M.D. (Luisito C. Gonzales, M.D.); Rachel Chua-Brown, M.D. (James M. Brown III, M.D.); and Emily Chua-Greenlee, M.D. (Jeremy Greenlee, M.D.). They have two grandchildren: Evan Anthony Gentile and Sydney Elizabeth Brown.

CHUA, HOWARD. Time Magazine Senior Editor. While still in college, Howard Chua, 36, applied for a job at two top publications: *Time* and the *Wall Street Journal*. He got a job as a secretary—one day a week. Chua seemed to have loved the publication atmosphere and he entered a journalism course at Columbia University in New York.

From Where Is He? Chua at the age of 20 quit the University of the Philippines in Quezon City, Philippines, where he took pre-medicine courses. He and his family headed for the United States in 1979.

New York, Here He Comes. Chua and his family probably got tired of California after six months, and left for New York, where he took English literature course at Columbia University, forgetting about becoming a doctor. "I wanted to write," he was quoted to have said in a feature story about him in the September 1996 issue of *Filipinas* magazine.

Chua was first appointed at *Time* as a reporter and researcher. He has been a senior editor at *Time* for the past five years.

CHUA, PHILIP S., M.D. Well-known Cardiac Surgeon. There are only a handful of Filipino heart surgeons in the United States, and Dr. Philip S. Chua, a cardiac surgeon in northwest Indiana, is without any doubt, among the most distinguished of them all.

Dr. Chua, the president of the Philippine Heart, Inc. (USA) and his Indiana team have just been granted by Dr. Potenciano V. Larrazabal, Jr., chairman and president of the prestigious Cebu Doctors' Hospital (CDH), an exclusive contract to provide cardiac surgery services at the Cebu Cardiovascular Center of CDH in Cebu City, Philippines. Dr. Chua who helped plan and establish the Cebu Cardiovascular Center in early 1996, and inaugurate it on November 21, 1997 by performing its first open heart surgery, was appointed chairman of the cardiovascular surgery department of this heart center.

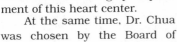

At the same time, Dr. Chua was chosen by the Board of Trustees of the Far Eastern University to deliver the coveted 1998 Dean Lauro H. Panganiban Memorial Lecture on January 14, 1998 at FEU Hospital in Manila.

Flashback. On March 13, 1972, while a Fellow in Cardiovascular Surgery at the world-renowned Texas Heart Institute in Houston, Texas, he organized the Residents and Fellows at THI and founded the Denton A. Cooley Cardiovascular Surgical Society, naming it in honor of his mentor, the surgeon-in-chief of the Texas Heart Institute. Dr. Chua was elected its first president.

On March 7, 1997, the society celebrated its 25th year anniversary at the Westin Oaks Hotel in Houston and Dr. Chua led his peers in paying tribute to this teacher before a capacity-filled room of heart surgeons from various parts of the world. Dr. Cooley has trained more than 750 heart surgeons from 51 countries around the globe, including the United States.

"I told Phil it would not last a year...and here we are twenty-five years later," Dr. Cooley smilingly said in appreciation of the vision of this Filipino heart surgeon, a loyal student of his.

Dr. Chua, even as early as after his graduation from medical school in 1961, where he was consistently the president of his class, already had a brash with history. He was the pioneer medical volunteer of the Work-a-Year-with-the-People Project of then-Senator Raul Manglapus, Manuel Quezon, Jr., and Ramon Magsaysay, Jr. He was assigned to provide healthcare to the people of Palanan, Isabela, Philippines, where General Emilio Aguinaldo was captured by the Americans in 1901, the event that officially ended the Philippine-American War. Knowing this, Dr. Chua met with the town officials and then organized the community of Palanan for the erection of a monument honoring the gallantry of Aguinaldo and his men. This came to pass and the monument was unveiled July 4, 1962,

during the Philippine Independence Day celebration, and to this day, still stands proudly as a living testament to the Filipinos' valor and clamor for freedom against foreign invaders.

Benigno Aquino's Friend. During the Marcos dictatorship, this Indiana heart surgeon was with Ninoy Aquino the late husband of President-to-be Corazon Aquino), Senator Raul Manglapus, Senator Heherson Alvarez, Governor Bonnie Gallego, and others rallying the Filipinos in the United States and the U.S. government to topple the autocratic regime back home in the Philippines. These leaders met at his home in Munster, Indiana, about 20 miles south of downtown Chicago. In his last visit to Munster before he was assassinated in Manila, Aquino had a medical checkup by Dr. Chua. Earlier that year, he was a guest of the Aquinos in their home in Boston, Massachusetts.

Leads Balikbayan Movement. When he was president of the Association of Philippine Physicians in America (APPA) in 1986, Dr. Chua spearheaded a nationwide balikbayan movement among physicians in the United States. The massive homecoming that December witnessed President Corazon C. Aquino as the keynote speaker of the APPA General Assembly at the Manila Hotel. Then General Fidel V. Ramos (now President of the Philippines) addressed the balikbayan doctors the following day. This trek home has since been a yearly tradition of the APPA.

Editor and Magician. Dr. Chua has been the editor-in-chief of *the Philippine Surgeon* since 1975, and was the editor-in-chief of the *Lake and Porter Counties Medical Journal* in northwest Indiana for eight years, the first non-Caucasian to hold this prestigious post. He is also a member of the International Brotherhood of Magicians and has performed magic and illusions at medical meetings in various cities in the United States.

In Private Practice. Dr. Chua is in private practice of cardiovascular surgery in northwest Indiana under the name of Cardiovascular Surgery Associates, a corporation he started in September 1972. His two associates are Victor K. O'Yek, M.D. and James J. McFarland, M.D.

On Heart Surgeries in China. In 1989 and in 1991, Dr. Chua, his partner, Dr. O'Yek and their cardiovascular surgery team flew to the Orient and performed almost two dozen open heart surgeries at the First Teaching Hospital at the invitation of the Beijing Medical University in Beijing, China.

Awards. Dr. Chua is a former president of the Beta Sigma Fraternity, the Philippine Medical Association in Chicago, the Society of Philippine Surgeons in America (SPSA), and the American Heart Association (NWI). He was the recipient of the Sagamore of the Wabash Award in 1996, the highest civilian award bestowed by Governor Evan Bayh of Indiana. A graduate of the Far Eastern University (FEU Class '61) in Manila, he is currently the president of the FEU Medical Alumni Foundation in America.

Family. He is married to Farida Isip-Chua, M.D. of Macabebe, Pampanga, a pediatrician. They have five children, all of whom are physicians, and four married to physicians. Their grandchildren are Evan Chua Gentile and Sydney Elizabeth Chua Brown.

CLEMENTE, LILIA CALDERON. International Money Manager. One of the best money managers on Wall Street, Lilia Calderon Clemente is chairman and chief executive of Clemente Capital, Inc. (CCI), chairman of the Clemente Global Growth Fund, Inc. (CGGFI), and president and a director of the First Philippine Fund.

Gross Assets. The total gross assets of the above corporations, as of December 1997, were as follows:

Clemente Capital, Inc. — $163.9 million; 97.3 million sterling.

Clemente Global Growth Fund, Inc. — $73.0 million; 43.4 million sterling.

First Philippine Fund — $90.9 million; 54.0 million sterling.

The Clemente Capital is an active equity and fixed income advisor specializing in the Pacific Basin and in emerging markets. In 1995, Clemente Capital was awarded the California Pension Fund, an $83-billion account. Clemente is the first Asian American company to manage the New York City Pension Funds.

Investments. The Clemente Global Growth Fund, a closed-end fund, invests in companies in the United States and in emerging companies in such traditional markets as the US, Japan, Canada, and West Germany, and in such emerging blue chips markets as Spain, Thailand, Taiwan, and Korea. On the other hand, the Philippine Fund, a closed-end investment management company, invests in equity securities in Philippine companies.

Flashback. Born in the Philippines, Clemente came to the U.S. in 1960 to study at the University of Chicago in Chicago, Illinois, where she obtained a master's degree in economics. Eventually, she landed a job at the Ford Foundation, where she managed a $3- billion portfolio. Then she managed Paine Webber's Atlas Fund, a global mutual fund that became popular with smaller investors and was ranked the top global fund in 1985.

Husband-and-Wife Team. Lilia's husband, Leopoldo Clemente, runs the day-to-day operations of Clemente Capital, while she analyzes trends and plots investment strategy.

Praise. Asiaweek magazine called her the "Wonder Woman of Wall Street." *Financial World* dubbed her the "Philippine Tigress." And *Forbes* magazine tagged her "one of the very hottest of money global managers."

Award. For her accomplishments, Clemente received the *Pamana ng Pilipino* award in 1996 from President Fidel V. Ramos of the Philippines at award ceremonies held at Malacanang in Manila. She was one of the 45 outstanding overseas individuals and organizations that were given presidential awards.

CORONADO, WIL AND ZEN. Cosmetics Magnates. More than a decade ago, husband and wife Wil and Zen Coronado worked as part-time sales representatives of Fashion Dynamics, a distributor of skin care products, vitamins, and cosmetics. Eventually, Zen, after making big money, left her job as a clinical coordinator in nursing in a county hospital to work full-time in her business. Later, Wil, a senior mechanical engineer with the Bechtel Corporation, also gave up his job and joined his wife to work full-time as well. They worked as a team.

Turning Point of their Lives.
On the third year of its existence, Fashion Dynamics had revenues of over $13 million and the Coronados became the top leaders and "producers" of the company. But in 1986, the Coronados left the company, after Fashion Dynamics closed shop due to financial troubles, reportedly caused by mismanagement. The couple thought of an idea: Why not form a skin

care and cosmetic company for their existing distributors who had been with them since the beginning? And they did. In 1988, Wil and Zen established Zinnellé International, Inc., and kept the chemists of Fashion Dynamics in the newly established company. Today, Zinnellé International is a multi-million-dollar cosmetics company with revenues of $15.8 million a year.

Award. In 1996, in recognition of his accomplishments, Wil, who is president and CEO of Zinnellé International, was awarded with a Doctorate of Science Honoris Causa by the Adam Smith University of America in Iowa for his "leadership and contribution in the sphere of biochemical and health sciences." He received his award at a convocation and investiture ceremony held at St. George Church in Flushing, New York City, on November 23, 1996.

Comments about Their Products. Wil Coronado says, "While our competitors talk about how good their products are, we are slowly earning the respect of thousands of our distributors and customers because of the dramatic results our products give them."

For her part, Zen, who is the executive vice president of Zinnellé, says, "Great efforts have been made in choosing non-irritants. The key ingredients are natural, such as papaya enzymes; black tea; vitamins C, E, and A; jojoba oil, which is a natural oil and healing agent; and herbal extracts imported from all over the world. And we were also among the first to introduce fruit acid into the skin care industry."

International Publicity. Zinnellé International gained international publicity when it was chosen as an official sponsor of the 1994 Miss Universe Pageant held in Manila, Philippines. Their anti-aging hightech skin care and other products were used on all 78 candidates from different countries of the world. Moreover, each candidate was given gift packs of perfumes, cosmetics, skin care, and oral hygiene products. The Coronados flew to Manila to attend the Miss Universe Pageant (the only U.S. sponsor to attend the worldwide pageant.) In 1996, Zinnellé International again was an official sponsor of Miss Universe Pageant that was held in Las Vegas, Nevada. The Durafresh oral hygiene products were used by all the candidates.

Network Marketing. Zinnellé International manufactures such products as oral hygiene, skin care, perfumes, and cosmetics. The company is selling its products directly to customers through their network of distributors, in multi-level marketing. Its commercial accounts include beauty salons, boutiques, and dentists that sell products directly to consumers.

Inventory and Assets. Having distributors, not only in the United States, but also in Asia, Europe, and South America, Zinnellé International is now worth $100 million in inventory and $40 million in liquid assets. The company's biggest manufacturing plant is located in Sao Paulo, Brazil, aside from the other two laboratories in California.

Flashback. Wil is a graduate of the University of Santo Tomas in Manila, Philippines, while Zen is a graduate of the Philippine Women's University, also in Manila. They married in 1968 in the Philippines and left for the United States the same year. They have a son, Paul, who has a degree in business management, and who is the vice president for sales and marketing for the company. Their daughter, Zara, is in medical school and helps out her dad in the administration of the company.

CRUZ, JR., JOSE B. The Howard D. Winbigler Chair in Engineering, Ohio State University.

Jose B. Cruz, Jr. has attained distinction and recognition worldwide in his technical field of systems control, science, and engineering; in leadership in national and international professional organizations; in engineering education; and in engineering education administration.

Born on September 17, 1932, in Bacolod City, Philippines, Cruz came to the United States to attend the Massachusetts Institute of Technology, where he received his master's degree in electrical engineering.

Dean of College of Engineering. A graduate of the

University of the Philippines College of Engineering, where he graduated *summa cum laude*, he served as the dean of the College of Engineering at Ohio State University, 1992-1997. Before his appointment at Ohio State, Cruz was the associate head of the Department of Electrical and Computer Engineering from 1984 to 1986 at the University of Illinois where he obtained his doctorate in engineering. Next, he became chairman of the

Department of Electrical and Computer Engineering at the University of California at Irvine in 1986.

Awards. Among honors and awards he has received are the following: Membership in the National Academy of Engineering (NAE), where membership is considered as the highest honor that an American engineer can receive; Curtis W. McGraw Research Award from the American Society for Engineering Education (ASEE), 1972; fellow of the Institute of Electrical and Electronics Engineers (IEEE) that honored him with a Centennial Medal, 1984 and the Richard M. Emberson Award, 1989; fellow of the American Association for the Advancement of Science, 1989; Richard E. Bellman Control Heritage Award, the highest award of the American Automatic Control Council (AACC); member of the Board of Examiners for Professional Engineers in the State of Illinois, 1984 to 1986. Concurrently, he served as a member of the National Council of Engineering Examiners (NCEE). Cruz has also authored and co-authored six textbooks and has edited books in electrical engineering.

Family. Married to Stella E. Rubia, Cruz and his wife have five children: Fe Cruz Langdon; Rick Cruz; Rene Cruz; Sylvia Cruz Loebach; and Lori Cruz Spray.

DADO, SPEEDY (DIOSDADO B. POSADAS). Flyweight Boxing Champion.

Speedy Dado, who was known for his quick feet and hands, won the Pacific Coast Bantamweight championship in 1932.

Born in Honolulu in 1916, Speedy Dado didn't become a world champion, although he tried unsuccessfully for the world flyweight and bantamweight titles. As a boxer, he lost to then-champion Panama's Al Brown, in spite of the fact that he sent him to the floor eleven times. As a celebrity boxer, Dado mingled with Hollywood movie stars. He also made the *Esquire* magazine's list of the world's best-dressed men. However, he lost most of his money in gambling.

DADOR, DENISE. Rising News Anchor Star in Michigan.

Born in Warrensburg, Missouri, and raised in San Francisco, California, Denise Dador is a rising star as a health reporter and a news anchor on Channel 7 in Southfield, Michigan. Filipino Americans living in the Detroit area and other parts of the state are really proud of this news broadcast star as being of their own race.

From Fresno to Detroit. Four years ago, Dador came from her job in Fresno, California, to the Detroit, Michigan, area to work for Channel 7. Since then, her

rise to fame has been meteoric. Besides her job as a health reporter, she acts as the weekend news anchor and as fill-in weeknight anchor.

Flashback. Dador, 31, was left by her father when she was a year old. Being an only child, she was raised by her grandmother in San Francisco, California, while her mother pursued her education. (Her mother is currently a professor of Asian American studies at the University of Colorado.) At the age of 14, when her grandmother died, her mother moved in to the grandmother's San Francisco home.

Her first job was as a general assignment reporter for KMPH-TV in Fresno, California. She was a main anchor there before she left for Detroit. With her application for the Channel 7 job, Dador enclosed a photo of herself with Connie Chung, a former national network anchor, with whom she has often been compared. to.

DAYAO, FIRMO S. Police Commissioner, Honolulu, Hawaii. Considered as one of the most outstanding Filipino leaders in Hawaii, Firmo S. Dayao was appointed as one of the seven police commissioners in the Honolulu Police Commission in 1992. His appointment was unanimously confirmed by the Honolulu City Council. He was sworn in by Honolulu Mayor F. Fasi. His term of office expired on December 31, 1995.

Memberships. Dayao, the holder of a master's degree, has been president of the Oahu Visayan Council and president and governor of the Visayan Congress of Hawaii. He is married to the former Olivia Solis, owner of Inter-Travel of Honolulu.

DE CASTRO, ROLANDO A., D.M.D., M.S.D. Well-Known Dental Professor-Artist. A dentist who immigrated to the United States in 1968, Dr. Rolando A. De Castro once said, "I wanted an opportunity to use my talent as a dentist-artist like Dr. Frank H. Netter was a physician-artist and whom I greatly admired."

With Dr. Netter's encouragement, Dr. De Castro pursued his dream of becoming a successful dental artist. This was soon realized with the help from Dr. Maynard K. Hine who was then president of the American Dental Association and dean of the Indiana University School of Dentistry. Many years after, this dentist from Malabon, Rizal, Philippines, has produced many works of art, including a monumental work, "The Historical Mural," a 6 1/2 feet by 28 feet mural displayed at the Indiana University School of Dentistry in Indianapolis, Indiana.
The mural traced some 4,000 years of the history of dentistry. Besides being a dental professor, teaching for 25 years at the university, he was also the director of the Dental Illustrations Department.

Author. De Castro became an author. Co-authoring with Drs. Arens and Adams, their dental textbooks have been translated into several languages; they are now in use in many dental schools and private clinics in North America, South America, Italy, Spain, and other countries. In recognition of his services for 25 years at the Indiana University School of Dentistry, he was given the title of "Professor Emeritus," when he retired from his professorship post at the School of Dentistry.

Works of Art. One of De Castro's best works was a unique animated display about tooth decay prevention exhibited at the noted Children's Museum in Indianapolis. De Castro did an oil painting of Saint Apollonia, patron saint of dentistry at the Indiana University School of Dentistry. He also made a bronze sculpture of Dean Emeritus Ralph McDonald. His more than 100 artworks are in international and private collections.

Memberships. De Castro is a member of the American Dental Association; Indiana Dental Association and other organized dental associations; Omicron Kappa Upsilon; Association of Medical Illustrators; and other societies. He is a fellow of the American College of Dentists.

Awards and Honors. A member of the Association of Medical Illustrators, De Castro won numerous first prizes and other top awards for the Indiana University School of Dentistry in national contests for continuing education. He has also received awards and honors from other organizations, including one from the Cavite Association of America that gave him an award for being one of the Most Outstanding Filipinos in education in the Midwest in 1985.

Present Endeavors. De Castro is the consumer advocate member on the Indiana Board of Pharmacy. He was appointed and commissioned to the position for a four-year term by Indiana Governor Evan Bayh in 1994. At present, he is the president of C. M. De Castro, Inc., a family business enterprise that operates Concha's Oriental Cuisine.

Family. He was married to the late Concepcion "Connie" De Castro. His children are Evangeline Tarquinio, Marie Clemens, Rolando De Castro, Jr., and Arlene Robinson. All are married.

DELA CRUZ, PEDRO. Member, Hawaii House of Representatives. Pedro dela Cruz migrated to Hawaii and worked as a driver on a sugar cane plantation. Later, he became a foreman. In 1974, after working for ten years, he was charged by the Dole Pineapple Company, allegedly for incompetence. He and his union claimed that he was relieved of his duties for his union activities. He then engaged in business in Lanai City and then he entered politics. He lost twice in his bid for a seat in the Hawaii House of Representatives. In 1958, he won in his third attempt. That election resulted in his 16-year career in the territorial and state legislatures. In the state legislature, he served as vice speaker of the house. He was defeated in 1974.

DELACRUZ, PROSY C. ABARQUEZ. Administrator and Community Activist. Prosy C. Abarquez Delacruz is a southern California administrator, the highest ranking Filipino American peace officer in the California Department of Health Services' Food and Drug Branch, headquartered in Los Angeles, California. As such, she provides executive leadership and management oversight to regulations, law enforcement, compliance activities on various public health issues associated with the manufacturing of pharmaceuticals, medical devices, cosmetics, and processed foods in California. She supervises directly a team of 6 supervising investigators and indirectly over 30 plus investigators and clerical staff, with a budget of over $7 million.

As an administrator, she has participated in a number of initiatives to provide customer-oriented services in state government, including handling emergencies and disasters and streamlined licensing procedures for manufacturers. She is a member of the branch's leadership team, providing executive leadership, guidance, and oversight to branch activities and is a co-leader of the food program team for the entire state.

Flashback. Born and raised in the Philippines, Delacruz received her bachelor's of science degree in food technology from the University of the Philippines at age 19. Thereafter, she immigrated to the United States. While working full-time, she completed her juris doctor degree from Whittier College School of Law at age 29, having been on the dean's list for several semesters.

She has been nominated to the position of secretary to the Food, Drug, and Cosmetic Division of the American Society for Quality Control, which is a 130,000+ member organization. She has held memberships in the Southern California Association of Food and Drug Officials, the Western Association of Food and the Drug Officials, and Institute of Food Technologists.

Delacruz started as an investigator in 1979, and has been promoted five times since to advance to her current position.

Community Activist. As a community activist, Delacruz has served on many boards, among them the board of THE (To Help Everyone Clinic), and has completed a nine-month training course with the LDIR (Leadership Development in Interclinic Relations).

Awards and Honors. Among honors and awards she has received are: Philippine Women's Network, Recognition Award for Excellence, 1992; City of Los Angeles Human Relations Commission, Recognition Award for Cross-Cultural Understanding, 1991; and California Department of Health Services Food & Drug Branch, Recognition Award for Excellence, 1979, 1980, 1984-85.

Articles. She was the author of "Is It Because I Am a Filipino?," *Los Angeles Times*, November, 1992; and "LA's Rainbow Revolt-From Ashes to Multicultural Unity," *LA Filipino Bulletin*, November 1992.

Family. Delacruz enjoys tandem cycling with her family. She is married to Enrique B. Delacruz, Ph.D., a respected community leader and a University of California at Los Angeles-based administrator. They have two children: Corina, 13; and Carlo, 9.

DICHOSO, CARMELO C., M.D. Well-known Texas Physician. As a young boy, Carmelo C. Dichoso's obsession was to pursue a difficult—and, therefore, challenging—profession. After completing pre-law, he switched to medicine and found it to be the intellectual "nut that was hard to crack," what he was searching for. He graduated in the top five of his class at the Faculty of Medicine and Surgery, University of Santo Tomas, in Manila, Philippines. Before graduation, he received one of 12 coveted internship positions at the USAF Hospital at the Clark Air Force Base in Angeles, Pampanga Province, after passing rigorous oral and written examinations given by the hospital medical staff to medical students representing the major medical schools in the Philippines at that time.

Flashback. Born in Masbate, Masbate Province, Philippines, on July 7, 1940, Dr. Dichoso's dream was to broaden his medical training in a reputable U.S. medical center and be in the forefront of medicine. He realized that dream when he gained admission to Baylor College of Medicine in Houston, Texas, where he finished a three-year internal medicine residency course and a two-year nephrology fellowship training. Immediately thereafter, he accepted a full-time teaching position in the same institution as assistant professor of medicine. During this time, he participated in research and published several papers in medical journals as well as chapters in medical textbooks.

In 1979, Dichoso helped found the Texas Association of Philippine Physicians and became its president in 1980. Two years later, he involved himself in the Association of Philippine Physicians in America (APPA), initially as governor and later as editor-in-chief of the *APPA Quarterly* (the association's official organ which was later renamed *The Philippine Physician*).

To APPA Presidency. His outstanding performance catapulted him to the APPA presidency in 1988. His first move as president was to terminate the longstanding constitutional violation of allowing officers other than the treasurer to handle the money of the APPA. For the first time, after sixteen years of APPA history, the treasurer served as the constitutionally designated "custodian of the funds."

He also abolished the practice of reappointing certain well-entrenched individuals to important positions and, instead, appointed new and highly competent leaders. Almost simultaneously, he caused to be investigated the financial dealings of the APPA. All these moves led to turmoil and a lawsuit for libel filed by a non-reappointee against Dr. Dichoso, seven other officers, and the APPA itself. For lack of evidence, the lawsuit languished and a judge declared the defendants cleared of any wrongdoing. These developments solidified the foundations of the organization and enhanced APPA's credibility as an umbrella organization.

As APPA president, Dr. Dichoso conceptualized and carried to fruition the Annual PMA-APPA Congress. He also inaugurated the APPA Scholarship Program which has subsidized the training in the U.S. of physicians from the Philippines, after which were required to return to the Philippines to disseminate what they had learned. He also started the APPA Legal Defense Fund to be made available to Filipino physicians in the U.S. who might be victims of discriminatory practices.

Awards and Honors. Among Dr. Dichoso's many awards are: a plaque for being one of four outstanding teachers, Family Practice Residency Program, University of Texas Medical School in Houston; a certificate of Appreciation from Houston Mayor Jim McConn for "meritorious service to the community"; a plaque for "outstanding services as editor-in-chief from the APPA; a medallion for being the "conceptor" of the Annual Joint PMA-APPA Congress; an Apolinario Mabini Award for "academic excellence and outstanding contribution to the practice of medicine" from the APPA; and a Silver Jubilarian of the Year award from the UST Faculty of Medicine and Surgery.

Dr. Dichoso is married to the former Helen Jimenez.

DIRIGE, OFELIA, Ph.D., R.D., Nutritionist/Dietitian, Professor, and Founder of Kalusugan Community Services. A successful nutritionist, dietitian, and professor, Dr. Ofelia Dirige taught in Hawaii and is presently teaching at San Diego State University and California State University Los Angeles, California.

She is a founder and the executive director of the Kalusugan Community Services, an organization whose mission is to improve the health of Filipino Americans. Its program includes the prevention of violence, AIDS, smoking/drug abuse, and hypertension through proper nutrition and physical fitness. Projects are geared to the general population of Filipino Americans with emphasis on children and youth.

High School Dream. All her high school days, Dirige dreamed of being in the helping profession. She wanted first to be a medical doctor but being the second oldest from a large family of seven children, it was impossible for her parents to send her to a medical school. She next wanted to be a nurse but height requirement disqualified this aspiring 4 feet 11 inches Filipina from entering the University of the Philippines College of Nursing. She was not five feet tall, the college minimum height requirement.

Nutrition is a field closely related to the medical profession. Hence, she enrolled for a bachelor of science degree in nutrition and dietetics instead at the University of the Philippines, and interned at the Far Eastern University Hospital and Philippine General Hospital. She was topnotcher of the first Board Examination for Dietitians.

On to Hawaii. Before long, Dirige left for the University of Hawaii under an East-West Center grant and received her master's degree in nutrition. Later, she went to Los Angeles, California, where she obtained a doctorate degree in public health at the University of California at Los Angeles (UCLA). She supported herself through scholarship, research, and teaching assistantship.

Work Experience. Her work experience includes serving as a research associate at UCLA and a nutrition supervisor at the Los Angeles County Department of Health Services. She taught full-time at the University of Hawaii School of Public Health, San Diego State University Graduate School of Public Health, and at the California State University, Los Angeles Department of Health and Nutritional Science. She also taught part time at Pepperdine University in Los Angeles and at California State University at Long Beach.

They Are a Family. Her father, a lawyer, worked for the Philippine government agency that specialized in agrarian reform. Her mother was a school teacher. Both her parents (now deceased) joined Dr. Dirige in Santa Monica, California, in 1970. They were from Victoria, Tarlac Province, Philippines. All her sisters and a brother are residing in the United States. Her older sister, Perla Belo, is director of Asian Ministries for the American Baptist Church; Evelyn Resella is a commercial artist in Castaic Lake; Hector Dirige, her only brother, retired from the U.S. Navy and is working with the Immigration Department; Didi Orejudos, is a school nurse and a housewife; Julie Conte, a nurse, is director of a home health agency; and Lois Campagna is a business associate of a private company managed by her husband. Dr. Dirige lives in San Diego, California.

DITTMAR, MELISSA. 1995 Tournament of Roses Princess. Chosen as one of the six 1995 Tournament of Roses princesses during the Rose Parade in Pasadena, California, Dittmar became the second Filipina American to have been bestowed such a title. (The first, Erica Beth Brynes, was selected as one of the Tournament of Roses Princesses in 1994.) Dittmar was a senior at the Asian Beverly Hills High School in San Marino, California.

DRAVES, VICKY MANALO. U.S. Diving Champion. Born Victoria Taylor Manalo in San Francisco, California, Draves won both the high platform and low springboard diving gold metals in the 1948 Olympics in London. Later, she became a member of Buster Crabbe's swimming troupe. Afterwards, she became a member of the Aqua Follies.

DULDULAO, JULIE R. Former Hawaii State Representative.

A native of Bangui, Ilocos Norte Province, Philippines, Julie R. Duldulao is a former member of the Hawaii State House of Representatives. In 1988, She was elected for the first time to the Hawaii State House of Representatives. In 1990, she was reelected for a second term and in 1992, she was reelected for a third term. However, she lost when she ran for senator in the 1994 primary elections. For her college education, Duldulao attended Manila Central University, Immaculate Conception College, and Northwestern College in the Philippines. She also took some post-education courses in Hawaii.

ELVAMBUENA, ROLAND P. City Engineer, Gary, Indiana.

A native of Nueva Ecija Province, Philippines, Elvambuena has been the city engineer of Gary, Indiana, since 1988, becoming the first known Filipino ever appointed to a city engineer's position.

He immigrated to the United States in 1972. Before he was appointed as a city engineer by the then Mayor Thomas V. Barnes, he was the chief engineer of the Air and Land Pollution Control of the city of Gary, from December 1972 to December 1987. Earlier, he held the position of chief of party/instrumentman of the Lake County Surveyor of Crown Point, Indiana, from April 1972 to November 1972.

Memberships. Elvambuena's memberships include: Gary Sanitary District Board of Commissioners; Gary Planning Commission; Gary Contractor Licensing Board; Gary Development Committee; Mayor's Cabinet; Northwestern Indiana Regional Planning Commission, and Gary Port Authority Advisory Board; National Society of Professional Engineers; Water Environment Federation; Philippine Professional Association (president, 1986); and Philippine Engineers and Scientists Organization.

Awards and Honors. Due to his accomplishments as an engineer, Elvambuena is the recipient of such awards as the most outstanding Filipino in the Midwest in the field of technology in 1988 from the Cavite Association of America, a Distinguished Award from the Philippine Professional Association; and an Outstanding Engineers/Scientists Award in 1990 from the Philippine Engineers and Scientist Organization.

Family. Married to the former Aurea Biscocho of San Juan, Batangas Province, Elvambuena and his wife have three children: Ariel, Rachel, and Eric.

ENRIQUEZ, JOCELYN. Queen of Free Style.

Enriquez holds the distinction of being the first Filipino American to make it in the mainstream music industry. Dubbed as the new "Queen of Freestyle," Enriquez was the first artist to be signed by Classified Records, a Filipino-owned recording company when it was established in 1993. When Enriquez's first single became a success, larger recording companies began to take notice.

Born and raised in San Francisco, California, Jocelyn Enriquez is the daughter of Filipino parents from Manila and the province of Pangasinan.

Do You Miss Me? By late April 1997, Enriquez's first single *Do You Miss Me?* had placed 49th on the *Billboard* Top 100 singles chart, 7th in Singapore, and among the top 20 in Canada. Then she had the hit song, *A Little Bit of Ecstasy.* By August 1997. every day in New York City, one could hear *Do You Miss Me?* or *A Little Bit of Ecstasy* booming from one's vehicle speakers.

At Age 3. At the age of 3, Enriquez had shown her prowess as a singer. Her first performance was a rendition of the Anita Ward hit *Ring My Bell.*

From the Living Room to Fame. From the living room coffee table, where she performed a song, Enriquez performed for ten years with the San Francisco Girls Chorus. She also sang as a part of a top-40 cover band that her parents managed. Enriquez and the band performed before Filipino social activities. She also sang in churches.

As a teenager, she became involved in a community outreach program called the Young Filipino Entertainers' Club.

From that time on, there was no turning back for Enriquez. The break that she was waiting for came when she first signed with the Bay-area based Classified Records. It was Glenn Gutierrez, a Filipino American producer and composer, who convinced her to try dance music. She tried it. *I've Been Thinking About You* became a hit and it led to an album. Two years later. she had two songs on the charts.

Kormman Roque, president of Classified Records says, "They couldn't believe that a small independent label could put out that song, and hold on to it for that long."

Now, a truly successful music career awaits this Filipino American artist. She, however, is no longer connected with Classified Records, but with another recording company that earlier merged with and then separated from Classified Records.

ESPALDON, ERNESTO M., M.D. Plastic Surgeon, Six-Term Guam Senator. On one of the southernmost islands of the Philippines, one bright-moonlit night, a young mother ran her fingers through the hair of her five-year-old son and said, "I wish you would become a doctor when you grow up."

As the years passed, the boy, Ernesto M. Espaldon never forgot his mother's words. He was in his junior year in high school when World War II broke out in December 1941. The following year, at the age of 16, he joined the guerrilla movement as an enlisted man and was promoted to commander, the youngest in the Sulu Area Command.

Today, Dr. Espaldon's skills as a plastic surgeon, his intense passion for medical missionary work, and his exemplary service to the public as a six-term Guam senator, have made Espaldon a living legend in the progressive U.S. territory of Guam.

Back to Home Town After the War. After World War II ended in 1945, Espaldon returned home, where he completed his secondary education at the Zamboanga City High School in 1947. Although a straight "A" student, the prospect of continuing on to college was very slim for Espaldon. His parents had moved from Sulu to Zamboanga and could not find jobs. While strolling one day with a friend along the pier where American vessels were docked, Espaldon picked up a newspaper that contained an article about a surgeon performing plastic and reconstructive work at the Valley Forge General Hospital in Philadelphia, Pennsylvania. His name was Dr. James Barrett Brown.

"This is the medical specialty I want," Espaldon said, showing the article to his friend.

Then to Manila. After graduation from high school, the young man managed to reach Manila, worked his way through college and, by sheer determination, successfully completed his medical education at the University of Santo Tomas in Manila, Philippines, in 1954.

Later, to the U.S. Dr. Espaldon left for the United States for post-graduate training. He completed his general surgery residency at the University of Oklahoma Medical Center in 1959. The young surgeon's aspiration was to ultimately become a plastic surgeon. At that time, there were only eight medical centers that offered this type of training. The most prestigious among them were the Washington University School of Medicine and the Barnes Hospital Group located in St. Louis, Missouri. As he had feared, he was rejected by every medical center. But two months later, before the start of the training program, Espaldon received a hand written letter from Dr. James Barrett Brown, now professor and chief of plastic surgery at the Washington University School of Medicine and The Barnes Hospital Group. (Then he remembered the article in the newspaper along a Philippine pier, where he had launched his dream of becoming a plastic surgeon.) Dr. Brown asked him if he was still interested in plastic surgery. Until this day, Dr. Espaldon

believes that "more things are wrought by prayers than man will ever know."

Back to the Philippines. After his training and passing the exam given by the American Board of Plastic Surgery, he left for the Philippines to serve his own people. He was one of the first two Filipino American diplomates in plastic surgery.

Destiny Intervenes. Goes to Guam. Espaldon and his wife, Dr. Leticia Virata Espaldon, an anesthesiologist, answered a worldwide appeal by the island government of Guam for volunteer doctors. Guam was struck by a devastating typhoon. Their work on Guam was to be only for six months, maybe a year. One year passed, then another. The couple had fallen in love with the place and its people.

In 1964, he was appointed chief of surgery at Guam Memorial Hospital, and a year later he was elected president of the Guam Memorial Hospital Medical Staff. During his tenure as president, the hospital received its first accreditation by the Joint Commission on Hospital Accreditation in 1965. He was elected president of the Guam Medical Society in 1971. A year later, mainly through Dr. Espaldon's efforts the Guam Medical Society was brought under the wing of the American Medical Association (AMA). He was elected as the first Guam delegate to the AMA, making him also the first Filipino American physician to be a member of the AMA House of Delegates.

The Call of Politics. In 1974, Dr. Espaldon entered the political arena. He was elected senator to the 13th Guam Legislature, the first physician to achieve this honor, and later the first Filipino American to be elected for six terms.

Espaldon is very much involved in leading medical mission groups to the Philippines and Micronesia, on a biannual basis, through the Guam Balikbayan Medical Mission which he founded, and the Hawaii-based Aloha Medical Mission which he co-founded.

Espaldon is also involved in cause- and service-oriented projects in the Philippines, such as the College Assurance Plan (CAP), the first and largest pre-need educational plan in the country, as one of its founders and a member of its board of directors. Dr. Espaldon is also the author of a recently published book, entitled *With The Bravest* (The Untold Story of the Sulu Freedom Fighters of World War II). The foreword of his book was written by Philippine President Fidel Ramos. The proceeds from the book will go to an educational scholarship fund for deserving descendants of the Sulu Freedom Fighters.

Awards. Dr. Espaldon has received numerous awards for his accomplishments and services. Among them are: Most Outstanding Filipino American leader of Guam, from the Filipino Community of Guam, 1980; Outstanding Filipino Overseas Award for Public Service, from the Philippine Government, 1981; Most Outstanding University of Santo Tomas Alumni Achievers Award for Public Service, 1981; Raja Baguinda Award for Humanitarian Services from the Autonomous Government of Mindanao, 6th Centennial Celebration of Islam in the Philippines, 1982; Man of the Year Award for Humanitarian Endeavors, from the Institute of the Philippine American Affairs, Honolulu, Hawaii, 1983; Thomas Jefferson Award for

Outstanding Public Service, Washington, D.C., and the *Honolulu Advertiser*, 1984; featured in *Filipino Achievers in the USA and Canada: Profiles in Excellence* by Isabelo T. Crisostomo, 1996; and listed in *Who's Who in America, 1990-1991*; and listed in *Who's Who in the World, 1991-1992*.

Family. Born on November 11, 1926, in Simunul, Sulu Province, Philippines, Ernesto was the second oldest of nine siblings of Cipriano Acuña Espaldon and Claudia Cadag Mercader, pioneer educators from Sorsogon, who volunteered to go to Sulu to help educate Filipino Muslim children before World War II.

He is married to Leticia Virata Espaldon, M.D., and they have six successful grown children: Arlene, the oldest, holds a BA in biology from Cornell University, and an MA from Boston University; Vivian, who has a BS in Education, and a BA and MA in sociology from the University of Pennsylvania; James Albert, who took up political science at the University of Pennsylvania, holds a BS in business administration from Menlo College, California; Diane Marie earned a BA in international relations (cum laude) from Harvard University and an MA in international affairs from Columbia University; Karl Patrick received a BA in political science from Yale University, and a juris doctor from the William S. Richardson College of Law, University of Hawaii; and Ernesto V. Espaldon, Jr., the youngest holds a BS in the joint major of applied science and business from the University of San Francisco.

EVANGELISTA, JOSE L., M.D. Member, National Committee on Foreign Medical Education and Accreditation (NCFMEA).

The recipient of many awards, including a Banaag Award from President Fidel Ramos of the Philippines, Dr. Jose L. Evangelista was appointed by President Clinton to the National Committee on Foreign Medical Education

and Accreditation. He was selected from a number of potential candidates because he represented Asian medical graduates, particularly those from the Philippines. Dr. Evangelista, one of the most well-known Filipino American doctors in the United States, is very active in Asian medical affairs, particularly in promoting the welfare of foreign medical graduates, such as Filipino physicians.

Association President. A practicing cardiologist in Michigan, Dr. Evangelista is a former president of the Association of Philippine Physicians in America (APPA) and a former president of the University of Santo Tomas Medical Alumni Association in America (UST-MAAA). It was Dr. Evangelista who spearheaded the formation of USTMAAA, a national association. He is also a former president of the USTMAA Foundation.

In 1994, Dr. Evangelista was one of those selected by the Commission on Filipinos Overseas to receive Banaag Award in recognition of his humanitarian

work and financial contributions to his native Pampanga Province and to the Philippines in general. The award was presented to him by President Ramos.

He is a delegate to the Wayne County Medical Society in Michigan and chief of staff-elect of St. Mary's Hospital in Livonia, Michigan, from 1997-1998.

With his wife, Dr. Stella Evangelista, M.D. they have been inducted as the first Filipinos and the first couple into the 87-year old International Institute of Metropolitan Detroit's International Heritage Hall of Fame.

Training. Dr. Evangelista underwent a residency in internal medicine at the Sinai Hospital and at the University of Illinois. He had a pulmonary fellowship at the Wayne County General Hospital in Michigan from 1971 to 1972. From 1972 to 1974, he was a cardiology fellow at St. Joseph Hospital in Ann Arbor, Michigan, and Sinai Hospital in Detroit, Michigan. He passed the Michigan state board examination in 1973, and is affiliated with St. Mary's Hospital in Livonia, Michigan, as well as the Annapolis Hospital in Wayne, Michigan. He also received fellowships from the American College of Cardiology, the American College of Physicians, the American College of Internal Physicians, the American College of Chest Physicians, and the Royal College of Physicians and Surgeons of Canada.

A Natural Leader. Dr. Evangelista has been a leader as far as he can remember. "Since my grade school, for some reason," Dr. Evangelista recalls, "I have always been elected as president of the class from the grade school to high school up to the time I graduated from the College of Medicine."

Character Traits. Describing himself, Dr. Evangelista quips, "I am a doer, a thinker, and an achiever. When I plan things, all the ancillary parameters are going to be meticulously thought of for the realization of whatever project I have in mind."

Awards and Honors. Among awards and honors he has received in recognition of his leadership and community service are as follows: National President's Award for Outstanding Leadership from the Michigan State Medical Society, 1988; the FLA Award, 1994; Physician of the Year Award from the APPA, 1994; 1990; Thomasian Outstanding Medica Alumni Award in the field of leadership from the UST Medical Alumni, Philippines; Archbishop Medallion Award for Most Outstanding Professional and for Philanthropic Services, Pampanga Province, Philippines; Outstanding Leadership and Presidential Citation Award from the Philippine Medical Association of Michigan, and Outstanding Pampangueño Award for Humanitarian Services and Medicine, from Governor Bren Guiao of Pampanga.

Flashback. The youngest son of the late former Mayor Jose Evangelista, Sr., of Candaba, Pampanga Province, Philippines, and Aurora Limjuco, Dr. Evangelista was born in Candaba on January 21, 1944. In 1956, he graduated as valedictorian at the Candaba Elementary School. In 1960, he was valedictorian in high school at the St. Andrew Academy in Candaba. He was a *summa cum laude* in pre-medicine in 1963 from the Faculty of Medicine and Surgery, University of Santo Tomas (UST) in Manila. He obtained his medical degree from the same institution in 1968.

Family. He is married to Dr. Stella S. Evangelista, M.D., whom he met during their college days at UST. At the same university, Dr. Evangelista was the president, and his would-be wife, Stella, was the vice president of the Medicine Interns Organization. They immigrated to the United States in 1968. They have 6 children, ages 14 to 29. Maria Cristina is a graduate of Pepperdine University School of Business and is now property manager of Royal Management Company, the family's real estate company; Edmund is a graduate of the Tufts University School of Medicine and is in residency in physical medicine/rehabilitation at the University of Southern California, Irvine; Marcus is pursuing a J.D./MBA degree at Boston College Law School; Jose III is a freshman, studying premedicine at the University of Michigan; Maristella is a high school sophomore at the Academy of the Sacred Heart and Augustus Peter is in the eighth grade at St. Hugo of the Hills Catholic School in Bloomfield Hills, Michigan.

EVANGELISTA, STELLA, M.D. Michigan Hall of Famer and Former Member, Michigan State Board of Medicine.

Dr. Stella Evangelista, M.D., holds the distinction being the first Filipino and the first Asian to be appointed to the Michigan State Board of Medicine, the body that regulates medical practice in the state.

Dr. Evangelista was elected president of the Association of Philippine Physicians in America (APPA) in 1993, the first woman to assume that position. She and her husband, Jose, became the first Filipinos and the first couple to be inducted into Detroit's International Institute Heritage Hall of Fame.

Training. In 1968-1969, Dr. Evangelista underwent her postgraduate internship at the Columbus-Cuneco Medical Center in Chicago, Illinois. From 1969 to 1971, she underwent her pediatric residency at the Cook County General Hospital in Chicago, Illinois. Then she went to the Wayne County General Hospital in Michigan for a pediatric fellowship. Certified by the American Board of Pediatrics, she passed the Michigan State Board exams in March 1973.

Positions. Dr. Evangelista is the president-elect of the USTMAAA. She was the vice chairman of the Congressional Asian Pacific American Caucus Institute (CAPACI), a non-partisan, nonprofit, educational corporation that aims to increase and promote the participation of Asian Pacific Americans in public policy on a national level; and member of the board of directors of the American Citizens for Justice. She is also a member of the board of directors of World Medical Relief; a member of board of directors of International Institute of Metro Detroit, and the executive director

of the UST Medical Alumni Association in America and its Foundation.

A Leader. Since she was a child, Dr. Evangelista, has been an outstanding leader. She recalls, "I was always chosen to lead either by the teachers or by the students themselves. I like being a leader because I find it very rewarding and challenging. My involvement in all aspects of school life—curricular and extra-curricular—made me a leader. I feel very accomplished as a leader."

Character Traits. Commenting on Dr. Evangelista's leadership, Dr. Fred Quevedo, past president of the APPA, says, "She has the ability to inspire people to work together as a team. She has the most number of innovative and creative ideas which she can easily translate into concrete goals and objectives."

Dr. Evangelista's friends describe her as "a kind, compassionate, and generous person." In describing herself, she says, "I am strong-willed but flexible. I am principled and will never compromise my principles. I am honest, friendly, and sincere, always ready to help others in need. I am motivated and goal oriented."

Awards and Honors. She is the recipient of numerous awards from various organizations. Among her awards are as follows: the Physician of the Year Award from the APPA, 1992; Most Outstanding Couple Award from the UST Medical Association, Philippines; voted one of the Twenty Outstanding Filipino Americans in the United States by *Fil-Am Image* in Washington, D.C.; Outstanding Filipino Woman of the Year, 1988; Outstanding Service Award from the Circulo Pampangueño of Michigan; Community Service Award from the Asian American Journalists Association; and Community Service Award from the American Citizens For Justice.

Community Involvement. Dr. Evangelista is very active in community activities. She is responsible for chairing various fund-raising activities. She chaired the first Henry Ford Hospice Annual Fund Raising; City of Hope Charity Dinner; Asian American Journalists' Association Scholarship drive; APPA's Philippine Earthquake Relief Drive; Circulo Pampangueño of Michigan's fund-raising for Mt. Pinatubo victims; World Medical Relief Annual fund-raising dinner and the Pilipino-American Community Center of Michigan's fund raising event. Her most recent achievement was to raise $50,000 during her APPA presidency for the International Kiwanis Foundation's IDD (Iodine Deficiency) program in the Philippines.

Family and Educational Background. A practicing pediatrician for 25 years in Livonia, Michigan, Dr. Evangelista was born in Bantayan, Cebu, Philippines, on April 30, 1945, to Salvacion Villacin and Pedro Salgado, In 1956, she graduated as valedictorian at the Zapatera Elementary School in Cebu City, and in 1960, as salutatorian at the Girls High School in the same city. She received her bachelor of science in premedicine, *magna cum laude*, from the Cebu Institute of Technology. She graduated in medicine as *benemeritus* from the University of Santo Tomas, Faculty of Medicine and Surgery in Manila. She and her husband have six children,

FABITO, DANIEL C. M.D. General and Vascular Surgeon and Missionary Worker. Born in Santa Barbara, Pangasinan Province, Philippines, Dr. Daniel "Danny" C. Fabito is the founder and chair of Operation Bayanihan and the organizer of APPA-PMA Medical Aid Assistance, Inc. These two organizations are sending doctors to the Philippines as part of medi-

cal-surgical missions to perform surgeries and offer free medical education to Filipino physicians in the art of surgery.

Dr. Fabito became the president of the Association of Philippine Physicians in America (APPA) in 1980. In the same year, he formed the first APPA-sponsored mission with the Philippine Medical Association of St. Louis, Missouri.

Dr. Fabito himself headed missions to Lucena, Quezon Province; Dagupan City, Pangasinan Province; Trece Martires, Cavite Province; St. Martin de Porres Charity Hospital, San Juan, Metro Manila; FEU Charity Hospital, Manila; Orani Hospital, Orani, Bataan Province; Davao Province; and Batangas Medical Mission, Batangas Province.

Commenting on why such missions are being conducted, Fabito says, "There is a great need to help medically the underserved poor. In the Philippines today, indigent patients abound, be that in the city or the rural area...An integral part of the mission is post-graduate education for the local doctors and the residents in training. All missionaries give lectures and demonstrate in clinics. The residents assist in surgery and they are always eager to learn new procedures." To Fabito, the forming of APPA-PMA Medical Aid Assistance is the fulfillment of a dream of a continuing effort to serve humanity through his beloved Philippines.

Flashback. Dr. Fabito, a 1964 graduate of the Far Eastern University Medical School, Philippines, is currently a general and vascular surgeon in St. Louis, Missouri, where he has been in private practice since 1973. He had his rotating internship at the Evangelical Deaconess Hospital in Milwaukee, Wisconsin, from 1965-1967; undertook his general surgery residency at the same hospital from 1966-1967; had his general surgery residency at Missiouri Baptist Hospital; and he took his preceptorship in vascular surgery from 1971-1973.

Affiliations. Dr. Fabito is affiliated with the St. Anthony's Medical Center, Missouri Baptist Medical Center, and Lutheran Medical Center, all in St. Louis.

Awards and Honors. His awards and honors include an award for outstanding leadership as president of the PMAGSTL (Philippine Medical Association of Greater St. Louis); most outstanding F.E.U. Medical Alumnus; most outstanding member of PMAGSTL for leadership as president of the national APPA; most outstanding member of the Filipino Association of

Greater St. Louis; a plaque of appreciation as president of Lutheran Medical Center medical staff; a plaque for serving as president of Society of Philippine Surgeons in America; a peace presidential plaque for his contribution to the community of underprivileged Filipino children and artesian wells construction in the Philippines; an award for serving the LMC governing board; an award for outstanding contribution to the continued success of the FEUDNR Medical Foundation; outstanding service to the PMAGSTL CME program; an award for 25 years of service on the medical staff of Lutheran Medical Center; and an award for 25 years of service on the medical staff of Missouri Baptist Medical Center.

Family. Dr. Fabito is married to Melinda Ayala-Fabito, B.S.N. They have three grown children: Melissa Gayle, B.S.N., a nurse; D. Marc, J.D., attorney-at-law; and Daniel Everett, a premed student at Boston University.

FAJARDO, JUVENTINO "BEN." Mayor, Glendale Heights, IL. Juventino Fajardo, 50, as of this writing, the current mayor of Glendale, Illinois, is the first Asian to be elected a mayor of a Dupage county municipality. In the April 4, 1995, election, he beat Charles Wheeler, an African American trustee.

Before his election to the mayoralty post, Fajardo acted as the village president after the death of the then-Mayor Michael Camera in 1994. He was a trustee of the municipality in 1989. He was reelected for a four-year term in 1993. Then in 1990, he was appointed deputy mayor.

He is a certified public accountant and a systems consultant for information technology with the Dean Witter, Discover & Company. A native of Santo Domingo, Albay Province, Philippines, Fajardo obtained his bachelor's degree in commerce, majoring in accounting from the University of Nueva Caceres in Naga City, Philippines. He immigrated to the United States with his wife, Adeline, in 1973. He and his wife, Adeline. They have four children: B.J., Julie, Tony, and Melissa.

FAJARDO, PETE. Mayor, Carson, California. First elected to the city council of Carson, California, Pete Fajardo is the first Filipino American to be elected mayor of a progressive city in the United States through a direct vote of the people. Fajardo, who won against three other candidates, including incumbent Mayor Mike Mitoma, was elected mayor by the people of Carson, a bustling suburb south of Los Angeles, California, with a population of about 100,000. He was Carson's mayor protem prior to his election in early 1997.

Immediately after the last vote was counted, Fajardo said, "We should immediately start the healing process among the candidates and their supporters. This election has divided our community."

Supporters. Even before the announcement of his narrow lead against his closest rival Fajardo started to thank all those who had spent their efforts to make him win the mayoralty race. Fajardo's supporters came from all parts of southern California. They were able to come up with much-needed funds and to walk precincts during the few weeks campaign before election day in March 1997. Moreover, his colleagues from the Filipino American Press Club of Los Angeles, led by its president, Dante Ochua, donated literature and funds.

Fajardo also received strong support from U.S. Congresswoman Juanita Millender-MacDonald; Carson City Councilwoman Kay Calas; George Kiyama, Board of Education member of Los Angeles; Marty McHale, vice-chair of the Carson Mobile Home Review Board; and former members of the State City Employees Union.

Advice. In advising Filipino Americans to strongly be involved in politics, Fajardo said, "Be volunteers for community service for all groups, not just particular ethnic groups. Support projects that will make you politically active. Network with civic leaders. Get to know the issues that count."

Fajardo came to the United States in the 1960s and first worked as a social worker for the County of Los Angeles.

FRANCISCO, ALICE NEPOMUCENO, M.D. Radiologist, Outstanding Physician.

A Diplomate in Diagnostic Radiology, Dr. Alice Nepomuceno is a multi-award winning physician. She was selected as one of the Twenty Outstanding Filipino Americans in the United States for 1992-1993 by the *Fil-Am Image* magazine in Washington, D.C. The immediate past president of the Association of Philippine Physicians in America (APPA), she is the owner of Whiting X-Ray, P.A. in Whiting, New Jersey.

Education. Dr. Francisco graduated from the University of Santo Tomas College of Medicine in Manila, Philippines, as *Meritus*, (Class 1961). She trained at St. Luke's Hospital in New York City. She was the former director of Radiology at Harlem Hospital-Columbia Affiliation and the former attending radiologist of Bronx-Lebanon Hospital. She also held academic titles of assistant clinical professor at Columbia University and at Albert Einstein College of Medicine.

Federal Consultant. Dr. Francisco is presently a federal consultant of the Medical Radiation Advisory Committee (MRAC) of the Center for Devices and Radiological Health in Rockville, Maryland. The committee is the center's advisory body on policies and programs relating to the application of medical radia-

tion in the healing arts and receives an overview of the medical device approval process.

Memberships. Dr. Francisco is a member of the New Jersey Medical Women's Association, the Radiological Society of North America, Roentgen Ray Society, and the New York Roentgen Society. She is the president of the Bergen Phil-Am Lions Club of New Jersey; a member of the board of directors of the Association of Filipino Americans in Bergen County, New Jersey; a member of the board of trustees of the Philippine Association of Medical Societies of New Jersey Foundation (PAMSNJ) and of the Good Samaritan Foundation; and an adviser to the Philippine Medical Association in America. She is a former president of the Philippine Medical Association in America,1986; a former hermana mayor of the San Lorenzo Ruiz Association in America, 1986; a former member of the board of governors of the Association of Philippine Physicians in America, 1987-1989; and a former member of the legal committee of the Bronx Medical Society.

Awards. Dr. Francisco's awards include a Humanitarian Award from the Lord of Pardon Association, 1996; a Humanitarian Award from the Kahirup Club, USA, 1950; a Humanitarian Award from the St. John's University Filipino Society, 1994; a Distinguished Service Award from the New York Jaycees, 1994; and a Good Samaritan Award.

Family. Dr. Francisco is married to Aris Francisco, a New York attorney. They have four grown children: Christan is a graduate of Fairleigh Dickinson University and is presently an auditor of the Intercontinental Hotel in Manhattan, and is married to former Ersylin Uriarte; Armel is a graduate of Columbia University and is now with Prudential in New Jersey; Aris Victor is a graduate of Rutgers University, with an M.B.A. from Fordham University and is an assistant vice president of Banker's Trust; and Alice Regina is a graduate of the College of Business Administration at Fordham University, where she majored in accounting, and is a manager at KPMG Peat Marrick, one of the largest accounting firms in the country.

In All Affairs. Dr. Francisco and her family are all active in the social, cultural, professional and political affairs in New Jersey and in the tri-state area of the eastern seaboard. Well-known for her generosity and philanthropy, Dr. Francisco has many underprivileged high school, college, and seminarian scholars studying under her patronage in the Philippines.

GABRIEL, ROMAN. Former Los Angeles Rams' Quarterback.

A half-Filipino, Roman Gabriel is the first known Filipino American quarterback. Named the National Football League's Most Valuable Player in 1969, Gabriel played eleven years in the NFL. He was an all-American quarterback from North Carolina State University.

First Honoree for Walk of Fame. In 1997, Gabriel, a native son, was selected as the first honoree for the Walk of Fame in Wilmington, North Carolina. He was chosen by a committee from a list of candidates, including Michael Jordan, Sugar Ray Leonard, Meadowlark Lemon, Charlie Daniels, and Woodrow Wilson. "Considering who has come from my hometown, it's a neat award and honor," the former NFL quarterback says of the star that is emblazoned with his name on the sidewalk outside the Cotton Exchange in downtown Wilmington. He adds, "People say it's because I haven't forgotten where I'm from."

1969 MVP Season. In 1962, Gabriel was the top draft pick of the NFL's Los Angeles Rams and the AFL's Oakland Raiders. He picked the Rams. His stay there lasted 11 years, including his 1969 MVP season. In that year alone, he threw for 2,549 yards and had a league-high 24 touchdowns.

GACOSCOS, PAT. Member, School Board, Union City, California.

Incumbent board member Pat Gacoscos was reelected to the New Haven Unified School District Board in the November 1996 elections. She placed second at the November 5 elections to serve for another four years. She was first elected into office in 1992. The New Haven Unified School District is composed of 11 schools—6 elementary schools, 3 middle schools, 1 high school, and 1 continuing high school. Gacoscos has been a resident of Union City since 1979.

GAN, JOSE C., Ph.D. University Professor.

Dr. Jose C. Gan is a professor of biochemistry in the Department of Human Biological Chemistry & Genetics at the University of Texas Medical Branch in Galveston, Texas.

Born in Pavia, Iloilo Province, Philippines, on November 30, 1933, he finished high school at Central Philippines, in Jaro, Iloilo. Upon graduation, he came to the United States to study.

Degrees. Dr. Gan obtained the following degrees: a B.S. in Pharmacy from the University of Wisconsin in Madison, Wisconsin (1953-1957); M.S. in Hospital Pharmacy from the State University of Iowa in Iowa City, Missouri, 1957-1959; and a Ph.D. in Biochemistry from the University of Illinois Medical Center in Chicago, Illinois, 1960-1964; He was an Alameda County Heart Association's postdoctoral fellow in physiology at the University of California at Berkeley, California, 1964-1966; and a San Francisco Heart Association's postdoctoral fellow in Hormone Res. Lab., at the University of California Medical School in San Francisco, California 1966-1968.

Professor. Dr. Gan was appointed and served from assistant professor to associate professor from 1968-1974, and has been professor since 1981 in the Department of Chemistry and Genetics at the Texas Medical Branch in Galveston, Texas. He is a member of the American Society for Biochemistry and Molecular Biology and Philippine-American Academy of Science.

Research Interest. His research interest is in the metabolism of proteins and amino acids as well as the biosynthesis, chemistry and biological activity of gly-

coprotein hormones and proteinase inhibitors. He has taught medical biochemistry and graduate biochemistry courses. Also, he has supervised several doctorate students and has published many articles in biochemical journals.

Family. Dr. Gan is married to Norma Estoque Gan, and they have two grown children: Yvonne Gan Bennett, and Karen Gan Abrams. They have three grandchildren: Andrew, Caitlin, and Madeline Bennett; and sons-in-laws: Jeff Bennett and Todd Abrams.

GARCIA, CEFERINO. Middleweight Champion of the World.

Known for his "bolo" punch, Ceferino Garcia won the world's middleweight championship on October 2, 1939, when he knocked out Fred Apostoli in seven rounds in New York City.

Before that, in 1937, he tried twice to win the world's welterweight crown. The fights were against Barney Ross in 1937 and with Henry Armstrong in 1938. Born in Manila, Philippines, in 1919, Garcia's boxing career started in 1932 and ended in 1945. This boxing great won 88 fights and lost 25 fights. Thousands of Filipinos in the United States saw him fight. He had 62 knockouts and 9 draws.

GARCIA, NESTOR R. Hawaii State Representative.

Nestor R. Garcia, 40, serves as a member of the majority leadership team in the Hawaii State House, as majority whip for the Democrats. He was reelected to the State House in the November 1996 elections, representing the 37th district. He was first elected in the November 1994 elections.

House Committee Memberships. Garcia is also a member of the Policy Committee for House Democrats. With respect to the House standing committees, Garcia serves as the chairman of the Public Safety and Military Affairs Committee, with jurisdiction over the state prison and parole system, and oversees matters of interest and concern between the state and the U.S. Armed Forces. He is also a member of the Consumer Protection and Commerce Committee, the Water and Land Use Committee, the Energy and Environmental Protection Committee, and the legislative Management Committee. He is also a co-chair of the bipartisan Small Business Caucus, which also includes state senators and members of the private sector. Garcia was first elected to the State House in 1994, representing the 37th district. He is also a vice-president with City Bank, a Hawaii-based financial institution, a key subsidiary of CB Bancshares, Inc., the third-largest bank holding company in the state.

Education and Work Experience. Garcia graduated from the University of Hawaii in 1980, with a B.A. in journalism. While he was earning his degree, he was working as a part-time newsroom assistant for the former NBC affiliate in Honolulu, KHON-TV. He became an on-camera reporter for KHON in 1981, a station that became number 1 in its market for news and programming. In 1991, he joined the staff of Hawaii's senior U.S. Senator, Daniel K. Inouye, as press secretary. After two years in Washington, D.C., Garcia returned to Hawaii, and later became a senior consultant with the state's premier public relations firm, Hill and Knowlton-Hawaii.

First Bid for Public Office. In 1994, Garcia launched his first bid for public office, winning the vacant seat in the 37th district of the State House. That year, he also became a vice-president with the Retail Banking Division of City Bank.

Memberships. Garcia sits on the boards of several community organizations, including the chairman of the Community Advisory Group to the Waipahu Family Planning Clinic; member of the board for the Leeward YMCA; member of the board for the Hawaii Community Services Council; member of the board for the Children's Advocacy Centers; member of the board for the National Kidney Foundation of Hawaii; and member of the advisory board for the Waipahu High School Academy on Finance. He is also a member of the Waipahu Businessmen's Association, the Leeward Lion's Club, the Filipino Chamber of Commerce of Hawaii, and he Waipahu Town Task Force.

Garcia's Dream. It has always been a dream of Garcia to be able to "be in a position to help others." When he was a TV news reporter, he was approached constantly to consider public office. "But at the time, I felt I could best serve as a role model for young Filipinos by remaining in a profession that seldom sees Filipino, much less Asian Pacific, males. We need to have a presence not just in politics, but in all walks of life." However, when an opportunity to serve in government presented itself, Garcia tossed his hat into the ring "because during my time in Washington, I witnessed how being in a position of influence could afford someone the chance to make some kind of contribution to the happiness and well-being of people."

Role Models. Garcia counts on role models such as Senator Robert Kennedy "because of his passion for doing things and helping the disadvantaged, the poor, and children."

Garcia is married to the former Karen Mun, and they are the proud parents of two daughters, Lyndsey, born in 1985, and Cara, born in 1988.

GASENDO, LEONARDO M. Award-Winning Engineer-Inventor. A holder of a bachelor's degree in chemical engineering from Adamson University in Manila, Philippines, Leonardo M. Gasendo is the only known award-winning Filipino engineer-inventor in the United States.

Gasendo, who has 10 patented inventions, won an award in 1983 from the American Institute of Chemical Engineers (AICHE) for his major invention, the Super Windmill, which is designed to help solve shortages

in electric power and water in developing countries, such as the Philippines. According to Gasendo, the windmill has the ability to capture unlimited supply energy from the wind. The windmill, with a diameter of 100 feet and 12 sails (optimum) has the ability to generate more than 1,000 horsepower at 35 miles-per-hour wind velocity.

In this connection, Gasendo, who formed his own firm, the Gasendo Company, has submitted a proposal to Chile for converting the country's wind energy into cheap electricity using his Floating Super-windmill invention. A few of these units offshore will supply electricity to Chile, Argentina, and a few other countries in South America.

Flashback. Gasendo, who was born in Bacolod, Negros Occidental Province, Philippines, in 1924, joined the Coca-Cola Company in Bacolod immediately after graduating from Adamson University College of Engineering. In 1959, he moved to the Bataan Refining Corporation, where he served as a process superintendent.

In 1967, he left the Philippines for the United States. He settled in Los Angeles, California, where he was employed with the Fluor Corporation as a principal process engineer, responsible for the design, engineering, and startup of their oil refineries and chemical plants in the U.S. and abroad. Among the projects he supervised were the Trans-Alaska Oil Plant Pipeline; the Iranian Oil Company oil refinery in Tehran, Iran; the Chinese Petroleum Corporation ethylene plant in Toufen, Taiwan; and the Mobil Oil Corporation petroleum refinery in Joilet, Illinois. He was instrumental in the building of a natural gas processing plant for the Chinese Petroleum Corporation in Tungsiao, Taiwan, and the Exxon Chemical Company low-density polyethylene in Baton Rogue, Louisiana, among other projects.

In 1978, he moved to the Ralph M. Parsons Company in Los Angeles as the principal project engineer. Then in 1983, he joined GLM Associate Consultants, which is based in Pasadena, California, as vice president.

Awards and Honors. Besides winning an award from the American Institute of Chemical Engineers, Gasendo received other awards, which include a Best Energy Invention Award in 1991 from the Inventors International; a Ninoy Aquino Memorial Award for his 10 patented inventions, and a Science and Technology Award from Adamson University for his scientific inventions. The university also conferred on him an honorary degree of Doctor of Chemical Engineering, being one of its outstanding graduates.

Family. Married to Conchita J. Gasendo, a hospital administrator in Los Angeles, California, Gasendo and his wife have a daughter, Leah, who is a practicing lawyer.

GILLESPIE, TITA DIOSO. *Newsweek's* General Editor. Tita Dioso Gillespie who has the equivalent of a master's degree in French language and civilization from the Sorbonne, Paris, France, is a general editor of *Newsweek*, the prestigious New York-based international magazine. She is also a copy edi-

tor of *Copy Editor*, a newsletter for professional copy editors, and copy-edits and proofreads on a freelance basis for such book publishers as Alfred Knopf, Henry Holt, and Putnam Penguin, and for such magazines as *Conde Nast Sports for Women* and *New York*.

From Manila to the U.S. Born in the Philippines, Gillespie had just finished her sophomore year at the University of Santo Tomas in Manila in 1960, when her father, Leocadio Dioso, a diplomat with the Philippine Department of Foreign Affairs was assigned to the Philippine Mission in the United Nations. Thus started Gillespie's life in New York City.

She enrolled at Hunter College in Manhattan, where she received her bachelor's degree in English and philosophy in 1963.

Commenting on how she started in journalism, she was quoted in the *Filipinas* magazine issue of September 1996 as saying, "I had one of those student aide jobs where I was proofreading the college bulletin for a dollar an hour."

To England. After getting her degree from Hunter College, Gillespie left for England to pursue studies in 17th-century English history at Oxford University, where she was awarded a certificate.

Then Paris, France. In 1968, Gillespie headed for Paris, France, where she studied French language and civilization, focusing on medieval French literature at the Sorbonne, University of Paris.

Back to New York. After four years' studies in Europe, Gillespie returned to New York. In the Big Apple, she started working as a proofreader of *Woman's Day* magazine.

Hi California! After marrying Brette Gillespie, then recently discharged from the U.S. Navy, the couple headed for San Francisco, California, where she worked for McGraw Hill and later for John Wiley & Sons in Palo Alto.

New York, Here I Am. Continuing her search for an interesting job in publishing, Gillespie returned to New York. There she worked for the *Free Press*, a subsidiary of MacMillan Publishing Co., as an editing supervisor. She was promoted to acquisitions editor, where she was put in charge of the history, political science, and international relations lists. Later she moved to *Newsweek* magazine to work as an associate editor.

Vienna, Instead of Geneva. After a stint at *Newsweek*, Gillespie decided to give the United Nations a try. However, she was assigned to Vienna, instead of Geneva, where she had hoped to make use of her

knowledge of French. She worked for the publishing section of UNIDO.

To New York Again. Two years later she was back at *Newsweek* in New York, having responded to a plea for help from the magazine's copy chief. She was put in charge of the magazine's style, and in 1992 she was promoted to general editor.

GONZALES, DENNIS. Postmaster, Daly City, California. An engineer by profession, Dennis Gonzales is the third Filipino American to become a postmaster in the United States. He is the current postmaster of Daly City, California, which has about 30 percent Filipino population. (Mill Valley and Union City are the two other cities known to have postmasters of Filipino descent.)

A graduate of the University of Santo Tomas in Manila, Philippines, where he obtained his engineering degree, he is also a graduate of Alameda College, where he majored in mathematics. He also attended Laney College, where he majored in computer science. Gonzales was a consistent honor student from the first grade through senior

high school. An achiever, he has received awards, honors, and recognition from the U.S. Postal Service. He lives with his wife, Ivy, and their son, Denny, in Oakley, California.

GONZALEZ, N.V.M. Novelist. A novelist, journalist, teacher, and critic, N.V.M. Gonzalez was born in Romblon, Romblon Province, Philippines, on September 8, 1915. Romblon is near to his heart, that's why it became the setting of some of his earliest work. For instance, Gonzalez earned his first peso by playing the violin. He relived this young musician in his short story *The Bread of Salt*, in which the 14-year-old narrator attempts to woo the niece of a wealthy Spaniard. There is, actually up to now, the site of the Spaniard's mansion mentioned in the short story; it is there where the wedding party is held and where the young musician plays in *The Bread of Salt*.

Recent Books. Gonzalez has added three books to his list of work: *Work on the Mountain* (1995), *The Novel of Justice (1996)*, and *The Grammar of Dreams* (1996).

Earlier Books. His earlier books of fiction are: *The Winds of April; Seven Hills Away; Children of the Ash-Covered Dancers; Look Stranger, On This Island Now; Selected Stories; and Kalutang: A Filipino in the World.*

Fellowship and Professorships. In 1949, Gonzalez's second book, *Seven Hills Away*, a collection of stories, won him a creative writing fellowship at Stanford University. In 1950, he began teaching at the University of the Philippines. In 1968, he became a professor at the University of California at Santa Barbara, California; University of California at Los Angeles; University of California at Berkeley, California, and the University of Washington and at other schools. In 1983, he retired as professor from California State University at Hayward, after which he returned to the Philippines to teach at the University of the Philippines. Gonzalez still maintains a residence in California where he comes occasionally for a visit.

Awards. In recognition of his achievements, Gonzalez has won literary awards and received honorary degrees from various institutions.

GRAULTY, REYNALDO. Hawaii State Senator.

Born in the Philippines 48 years ago of an American father and a Filipino mother, Reynaldo Graulty was elected to the Hawaii State Senate in 1992. Graulty first entered public service in 1982 when he was elected to the State House of Representatives. He was reelected without opposition in 1984. He left the State House in 1986, but he ran for public office and was elected to the State Senate in 1992.

Graulty received his undergraduate education from the State University of New York at Albany, New York, where he obtained his bachelor's degree in political science, *magna cum laude.* He earned his doctorate in jurisprudence from the University of Hawaii School of Law in 1979.

Honors and Awards. Among honors and awards Graulty has received are Senator of the Year Award from the Hospital Association of Hawaii for his work on health-care issues; Eva H. Smyth Award for his efforts on behalf of the blind people of Hawaii; and Outstanding Achievements in Government Service Award from the Ateneo de Manila High School Class of 1966. As a practicing lawyer, Graulty is the senior partner of his law firm, Graulty, Evangelista & Quilban. he is married to Gig and they have two children, Erinn, and Stephanie.

GUINGONA, MICHAEL, JR. Mayor, Daly City, California.

In a special meeting of the city council on November 30, 1995, Guingona, Jr., was unanimously voted as its new mayor. During his term of office as a council member, Guingona worked for the creation of the Daly City-Quezon City (Philippines) Sister Committee which established cultural, economic, and educational ties between the two cities.

HAGEDORN, JESSICA. Famous Novelist.

A novelist, poet, singer, performing artist, and teacher, Jessica Hagedorn, is the author of *Dogeaters,* which was featured by the *New York Times Book Review* on its cover in its issue of March 25, 1990. The book eventually was chosen as a finalist for the National Book Award for fiction. Her second and most recent novel, *The Gangster of Love,* published by Houghton Mifflin, garnered generally good reviews. *The Gangster of Love* sold well, as expected in New York City and on the West Coast. The book also sold in Chicago, Illinois; Houston, Texas; Denver, Colorado; and Minneapolis, Minnesota—cities that were not included on the tour to promote the *book.*

After the *Dogeaters* was published, Hagedorn spent six years in performing and writing for theater

and film. It was also during this time that she edited *Charlie Chan is Dead: An Anthology of Contemporary Asian American Fiction.* Works of 48 writers she selected are represented in the book—writers with different literary styles and cultural backgrounds.

The American Experience. While the *Dogeaters* is about her Philippine experience, Hagedorn's *The Gangster of Love* narrates her American experience. She says, "...I figured I've lived here long enough; it was time to take a look at my own backyard."

Fact or Fiction? Hagedorn seems to like playing with fact and fiction. In her novel, *The Gangster of Love,* her heroine, Rocky Rivera, is the singer of a rock band, like Hagedorn who was the lead singer of her disbanded band.

Knowing three languages: English, Tagalog, and Spanish, Hagedorn, in order to have genuine Filipino characters, sprinkled *Dogeaters* with Spanish and Tagalog words, which she says irritated some American critics and readers. In actuality, Tagalog words, with some Spanish words, are mixed with English in common conversation on the street, in movies or on television in the Philippines. They call it Taglish—a combination of Tagalog and English. Moreover, the Tagalog dialect contains many Spanish words.

Hagedorn currently is busy touring the country— attending readings and teaching writing courses.

Flashback. Born in the Philippines, Hagedorn moved in the early 1960s to San Francisco, California, with her mother and two brothers. Her brothers, however, didn't like the life in America, so they returned to the old country.

Recalling her early years, Hagedorn was quoted to have said, "I had no role models while growing up. I basically had to invent myself."

Hagedorn studied at Lowell High School in San Francisco, While she didn't attend college, her English literature teacher at Lowell has had an influence on her—opening her eyes to the beauty and rewards of writing.

Kenneth Rexroth, a poet and translator in San Francisco, noticed her talent in writing. Hence, he took her under his wing when she was only 14 years old. It was also Rexroth who took her onstage at the Straight Theater in San Francisco to read some of her poetry. Hagedorn's first book of poetry was published by McGraw-Hill.

Family. Hagedorn lives in New York City with her husband and two daughters, Paloma and Esther,

HALEY, MARIA LUISA MABILANGAN. High-Ranking Filipino American Official in Clinton's Administration.

When Maria Luisa Mabilangan Haley disembarked from the presidential plane and once more stepped on Philippine soil on November 12, 1994, she felt that it was one of the most memorable moments in her life. "It was a wonderful experience," she says, reminiscing her visit to her homeland. "It was something I never thought would happen—going back to the country of my birth with the President of the United States."

Considered the highest-ranking Filipino American in the Clinton administration, Haley, as a member of the board of directors of Export-Import Bank, maintains close ties with President Clinton.

Flashback. Born in Manila, Philippines, in 1940, Haley is the daughter of Philippine Ambassador Felipe Mabilangan, Sr., a diplomat whose overseas assignments included India, Laos, Pakistan, and France. She was 10 when the Mabilangan family moved to India, where they lived for five years. Later, her father was assigned to Pakistan where they settled for two years. At age 22, her father sent her to Madrid, Spain, to study with her friend, Conchitina Sevilla, a top Filipina model, at the Universidad Central de Madrid. After staying there for a year, they returned to Paris, where Sevilla trained in modeling.

Upon returning to Manila, the two friends established the Karilagan Finishing School. However, after a year, Haley changed her career when she was hired by Hilton International in Manila, where she held a management position. While working at Hilton, she met and married John Haley, an international attorney from Arkansas.

To the U.S. with Love. Upon getting married in Hongkong, Haley and her husband headed for his home state of Arkansas and they settled in Little Rock. She worked in several private companies, where she was exposed to planning, budgeting, operations, and marketing strategies.

In 1979, she was employed at the Arkansas Industrial Development Company AIDC, where she was a trade and marketing specialist. This position resulted in her close association with then-Governor Bill Clinton. Later, she became the international marketing consultant of AIDC, which took her, with President Clinton, to various cities in Asia and Europe in search of international trade for the state of Arkansas. Haley recalls, "I was an international saleswoman for Arkansas, traveling all over the world selling Arkansas products."

She worked there until Clinton was elected president in November 1992. She was appointed to the President-elect's transition team as deputy assistant director for political affairs. Afterwards, she was appointed as special assistant to the President and associate director of Presidential Personnel for Economics, Trade, and Commerce at the White House. She was later appointed as a member of the board of directors of Export-Import Bank, where she is still assigned.

Turning Point in Life. The turning point of Haley's life was "when I decided to work for the State of Arkansas when Bill Clinton first became governor."

Traits. Dave Harrington, former executive director of AIDC, says of Haley, "Maria is a focused, determined and committed person. She has tremendous organization skills...."

Del Boyette, executive director at AIDC, comments, "During that time, I discovered that Maria is more than an energetic and enthusiastic colleague, she is a true friend."

Award. On May 19, 1997, Haley received the 1997 Ronald H. Brown Export Enhancement Award from the Small Business Exporters Association (SBEA) at a ceremony held in New York City.

Goals. Haley, who is childless and is divorced from her husband, speaks several languages: Pilipino (Tagalog), English, Spanish, and French. Commenting on setting goals, she says, "I've had to change plans many times in my life. I've lived in eight countries and have had five different careers. Change does not intimidate me, instead it fuels my growth. Yes, I set goals and deadlines." As a member of the board of directors of Export-Import Bank, Haley focuses her attention on the expansion of the role of small businesses in the export market.

HARU, SUMI SEVILLA. Actress, Activist. A Filipino American actress who was cast by producer Ralph Nelson in 1964 in "Soldiers in the Rain," which starred Steve McQueen and Jackie Gleason, Sumi Sevilla Haru is vice president of the Screen Actors' Guild (SAG). She is also the coordinator of the performing arts division of the Los Angeles Cultural Affairs Department. A vice president of AFL-CIO, Haru is the first Asian and Filipino American on the AFL-CIO's executive council.

Haru was born in Orange, New Jersey in 1939, but she was raised in Arvada, Colorado. She obtained her bachelor of arts in music degree from the University of Colorado. She was married in 1956 but she was divorced in 1963.

Haru's first feature film was *Krakatoa; East of Java* in 1967 after she moved to Los Angeles. She was always cast as a geisha girl. Thereafter, she changed her name from Mildred Sevilla to Sumi Haru, her Japanese stage name. But Haru still carries her maiden name, Sevilla. She says, "It gives you a sense of the importance of who you are and where you came from." She also appeared on such TV shows as *Ironsides, The Young and the Restless*, and *The Partridge Family*. She was cast as an attorney in *Hill Street Blues*. Haru, whose family hails from Ilocos Norte Province, Philippines, still looks forward to the day when she can play a woman her age in any dramatic series.

IGARTA, VENANCIO. Filipino American Master Colorist. Venancio Igarta, the oldest and most celebrated Filipino American master colorist of the visual art scene, is the recipient of the *Pamana ng Pilipino* Award from President Fidel Ramos as one of the most outstanding overseas Filipinos in 1996.

During ceremonies held at Malacañang, Philippines, President Ramos paid tribute to 45 outstanding overseas Filipinos (including Igarta) and organizations whose exemplary deeds and contributions to the Philippines have uplifted the lives of many of their countrymen. The awarding ceremonies were part of the observance of the "Month of Overseas Filipinos."

Praise. Writer Celia Aborro, Igarta's biographer and friend, in the April 5-11, 1996, issue of the New York City-based *Filipino Reporter*, was quoted as saying, "Igarta is extraordinary, he's an original, he's a master and he's a breakaway artist because his art is not a traditional art you associate with. Igarta has departed from academic images that we used to, making him a master artist."

From Ilocos Sur to the U.S.A. Born in Sinait, Ilocos Sur Province, Philippines, on May 18, 1912, Igarta, left his hometown in 1930, when he was 18 years old, to seek his destiny in the United States. He settled in San Francisco, California, and worked as a laborer on farms and in factories. After four years in California, Igarta moved to New York City.

His Talent Discovered by a Nurse. After holding odd jobs, he was employed as a houseboy in a psychiatric hospital on Park Avenue in New York City. At that time, his nurse supervisor painted designs on meal metal trays that were used for serving meals. One day, Igarta found an unfinished tray design and he completed it. The nurse supervisor was amazed at what he drew and she encouraged him to study art. Igarta attended art classes at the National Academy of Design and other art schools.

At Last, a Door Is Opened! Eventually, his work was exhibited in a commercial gallery. Then other paintings were shown in well-known institutions. One of his great works, *Northern Philippines*, an oil painting, was shown at the Museum of Modern Art in New York City. In 1940, this same painting was reproduced and featured in *Fortune Magazine*. Later, his fame as an artist reached his native Philippines.

A Twist of Fate. Igarta's marriage to an Englishwoman, however, resulted in a bitter divorce that made him broke. Depressed, he burned many of his drawings and paintings, including his masterpiece "Northern Philippines." Only a few of his early works were spared.

He spent his next 25 years without painting. However, he continued to work in his regular job as a master colorist, retiring in 1982 at the age of 70.

The Call of His First Love. Upon retirement, he felt the urge to paint again. And he did—creating a number of masterpieces. He became famous again with his drawings, watercolor, oil, and acrylic paintings.

"I'm Going Home!" Igarta, after an absence of 62 years, might have said, "I'm going home!" when he went home to the Philippines in 1992 to have an exhibit at the Metropolitan Museum of Arts in Manila. More than 50 of his art pieces, mostly done from 1982 to 1992, were exhibited at the show.

Larry Itliong, Labor Leader. At the age of 16, Larry Itliong, with a sixth-grade education, left Pangasinan Province in the Philippines to follow a dream: to become a lawyer and politician. One year after his arrival in the United States in 1929, Itliong joined striking lettuce pickers in Washington State. Later, he helped establish the Alaska Cannery Workers Union in the 1930s.

As a Worker. Itliong, like any other workers, among others, worked in canneries in Alaska, harvested sugar beets in South Dakota and Montana, laid railroad track, and worked everywhere where he could find a job. Anytime and anywhere that Filipinos had a problem, he was always there.

Union Activities. In 1953, Itliong became the vice president of the Cannery Workers Union in Seattle, Washington. After that, he organized the Filipino Farm Labor Union in 1956. In 1965, he and Pete Velasco led the Filipinos in striking against grape growers in the Coachella Valley in California, obtaining higher pay for the workers. Then he led a strike against grape growers in Delano, California, the center of grape vineyards. It was during that time that Cesar Chavez's union joined the Filipino strikers. Later, the Filipino and Mexican unions were formed into one organization, which became the United Farm Workers of America, AFL-CIO. The strike, ending in July 1970, resulted in the hike of wages and a medical plan for workers. In 1971, in a dispute with some union officials, he resigned as second-in-command of the UFW.

The Work Continues. After he was out of the UFW, Itliong continued his fight for the rights of retired Filipino workers. He founded the Filipino American Political Association.

Family. For a short time, Itliong was first married to a woman he met at the New Continent Pool Hall in "Little Manila" in Seattle Washington. His second wife bore him three children, but left him. When he went to Manila, he met and married his third wife. His fourth wife was a Mexican woman and they had one child. All in all, Itliong had seven children. Born in 1914, he died in 1977.

JAO, RADMAR AGANA. Up and Coming Actor. Theodore Roosevelt once said, "Far better it is to dare mighty things, to win glorious triumphs, even though checkered by failure, than to take rank with those poor spirits who neither enjoy much nor suffer much, because they live in the gray twilight that knows no victory nor defeat."

It is in that spirit that Radmar Agana Jao initially took the challenge of becoming an actor and is now one of a handful of up-and-coming Filipino Americans who are making a name for themselves in Hollywood. Against all odds, he has worked hard to earn the privilege of being called a "working actor" among his peers.

From the day he started acting, he has never looked back. Today, Jao (pronounced "how"), plays a Tagalog-speaking cook, named Kim on NBC's hit comedy "Union Square," which airs on Thursday evening at 8:30 p.m. Jao said his Tagalog-speaking character is nonetheless "a great thing for the Filipino American community."

"Ideally, my character would have no accent, and not play a cook, but at least there is representation of the Filipino culture, which I'm totally, totally proud of," Jao explained to Corin Ramos, a correspondent of the *Philippine News*.

Actually, the producers wanted a Vietnamese to play the role of Kim. However, they were impressed with Jao's audition that they didn't mind when they learned he was a Filipino.

Earlier Roles. Jao has appeared on such TV shows as *Seinfeld, Crisis Center, Boston Common, Nightstand,* and *Burning Zone.* Highlights of his film credits include the major motion pictures, *The Phantom* and *Contact,* and the independent features, *Shopping for Fangs, Fall 1990,* and *Debut* (by Filipino American filmmaker Gene Cajayon). However, Jao began his career in the theatre, working with the prestigious East West Players, the nation's first and foremost Asian American theatre company, based in Los Angeles, California. He received the LA Theatre League's 1995 Ovation Award for "Best Supporting Actor in a Musical" for East West Players' critically acclaimed production of *Sweeney Todd.*

A Career in the Art Is His Calling. Born and raised in Northwest Indiana, this actor who is commonly called Radmar, is the son of Dr. Rodolfo L. Jao and famed Filipina child star Tessie Agana (daughter of Linda Estrella). Obviously, performing has always been in his blood. Ever since he and his eight other siblings began performing together at medical functions and other family get-togethers, Jao knew that a career in the arts was his calling. However, in typical Filipino fashion, academic excellence was what was important. The arts was only a hobby. So he decided to follow in his father's footsteps and set his sights on becoming a doctor. Despite excelling in academics during his high school and college years, the medical profession just kept eluding him. The arts was calling him.

Focuses on His Career. Jao received his bachelor of arts in telecommunications, with a a minor in Theatre, from Indiana University. He set his goals on becoming a film and television producer/director. He moved to Los Angeles in 1989 and began working as an assistant to the executive producer of *China Beach* then moved on to work for other producers on such shows as *Life Goes On* and *Under Cover,* among others. It was while taking an acting class at East West Players that he was "discovered" by Amy Hill and asked to audition for the Berkeley Repertory Theatre's production of *Dragonwings.* Needless to say, he got the part and continued touring with the show for the next two years in New York, Seattle, and Atlanta. He has since worked in all aspects of the entertainment industry, in front of and behind the scenes, trying to make a positive impact, not only as an Asian American, but also as a Filipino American.

Currently, Radmar Agana Jao is proud to be working with a group called INSIDE/OUT. This is a collection of artists from various backgrounds and disciplines, whose mission is to work with inner city junior high school students and help them express themselves in a positive and creative way, thus providing them with an alternative to the violence and negativity that surrounds them. He continues to balance working in the Los Angeles theatre scene with film and television work and dares to be the first Filipino American to receive an Academy Award. As his credits continue to grow, this seemingly impossible goal may soon become a reality.

JAYA, Singer. A Filipina American and a Filipina/African American, and daughter of Elizabeth Ramsey, Jaya had the first Filipino single to hit the charts. That was in 1989. Her song *If You Leave Me Now* almost hit the Top 40 list and stayed for a record-breaking 26 weeks, according to the song's co-producer Glen Gutierrez.

Her Filipina mother, Ramsey, was one of the top comedians on stage, television, and movies in the 60s and 70s in the Philippines.

Jaya, a former San Jose (California) resident, who now lives in the Philippines, was named the Best New Artist and Best Pop Female Vocal artist Performance at the third Annual Katha Music Awards held in 1997 at Cinema 2 of EDSA Shangrila Hotel in Manila, Philippines.

JIMENEZ, JOSEPHINE, CFA. Montgomery Money Manager. A founding partner of the emerging markets discipline at Montgomery Asset Management (based in San Francisco, California), Josephine Jimenez manages over $2.5B of investments, including the Montgomery Emerging Markets Fund. She received a master of science degree from the Massachusetts Institute of Technology (M.I.T.) in 1981 and a bachelor of science from New York University in 1979.

Prior to joining Montgomery Asset Management in 1991, Jimenez worked for five years at Emerging Markets Investors Corporation, where she managed over $300M. During 1984-1987, she was an investment officer at Shawmut Corporation, and from 1982-1984, she was an analyst at the Massachusetts Mutual Life Insurance Company.

Learning the Values of Life. Jimenez was born in Lucena, Quezon Province, Philippines, on June 6, 1954. She spent her childhood in Lucena and in Olongapo, Zambales. A family setback led to her being placed as an intern at Hospicio de San Jose, operated by Hijas de Caridad (Daughters of Charity) from 1962 to 1965. Jimenez recalls those years at Hospicio as "happy days at a fine finishing school," where young girls were taught the values of life. She later attended St. Joseph's School in Olongapo. She completed her secondary education at the University of the East in Manila in 1970.

Immigrates to the U.S. Immigrating to the United States in 1972, Jimenez financed her undergraduate education by working full-time. With some savings and a strong determination to succeed, she later studied full-time at M.I.T. Upon completing her studies, Jimenez relentlessly pursued a career in emerging markets investments. Not only did she believe in the investment potential of these countries, but she also found the pursuit intrinsically rewarding for she believes that by investing in these countries, she would be able to help others as more jobs are created; thus, contributing to the world's social and economic development.

Rising Market Portfolio Manager. In 1985, inspired by the challenges presented by hyper-inflation in Argentina and Brazil, Jimenez developed a proprietary stock valuation model for inflationary economies, under the guidance of her former thesis advisor at M.I.T., Dr. Franco Modigliani, recipient of the 1985 Nobel Prize in Economics. Jimenez has built a reputation as one of the best emerging markets portfolio managers and is cited in *Who's Who in the World.* She has been frequently interviewed and featured in several publications, including the *Wall Street Journal,* and has appeared as a guest on several television shows. She is an elected member of the board of trustees of the M.I.T. Corporation.

KIM, DONNA MERCADO. Councilmember, Honolulu, Hawaii.

With a strong desire to participate in government, Donna Mercado Kim's political career began with her election in 1982 to the State House of Representatives for District 40, in which she was elected for two terms, 1982-1986. She resigned in 1985 and successfully ran in a special election for the Honolulu City Council. She was then reelected in 1986, 1990, and 1994 and is currently serving her third full term as a councilmember where she has been, since 1987, the chair of the powerful Zoning Committee.

Before Entering Public Office. Prior to holding an elective office, Kim was the executive director of a local modeling agency. She has served as a member of the National League of Cities - Economic Development Steering Committee, the President's National Committee on Transportation, and the YMCA Century Club. She also served as a director of the Asian Pacific American Municipal Offi-  cials, Hawaii's Junior Miss Program, Kalihi Business Association, and Planned Parenthood and Bank of America-Hawaii. At present, Kim is a member of the board of trustees of Palama Settlement, and member of the Filipino Chamber of Commerce and the Hawaii Korean Chamber of Commerce. She was voted one of Hawaii's Three Outstanding Young Persons in 1988 and was named the 1997 Outstanding City & County Administrator.

Aims. She considers herself pro-economic and believes that government must work in partnership with the private sector to utilize all resources to stimulate and diversify our economy. Her main focus is to upgrade the city's infrastructure, lower government spending by scrutinizing all budget requests, cut unnecessary and excessive expenditures and improve the island's transportation system.

Kim's formula for success is, "To achieve all that is possible, you must attempt the impossible."

Education. Kim was born and raised in Kalihi-Palama, Hawaii, and is a graduate of Farrington High School. She attended the University of Hawaii from 1970-1972 and completed her education at Washington State University, graduating with a B.A. in recreation, *cum laude.* Kim is married and has an eight-year-old son.

LANDERO II, REYNALDO "Rey" R., M.D. Noted Internist-Pulmonologist/Political, Civic, and Community Leader.

While a man of medicine, Reynaldo "Rey" R. Landero is one of the Filipino American "movers" and "shakers" in political and community circles.

As a politician and leader, he is the founding chairman of the Confederation of Philippine-United States Organizations (CONPUSO), which is billed as an umbrella organization composed of the presidents of about 300 various Southern California organizations. "While Filipinos are the largest Asian minority in California, they need to cross those lines of division," according to Landero. "We have a lot of things to do here as a minority," he says.

"I want to work the issues directly affecting and uplifting the Filipino Americans here, rather than worry about the political shenanigans in the Philippines," he pointed out, clarifying his stand in organizing CONPUSO. "The effectiveness of banding the leaders from Los Angeles area is important to the political, economic, and social upliftment of the Filipinos," he adds.

Emphasizing the need of Filipinos to participate in the mainstream America, he says, "We should encourage Filipino Americans for political empowerment and legislative involvement."

As a political leader, Landero has also been involved in fund-raising and policy making of both Filipino American candidates and American politicians who are supportive to the Filipino endeavors. Landero's dynamic leadership and expertise naturally catapulted him into the helm of leadership in the Filipino American community. It was his appointment as a commissioner to the Cultural Heritage Commission during the administration of Los Angeles City Mayor Tom Bradley that strengthened his credibility as a leader. At the same time, he engineered the appointment of several Filipino leaders in the policy making body in the State of California during Governor Brown's administration. Some news writers called him the virtual "King of the Hill." He calls the shots on almost every community undertakings in his capacity as head of this or that organization. Being the acknowledged leader of the Filipino Americans in Southern California, his presence at gatherings as emcee or speaker is a social event in itself.

Flashback. Born in Manila, Philippines, on October 3, 1940, Dr. Landero graduated from the Manila Central University in Manila with a the degree of doctor of medicine in May 1967. He took his rotating internship at the North General Hospital and subsequently took an intensive training in internal medicine at the UP-PGH, both in Manila. In the same year, he passed both the Philippine National Medical Board and the ECFMG (Educational Council for Foreign Medical Graduates) exams. He soon took up his rotating internship at the St. Thomas Hospital in Akron, Ohio, with rotation to the famous Children's Hospital of Akron.

Dr. Landero moved to California the following year, to take his internal medicine residency at the Long Beach VA Medical Center and University of California in Irvine. He had his pulmonary fellowship at the Wadsworth VA Medical Center-UCLA with rotation at Harbor General Hospital. He passed his California FLEX board exam and was licensed in 1972. He taught as a clinical instructor in medicine at the University of Southern California from 1973-1985. He is a practicing internist and a pulmonary consultant in several South Bay Hospitals.

Landero has been president and board chairman of several professional, religious, business, social, and cultural organizations. He holds memberships in local, county, and national medical associations and specialty societies.

Awards and Honors. Dr. Landero is the recipient of an award bestowed on him by the *Fil-Am Image* magazine, as one of the Twenty Outstanding Filipino Americans in the United States in 1992. His other awards include Outstanding Community Leader from County Supervisors and Outstanding Community Leader from Los Angeles Mayor Bradley. He is listed in *Who's Who in California* (1983-1984); *International Who's Who in Education,* (Cambridge, England, 1982); *Who's Who Among Asian Americans,* and *Quien es Quien* among Hispanics in 1994. He was very elated when he was chosen to give the prestigious 27th FD Tanchoco Memorial medical lecture, during his Silver Jubilee homecoming celebration in Manila on December 21, 1992. He is presently active in the celebration of the Philippine Independence Centennial, acting as vice-chairman.

Family. Landero and his wife, Lynda, reside in Santa Ana, California. They have five children: Rey Raleigh III, Lorelei, Rosanna, Rey Rainier IV, and Rey Randall V, all independent and on their own with families.

LARETA, ALFRED. Lawyer, Hawaii Judicial Circuit Judge.

Born in Oahu, Hawaii, but grew up in Maui, Hawaii, Alfred Lareta was appointed by Governor John A. Burns in 1969 as judge of the fifth judicial circuit, which encompassed the county of Kauai. He served as director of the Department of Labor and Industrial Relations under Governor Burns from 1962 to 1967. He became the first Filipino American to hold a state cabinet position in the United States.

Lareta was a self-supporting student at the University of Hawaii. He received a scholarship to Fordham University School of Law, where he obtained his law degree. He returned to Honolulu, where he formed a law partnership with George Ariyoshi, who became Hawaii's third governor in 1975, and Bernaldo D. Bicoy. Bicoy was elected to the Hawaii House of Representatives in 1958.

LASERNA, ROSARIO "SARI," M.D. Obstetrician-Gynecologist.

A graduate of the University of Santo Thomas in Manila, Philippines, Dr. Rosario Guanzon Laserna has been in practice for over 20 years. She is executive vice president of the Obstetrics and Gynecology Associates of Fredericksburg, P.C. in Fredericksburg, Virginia. She is also the medical director of the Spotswood Medical Center and president and CEO of SMC Alternative Health Care and Anti-Aging CTR.

Dr. Laserna is not only known for her excellence  as a physician, but also for her being a civic-minded person. She is currently the president of the Philippine Economic and Cultural Endowment (PEACE), which is a humanitarian and civic organization currently preoccupied with constructing artisan wells in rural areas in the Philippines. In 1996, Dr. Laserna received from President Fidel Ramos the LINKKAPIL Award on behalf of PEACE. The award is conferred on overseas Filipino associations or individuals for their contribution to Philippine national development efforts. It is one of five categories of presidential awards for overseas Filipino individuals and organizations.

Flashback. Dr. Laserna is a member of the rich and famous Guanzon family in Manila, Philippines. She is one of five sisters who were known as Farmacia Oro's "5 Golden Girls." Together, they formed a formidable team, the five golden girls of Oro Laboratories, Farmacia Oro, and the Guanzon-Guidote Enterprises. The sisters have been known not only for their beauty, but also for their being talented, educated, and business-minded.

During her stay in the Philippines, back then, Laserna was the medical and marketing director of Oro Laboratories, in addition to being the company physician of three other corporations.

Dr. Laserna, in explaining why she took medicine, recalls, "My father was the one who selected medicine for me. I personally preferred commerce. So every time he traveled, I shifted to commerce. And when he came back, he made me shift back to medicine. It was always like that until I graduated."

After being a doctor in the Philippines for several years, Laserna decided to take post-graduate training in the United States. She met her would-be husband when she undertook her residency at the St. Vincent's Medical Center in New York City. "I trained under him for about three years," she recalls.

Affiliations. A diplomate of the American College of Ob-Gyn and an American College of Ob-Gyn fellow, Laserna is a member of Special Task Force of FMGs-Medical Society of Virginia, Fredericksburg Area Medical Society, Mary Washington Hospital Medical Society, Society of Philippine Surgeons in America, and lifetime member of PEACE.

Special Award. Laserna, as a car driver, won special awards as the only "Woman Shell Car Rally Champion for AA Division (Philippines) from 1966 to 1970.

Family. Dr. Laserna is married to Dr. Oscar Laserna, a gynecologist. They have three children: Ace, 24; Marisol, 20; and Anthony. 17. They live in Fredericksburg, Virginia.

LEIGHTON, VERONICA V. Editor/Publisher and TV Show Producer. One of the most well-known Filipino Americans in Chicago, Illinois, Veronica V. Leighton is the editor/publisher of *Via Times* and producer of the *Chicago Philippine Reports*, the only locally-produced weekly television program for Filipino Americans in Chicago.

Using desktop publishing and working from her home, Leighton, a former columnist for a national Filipino American newspaper, has come a long way since she started publishing *Via Times* 15 years ago. Today, the monthly newsmagazine has a readership between 50,000 and 60,000. Although she didn't need a big capital in starting her publishing, it was a real struggle for her along the way to success.

"People really watched for me to fall, especially since I'm a woman, " she was quoted as saying in an interview in *Your Money* magazine (February 1987) issue. She attributes her success to "a lot of trial and error, a lot of struggle, persistency, guts, and determination."

Projects and Activities. Besides being an editor/publisher and TV program producer and president of Veron Publishing, Inc., Leighton is the president of Verrene, Inc.; producer of the Annual Presentation of Chicago's Prettiest Filipinas; producer of Chicago's Filipino American Hall of Fame and producer of America's Fil-Am Heritage Award, and Midwest coordinator of the Philippine Children's Fund Midwest; member of the board of advisors of the Society of Young Filipino American Professionals and the Philippine Centennial Celebration's 1998 Field Museum Exhibition.and Chicago coordinator for the Philippine Children's Fund and the Chicago marketing director of *TV Patrol* (ABS-CBN, Philippines).

Awards and Honors. Leighton, the holder of a bachelor's degree in foreign service from the University of the Philippines, is the recipient of numerous awards and honors. They include Who's Who Among American Women; Most Outstanding Asian from Asian American Coalition; Most Outstanding Asian in Journalism as chosen by Asian Human Services; Community Builders Award from Mason Lodge No. 937; Most Outstanding Filipino in the Midwest in Journalism by the Cavite Association of America; Publisher of the Year 1989 award from the City of Chicago's Minority

Enterprise Development; award from the Philippine Chamber of Commerce's "Recognition Night for Filipino Entrepreneurs in 1990"; Women's Voices award from Women in Business Yellow Pages; one of 100 Chicago Women to Watch as chosen by *Today's Chicago Woman;* One of Twenty Outstanding Filipinos in America as chosen by *Fil-Am Image* magazine in Washington D.C.; Women's Hall of Fame '90 award from the City of Chicago; Media Award 1993 from the Philippine Department of Foreign Affairs; and Woman of the Year 1996-1997 award from Reflections VIII, in Los Angeles, California."

LEWIS, LOIDA NICOLAS. Lawyer, Author, and Entrepreneur. Loida Nicolas Lewis is chairman and CEO of TLC Beatrice International Holdings, Inc., a multinational food company with sales in 1996 of $2.2 billion. One of the best known Filipino Americans, she was once on the covers of the *Working Woman* and *Filipinas*, a Filipino American magazine in the United States. She has been cited as one of the most successful women business executives in the corporate world. She has also been honored, together with six other Asian American Achievers as part of *A. Magazine's* 1997 Bridge Builder Awards in New York City. She recently received the Ronald H. Brown Leadership Award from the U.S. Department of Commerce.

Assumes Leadership of TLC Beatrice. An attorney by profession and admitted to practice in the Philippines and in New York, Lewis served as an informal adviser and confidante to her late husband, Reginald F. Lewis, TLC Beatrice's first chairman and CEO. She assumed the leadership of the company in February 1994, a year after her husband's death. She moved quickly to cut costs, sell non-core and under-performing assets, reduce debt, and strengthen her management team.

Reginald Lewis acquired Beatrice International in December 1987 in a $985 million leveraged buyout. He moved quickly to reduce debt by disposing of non-core assets and repositioned the company around a group of diversified food companies in Europe.

TLC Beatrice is a major manufacturer and marketer of ice cream in Spain and the Canary Islands, and it is the leading manufacturer of potato chips in Ireland. It also has beverage operations in Holland, Belgium, France, and Thailand.

Lewis was the first Asian woman to pass the New York State bar exam without having studied law in the U.S. After winning her discrimination complaint on the basis of race, sex, and national origin against the Immigration and Naturalization Service (INS) in 1979, she served as general attorney with the INS until 1990.

Book Author. Lewis has written three books on U.S. immigration law. The latest is *How to Get a Green*

Card, now a bestseller in that genre. In 1972, she established a monthly magazine for the Filipino American community and served as the magazine's publisher until it merged with another publication in 1979.

She has spoken to audiences around the country and the world to promote the biography of her late husband, *Why Should White Guys Have All the Fun?...How Reginald Lewis Created a Billion Dollar Business Empire*.

Memberships. Lewis, one of the founders of the Asian-American Legal Defense & Education Fund, is a member of the Business Roundtable, the Council on Foreign Relations and Jack and Jill. She serves on the boards of the Dance Theater of Harlem, the National Foundation for Teaching Entrepreneurship, and the Black Patriots Foundation.

Flashback. She is a graduate of the University of the Philippines College of Law and a *cum laude* graduate of St. Theresa's College, two of the Philippines' premier educational institutions. Lewis comes from a family of entrepreneurs: her father started one of the Philippines' largest furniture manufacturers. Born in the Philippines, she currently resides in New York City. Presently learning Chinese, she speaks several languages: English, French, Spanish, and Pilipino. She and her husband have two children.

LIDDELL, GENE CANQUE. First U.S. Filipina American Mayor. The daughter of Filipino farm workers in Hawaii, Gene Canque Liddell is considered the first Filipino American woman to become a city mayor in the United States. She was unanimously elected by the city council of Lacey City, a suburb of Seattle, Washington, as its mayor on April 11, 1991.

Liddell, who obtained a bachelor's degree in science from Washington State University in Seattle, Washington, in 1964, earned her master's degree in science from the University of Oregon in 1978. In 1964, she became a junior high school physical education teacher in the Auburn School District of Washington. From 1966-1973, she was a high school teacher in the Olympia School District. She later became an administrative intern in the Office of Superintendent of Public Instruction. A community leader, Liddell was appointed as director of Washington's Department of Community Development by Governor Mike Lowry in July 1993.

MADEIROS, GLEN. Singer. A Filipino American from Hawaii, Glen Madeiros, made the hottest singles list with his ballad, *Nothing's Gonna Change My Love for You* in the 1980s.

MALAPIT, EDUARDO E. Hawaii Elected Mayor. Eduardo E. Malapit became the first Filipino American to be elected mayor in the United States. Before being elected mayor of Kauai, Hawaii, Malapit served several terms on the Kauai County Council.

MANAYAN, HENRY. Mayor, Milpitas, California. Henry Manayan, a Milpitas council member, won by a clear landslide to clinch the top position of that Silicon Valley's city government during the elections of November 5, 1996. He garnered 5,164 votes, giving him a 12 percent margin over his closest rival, Jim Larson, in this city of 65,000 people.

With a Filipino father from Ilocos Norte Province, Philippines, and a Chinese mother, Manayan declared after the elections, "Thank you for your enthusiastic and general support." Milpitas has over 12,000 Filipinos, making them the largest immigrant group. The Chinese rank second in the Asian population. Whites make up the majority.

Manayan

Three years ago, Manayan was elected into one of two hotly contested seats for the city council of Milpitas by a margin of 107 votes during the November 1994 elections. Son of Dr. Henry and Lorraine Manayan, Henry was born in New York City. As a young boy, his parents moved to Hawaii, where he became fluent in Japanese, Chinese, and German.

Education. After graduation from high school, Manayan returned to New York. He studied at Syracuse University, where he obtained a B.A. from the Maxwell School of Citizenship and Public Affairs and Oxford University. Later, he received his juris doctor from the University of Santa Clara School of Law where he met his future wife and law partner, Anna, who is of German, Polish, and Japanese descent.

Affiliations. Manayan's affiliations include the American and Hawaii Bar associations, the San Jose Metropolitan Chamber of Commerce, and the San Jose Real Estate Board.

Awards. In 1992, he received an award as Businessperson of the Year from the Filipino Chamber of Commerce.

MANDAC, EVELYN. International Lyric soprano. Born in Malaybalay, Bukidnon Province, Philippines, Evelyn Mandac is the recipient of the *Pamana ng Pilipino* award granted during the awarding ceremonies for the 1996 Awards for Outstanding Filipinos and Organizations at Malacanang in December 1996. The yearly presidential awards are given to outstanding overseas Filipinos and organizations in recognition of their exemplary deeds and contributions to the Philippines.

Singing with Placido Domingo. Mandac, the first Filipino to sing with world-reknown Placido Domingo at the world-famous Metropolitan Opera in New York City, had her debut at the Metropolitan Opera in 1975 as Lauretta in six performances of *Gianni Schicchi*.

Other Performances. She also performed at the Met as Zerlina in *Don Giovanni*; played the lead roles in Massenet's *Manon*, in Stravinsky's *Rake's Progress*, and in Puccini's *La Boheme*. She toured Europe, where she had a great success performing in Mozart's *Marriage of Figano* under the baton of Herbert von Karajan. She also performed at the Promenade Concerts at the Royal Albert Hall in London and at the Glyndebourne Opera Festival in England.

Residing in New York, Mandac is married to Sanjoy Bhattacharya, an investment banker from India.

MANIBOG, G. MONTY. Three-term City Mayor, Monterey Park, California. A practicing lawyer for the past 30 years, G. Monty Manibog is one of the best-known Filipino city mayors in the United States. The Philippine American Bar Association has bestowed upon him, the Distinguished Service Award in recognition of his pioneering endeavors and accomplishments both in law and in politics.

A graduate of the University of the Philippines, Manibog represented the Philippines in the World Olympics of 1952 held in Helsinki, Finland, as a Philippine national wrestling champion. Married to Jean Gingerich, of Cincinnati, Ohio, Manibog and his wife have six grown children: Monty, Jr., Lisa, Lana, Ricky, Dean, and Darren.

MANUEL, EDUARDO G. Former Mayor, Hercules, California. When he was little, Eduardo "Eddie" G. Manuel had a dream: to be of service to the community and to walk on the streets in California. From November 23, 1993, to December 4, 1994, he didn't only walk on the streets of California; he was the city mayor of Hercules, California.

Flashback. Born and raised in Pasig, Rizal Province, Philippines, to Ilocano parents, Manuel studied at the Pasig Catholic School (now College), operated by Belgian Fathers of the CICM Order.

Graduating from high school as valedictorian in 1957, he attended the Mapua Institute of Technology in Manila to study engineering. Later, however, he decided to take up foreign service, and he went to the Lyceum of the Philippines, where he was involved in student activism. As he hobnobbed with student leaders, Manuel was influenced by them to add political science and journalism as his other fields of dreams. He became a journalist in Manila. He also became a good public speaker; he would often go on stage and recite poetry. He later became a poet—his poem, *Had I Been Born to Fame and Fortune*, was certified as a semi-finalist in the 1995 North American Open Poetry Contest, sponsored by the National Library of Poetry, with main offices in Ownings Mills, Maryland.

Bitten by the Bug of Politics. Manuel became interested in politics. In fact, in the 1960s after he had become a political leader of Frisco San Juan, who became a congressman in Rizal Province, Manuel was groomed to be a candidate for councilman in Pasig.

To Pursue His American Dream. Manuel left Manila for the United States in March 1968. He first worked at the Washington Gas Company in Washington, D.C., where he met his would-be wife, Norma Alano, of Quezon Province, who was then a nurse with the Doctors' Hospital in the nation's capital. The two later married and left for the West in 1972, thinking of his dream of "walking on the streets of California." For some time, they settled in Sacramento and Daly City, California. Eventually, they settled in Hercules, California, where he immediately became involved in community services and political affairs.

Turning Point in Life. The turning point of his political life came when he was appointed in November 1991 to the Hercules City Council seat previously held by another Filipino, Goni Solidum, who had resigned. Then, on November 4, 1992, he was elected as a council member to the seat he had held the past year by appointment. In 1993, he was unanimously elected city mayor by the city council.

Special Talents and Skills. Manuel, who obtained a master's degree in public administration from Golden Gate University in San Francisco, has special talents and skills. For instance, besides being a poet, he sings and composes music. His singing ability is one of the keys to his popularity in the community, "I am usually the life of the party," Manuel says. He composed the theme song of the football team San Francisco '49ers, after their 1989 Super Bowl Victory, which he titled '49ers Fight Song. His two other compositions are *Hercules Lions Song*, and *America Beloved.* Manuel continues to work as a full-time deputy clerk in the U.S. Court of Appeals in San Francisco.

Positions Held. Manuel's positions held, past and present, include chairman, West Contra Costa Mayors and Supervisors Association, June 1994-December 1994; director, West Contra Costa Transit Authority (1991-present; alternate delegate of the Contra Costa Mayors Conference to the Association of Bay Area Governments (ABAG), January 1970-July 1995; California delegate to the White House Conference on Library and Information Services, July 1991; and board member, Filipino American Political Association.

Awards and Honors. Manuel's various awards and honors include a resolution of recognition from the City of Hercules for services as mayor of Hercules, December 18, 1994; Contra Costa County Supervisors Certificate of Commendation for his services, March 1995; Political Leader of the Year Trophy from Filipino Media Production (San Francisco), February 1995; and State of California "All-Star Awardee" as the best community partner in the Partnerships for Change Program, 1990.

MARCIAL, GENE G. Senior Writer, Business Week. A senior writer of *Business Week*, Gene G. Marcial writes the column "Inside Wall Street" in the national publication. He is the author of the book *Secrets of the Street: The Dark Side of Making Money*, published by McGraw-Hill. *The Secrets of the Street*, a controversial, gripping tale of how Wall Street really makes its money, was released in 1995.

Marcial is one of three former staff members of the *Manila Chronicle* who made good in the United States. (The other two are Veltisezar B. Bautista, successful author-publisher, and Alberto Alfaro, editor-in-chief of the *Manila Mail*, based in Washington D.C.)

Marcial joined *Business Week* on August 3, 1991, to purposely write the column. Before he joined the publication, he was a senior writer at the *Wall Street Journal*, where he wrote the columns "Heard on the Street" and "Abreast of the Market." Prior to joining the *Wall Street Journal*, he was a copy editor at the AP-Dow Jones News Service.

A graduate of the University of Santo Tomas, Manila, Philippines, where he received a bachelor of literature in journalism, Marcial obtained a master's degree in politics from the New York University in New York City.

MARIANO, ELEANOR CONCEPCION, M.D. President Clinton's Personal Physician. The daughter of Filipino immigrants and a valedictorian of her San Diego, California, high school class, Dr. Eleanor Concepcion Mariano, 42, is President Bill Clinton's personal doctor. The medical team headed by Dr. Mariano takes care of the health needs of Vice President Al Gore and all employes in the White House as well.

The Doctor Is a Commander. Dr. Mariano, a commander in U.S. Navy, assumed the position in February 1993 after Army Colonel Lawrence Mohr retired from the service. An honors university graduate, she is a board-certified general internist and fellow of the American College of Physicians.

MARINO, SALVADOR (DADO). Flyweight boxing Champion. Dado Marino, born in 1916 in Honolulu, Hawaii, the world's flyweight boxing champion when he defeated Terry Allen in a bout in Honolulu in 1950. A year before, he lost as a bantamweight contender to Manuel Ortiz.

MARTIN, ARSENIO R., M.D. Medical Director, Marathon and Olympic Torch Runner. As a growing boy in Cabatuan, Isabela, Province, Philippines, Arsenio R. Martin didn't dream to be a physician and he never imagined to be in America. However, "When I went to college and in my last years in medicine, I raised my expectations and aimed to the West (America) and I came to the United States in 1967." As a foreigner, he had to work harder to fit in with the American life. Then he was awarded the Most Outstanding Intern and again as a chief resident in one of the top training institutions in the U.S.

"I continued to raise my goals and dreams and choreographed my life from it," he says. "As someone once said," he continues, 'If you can dream it, you can have it."

"Pinnacle of My Dreams." Thus he reached, what he called "the pinnacle of my dreams." He was honored to be "one of the Most Outstanding Philippine Physicians in the United States in 1992 by the Association of Philippine Physicians in America. He has been a Texas delegate to the APPPA for the past three years. He was also voted as the Most Outstanding Alumni FEU-Medicine in 1992.

Dr. Martin, a pulmonary specialist, is currently the medical director of the Respiratory Department, chairman of the Department of Medicine, and member of the governing board of the St. Mary Hospital in Port Arthur, Texas. He is board certified and a diplomate of the American Board of Internal Medicine.

Training. Dr. Martin took his rotating internship at the Grant Hospital of Chicago (Most Outstanding Intern) during 1968-1969 and his residency in medicine in the same hospital during 1969-1970. From 1970-1972, he was an internal medicine resident at Cook County Hospital in Chicago, Illinois. From 1972-1973, he took his fellowship in pulmonary disease at the same hospital, where he also became chief resident in medicine. From 1973-1974, he underwent his fellowship in pulmonary medicine at Hines V.A. Hospital in Hines, Illinois. From 1974-1979, he was an attending consultant at the pulmonary section at the same hospital. Also, he was on the faculty at the Loyola Stritch School of Medicine.

Memberships. In Texas, Dr. Martin became president of the Filipino American South Texas and president of the Texas Association of Philippine Physicians. He was also chairperson, along with his wife, for the Charity Fund Drive (Heavenly Ball) for St. Mary Hospital that brought a national celebrity to the area. He also chaired the fund drive to aid the victims of Mt. Pinatubo in the Philippines, including two musical extravaganzas featuring Jaime Rivera (fresh from the *Miss Saigon* show in London) in Beaumont and Houston, Texas. He is on the board of directors of FACOST (Filipino-American Council of South Texas), the governing organization of all Filipino American organizations in southern Texas. Dr. Martin has been on the board of the FEU Dr. Nicanor Reyes Medical Alumni Foundation as a chapter president of the board of governors since 1982.

Carries the Olympic Torch. As a hobby, Dr. Martin ran for many years until a recent injury related to his running. He has participated and completed 15 marathons (26.2 miles) all over the country, including three Boston Marathons. One of the highlights of his life was his selection to carry the Olympic Torch in 1996 in Texas. "Through a long distance runner's perspective, the relay was just a mere kilometer, a small fraction compared to the 26.6 miles of a marathon," Dr. Martin comments on his participation in the carrying of the Olympic torch.

Family. **Dr.** Martin and his wife, Fe Mercado Martin, a board certified pediatrician, have two sons and one daughter: Ronald, who is attending the University of Texas; Ryan, who is attending the University of Notre Dame; and Regina, who graduated from Kelly High School in Beaumont, Texas.

MATTINGLEY, AIDA SANTOS. Librarian-Teacher, Facilitator, Speaker, Performing Artist, Community Leader, Chair of Utah Governor's Council for Asian Affairs. The first Filipina American appointed by the Utah governor to serve for a second term to the Governor's Asian-American Advisory Council, Aida Santos Mattingley is also the first Filipina American to receive the Utah Centennial Asian-American Leadership Award and the Governor's Leadership Award.

A graduate of the University of Santo Tomas in Manila, Philippines, with a bachelor of science in education, majors in English and Library Science, she immigrated to the United States in 1975 to join her family in San Francisco, California. In November 1975, she moved to Salt Lake City, Utah to seek the oasis of her religion. Mattingley is a Mormon, a member of the Church of Jesus Christ of Latter Day Saints (LDS Church).

Accomplishments. Twenty-two years passed and a litany of accomplishments deck her name. Just to name a few: chair of the Board of Trustees and director of the Filipino Performing Arts of Utah (FPAU) (this group received the Utah Ethnic Arts and membership to the State Office of Education Multi-Ethnic Bank and the Utah Arts Council Folk Arts Program); chair, Salt Lake City-Quezon City Sister Cities Committee; second term council member, West Valley Arts Council; second term appointee, Utah Department of Health Committee; court interpreter for the State of Utah; translator for the LDS church; network correspondent for *Philippine News* based in San Francisco, California and a community volunteer.

Librarian-Teacher. Mattingley is in the process of organizing the Utah chapter of FANHS (Filipino American National Historical Society) and Empowerment of the Youth through learning its heritage. She is a librarian-teacher in the Spanish-Philippine section of the Genealogical Library in Salt Lake City. It has always been her passionate dream to help the small people whatever the cost. She has lobbied for the Utah Asian Americans, especially the Filipinos, whether for welfare reform, diversity training, the arts, fundings for ethnic health special population surveys, or even fighting discrimination in the workplace.

Mattingley's service is for everyone and everything positive for the community and family. She has pioneered the largest April/October Filipino conference. She has also chaired the Governor's Initiative On Families Today (G.I.F.T.) Program. These two great events focus the Filipinos in general throughout the state of Utah and its neighboring states.

Family. She met Kent Mattingley, her would-be husband, at Brigham Young University in Provo, Utah. She taught at BYU for a year prior to getting married. Kent graduated from the same university with a bachelor of arts in international relations and Japanese. Her husband served an LDS mission in

Fukuoka, Japan, and is currently pursuing his master of arts in organizational management while being a full-time officer for the Salt Lake County Sheriff's Department. Their only child, a son, Kenton, Jr., is a high school honor student and a member of the National Honor Society.

MCCOY, NEAL. Up-and-Coming Country Music Star. The young Neal Mccoy was different from other kids. When the rodeo would arrive in Jacksonville, Texas, where McCoy was born, the other kids would watch the cowboys. Meanwhile, he would see the entertainers and the television and the country music stars who performed after the rodeo.

At the age of nine, when he saw Michael Jackson singing and dancing on television, McCoy envisioned himself to be an entertainer, too.

Today, McCoy, the son of a Filipino mother and an Irish American father, Neal McCoy is an up-and-coming country music star. Two of his hit songs have gone platinum; that is, they have sold a million copies.

Failure, Then Success. After his first two albums failed to be successes, McCoy didn't get discouraged. Atlantic Records that had signed him, didn't get discouraged, either. Finally, his third album and its big hit, *No Doubt About It*, went to the top of *Billboard's* country music list in 1994. Next followed the hit single *Wink*. McCoy's two songs, *No Doubt About It* and *You Gotta Love That* have gone platinum. Among his other country hits were *If I Was a Drinkin' Man*, *For a Change*, and *They're Playing Our Song*.

Not American Indian, But Filipino American. According to Rick Blackburn, president of Atlantic Records, most people are not aware that McCoy is Filipino. Rather, many people think he is an American Indian. McCoy calls himself a "Texapino" which means half-Texan, half Filipino. He says he feels his looks, with long hair and a little darker skin, make him interesting to some people. Although he wears a Stetson hat and black western boots when he performs, McCoy looks more, not as a cowboy, but as a hillbilly. He inherited his little darkness from his mother, Virginia, who married his father, Hubert, in the 1950s in Manila. McCoy's mother is Filipina and his father is Irish American. His father was at that time with the U.S. Army. The family moved to Jacksonville, Texas, where McCoy was born. McCoy has a brother, Gary, and a sister, Barbara. His parents divorced after 23 years of marriage. McCoy derived from the name McGoy, (his previous name), an abbreviation of his original name, McGaughey.

This fast-talking, tight-jeaned Filipino American with a rich Texas twang, says, "Music should be a diversion. There are enough problems in the world without singing about them." In view of this, when he sings, he wants to have fun, as much as his fans do.

In 1989, 16th Avenue Records signed McCoy. But the company closed shop. Later, he signed with Atlantic Records that launched his career. the *Dallas Morning News*, describing him in one of his shows (as published in *Filipinas Magazine*) says, *"If I Was a Drinkin' Man* proved to be his best vocal performance of the night. The breezy, R&B-soaked ballad showcased the way he dips from baritone to bass without ever losing control of his pitch. It's those R&B-tinged songs, including 'No Doubt About It,' 'For a Change,' and the new single 'They're Playing Our Song,' that work for Mr. McCoy's soulful voice." The *Tampa Tribune* calls him, an "Irish Filipino hunk."

Family. McCoy, 39, is married to Melinda. They have two young children: Miki and Swayde. They live in Longview, Texas. The Neal McCoy Fan Club's address is P.O. Box 9610, Longview, TX 75608-9610.

MENDEZ, FERNANDO M. New York City Magazine Publisher. A winner of 30 awards in art and advertising, Fernando M. Mendez is the publisher of *Special Edition Press: Philippine American Quarterly*. published in New York City. The magazine focuses on a single topic, event, or issue, and has regular feature sections such as nutrition, financial services, and movie reviews.

Mendez, while studying at the University of Santo Tomas in Manila, Philippines, became art editor of the official student magazine of the university for two years. Upon graduation, with a degree in fine arts, he held several art director positions in numerous advertising agencies in Manila.

To the U.S. Mendez immigrated to the United States in 1982. After working as an art director of an advertising agency in Billings, Montana, he established his own shop, Mendez Designs. He moved his family to New York and worked at Comprehensive Services, Inc., as an art director. His next job was as a graphics designer. Deciding to be on his own, he revived his former company, Mendez Designs, in New York City.

The Launching of a Magazine. In 1992, in recognition of the need for a different Filipino American magazine, Mendez launched the *Special Edition Press* with an initial print of 10,000 copies. Distributed nationwide, the magazine is available, by subscription, and in bookstores and through the network of Ingram Periodicals that includes B. Dalton Booksellers stores, Barnes & Nobles Bookshops and a few Filipino stores.

Awards. Among awards received by Mendez in the United States are: First Place, Billings Flag and Seal Design Competition; three first places and one Award of Merit, Great Montana Advertising awards; three First Places and one Second Place, Great Montana Advertising Awards; Award of Merit, Printing Industries of America; and two Desi Awards of Excellence, New York City. He also received several awards in national art and advertising competitions in the Philippines.

Memberships. His memberships include Association of Publication Designers, MacUsers Groups, and Philippine American Jaycees in New York City.

Family. Born in Caloocan City, Philippines, on October 24, 1953, Mendez is married to Milagros, who is the advertising and circulation director of *Special Edition Press*. They have two children: Nathaniel 19, and Mervin, 16.

MENOR, RON. Hawaii State Representative. Ron Menor was reelected to the State House of Representatives when he defeated his Republican opponent Thomas White by a wide margin: 6,554 to 3,132 in the November 1996 elections. Representing the Milihani-Wahiawa district, Menor is the son of the first Filipino Hawaii Supreme Court Justice, the late Supreme Court Justice Benjamin Menor.

MONTALBAN, PAOLO. Television Movie Actor/Singer. Paolo Montalban, originally from Manila, played the role of Prince Charming in the ABC's television musical version of *Cinderella* aired on November 2, 1997. Montalban's family moved to New York City from Manila in 1974 when he was four years old. He attended Rutgers University in 1989. In 1993, he was cast in a national tour of Man of La Mancha. Before he was featured in *Cinderella*, he got a role as a member of the chorus of the Broadway revival of *The King and I* for 15 months.

MONTERO, JUAN M., II, M.D., F.A.C.S. Surgeon, Assistant Professor, Leader, and Speaker. Dr. Juan M. Montero is one of the well-known Filipino American physicians in the United States. He is the recipient of a number of honors and awards for his accomplishments as a physician and his services to the community.

Dr. Montero's turning point in life came when he was certified by the Educational Council for Foreign Medical Graduates, paving his way to the United States.

Montero came to the United States in 1966 at age 24 to pursue a post-graduate training in general surgery at DePaul Hospital in Norfolk, Virginia, and a fellowship in thoracic surgery at the University of Virginia Medical Center. In 1972, he joined the private practice of Dr. William S. Hotchkiss, a prominent thoracic surgeon in Norfolk (who eventually became president of the American Medical Association, 1987-88. Dr. Montero is an assistant professor in surgery at Eastern Virginia Medical School.

Community Projects. Following his American Board of Surgery certification, fellowship of the American College of Surgeons, and a thriving general and thoracic surgery practice, Dr. Montero embarked on numerous community projects continuing to the present. He also became involved in many civic and professional organizations both locally, statewide, and nationally. He subsequently served as president of a few associations of physicians. He was the president of the Association of Philippine Physicians in America, 1983-1984, and the Society of Philippine Surgeons in America, 1986.

Publications. Dr. Montero has authored or co-authored over a dozen papers and presented them at professional meetings.

Awards and Honors. For many years, Dr. Montero has helped the very poor migrant workers on the eastern shore of Virginia through a mobile clinic. Moreover, he has also provided free health care to the uninsured working poor in the Hampton Roads area through the Chesapeake Care Free Clinic he founded in 1992. His humanitarian endeavors have brought him numerous honors and citations. To name a couple, he is the recipient of the Medical Society of Virginia Most Outstanding Community Service by a Physician Award in 1992 and the Governor's Award for Volunteering Excellence (gold medal) in 1993.

Autobiography. At the age 35, Montero wrote his autobiography, titled *Halfway Through.* He was profiled as one of the 21 Asian Americans in a high school reference book, *Asian American Biographies,* copyright 1994. The Montero family appeared on NBC television *Evening News* with Tom Brokaw which featured the "New Pilgrims" on November 21, 1984.

In June 1995, Congressman Norman Sisisky officially submitted the name, Juan M. Montero, II, M.D., to the White House for consideration for possible nomination for the position of Surgeon General of the United States. At Old Dominion University, where he sits on the Board of Trustees of the Educational Foundation, Dr. Montero is spearheading the establishment of a Filipino-American Student Cultural Center.

"Designated" to Be a Physician. According to Dr. Montero, he was "designated" by his family at age six to be the physician among seven children. "My mother instilled among us volunteerism, discipline, and hard work while my father supplied the sense of honor to the above," he says.

Family. Dr. Montero is married to the former Mary Ann Goodsell. They have four children who are all now in college. They live in Chesapeake, Virginia.

NATIVIDAD, IRENE. Political Activist. In

1968, Irene Natividad, 48, participated in a political rally and passed out leaflets for Eugene J. McCarthy, a presidential aspirant. That event led her to a life of being a political activist. Years later, she was elected as president of the powerful National Women's Political Caucus (NWPC) in 1985. She was reelected to the position in 1987.

Presidential Awardee. Natividad is the recipient of the *Pamana ng Pilipino* award from Philippine President Ramos, in connection with the 1996 Presidential Awards for Outstanding Filipinos and Organizations held in the Malacanang Palace Heroes Hall in December 1996. The awarding ceremonies were part of the observance of the "Month of Overseas Filipinos."

Flashback. Born in Manila, Philippines, Natividad is proficient in several languages such as Spanish, Italian, French, and Greek. When asked if she ever dreamed that she would be a a political activist, she says, "No. But I was the eldest and my siblings told me that I 'bossed' them around." *Working Mother* magazine, in a write-up in its February 1997 issue, described her as follows: "Natividad, a native of the Philippines, has devoted her career to promoting the political and economic power of women. A masterful politician and a brilliant public strategist, she is known for bringing people together to push a common agenda."

Education. Natividad has a bachelor of arts degree, *summa cum laude,* from Long Island University, 1971; master of arts degree, with high honors, from Columbia University, 1973; and doctor of philosophy candidate (AbD), MPhil., orals, 1976.

Family. The oldest of four children, Natividad is the principal of the Natividad & Associates, and the chairwoman of The National Commission on Working Women. She is married and has a 12-year-old son. She is also director of the biennial Global Summit of Women.

NATORI, JOSIE CRUZ. International Fashion Magnate. Josie Cruz Natori, a native of Manila, Philippines, is the founder and chief executive officer of The Natori Company, a fashion business empire that is forecast to reach and possibly exceed $100-million sales a year by the year 2000.

In recognition of her business acumen and achievements, Natori received last year the prestigious 1997 Business Woman of the Year Award from the New York City Partnership and Chamber of Commerce, in New York City, the center of international trade.

Richard Parsons, president of Time Warner Inc. and chairman-elect of the New York City Partnership and Chamber of Commerce, says of Natori, "Josie Natori is a genuine risk taker who embodies the spirit of our award. A true role model, she drew on her previous life experience to strike out on her own and create a successful enterprise."

Greatest Contributions to Fashion Industry. Natori, head of her company that operates in New York City; Paris, France; and Manila, Philippines, is credited with having revolutionized the lingerie business by eliminating "barriers" between inner and outer wear. She is also often credited with having spearheaded the resurgence of lingerie-influenced ready-to-wear for day and evening.

Products. The Natori Company's products include the Natori Collection of luxury lingerie, at-home-wear, evening wear, and the Josie Line. Furthermore, in an alliance with Avon, Natori introduced her first signature fragrance, "Natori," in the spring of 1995. Last year, the company introduced her second fragrance, "Josie."

Flashback. Natori who was born in Manila on May 9, 1947, graduated from Maryknoll (now Miriam) College High School in Manila in 1964. She joined the Bache Group in New York City to work as an investment banker immediately after graduating, with a bachelor's degree in economics with honors from Manhattanville College in Purchase, New York in 1968. A few months later, she was instructed by her company to establish an office in Manila. It was closed down after two years by Bache.

Returning to the United States in 1971, she joined Merrill Lynch as an investment banker to continue her career on Wall Street.

After seven years, Natori quit her Wall Street career after she had a meeting with a Bloomingdale's buyer who suggested that she produce nightshirts from Philippine embroidered shirts. In only three month's time, she had already received orders from major department stores in New York City. From then on, she never looked back; she was on her way to destiny.

Today, The Natori Company has exclusive shops in 40 countries, including the Philippines. The 3,500-square-foot Natori Boutique in Manila has wholesale offices, where Natori products are sold for distribution to other Southeast Asian countries.

Character Traits. Natori, who is the daughter of a well-known contractor in Manila, describes herself as "very intuitive," "very driven," "tenacious," "full of ideas," and a person "who doesn't stop." *Working Woman* magazine that featured her in one of its issues has dubbed her as "the Luminary of Luxury Lingerie."

Awards. Natori is the recipient of the Galleon Award from former Philippine President Aquino, the New York City Asian American Ward, the Philippine American Foundation Friendship Award, and the 1987 Harriet Alger Award from *Working Woman* magazine.

Affiliations. Natori serves on the boards of directors of the Educational Foundation of Fashion Industries, the Alltell Corporation, The Philippine American Foundation, and the Calyx & Corolla. She is a trustee of Manhattanville College, the Asian Cultural Council, and The Asia Society.

Family. In 1972, she married Kenneth Natori, who was with Smith Barney as an investment banker. (Kenneth joined The Natori Company in 1985 after he quit his job as senior executive vice president at Shearson American Express in New York City.) Her husband is involved in the operation of their business, except design. They have a son, Kenneth, Jr.

NOCON, JR. Multi-Award Winning Florist. Born in General Trias, Cavite Province, Philippines, JR Nocon, now an American citizen and co-owner of a well-known flower shop in Escondido, California, has become a top U.S. florist and a living legend in the American floral industry. He accomplished this by vir-tue of receiving first place in the 1992 National America's Cup Design Competition in Orlando, Florida. The contest, held every four years, is considered the Olympics of floral design. Nocon's achievement in this contest was covered by the Orlando and San Diego newspapers. Winning the national level led him and his business partner and design-assistant, Paul R. Lopez, to represent the United States in the 1993 INTERFLORA World Cup competition in Stockholm, Sweden. No American has yet won the championship title in the 40-year history of the competition.

Florist Competition Judge. Nocon, also a noted florist competition judge, broke the barrier for future American competitors by winning the Bronze Medal for the United States. This event was captured on tape by CNN News Paris. CNN fed its tapes via satellite to all of Europe and the United States. The Southern California District of F.T.D. passed a resolution to provide a lifetime tribute to his historic achievement by naming its annual awards banquet in Los Angeles as the JR Nocon Awards, which honors local artists for their floral design excellence.

Altar Boy. According to Nocon, his first exposure to floral designing was at age 10 as an altar boy in his hometown in the Philippines. He went on to a seminary in Guadalupe, Makati, Rizal Province (now Metro Manila.) He enrolled later for an engineering course at Mapua Institute of Technology.

From Manila to Guam to California. He left Manila for Guam in 1969. There was no engineering job on the island, so he left for the mainland and settled in Hollywood, Los Angeles, California. He worked in a flower shop near Beverly Hills, and had the opportunity to make casual acquaintances with Hollywood celebrities. Then he and his partner, Lopez, decided to start their own company in Escondido.

Awards and Honors. Among the awards and honors Nocon has won are as follows: chair, Professional Design Competition, Del Mar Fair, Del Mar, California, 1995-97; Lifetime recognition from the "JR Nocon Awards Banquet" FTD District, Los Angeles, CA, 1995, featured designer, FTD National Convention, Anaheim, CA, 1994; National Winner, FTD America's Cup Competition in Orlando, Florida, 1992; national finalist, FTD Selection to World Cup, Tokyo, Japan, 1989; West Coast Winner, FTD America's Cup, Boston, Massachusetts, 1988; winner, California State Gold Cup & Best Designer, Palm Springs, CA, 1987; and commendation from the International Olympic Committee for his Olympic floral designs, Los Angeles Summer Olympics, 1984.

OADES, RIZALINO "RIZ" AQUINO, Ph.D. History Professor, Community Leader, Newspaper Columnist, and Co-Founder of *Kalusugan* Community Services. One of the few tenured Filipino professors in the United States, Dr. Riz A. Oades has successfully developed and taught East and Southeast Asian history courses at San Diego State University (SDSU) in San Diego, California, since 1970. Besides teaching European history, he pioneered such courses as *Premodern and Modern Southeast Asia; Social Change and Revolution in Asia; Contemporary Philippine Society and History; Southeast Asian and Filipino Experiences in America, Social and Cultural Change in Indonesia and the Philippines;* and *Contemporary Issues in the Filipino American Communities.*

Education. Oades was born in Lumban, Laguna Province and raised in Pasay City, Philippines. The eldest son of Lorenzo and Beatriz Oades, he finished his high school education at the Jose Abad Santos High School (Arellano University) in Pasay City, as salutatorian. He obtained his Bachelor of Arts in History *(magna cum laude)* from Far Eastern University (FEU) of Manila; MA in Asian History from the University of Hongkong; and Ph.D. in East and Southeast Asian History from the University of Hawaii. He also did a postgraduate study at New York's Cornell University on a Fulbright/Smith-Mundt scholarship grants.

To the U.S. In trouble as a student activist, Dr. Oades began to focus on graduating at the top of his class, which shortly led to a university lectureship appointment. He then competed and garnered the best fellowships and scholarships open to Filipinos for study abroad. He first came to the United States as a Fulbright scholar at Cornell University in August 1961. The second time that he came here as a Ph.D. candidate at the University of Hawaii (UH) was in the summer of 1966. He applied for an immigrant status in 1967 in Honolulu, Hawaii.

Work Experience. His work experience includes: statistician and head of FEU Training Hospital Medical Records Department; history lecturer at the FEU and University of Hawaii College of Extended Studies; coordinator of the U.S. Peace Corps Asian/American Studies Program, Hilo, Hawaii; and history professor at San Diego State University.

Thesis and Publications. His thesis and publications include *Chinese Emigration Through Hong Kong to North Borneo Since 1880; The Social and Economic Background of Philippine Nationalism 1830-1892; The world of Southeast Asians and Filipinos in America: A Reader; Filipino Migration and Labor Movement in America; Defining Ourselves: Voices and Images of Second-generation Filipino Americans; Project Kalusugan: Getting and Keeping Filipinos Involved in Social and Health Issues; Interview Strategies: What Every Filipino Job-Hunter Needs to Know; Kabataan Filipino: Youth Gangs in San Diego; The Philippines: The Birth of a Nation.*

Oades has written some 200 newspaper and scholarly journal articles that covered varied subjects on Asian and Filipino American cultures, society, history, and public health.

Civic Leader. A well-respected educator and tenacious civic leader, Oades is an outspoken critic of Filipino American politics and an advocate for much-needed community projects and programs in San Diego, addressing such issues as affirmative action, youth gang violence, teen suicide, substance abuse, high-school dropout, and higher education.

He has actively participated in community-based organizations, such as the Council of Philippine-American Organizations (COPAO), and co-founded the *Kalusugan* Community Services (KCS), a coalition of community leaders and health professionals. He served as vice chair of the former organization for five years and is the incumbent president of the latter. He has also served as an advisor or consultant to numerous student, professional and civic associations, and government boards or task forces.

For the past 25 years, Dr. Oades has been supportive of Filipino student organization and programs, especially SDSU's AB *Samahan's* sports events, cultural nights, and annual high school conferences. Off-campus and through community-based organizations, he has pioneered ongoing Tagalog and Philippine history classes, and administered funded projects that address the social and mental health problems of Filipino youth and elderly. He has also run columns in the *Asian Journal* (i.e., *Voices & Images* and *Growing Up in America*) and *Philippine Mabuhay News* (i.e., "Portraits") and periodically contributing feature articles to mainstream newspapers and magazines.

Textbook Reviewer, Commentator/Narrator. Oades served as a textbook reviewer for West Publishing Company; editorial consultant to SDSU's Center for Asian Studies Asian-Pacific Horizons publication; and commentator or narrator in TV documentary films. The most notable of the latter were *In No One's Snadow,* sponsored by KPBS and *The Challenge of Diversity: Becoming American,* sponsored jointly by SDSU College of Education and San Diego City College for the San Diego County Office of Education.

Awards. Dr. Oades has been a recipient of numerous outstanding awards that include the Fulbright/Smith-Mundt combined scholarships; British Council Southeast Asia Fellowship; National Conference of Christians and Jews Awards in Journalism; two U.S. Congressional Awards for Outstanding Community Services; Asia Foundation Research grant; Association for Philippine Graduate Education Award for Meritorious Service, SDSU Affirmative Action Faculty Research Grant; Filipino American Lawyers of San Diego Award; SDSU AB Samahan Outstanding Faculty of the Year Award; and SDSU Mortar Board Chapter's Outstanding Faculty Award.

Family. Dr. Oades has four children: Wai-ling Oades-Rubic, 34; Kimo, 31; Kahuku, 26; and Krizpin, 19.

OSTREA, ENRIQUE M., JR. Famed Pediatrician, Professor, Inventor. Recognized as one of the best 500 doctors in the national publication, *The Best Doctors in America*, Dr. Enrique "Buddy" M. Ostrea, Jr., is best known for his patented method for detecting maternally transferred drug metabolites in newborn infants.

Inventor. As a researcher, Dr. Ostrea is the recipient of two patents from the U.S. Patent office: (1) U.S. Serial #07/264,131, Method for Detecting Maternally Transferred Drug Metabolites in Newborn Infants; and (2) U.S. Serial #5,185,267, Improved Method for Detecting Maternally Transferred Drug Metabolites in Newborns. The patents, used by clinical laboratories or drug detection kit man-

ufacturers, are assigned to Wayne State University (WSU) in Michigan. It's the university, not Dr. Ostrea, who collects royalties on the inventions.

According to Dr. Ostrea, "The inventions are a method of analyzing infant's meconium (first stools after birth) to determine if the infants have been exposed to illicit (e.g., cocaine) and licit (e.g., nicotine, alcohol) drugs during pregnancy."

Positions. Currently, Dr. Ostrea is the chief of the department of pediatrics at the Hutzel Hospital in Detroit, Michigan, a position he has held since 1972. He joined the WSU faculty in 1972, during which he was appointed as an assistant professor, later becoming an associate professor, and then a professor. He is also the director of the University Service Nurseries at Hutzel University, also in Detroit.

Flashback. Dr. Ostrea studied at the University of the Philippines, in Quezon City, Philippines, where he obtained his degree in medicine, *cum laude*, as class valedictorian in 1965. He took his internship and residency in pediatrics at the Philippine General Hospital in Manila.

In the United States, he was appointed as a junior assistant resident in pediatrics at the Children's Hospital Medical Center in Boston, Massachusetts from 1968 to 1969. He became a fellow in neonatology at Johns Hopkins Hospital in Baltimore, Maryland, from 1969 to 1972.

International Lecturer. Dr. Ostrea is an international scholar and lecturer. The 1989-90 president of the Philippine Medical Association of Michigan, he is a world-renown authority on neonatology. He has published 42 original papers and co-authored 24 books, chapters, and monographs on a variety of subjects. More than 100 of his published abstracts were presented at different national and international meetings and conferences

Awards and Honors. Dr. Ostrea's awards and honors include: Winthrop Stearns scholarship in 1964; Philippine Medical Association award for Most Outstanding Medical Graduate, 1965; Mead Johnson Pediatric Research Award (first prize), 1966; Most

Outstanding Filipino Physician in Medicine in the Midwest, 1986; Most Outstanding Educator Overseas Award of the University of the Philippines (U.P.) Medical Alumni Association, 1990; Wayne State University Board of Governors Faculty Recognition Award, 1991; U.P. Alumni Association of Michigan Professional Achievement Award for Academic Excellence and Research, 1991; and U.P. Alumni Association of America Award as Outstanding Alumnus in Medicine, 1991.

PARAS, ANDY. Member, City Council of Hercules, California. A native of Manila, Philippines, Andy Paras won first place in the city council elections in November 1996. He was the topnotcher, getting 2,989 votes, some 205 votes over his closest rival. Five candidates vied for three seats.

Upon his election, Paras declared, "I give credit for my victory to the work that the Filipino community did at the time. There were a lot of volunteers and the message really came across." Currently president of the Filipino American Political Association (FAPA) in Hercules, Paras served a two-year term with the Community Service Commission.

It was 12 years ago when Paras and his wife, Daisy, immigrated to the United States. They have made Hercules their home ever since. Paras estimates that Filipinos comprise 33 percent of the city's population. "This makes me feel at home," he said.

PARDO, LILLIAN GONZALEZ, M.D., M.H.S.A. Pediatric Neurologist, Community Leader. Dr. Lilian Gonzalez Pardo is a clinical professor of pediatrics and neurology at the University of Kansas Medical Center, where she has been on the faculty since 1975.

Flashback. Dr. Pardo obtained her medical degree

from the University of the Philippines in Quezon City, Philippines, in 1962 and pursued a postgraduate training in neurology, child psychiatry, pediatric neurology, pediatrics, and developmental pediatrics at the University of Kansas. She was awarded Master's degree in health services administration at the University of Kansas in May 1996. In the same year, she assumed the position of medical director of Teva Marion Partners, a pharmaceutical company based in Kansas City.

As the first Asian American president of the American Medical Women's Association (AMWA), she initiated several projects, including the Asian American Women Physician's History Project in cooperation with the Medical College of Pennsylvania. Her clinical work, publications, and presentations reflect her diverse interest in children's and women's health issues. Dr. Pardo is a fellow in the American Academy of Pediatrics and a diplomate in neurology with special certification in pediatric neurology.

Volunteer Work. In her thirty years in Kansas City, she has made a strong commitment to her volunteer work in the Filipino Association of Greater Kansas City, with her strong belief in the promotion and preservation of her cultural heritage, particularly the support of the association's Sinagtala Dance Troupe. As a first generation immigrant to this country, she successfully acculturated and embraced the best of both worlds—the dignity of labor and the work ethic, and the preservation of the cultural attributes that espouse family traditions, respect for elders, and pursuit of higher learning

Awards. Dr. Pardo has received numerous awards from national medical and civic organizations, including an Outstanding Alumna Overseas Award from her alma mater, 1991, and an Excellence 2000 Outstanding Asian American Award, 1993, from the Pan Asian American Pacific Chamber of Commerce based in Washington D.C. She has provided a good role model and a positive image for Asian Americans and certainly a sense of pride for the midwest.

Family. Dr. Pardo is married to Dr. Manuel P. Pardo, a psychiatrist in private practice in the Kansas City area. They have three grown children: Dr. Manuel Pardo, Jr., who graduated from the UCLA School of Medicine and is currently on the faculty and staff at the University of California in San Francisco in the Department of Anesthesia; Lillie Pardo, who graduated from the University of Kansas where she majored in Spanish and journalism; and Patrick Pardo, who graduated from Sarah Lawrence College, with a major in art history and is currently in the New York's New School of Master's program in creative writing.

PEDROSA, VERONICA. CNN News Anchor.

Veronica Pedrosa is an anchor for CNN International (CNNI), the 24-hour global news network. Based in the network's Atlanta, Georgia, headquarters, Pedrosa anchors the Friday and weekend editions of "CNNI World News," CNN's flagship international news program, from 17:00 to 21:00 (Hong Kong time). She also anchors the Friday edition of "CNNI World News Asia," a daily newscast. This British-accented broadcast journalist has really gone a long way from her native Manila, Philippines, where she was born.

Flashback. Pedrosa, the daughter of Alberto Pedrosa and Carmen "Chit" Pedrosa, was four-and-a-half years old when the family moved to London in 1972. At that time, her father traveled abroad on business trips on behalf of the wealthy Eugenio Lopez family that owned the *Manila Chronicle*, where her mother used to work as a member of the editorial staff. Her mother wrote the book *The Untold Story of Imelda Marcos.*

Pedrosa first studied at St Paul's, a private all-girls' school in London. She attended Newham College and obtained a master's degree in English from Cambridge University.

Before Coming to the U.S. Pedrosa, before coming to the United States, worked for Manila's ABS-CBN TV, where she wrote for the news programs "The World Tonight" and "TV Patrol." She also worked as a part-time correspondent for *The Times of London*, National Public Radio (NPR), and other broadcasting organizations. Her work at ABS-CBN International introduced her to the CNN "World Report" program. Eventually, Pedrosa, who speaks fluently in English and Tagalog and with knowledge of Spanish and French, was offered at job at CNN International. The rest is history.

PELAYO, LIBERTITO "BERT." Publisher and Editor of *Filipino Reporter.*

A former member of the defunct *Manila Times*, Libertito Pelayo is the publisher and editor of the New York City-based *Filipino Reporter.* He is a member of the New York Press Club.

Outstanding Filipino American Awardee. Pelayo, being an outstanding Filipino American, has been honored, together with three Filipino Americans, with the 1997 Outstanding Asian Pacific Americans Award, in celebration of the annual Asian Pacific American Heritage Month in Hudson County, New Jersey. The award ceremony was held at the rotunda of the Justice Brenan Courthouse on Newark Avenue in Jersey City. The affair was sponsored by the County of Hudson, Hudson County Executive Robert C. Janiszewski, Hudson County Board of Chosen Freeholders, and the Hudson County Cultural and Heritage Affairs, in cooperation with the Asian American Civic Association, Inc.

In June 1996, he was named the grand marshal of the 99th Philippine Independence Day parade and celebration in New York City.

Flashback. Pelayo covered the Department of Defense and he spent a year in Vietnam. He came to the United States in the early 1970s and settled in New York City, where he established the *Filipino Reporter.*

Pelayo, during his college days, became the editor-in-chief of the *Advocate*, a student publication of the Far Eastern University in Manila.

Family. Pelayo is married and has three children. The family lives in Jamaica Estates, New York City.

PEEPLES, NIA. Actress and Singer.

A popular television actress in the 1980s, Nia Peeples appeared in *Fame* and the *North Shore* (1987). She also hosted the musical show "Party Machine." As a singer, she has released, "Nia and Troubles," "Street of Dreams," and "Think Twice."

PHILLIPS, LOU DIAMOND. Movie Actor.

Born to a Filipina and a U.S. Navy man, at the Subic Bay Naval Station in Olongapo, Zambales Province, Philippines, 35 years ago, Lou Diamond Philips is one of a few successful movie stars in Hollywood of Filipino descent. His mother married another naval man, George Phillips, after his father died.

Being Part-Filipino: an "Added Plus." Commenting on ethnic roles, Phillips says that it was an "added plus" when people knew he was part Filipino. He says he is Scot-Irish-Cherokee on his father's side and mostly Filipino on his mother's, with a little bit of Hawaiian, Chinese, and Spanish.

La Bamba. In 1987, this half Filipino, half Scotch-Irish-Cherokee gained international fame when he played rock and roll legend Ritchie Valens in the film *La Bamba. In* the film *Dark Wind,* Phillips called a character played by Han S. Ngor in the credits as *Tatay* (a Pilipino language word for father). He has also appeared with Meg Ryan in the box office smash military drama *Courage Under Fire.* He has also appeared in movies such as *Stand and Deliver,* in which he played an East Los Angeles Chicano hoodlum and *Shadow of the Wolf,* where he played the role of an Inuit. Phillips, not only played, but also wrote and directed several small movies.

Role in The King and I. In 1996, a great challenge of his life came, when he played the Broadway role of the king in *The King and I,* for which he was nominated for a Tony Best Leading Actor award.

The offers of roles in *The King and I* and Edward Zwick's *Courage Under Fire,* came at the same time. Phillips says, "They just came out of the blue, like *La Bamba.* All of a sudden, two of the best roles in my career, back to back in the same week."

Acting Education and Training. Phillips graduated from the University of Texas with a bachelor of fine arts in theater. His early acting involved interscholastic drama. After he performed in the Dallas-Fort Worth area, he won over 500 other aspirants around the country for the role of the doomed Ritchie Valens in the 1987 movie *La Bamba.*

Phillips' first wife was filmmaker Julie Cypher. In 1994, he married model Kelly Preston. In October 1997, Phillips, 35, and Kelly, 29, became parents to Isabella Patricia and Grace Moorea in Santa Monica, California.

PRINCE (THE ARTIST). Prince, who needs no introduction, according to the article *Prince in Exile,* by Scott Isler in the October 1984 *Musician* is part Filipino.

PUNSALAN, ELIZABETH. U.S. Ice Dance Champion. Five-time and current U.S. dance champion and 1994 and 1998 Olympic competitor, Elizabeth Punsalan received awards from two organizations last year for her ice skating achievements. She received an award from the Filipino American Human Services Inc. (FAHS) in salute to an Outstanding American of Filipino Descent on May 4, 1997, in New York City.

Before receiving the award, Punsalan said, "I'm very proud to be a Filipino. While I was growing up, I didn't realize the significance of it. As I got older, I realize how special it is and I'm very proud of the Filipino heritage."

On May 5, 1997, Punsalan and six professional and amateur Asian American athletes were honored by the Asian American Federation of New York at its "Tribute to Excellence in Sports Gala" in New York City.

Olympics Participation. Punsalan, married to her skating and life partner, Jerod Swallow, participated in the 1994 Olympic Winter Games in Lillehammer, Norway, a few weeks after the death of her father. They dedicated their Olympics performance to her father's memory. Her father, Dr. Ernesto R. Punsalan,

57, a native of Davao, Philippines, and a renowned surgeon in Ohio, was stabbed to death in the family residence in Sheffield Lake, Ohio, by his son Ricardo, 21. Dr. Punsalan was dead on arrival at St. Joseph Hospital in Lorain, Ohio. The killing happened on February 4, 1994. The son was later declared by two psychologists as mentally incompetent to stand trial.

Punsalan

(Dr. Punsalan and his Irish American wife, the former Francisca Rancoma, met in Buffalo, New York, where he received a medical degree from the University of New York.)

Loves Philippine Culture. Born on January 9, 1971, in Sheffield Lake, Ohio, Punsalan didn't learn the Filipino language, Tagalog, or Pilipino. However, she said the "unique warmth and kindness" of the Filipino people taught her to love the Philippine culture. "I started learning Tagalog when I was very young and I was getting the two languages (the other English) mixed up, so my dad decided not to continue it," the *Filipino Reporter,* a New York City-based weekly newspaper, quoted her as saying. Punsalan loves to cook and eat *pansit* (rice noodles) and *adobong manok* (chicken cooked with minced garlic, spices, vinegar, and salt and/or soy sauce.) Her father instilled in her mind a strong work ethic: "There is no mountain too high to climb."

First Skating Lessons. At age 7, Punsalan took her first skating lessons with her older siblings in Cleveland, Ohio. At the age of 14, she moved to Michigan by herself to undergo an intensive ice dance training. Later, in her senior year in high school, she moved to Colorado Springs to further her skating training. When she went to college, Punsalan met Swallow who became her partner. Their relationship culminated in marriage in 1993.

Punsalan, 27, and Swallow, 31, live in Pontiac, Michigan.

QUIDACHAY, RONALD E. California Municipal Judge. Born in San Francisco, California, in 1947, Judge Ronald E. Quidachay is a law and motion judge in the Municipal Court, Civil Division, in San Francisco, California. He twice ran unopposed, first elected in 1986, then reelected in 1992. His current term ends in 1998. A half-Filipino and half-Irish, Judge Quidachay grew up in Guam. He returned to San Francisco when he was 17 years old to attend the San Francisco State College, (now a university), where he majored in pre-law. He graduated from the University of California at Berkeley, where he obtained his law degree.

QUISMORIO, FRANCISCO P., JR, M.D. Physician, University Professor, and Medical Researcher. Dr. Francisco P. Quismorio is currently a professor of medicine and pathology (with tenure) at the University of Southern California School of Medicine in Los Angeles.

Flashback. Born in the Philippines, Dr. Quismorio grew up in Candon, Ilocos Sur. After graduating from the College of Medicine, University of the Philippines, in 1964, he obtained a postgraduate training at the Philippine General Hospital in Manila, the University of Pennsylvania Hospital in Philadelphia, and the Los Angeles County-USC Medical Center in Los Angeles.

Board certified in internal medicine, rheumatology subspecialty and diagnostic laboratory immunology, he is a fellow of the American College of Physicians and the American College of Rheumatology. His academic career at USC involves the areas of medical education, scientific research, and patient care. He teaches medical students and residents in internal medicine. He has helped train over 50 rheumatologists from the USA and other countries, many of whom have become outstanding academicians and successful practitioners.

Research Interest. The major area of Dr. Quismorio's research interest is the study of arthritis and rheumatic diseases. He is the director of the Lupus Clinic at the LAC+USC Medical Center, which provides health care to a large population of urban poor and minorities.

Writings. Over 100 of his writings have appeared in peer-reviewed scientific journals and books. He is a member of the editorial board of *Postgraduate Medicine* and *Lupus Erythematosus* and is a reviewer for many medical journals. He has served the Medical Board of California as a commissioner for oral and clinical examinations for physicians.

Awards and Honors. Dr. Quismorio is a recipient of several honors including: Listed in *Best Doctors in America, Who's Who in Medicine & Health Care; Who's Who in the West;* Fleur de Lis Award and Community Service Award (American Lupus Society); Service Award from the (Arthritis Foundation); Outstanding Alumnus (U.P. College of Medicine); Burke Award from the Philippine Heart Association; and research grants and contracts from private foundations and government agencies.

Memberships. Dr. Quismorio is currently the vice chief of the Division of Rheumatology and Clinical Immunology at the USC School of Medicine. He is a member of several professional, scientific, and civic organizations and has served in various official positions. He has a particular interest in Philippine history and is a member of the Philippine History Group of Los Angeles.

Family. Dr. Quismorio is married to Violeta Consolacion, RN, of Tamurong, Ilocos Sur Province, Philippines. They have two grown children: James, a graduate of the Wharton School of the University of Pennsylvania, 1994; and Anne, a graduate of Smith College, 1995.

RECANA, MEL RED. Presiding Judge, Los Angeles Municipal Court, California. Judge Mel Red Recana made history when the governor appointed him to the California Judiciary in June 1981. In the Governor's words, "Judge Recana is the first and only Filipino judge in the Western Hemisphere." Actually, being first is not new to him. Back in 1974, he became the first Philippine-educated and trained lawyer to pass the California Bar Examinations without going to an American law school.

First Filipino Deputy District Attorney. In 1977 Recana also became the first Filipino Deputy District Attorney in the County of Los Angeles. In 1979, he passed another tough bar examinations for criminal

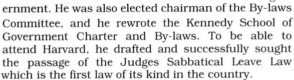

law specialists. In 1984 he started to teach trial technique and procedure at Pacific Coast University School of Law.

By 1993, he had graduated with a master of arts degree in public administration from the Kennedy School of Government, Harvard University. At the Kennedy School, where 56 countries were represented, Judge Recana was elected representative to the student government. He was also elected chairman of the By-laws Committee, and he rewrote the Kennedy School of Government Charter and By-laws. To be able to attend Harvard, he drafted and successfully sought the passage of the Judges Sabbatical Leave Law which is the first law of its kind in the country.

In May 1995, in Washington, D.C., he graduated class valedictorian of the National Center for State Courts and was conferred the title Institute for Court Management Graduate Fellow, the first California judge to be conferred this honor.

Reelected Presiding Judge. In 1996 the judges reelected Recana as presiding judge of the Los Angeles Municipal Court with 89 judges, 25 commissioners, eleven courthouse facilities and a revenue of $108 million, easily making it the largest court of its kind in the world. The presiding judge is the corporate counterpart of the president, chairman, and CEO. He was also elected president of the California Asian Judges Association whose membership includes two judges of the Supreme Court, a justice of the United States Court of Appeal, several appellate justices, and, of course, Judges Ito and Fujisaki of the O.J. Simpson case.

In December 1996, President Fidel V. Ramos of the Philippines honored him with a Presidential Award "for exemplifying the best of Filipino talent and excellence in demonstrating consistent and outstanding professional performance and exceptional competence as a Philippine-trained lawyer and member of the judiciary in the United States. Mayor Lim also awarded him with the ceremonial key to the City of Manila.

Flashback. Married to the former Aurora Lapuz of Candaba, Pampanga Province, Philippines, Judge Recana in the prime of life has made his mark and reached a summit in his career. He has come a long away—from his native town of Guinobatan, Albay Province, Philippines, where he was born, to where he is now. During his youthful years, he had to walk 14 kilometers a day to go school, and yet he graduated as valedictorian in grade school and in high school and was a college scholar. It was in Manila where he studied in college and initially practiced law. At last, it was in America where he reached his mountain top.

REYES, HERNAN M., M.D. Pediatric Surgeon, Professor, and Chairman of Department of Surgery. As a young boy, Hernan M. Reyes had dreamed to be a physician or a lawyer. He recalls, "I enjoyed acting as the doctor with other kids. My father's death in World War II, when I was 9 years old turned me off from being a lawyer."

According to Dr. Reyes, her mother influenced him a lot, especially with her dedication to her profession as a grade school teacher. "Aside from my clinical work," he says, "I have been very active in academic work: teaching medical students and residents and doing research and other scholarly activities."

Now, as chairman of the Department of Surgery at Cook County Hospital in Chicago, Illinois, Dr. Hernan Reyes belongs to a select group of academic department chairs in the United States. He is an associate examiner of the American Board of Surgery in general surgery and pediatric surgery. Since 1993, he has been a member of the Residency Review Committee for Surgery of the Accreditation Council for Graduate Medical Education, a 12-member group representing the American College of Surgeons, American Board of Surgery and the Council on Education of the American Medical Association, whose responsibility is to review residency programs in general, vascular, pediatric, and hand surgery in the U.S.

Flashback. Dr. Reyes's academic career started with the Stritch School of Medicine at Loyola University in the United States and continued at the University of Santo Tomas College of Medicine in Manila in 1966.

In the summer of 1967, he returned to the United States and joined the Pritzker School of Medicine, University of Chicago in 1969, where he was promoted from assistant professor to associate professor of surgery. For a time, he served as acting chief of section of the Department of Pediatric Surgery in 1973. Three years later, he accepted the position as chairman of the Division of Pediatric Surgery at Cook County Hospital Children's Hospital and professor of surgery and chief of Section of Pediatric Surgery at the University of Illinois College of Medicine in Chicago, a position he held until 1992,1994, and 1990 respectively.

On January 6, 1987, he was appointed chairman

of the Department of Surgery at Cook County Hospital with administrative oversight of all the various surgical specialties representing divisions in the department. He also serves as professor of surgery at the Cook County Graduate School of Medicine. He is currently a professor of surgery at Rush Medical College/ Rush University and assistant dean for surgical programs at Cook Country Hospital for Rush. Throughout his career, he has been involved in teaching, surgical research and patient care.

His career can be summarized by a recommendation made by a colleague at the University of Chicago Prizker School of Medicine who wrote, "I have known and admired Dr. Hernan M. Reyes, a pediatric surgeon for over 25 years. From the moment I saw him do his first case, I knew he was a brilliant surgeon. He developed into much more, identifying himself as a teacher (he and one other) were the only surgeons selected by the 4th year students to have their pictures alongside of students from the class photos for several years as well as a clinical investigator."

Publications. A member of 27 surgical organizations serving in various committees and as an officer in some of them, he has 68 publications in peer-reviewed journals, 21 book chapters, 40 published abstracts, and numerous presentations at regional and national meetings. His publications on pediatric trauma care became a catalyst leading to the evaluation of pediatric trauma care in the metropolitan Chicago area, so much so that in 1986, he was appointed by the Commissioner of Health of the City to serve as chairman of the Pediatric Trauma Oversight Committee of the Department of Health.

Memberships: Dr. Reyes is the founding president of the Society of Philippine Surgeons in America in 1972. He initiated the annual Continuing Medical Education Program of the society and remained as chair of the CME committee for 10 years. It was during his tenure that the continuing education program of the society was approved by the Accreditation Council for continuing medical education of the AMA for Category 1 CME credits.

He served as a member of various hospital committees and specialty societies and as president of the following organizations: Illinois Pediatric Surgical Association, 1978; Wood Street Branch, Chicago Medical Society, 1993; Chicago Committee on Trauma of the American College of Surgeons, 1994-1997; Illinois Surgical Society, 1995; and vice president, Chicago Surgical Society, 1988.

His civic and local government appointments include: member, Mayor Harold Washington's Advisory Committee on Asian American Affairs, City of Chicago, 1983-1989; member and later vice president, Chicago Board of Health, 1985-1989); chairman, Pediatric Trauma Oversight Committee, Department of Health, City of Chicago, 1986; member search committee, Mayor's Office for Commissioner of Health, Bureau Director and AIDS director, 1987-1988; member, Pediatric Trauma Technical Advisory Committee for the city of Chicago, 1989; member, Forensic Advisory Board, Attorney General's Office, State of Illinois, 1994; and member, Medical Licensing Board of the State of Illinois, 1996-2002, as appointed by the governor.

Awards. Dr. Reyes is a recipient of numerous awards from students, residents, and medical societies.

Family. Dr. Reyes is married to Lory, his wife of more than 35 years. They have five children and two grandchildren. The oldest, Cynthia, is completing her thesis for her doctorate degree in education at the University of Illinois in Chicago. Michael is a third-year medical student at Loyola University in Chicago, having switched gears following a career in economics (bachelor's and master's degrees in economics at Boston University). Maria recently completed a residency in internal medicine at Rush-Presbyterian-St. Luke's Medical Center and is board certified in her specialty. Patricia is in her last semester at George Washington University in Washington, D.C., for her master's degree in international relations with a major in economics (undergraduate at UCLA). The youngest, Catherine, who graduated last year with a bachelor's degree in fine arts, fashion design from Parsons School of Fashion Design in New York City, is working for Banana Republic as an assistant designer.

RIVERA, EVELYN M. Biological Scientist.

Evelyn M. Rivera is professor of zoology at Michigan State University, where she has been since 1965. She received her A.B., M.A., and Ph.D. degrees in zoology at the University of California, Berkeley. After completing her doctorate in 1963, she worked in England (Reading and Oxford) on a postdoctoral fellowship from the American Cancer Society, 1963-1965. Her field of specialization is endocrinology, and her research has focused on the normal and cancerous development of the mammary gland. Her research has been supported by grants from the National Institutes of Health and the Pardee Foundation.

Sabbatical Leaves. Rivera took sabbatical leaves at U.C. Berkeley, 1971-1972, and in London, England, 1978-1979, where she studied immunology with Nobel Laureate Sir Peter Medawar. She also worked for a brief period at the Salk Institute, La Jolla, California, 1983, with Nobel Laureate Renato Dulbecco to learn cell cloning techniques. Throughout her professional career, she has been active in regional and national scientific societies, serving as president or chairperson in several organizations. She was elected fellow of the American Association for the Advancement of Science, an honor accorded to less than one percent of the membership of scientists from all disciplines. She has served as consultant to the National Institutes of Health and to the National Science Foundation. For her biological research and to some extent, promotion of women in science, she received an Outstanding Woman Faculty Award, 1992, from the Michigan State University.

Affirmative Action for Minorities' Activities. In recent years, Rivera has been involved with affirmative action for women and minorities and has worked to improve race relations at her institution and in the community. She served as president of the Asian Pacific American Faculty and Staff Association of MSU and of the Asian Pacific American Women's Association of Greater Lansing. She is currently a board member of the Mid-Michigan Asian Pacific American Association. She received an Excellence in Diversity Award, 1997, from the Michigan State University.

Background. Born in Hollister, California, on November 10, 1929, Rivera is the daughter of Atanacio Rivera, 1903-1953, and Anselma Dangtayan Rosario, 1911-1993, of Banayoyo, Ilocos Sur Province, Philippines. She is the eldest of eight siblings (Andrew, Benjamin, Katherine, Jane, Romeo, Douglas, and Victoria), all born in California. Children of the depression, Rivera and her siblings grew up in San Luis Obispo County on the central coast of the state. Her youthful ambition was to become a physician, and although she was an alternate in the early 1950s at what was then Women's Medical College in Philadelphia, she could not provide assurance of financial ability to pay for the medical training. Her father had died in an automobile accident.

Loves the Biomedical Field. Still interested in working in the biomedical field, Rivera enrolled at University of California Medical School, San Francisco, in the medical technology curriculum, became certified, and stayed to work at the Cancer Research Institute (1953-1956). She then worked as a cytologist at a cancer center in Nancy, France. After eight months in Nancy, and after becoming fairly proficient in the language, she left for Paris to complete her year in France by enrolling at the Sorbonne University for a course in French civilization.

After realizing that she wanted to do an independent research, she returned to the University of California in Berkeley in January 1958 for her master's and doctoral degrees. Five years later, she returned to Europe as a postdoctoral fellow in biochemistry.

ROBERTO, JOSEPHINE "BANIG." Singer.

Josephine Roberto is a rising Filipino American singer known as "Banig." Banig, a child star who won the Star Search Grand championship, appeared on the Arsenio Hall and Rick Dees shows.

"Can You Feel My Heart?" She made her debut CD album, "Can You Feel My Heart," and ever since she has been trying to penetrate the mainstream audience. Some say she has the voice quality of Whitney Houston and Mariah Carey. Moreover, they say, she has the moves of Janet Jackson. Although she has not hit the big-time charts yet, Banig's album *Can You Feel My Heart*, made #8 on the best-selling list at Virgin Megastore, one of Los Angeles' largest record stores.

RODRIGUEZ, MANUEL, SR. Father of Philippine Graphic Arts.

Born in Cebu City, Philippines, on January 1, 1915, Manuel Rodriguez, Sr., is the father of Philippine graphic arts and one of the most famous Filipino American artists in America. Rodriguez, a multi-awarded printmaker, has made New York City his home since 1976 returned to Manila, Philippines, for a few days in 1996 to exhibit both his prints and paintings with two of his equally famous sons, Boy, Jr., and Beboy Marcelino.

Flashback. Rodriguez finished his elementary education in Argao, Cebu, Philippines, and his secondary education at Southern Institute (now the University of Southern Philippines). Orphaned in early childhood, the ambitious Rodriguez left home in Cebu for Manila to chase his dream. In 1939, he obtained his bachelor of science in fine arts from the University of the Philippines School of Fine Arts on Padre Faura Street in Manila.

After World War II, Rodriguez introduced printmaking in the Philippines. At that time, he had already won painting awards. He put up "Art in Action," a printmaking project sponsored by the Art Association of the Philippines at the showroom of Northern Motors on United Nations Avenue in Manila.

Later, while he was employed as a resident artist at Clark Field Air Base, home of the U.S. Air Force in Angeles, Pampanga Province, he produced greeting cards of Philippine scenes. He became successful in this endeavor, so much so that other well-known artists followed, including Magsaysay Ho, Malang, Manansala, Ang Kiu Kok, Lyd Arguilla, and Larry Alcala.

He left his job at Clark Field and established the Contemporary Art Gallery on Mabini, Malate, Manila. At the same time, he offered classes in printmaking, silkscreen, and woodcutting to support his wife and eight children. He also sold prints at P10 per piece, in which he was quite successful.

In the 1950s, Rodriguez was among those "progressive conservatives" when art was transforming from the "traditional" of Fernando Amorsolo to the "modern" art of Victorio Edades. "I was the *rebel* against the group of mainstream modernists," Rodriguez once said. "I was an *individualist*, exploring non-traditional materials like sticks and textiles."

The Chance of a Lifetime. In 1960, a chance to go abroad came when Rodriguez obtained a Rockefeller Grant for the Graphic Arts for a year of intensive study in New York City. He settled in Manhattan and trained at the Pratt Art Center. His one year study was extended to another six months. In 1961, he worked at the Museum of Modern Art in New York City as a trainee in the print department. He also worked under a training program with Mauricio Lasansky, a well-known lithographer in Iowa. Later, he went to Paris, France, and studied under William Stanley Hayter, a British pioneer printmaker at Atelier 17 in the French capital.

Returns to Manila. When Rodriguez returned to Manila in 1962, where he became an immediate celebrity, he was interviewed by journalists who eventually called him the "Father of Graphic Arts." His biggest accomplishment was improvising machines and materials for etching on metal. He invented a roller press and metal plates from junk and scrap parts found at a jeepney factory.

Awards. In recognition of his accomplishments in printmaking, Rodriguez was granted the Cultural Her-

itage Award in Graphic Arts in 1967. Immediately after, he won the Araw ng Maynila Award.

To the U.S. In 1976, a few years after martial law was declared by President Marcos, Rodriguez, his wife and his younger children headed for New York City, where he maintains a studio to this day.

ROMERO, JOSE. World-Renowned Acrylic-Impressionistic Artist. As a boy growing up, Jose Romero painted murals in watercolor on manila paper. Today, Romero, a native of Tayabas, Quezon Province, Philippines, is an international acrylic-impressionistic artist whose works are exhibited in art galleries throughout the world. Currently, a lot of his works are displayed and are sold at the Ayala Museum, in Makati City, Metro Manila.

The Ayala Museum took interest in his paintings after he held a successful one-man show exhibit at the Cultural Center of the Philippines in 1994. During his solo exhibit, one of his works entitled *Clean and Green Landscape* was sold at an auction for P300,000 to Mary Tan, a Manila socialite. The money went to the

First Lady's (Mrs. Amelita M. Ramos) Orchidarium project at Rizal Park on Luneta in Manila. Romero held his first exhibit of fifty original paintings in Southfield, Michigan in 1974. He has exhibited his paintings in such cities as Paris, France; New York, New York; Chicago, Illinois; Beijing, China; and other cities in Canada, Europe, and other parts of the world.

A Visit to the Philippines. In 1997, nationally and internationally acclaimed artist Romero went home to the Philippines to receive an award as one of 1997's outstanding citizens of Quezon Province during the observance in Lucena City of the birthday anniversary of President Manuel L. Quezon.

On August 20, 1997, in conjunction with the 10th year anniversary celebration of the *Susi ng Tayabas*, this cultural group mounted a one-man exhibit of his paintings at the Case de Comunidad de Tayabas, in Tayabas, Quezon.

Back to the U.S. Romero in October 1997, held two exhibitions in Seattle, Washington. On October 11, he held a successful one-man exhibit at the *Bituing Filipino* at the Double Tree Suites at South Center Parkway, Seattle. The next day, he exhibited his paintings at the Seattle Asian Art Museum. The two shows benefited both the Pacific Aids Council and the Asian Pacific Islander Women and Family Safety Center. *Bituing Filipino* was a novel show that presented a collection of art, music, and dance that was produced for the first time by NR Productions.

Flashback. A graduate of a nursing in Lucena City, Quezon, Romero left for the United States in 1963 under an exchange program. He first worked as a nurse at St. Vincent's Hospital in Worcester, Massachusetts.

Then to Canada. After holding several jobs, Romero left for Chicago. It was there that he fell in love with impressionism, cubism, and modern art after he visited art galleries and museum. From there, he departed in 1966 for Ontario, Canada, where he worked as a nurse while taking art lessons from Agnes Depew.

Back to the U.S. He returned to the United States and studied to be a nurse anesthetist and then to work as such. Then he also enrolled at the Art Instruction School in Minneapolis, Minnesota. In 1974, he went to New York City to visit galleries and museums. It was there where he learned to "thin the acrylics to get a watercolor effect." It was this technique of painting that propelled him to be a well-known impressionistic artist.

Praise. According to Ella Steele of the *Oakland Press* (March 9, 1989,) women comprise the predominant theme in his works. For instance, in his painting, *Japanese Woman,* he mixed collage and acrylics. Romero has his own unique technique and style in painting: "My individual style grew stronger when I discovered acrylic wash. While I was studying, I would fill the whole canvas with colors and people would be at the bottom. This is my new technique, my style. I don't have a rough draft or lines to follow. I don't even know what's going to happen. I think that's exciting and I love the excitement of the unknown." Some of Romero's works depict a universal theme; for instance, one of his paintings shows the picture of several women strolling by the seashore in a fishing village. It can be a scene in any country in the world. It may be a scene on the Bahamas, in Thailand, or in the Philippines. Romero says, "People sometimes label me as an Asian or a Hispanic artist. I don't think of myself as representing a particular culture. I love to travel. I have experienced many cultures and I am always inspired by the beauty I see around."

In 1978, he studied at the Paris-American Academy Beaux de Artes in France.

Solo Beijing, China, Exhibit. Romero's solo exhibit in Beijing, China, in 1991 was a huge success. Lu Liyuan, a representative for the foreign ministry in Beijing said, "The subject, the color, the structure, and the technique combine wonderfully the Oriental art with western tone...It seems that each painting has a story behind it."

In praising Romero's paintings, Art critic James Bloch comments, "His travels to Europe, Africa, and the Far East have provided much of the grist for his aesthetic mill. But his painterly focus falls most frequently on women, their faces reminiscent of Modigliani, their souls charged with strength. Impressionism, a strong sense of motion, a warm palette, and the use of acrylic washes combine to lend his works as a multi-layered, almost auroral sort of depth. His most famous painting is the *Red Madonna*, a black outlined nearly apparitional figure, free-floating against a virginal background, her frock splattered and dripping with gunshots of red. But her tilted face and prayerful hands are strangely at peace."

Awards and Honors. Romero's honors and awards include: a degree of Doctor of Art *(honoris causa)* by the Marquiz Giuseppi Scicluna University Foundation in Malta; Michigan Annual Art Festival Merit Award,

1975; Outstanding Men of Michigan Award for Professional Achievement as an Artist and Anesthetist, 1976; Outstanding Man of the Year, Filipino-American Association of Michigan, 1976; *Who's Who In the Midwest; Marquiz's Who's Who in the World, 16th Edition; The Marquiz's Who's Who Publications Board,* 1978-79; Recognition in Men and Women of Distinction, International Biographical Centre, Cambridge, England, 1979; one of the 2,000 Outstanding People of the 20th Century; *International Directory of Arts,* 1979-80 (U.S., Europe); Lifetime Membership, The Scarab Club, Detroit, 1986; *Who's Who in American Art,* 1989-1990; *Who's Who in International Art, 1991; Einstein Academy Foundation Alfred Nobel Medal,* 1991; and One of the Best Three Award Winners, Michigan Annual Art and Competition, 1993. He was also cited as an Outstanding Quezon National High School, Class 56' alumnus, for being an international artist, 1994; and as a Quezon Memorial Hospital School of Nursing alumnus, for being an international artist, 1994.

Family. Romero is the fourth of eight children of Melanio Merca Romero and Teodorica Tabernilla Romero of Tayabas, Quezon Province. This acrylic-impressionistic artist is based in West Bloomfield, Michigan.

ROSCA, NINOTCHKA. Award-Winning Novelist and Short Story Writer. An outspoken radical, Ninotchka Rosca is the author of two novels: *State of War,* a bestseller book a published by Fireside/Simon & Schuster, that has been translated into German and Dutch; and *Twice Blessed,* the winner of the National Book Award in 1993. She is also the author of the nonfiction book *Endgame: The Fall of Marcos* that discusses the People-Power movement that toppled dictator Ferdinand Marcos' regime.

Rosca is the author of two short story collections, *Bitter Country and Other Stories* and *The Monsoon Collection. The Monsoon Collection* came out years after her release during the martial law regime from a military detention camp, where she was detained for six

months, "without charges, trial, nor even the vaguest reason for my incarceration." It was during her detention that she conceived her short stories in *The Monsoon Collection.*

Still Indignant. In an interview with writer Isabel Manalo of *The Progressive,* Rosca, in recalling the Marcos martial law regime and 1986 Philippine People-Power events, was quoted as saying, "I cannot find the words to express how deep my anger is. People like me spent practically our whole lives to get Marcos out. In the end, we are betrayed, and nobody paid except for us and the poor people. They got away with it."

Rosca is currently writing her new novel entitled *The Archipelago of Saint Lazarus,* the original name discoverer Ferdinand Magellan gave to a group of many islands to be known later as the Philippine Islands and more later as the Republic of the Philippines.

Flashback. Rosca obtained her bachelor of science degree in comparative literature from the University of the Philippines. From her college days to this day, she has been a defender of women's rights and human rights.

Upon graduation from college, Rosca joined the editorial staff of the *Graphic* magazine, where she later became its managing editor.

In 1976, Rosca flew to the United States after she received a writing fellowship at the University of Iowa. While on fellowship at the university, she wrote *The Monsoon.* After her stint in Iowa, she headed for Hawaii, where she taught Philippine literature at the University of Hawaii. Then she moved to New York City, where she obtained some fellowship awards.

Among other short stories written by Rosca were "Epidemic," published by *Missouri Review* and "Sugar & Salt," published by *MS Magazine.*

Besides being a fiction writer, Rosca is also a well-known journalist, having written a nonfiction book and columns and articles for Filipino American publications.

RUELAN, MIGUEL A., Ph.D. Scholar, Scientist, Educator, and Civic Leader. Dr. Miguel A. Ruelan has been professor of chemistry at Camden County College in Blackwood, New Jersey, since 1967. From 1967 to 1970, he was chairman of the Department of Chemistry and Physics of the institution.

Fifteenth Son of Twenty-Two Children. Born on September 29, 1936, he is the fifteenth son of twenty-two children of the late Mr. and Mrs. Pedro and Catalina Ruelan of Pio V. Corpus, Masbate Province, Philippines. A consistent honor student and scholar since grade school, Dr. Ruelan, also known as "Mike" to his friends and close associates, carries with his name a long list of honors and distinctions.

Flashback. He graduated as valedictorian in 1950 at Pio V. Corpus Central School (formerly Limbuhan Elementary School) where it took him only four years to finish his elementary education instead of six years because he was accelerated a couple of times during his elementary grades. When he finished high school in 1954 at Masbate Southeastern Institute in Masbate, he was again the valedictorian.

He left his hometown for Manila in 1954 at the young age of fifteen to pursue his college education as a working student. In 1958, he finished his Associate in industrial technology, with honors at Manuel L. Quezon University in Manila. In 1961, he received a Bachelor of Science in chemical engineering, also with honors at Polytechnic Colleges of the Philippines. In 1963, he left for Japan as a scholar of the Japanese government, where he obtained his Master of Science degree in chemical engineering at the Tokyo Institute

of Technology in Tokyo, Japan in 1965. In 1966, he became a Fulbright scholar and left for the United States, where he obtained his doctoral degree in chemical engineering and attained personal success. In 1974, he earned his Doctor of Science in chemical engineering (Ph.D.), with highest distinction at California Christian University in Los Angeles, California. He passed the licensure board examinations for professional chemical engineers in 1962 in Manila, Philippines.

Awards and Honors. As a scholar, Dr. Ruelan received several awards, scholarships, and fellowships. He was a recipient of the Balik-Scientist of the Philippines award from the National Science Development Board in 1976; recipient of a Kellog Fellowship at Drexel University, 1973-1975; recipient of the National Science Foundation in instrumental and analytical chemistry at Rutgers University, 1971; recipient of a Fulbright scholarship, 1966; recipient of a Japanese government Graduate Scholarship at Tokyo Institute of Technology in Tokyo, Japan, 1963-1965; and recipient of an industrial training grant from the Association of Overseas Technical Scholars in Japan, 1965. At Manuel L. Quezon University, he received a free tuition scholarship, 1954-1958 as well as from the Masbate Southeastern Institute, 1950-1954.

Dr. Ruelan received a number of commendations in recognition of his leadership and civic service. Among these are certificate of recognition as the Most Outstanding Filipino in America from the Delaware Valley Association of Filipinos; certificate of commendation for outstanding leadership from the Filipino-American Society of South Jersey; and certificate of commendation for distinguished leadership from the Filipino Executive Council of Greater Philadelphia. He was awarded the most outstanding alumnus of Masbate Southeastern Institute and Pio V. Corpus Central School.

Professional Experience. Dr. Ruelan's professional experience include working as a chemical technician at Marcelo Steel Corporation and Philippine Blooming Mills, Inc., in Manila, 1956-1958, where his work involved the analyses and quality control in the manufacture of steel products; research and development technician at Proctor and Gamble Company (Philippines), 1958-1959, where he worked on research and development of such edible oil and oil products as cooking oil, shortening, margarines, soaps, and detergents; chief chemist at General Textiles, Inc., in Quezon City, 1959-1966, where he was in charge of the Chemical Laboratory and Quality Control Department; professor at Technological University of the Philippines, 1965-1966, where he taught (part-time) chemical engineering, thermodynamics, and physical chemistry; research scientist at Shell Chemical Company, in Woodbury, New Jersey, 1966-1967, where his worked involved research and development of styrene and polystyrene polymers; and professor of chemistry at Camden County College, in Blackwood, New Jersey, from 1967 to the present time.

Ruelan: the Scientist. As a scientist, Dr. Ruelan has written and published in scientific journals, or delivered as lectures, dozens of technical and scientific papers on many aspects of his specialization. Among these papers are Characterization and Treatment of Automotive Waste Oils and Industrial Oil Wastes; Thermal Pollution in Aquatic Life; and Biological and Chemical Treatment of Waste Water, to cite only three.

Community Leader. As a community leader, he is the founder and past president of the following organizations: Masbateño Association of America, Inc., Filipino American Society of South Jersey, Inc., and The Maharlika Group. He was the past president of the Filipino American Association of Philadelphia, Inc., and director of the Philippine Chamber of Commerce of North America, and the Garden State Filipino-American Association. He is a member of the following organizations: New Jersey Education Association, American Association of University Professors, American Institute of Chemical Engineers, and American Chemical Society.

Dr. Ruelan has always kept his ties not only with the Filipino community and the scientific world, but also with the political circle, especially Filipino American affairs. He has been an active leader of the Filipino political action group of New Jersey known as the Filipino Action Committee Alliance or FACA. He served as one of the campaign leaders for former Governor James Florio of New Jersey. In 1978, he was invited by former President Jimmy Carter to spend a week in Washington, D.C., as a counselor on environmental issues.

Ruelan's Dream. Dr. Ruelan's dream, according to him, was "to become a successful scientist and to be able to help the less fortunate of his countrymen." His American dream was "to finish his lifetime career as a scientist and to become rich and famous." His secret formula for success is "set short- and long- term goals and make plans to accomplish them. Do it with positive attitude and perseverance, and use a lot of common sense."

Scholarships to Students. Dr. Ruelan initiated and still supports scholarships for deserving students in his native province of Masbate. At the last count, he had funded the education of more than one hundred talented boys and girls from that island province. "It's a way of sharing my success with others and helping the less fortunate of my countrymen and thanking God and my mother country for what they have given me," he says.

Family. This notable Filipino scientist, educator, and civic leader is married to his childhood sweetheart, Gloria Monares, a former beauty queen in Masbate. They have three children, all college graduates: Marel, a business administrator (married), Alma, a nurse (married) and Miguel, Jr., a doctor of chiropractor, who is still single. The Ruelans reside in a lovely house on a multi-acre estate with a lake in Blackwood, New Jersey, and they have plans to spend their retirement years in the Philippines.

SALONGA, LEA. Actress/Singer. As a young child, Lea Salonga's Philippine dream was to be a psychiatrist ("Believe it or not," she says). Then that dream turned into an American dream: "To one day perform on Broadway." ("Got it!" she says.)

At the age of two, Salonga often sang, using the living room coffee table as a stage and using a plug for a microphone. No wonder that in May 1991, she won the prestigious Tony award for best actress for her role as Kim in the musical *Miss Saigon* on Broadway.

Flashback. Salonga was born in Manila to Feliciano Salonga and Ligaya Imutan on February 22, 1971. Salonga stayed in Angeles City, Pampanga Province, for 6 years and then she moved back to Manila.

When she was 3, Salonga's aunt used to go to their house to babysit her and play the guitar, while

Salonga did the singing. At age 7, she made her professional debut in Repertory Philippines' production of *The King and I.* At age 10, she began her recording career, eventually receiving a gold record for her first album, *Small Voice,* and at age 13, she won three *Aliw* Awards for Best Child Entertainer during the years 1981, 1982, and 1893.

From London to Broadway. Salonga played the role of Kim in *Miss Saigon* in performances in London, where she won the Laurence Olivier Award. From London, she went to Broadway in New York City, where she garnered the Tony, Drama Desk, and Outer Critics Circle Awards. She also won the Theatre World Award.

Greatest Achievement. Referring to her greatest achievement, Salonga says, "That through whatever I've done, the image of the Filipino was made a little more positive, and that somehow, the Filipino was given the chance to smile and be proud. Hopefully, the world's awareness of the Filipino artist remains."

Special Appearances. Among her special appearances were in the presence of Her Royal Highness Queen Elizabeth II; President and Mrs. George Bush; First Lady Hilary Rodham Clinton at the Women's Forum during the Asian Pacific Economic Conference (APEC) in Manila; and at the 65th Annual Academy Awards, where she sang *A Whole New World,* and where the song won an Oscar. She also recorded the singing voice of Jasmine for the Walt Disney animated hit, *Aladdin.*

Special Skills. Languages speaks English and Tagalog, with the talents of several accents—British (cockney and fine British), American, and Filipino.

Tidbits: Culled from an interview with some people on the Internet at the TalkCity's Pavilion facilitated by *Filipino Today* newspaper were the following information:

People She Idolized While Growing Up: The Osmonds, The Carpenters, Olivia Newton-John, and Abba.

Training As a Singer: With Zenaida Amador (drama) and Baby Barredo (drama and voice) in the

Philippines and a year in London with Mary Hammond (voice) and a year, off and on, in New York City. "I do sing in the shower a lot," she says.

Role Model in Her Professional Career: "None really...I don't pattern my career from anyone else. I just go with my gut and do stuff that I love to do."

Goals and Aspirations for the Future. "To just continue to do quality work for as long as I can."

Where to Settle Down in the Long Term, Whether Abroad or in the Philippines: "That would depend on who I ended up marrying."

Theater Performances: Miss Saigon, Les Miserables, Grease!, Into the Woods, My Fair Lady, The Fantasticks, Annie, Paper Moon,; The Goodbye Girl, The Rose Tattoo, Fiddler on the Roof, Cat On a Hot Tin Roof, and *The King and I,* The performances were held in Manila, London, Singapore, and New York City.

Television Movie: Redwood Curtains telecast on national television (ABC) on April 27, 1995.

Filipino Films: Sana'y Maulit Muli, ("May It Be Repeated), *Bakit Labis Kitang Mahal (Why I Love You So Much),* and others.

Recordings: Her recordings include *The Nutcracker, Les Miserables 10th Anniversary Concert, People, Lea Salonga, The Little Tramp, The King and I, One Earth, Aladdin, Miss Saigon, Lea Salonga Christmas Album, Lea,* and *Small Voice.*

SANTOS, BIENVENIDO N. Well-known Writer of Fiction and Poetry. Bienvenido N. Santos, no doubt, was one of the most prolific Filipino writers in English. His works depict the life and times of Filipinos in the Philippines and in America. Most of them, however, were about the joy and sadness of being Filipinos in America and about the search for their own destiny in the United States. He was indeed a master story teller of the Filipino American experience, often times giving funny stories about themselves. He had books, stories, and poems published in the Philippines and in the United States.

Praise. Novelist Jessica Hagedorn, says of Santos, "I knew Bienvenido Santos to be a generous, kindhearted writer with a twinkling eye and a mischievous sense of humor. He seemed as proud of us younger writers as we were of him."

His Home in America. Greeley, Colorado, was Santos' home in America. However, each year, he spent several months in the Philippines. He was a visiting writer and artist in residence at De la Salle University.

Awards and Honors. For his accomplishments in literature, Santos received numerous awards and many honorary degrees. Among the awards he had received were a Guggenheim Foundation Fellowship and a Republic Cultural Heritage Award in Literature. Among his honorary degrees were from his alma mater, the University of the Philippines and the Bicol University in Legazpi City, which both rendered him honorary degrees in letters and the humanities. He also obtained an honorary degree in humane letters upon his retirement from Wichita State University, where he was a distinguished writer in residence from 1973-1982, the year he retired.

Novels. Among his novels are *The Man Who Thought He Looked Like Robert Taylor, Villa*

Magdalena, The Praying Man, and *What the Hell for You Left Your Heart in San Francisco.*

Taken Ill. When Santos, who was born in Tondo, Manila, Philippines, in 1911, was taken ill, he was brought by boat from his home in Sagpon, Daraga, Albay, to Naga City. Then he was flown to the Makati Medical Center in Manila for emergency treatment. Later, however, he was flown back home.

"I'm Glad I'm Home." According to novelist Hagedorn, "With subtle insight and great compassion, Ben wrote about love, loss, and the bittersweet yearning for 'home.'" Writer Leonor Aureus Briscoe, in her article *Home at Last* in the *Filipinas* issue of March 1996, says "The family chartered a plane and took him home to Sagpon, Daraga, Albay, There, in the comfort and peace of his "forever" house among the foothills and coconut groves of Mayon Volcano, he managed to push out words as only a Santos fictional character could speak—from the heart: 'I'm glad I'm home.'" The year was 1996.

SARMIENTO, CESAR C. Superior Court Judge, Los Angeles County, California. Judge Cesar Sarmiento, a superior court judge for Los Angeles County, State of California, has become the first Filipino to be assigned to such stature on the United States mainland. He was born at Clark Field Air Force Base in Angeles, Pampanga Province, Philippines.

Formerly a municipal court judge at the West Los Angeles Branch of the Los Angeles Municipal Court, he was appointed as a superior court judge by the former Governor Pete Wilson. He is a graduate of the University of California at Davis, where he received his law degree in May 1980.

Family. Judge Sarmiento is the second of three children of I.M. "Sammy" Sarmiento and Aurea Cabrera. He is married to the former Ellen Kold, currently a deputy district attorney for the Los Angeles County. They have four children: Allison, Jamie, Timothy, and Ryan.

SCHNEIDER, PILAR, School Board Member, Pacifica, California. The mother of actor Rob Schneider, a movie actor and star of the NBC television series, *Men Behaving Badly,* Pilar Schneider was reelected to the school board of the Laguna Salada Unified School District in the November 1996 elections. Schneider, president of the five-member board in 1995, was first elected to the board in 1992. The two-time winner placed second in the 1996 race. A half-Filipino, half-Caucasian, Schneider obtained her master's degree in education from the San Francisco State University. She was a teacher at Laguna Salada for about 23 before she ran for a seat on the school board.

SCHNEIDER, ROB, Movie Actor. The son of a Filipina American, Pilar Schneider, Rob Schneider is the star of NBC's *Men Behaving Badly.* At age 15, Schneider, a native of San Francisco, California, started writing jokes. He also appeared at local places such as the Holy City Zoo in that city.

To Europe and Back. After he graduated from high school, Schneider left for Europe, where he stayed for about half a year. After he came home, he decided to be in show business. In January 1988, after he had worked at the comedy club circuit, he moved to Los Angeles, California. There he worked as an agent and a manager for auditioning. On the sides, he wrote jokes and television specials for a few well-known comics.

Turning Point of Life. The turning point of his life came when Schneider performed on HBO's *13th Annual Young Comedians Special.* It was there where Lorne Michaels, executive producer of *Saturday Night Live.* "discovered" him. Schneider, not only wrote, but also performed on the series.

Film Roles. Schneider later obtained some feature film roles in *Home Alone 2: Lost in New York, Demolition Man,* and *The Beverly Hillbillies.*

In 1994, Schneider left the Saturday Night Live. He has co-starred with Sylvester Stallone in *Judge Dredd,* with Kelsey Grammer in *Down Periscope,* and with Martin Landau and Jonathan Taylor Thomas in *Pinocchio.* He also appeared in *Surf Ninjas* and *Martians Go Home.*

He also hosted the *Sports Illustrated Swimsuit '97 Special* that aired on February 22, 1997, on TNT. "As the sex symbol of the '90s, I was the natural choice to do this job," says Schneider. His swimsuit stint included a trip to Turkey, Monaco, and Venezuela with a group of barely-clad models.

SILVA, EULALIO BUENO. Internationally Renowned Artist.

By the age of six, Eulalio Bueno Silva had a dream to become an artist. He surrounded himself with books that contained reproductions of paintings, prints, and sculptures. Frequent visits to art galleries and museums as an adolescent allowed him to observe and become inspired by the masters. Those early years served as Silva's preliminary tools and foundation towards the development of his art.

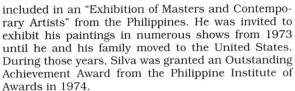

Silva was born into a large business-oriented family on August 20, 1941 in Baguio City, Philippines. He was encouraged by his family to study accounting. He received a bachelor's degree in business administration in 1965 from the University of the East in Manila, Philippines.

Chases His Dream. At twenty-four, Silva decided to realize his dream to become an artist, without any formal training, guidance, or degree in fine arts. He remained committed and determined to study art and develop his skills despite criticism that becoming an artist was a difficult field to provide a decent living.

In the late 1960s and the early 1970s, Silva opened a portrait gallery in Makati, Metro Manila. That experience allowed his painting skills to develop. A significant accomplishment in his young career culminated in 1970 when Silva received a Medal of Achievement citation, personally presented by His Holiness Pope Paul VI. In 1973, he was honored to be included in an "Exhibition of Masters and Contemporary Artists" from the Philippines. He was invited to exhibit his paintings in numerous shows from 1973 until he and his family moved to the United States. During those years, Silva was granted an Outstanding Achievement Award from the Philippine Institute of Awards in 1974.

His work was included for publication in 1975 and 1976 in textbooks in the arts and humanities curriculum at the University of the East, in Manila.

First International Group Exhibit. Exposicion de Pentores Filipinos, held in Madrid, Spain, in 1978, was Silva's first international group exhibition.

Moves to U.S. Still Following His Dream. In 1979, a year after his first international group exhibition, Silva and his family moved to the United States. They arrived in San Francisco, California, where he had his first American solo exhibition at the Philippine Consulate. Silva soon resettled in Sacramento, California, where he continued to support his family by painting landscapes and commissioned portraits. His paintings became recognized and he was invited to participate in several group exhibitions featuring international artistic exchanges.

Another significant experience in Silva's career came in 1985 when his oil painting, *Our Lady of the Beaterio,* commissioned for the Religious Order of the Virgin Mary, in the Philippines, was made into a commemorative national postage stamp.

Silva relocated his family to Fredericksburg, Virginia, where he continued to develop his artistic skills through museum visits and commission portraiture.

In 1987, he mounted a solo exhibition at Fredericksburg's Center for the Creative Arts-Silversmith House. He was recognized from that show with a limited edition lithograph, "Silversmith House," a Virginia State Top Honors Award and a National Semi-Finalist Award for the Take Pride in America competition. The national exhibition was held at the White House, in Washington, D.C.

Seeking the Opportunity for a Better Life. The opportunity for a better life for his family brought Silva to Chicago, Illinois, in 1987. For two years, Silva familiarized himself with Chicago's art scene, while exploring different avenues in painting. The color and composition of master artists like Cezanne, Gauguin, Matisse, and van Gogh became his new inspiration. These works brought Silva closer to his current style painting, a transition he embraced. "I no longer do the traditional way of mixing colors. I do not just mix colors anymore. I now have to use the colors, especially loud colors, in their pure state and pay attention to composition," he says.

Participation in Other Group Exhibits. Silva continued to exhibit his new paintings in several group exhibitions from 1990-1993. His works were included in an art exhibition of twenty internationally renowned artists at the Grove Street Gallery and Land of Lincoln's Gallery, in Illinois. From 1992-1994 Silva exhibited his work with a group of Asian artists's organization, called Destin-Asian, to bring their collective art experiences to the Chicago communities. Silva met artist and independent curator Phillip J. Turner in 1994. Turner's family-run and art consultation business, Curtis.Allen.Turner Fine Arts (CATFA), invited Silva to exhibit with them. In 1995, their mutual interests to develop a commission portrait business led to the formation of Margaret Emily Curtis Portrait Studios, a division of CATFA.

Solo Exhibitions. Silva began to exhibit with a number of galleries in Chicago, namely East+West (Walsh) Gallery; BAGIT; Gahlberg Gallery of College of DuPage; North Lakeside Cultural Center; Gallery 7000; and Curtis.Allen.Turner Fine Arts. His recent solo exhibition, "Passion & Chaos," was held at the Chicago Cultural Center. This mid-career retrospective chronicled his view of the world. Phillip J. Turner, director of CATFA, says of Silva's work, "Silva fuses a sense of western art composition with a Southeast Asian intensity of color...His view of the world is tempered by a sensory explosion of color and technique." Teresa J. Parker, curator for Elmhurst Art Museum writes, "The paintings evoke an other worldly sensation of 'passion under the surface'."

Family. Silva is married to Patria Clara Fabie Silva. They have four grown children: Eulalio III, married to Roseanne Rasmussen; Mary Jane, married to William Tam; Joanne, married to Hector Arreola; and Patrick. Eulalio III has followed in his father's footsteps, also pursuing a career as an artist.

SORIANO, EDWARD. First Philippine-born Soldier to Become a General.

Born in Alcala, Pangasinan Province, Philippines, Major General Edward Soriano, 50, is the first Philippine-born soldier to become a general in the Armed Forces of the United States.

Major General Soriano is currently assigned as the director of operations, readiness and mobilization

in the Office of the Deputy Chief of Staff for Operations and Plans of the U.S. Army at the Pentagon.

At present, there are only three Asian American generals in the Armed Forces of the United States, two of them Filipino Americans, Soriano and Taguba, and the other is Lieutenant General Eric K. Shinseki, a Japanese American.

"It's significant that we have two (Fil-Am) generals," Soriano told Ely Barros, a free-lance writer in San Francisco, California, for an article in *Filipinas Magazine*'s issue of October 1997.

Flashback. Soriano was seven years old when he, his mother, Encarnacion, and his sister, Blez, immigrated to Guam to join his father, Fred Soriano, who was in the U.S. Army. From Guam, they headed for Hawaii to begin a new life there.

According to Soriano, he and his sister, the only children of the Sorianos "enjoyed being 'army brats.'"

Later, in the 1960s, the Sorianos moved to Salinas, California, when the elder Soriano retired as a major in the U.S. Army. Upon graduation from high school in Salinas, the younger Soriano attended San Jose State University, where he received his bachelor's degree in management in 1970. He took the R.O.T.C. program at San Jose State University and he was inducted into the U.S. Army as a second lieutenant in the U.S. Army immediately after graduation. He took some courses in military schools. Later, he obtained a master's degree in public administration from the University of Missouri.

After taking the infantry officer basic, airborne, and ranger courses at the U.S. Infantry School in Fort Benning, Georgia, Soriano's first assignment was to the 82nd Airborne Division at Fort Bragg, North Carolina, as officer-in-charge of the Recondo School of the same outfit. He later took basic and advanced courses at the U.S. Army Command and General Staff College and the U.S. Army War College.

His stint in the U.S. Army included a three-year stay in Germany as a company commander in a mechanized battalion; as a liaison to the 1st Marine Expeditionary Force in Saudi Arabia during the Persian Gulf War; as a secretary of the Gulf War Report Team during Operation Desert Shield/Storm; as an assistant commander for the Army's First Infantry Division in Bosnia and as a director of personnel operations at the U.S. Army Total Personnel Command in Alexandria, Virginia.

In 1997, he was assigned to the Pentagon. He has been in the military for the past 27 years.

Family. Married to Vivian, he and his wife have two children: Melissa, 23, and Keith, 19.

TABACO, NATALIO D. First Filipino United Nations Secretariat Employee.

A World War II veteran, Natalio D. Tabaco holds the distinction of being the first Filipino to be recruited by the United

Nations Secretariat as an employee in 1946. Born on July 27, 1918 in the barrio of Taloto, Tagbilaran, Bohol Province, Philippines. Tabaco received the United Nations Peace Medal for outstanding service to the U.N. in 1976. This is the highest medal of honor given to an individual working for the cause of international peace through the United Nations.

Flashback. In 1939, after completing his Teacher's Course from the Philippine School of Trades (PSAT) in Manila, he taught in the industrial arts field in various city schools in Manila. He attended night classes at the University of Santo Tomas in Manila to major in vocational administration but didn't finish it due to the outbreak of Second World War.

Being an ROTC graduate from PSAT, Tabaco was called to active duty. He enlisted in the United States Armed Forces in the Far East (USAFE) and he was stationed in Cebu Province and later in Bohol Province for three years. In 1944, he was transferred to Leyte Province and stayed there for a year. He was a sergeant when he was discharged from the service. He married Venancia Catay and taught again in schools as an industrial arts teacher.

At the UN. He first worked as a clerk-typist and a projectionist with the U.N. Department of Public Information. During his tenure of service, he did research and made periodic reports on U.N. technical assistants' projects of underdeveloped countries that were members of the U.N., one of which was the Philippines. In 1947, the then Secretary-General Tryve Lie presented him with the First Staffer Medal in recognition of his being the first Filipino to be recruited by the United Nations. He retired from the United Nations at the age of 60 in 1976.

Author. Tabaco is the author of a three-volume book on the life and times of the late Carlos P. Romulo, former Ambassador and Secretary of the Department of Foreign Affairs of the Philippines.

Family. Tabaco lives with his wife in New York City. They have ten grown children who are all married and have children.

TAGLE, DANILO A., Ph.D. Geneticist. A scientist, Dr. Danilo A. Tagle is at the forefront of genetics research as part of the Human Genome project. The Human Genome Project is an international research program designed to construct detailed genetic and physical maps of the human genome, to determine the complete nucleotide sequence of human DNA, to localize the estimated 100,000 genes

in the human chromosomes, and to perform similar analyses on the genomes of several other organisms used extensively in research laboratories as model systems. Compared in magnitude to the space exploration program, the Human Genome Project is already yielding clues on the basic set of inherited "blueprints" for the development and functioning of a human being and will form the basis of future biomedical research.

Senior Investigator. Dr. Tagle has been a senior investigator at the National Human Genome Research Institute of the National Institutes of Health in Bethesda, Maryland, since 1993. He heads the Molecular Neurogenetics Section in the Genetic and Molecular Biology Branch. Research in his laboratory involves the identification and characterization of genes for inherited neurodegenerative disorders. His research program includes the development and refinement of methodologies for gene mapping and cloning, as well as the characterization and functional analyses of these genes for a better appreciation of their pathogenic mechanisms that will lead to therapy and intervention.

Cloning of the Genes. In this highly competitive field, Dr. Tagle has been involved in research collaborations that lead to the cloning of the genes for a number of brain disorders, among which include Huntington's disease, ataxia-telangiectasia and more recently, Niemann-Pick type C disease. He shares

international patent applications for these discoveries. He has published, on his own or jointly with other scientists, no less than 60 peer-reviewed articles and abstracts in internationally recognized scientific journals, 6 book chapters, and has participated in numerous scientific proceedings.

Education. After high school graduation from Colegio de San Juan de Letran in Manila, Philippines, Dr. Tagle started his undergraduate education at the University of Santo Tomas in Manila and later received his bachelor of science in 1982 and master of science degrees in biological sciences in 1984 from Wayne State University School of Medicine in Detroit, Michigan. He later obtained a Ph.D. degree in molecular biology and genetics in 1990 from the same institution. For his postdoctoral training, Dr. Tagle was a research fellow from 1990-1993 at the University of Michigan Medical Center under the mentorship of world-renowned geneticist, Francis S. Collins.

Memberships. Dr. Tagle has been on the Science Advisory Council of the Huntington's Disease Society of America, Inc., since 1994 and has served on the science review committee of the National Retinitis Pigmentosa Foundation (the foundation fighting blindness). He also serves as ad hoc reviewer for a number of scientific journals and is a member of several professional societies (American Association for the Advancement of Science, American Society of Human Genetics and American Society of Neuroscience). He is also in the editorial board of the International Electronic Journal of Biotechnology.

Flashback. As a boy growing up in Manila, the young Tagle had always been fascinated with God's creations. He says, "The weekend trips to beaches of Cavite and to the family farms in Bulacan and Bataan or even those lazy afternoons in the background were quickly transformed into my very own laboratory. My mind quickly filled with nostalgic memories of homemade exploding volcanoes, a plethora of exotic pets, shooting rockets, amateurish taxidermy, mining fools' gold, and powerful electromagnets. My dream of becoming a scientist was therefore not too surprising to my parents and teachers."

Explaining his career, Dr. Tagle says, "The successes that I have had in gene cloning have allowed me to be at par with the best and top-notched genetic researchers of the world and have a very active research program at one of the most prestigious research institutions in the United States."

Family. Dr. Tagle is the second of seven siblings (Maria Corazon, Maria Lourdes, Maria Theresa, Dioscoro Jr., Dennis, and Maria Cecilia), all established professionals in their respective fields. His parents, Lourdes (nee Angeles) and Dioscoro V. Tagle of Clinton Township, Michigan were originally from Bataan Province, Philippines. Dr. Tagle and his wife Maria Leilani (nee Domingo) have three children: Leanne, Danny, and Lorena. In addition to his scientific achievements, Dr. Tagle is also an accomplished chef and an active member of a local church.

TAGUBA, ANTONIO. Second Philippine-born Soldier to Become a General. A native of Manila, Philippines, Brigadier General Antonio Taguba, 46, is the second Philippine-born soldier to become a general in the Armed Forces of the United States.

At present, Brigadier General Taguba, the son of a U.S. military man, is temporarily assigned as a special assistant to the commanding general at Fort McPherson in Atlanta, Georgia, He has been with the military for the past 25 years. Before he was promoted, Taguba was previously the commander of the Second Brigade, Fourth Infantry Division in Fort Hood, Texas.

In an interview with Ely Barros, a writer in San Francisco, for an article in the *Filipinas* that came out in its October 1997 issue, Taguba, said, "I take it with great pride that we're able to assimilate ourselves with American society. We've shown we can contribute to society and at the same time preserve our Filipino heritage."

Flashback. Taguba was only 11 years old, when he, his two other brothers, and five sisters, moved with their mother to Hawaii. After graduating from the Leilehua High School in 1968, Taguba attended the Idaho State University, where he graduated in 1972. He immediately joined the military.

Taguba took courses at military training schools, including the U.S. Army Command and General Staff College, the College of Naval Command and Staff, and the U.S. Naval War College. He is a holder of master's degrees in public administration from Webster University, in international relations from Salve Regina College, and in national security and strategic studies from the U.S. Naval War College.

Taguba's stint in the U.S. Army include such assignments as commander of a tank company in Germany and battalion commander and later executive officer of the combined U.S. and Korean forces in South Korea.

Married to Debbie and residing in Peachtree City, Georgia, he and his wife have two children: Lindsey, 15, and Sean, 12.

TEJANO, NEONILO A., Well-Known Orthopedic Surgeon. As a child growing up in Loay, Bohol Province, Philippines, where he was born, Neonilo A. Tejano was impressed with the town's physician, and dreamed of becoming a doctor himself. Today, Dr. Tejano is the senior orthopedic surgeon and chairman of the board at The Hertzler Clinic, P.A., a multi-specialty clinic in Halstead, Kansas. He has been

a member (and has served as chairman) of the board of directors of the Heritage Clinic, P.A. for many years. Dr. Tejano was the chairman of the Department of Surgery of the Halstead Hospital, from 1974-1976 and again from 1994-1996. He is well-known for his pioneering use of bone-growth stimulators in lumbar fusion. The Hertzler Clinic is one of only eight centers in the United States approved by the Food and Drug Administration to conduct research on the use of Spf 100 in lumbar fusions. Dr. Tejano leads that research initiative.

Dr. Tejano, who specializes in spinal and reconstructive joint surgery, flies all over the country treating patients. Many of the people he treats say that they wouldn't have been able to walk again except for his surgical talent.

Flashback. While a student, Dr. Tejano studied hard even in the elementary grades. He was the valedictorian in high school at the Holy Trinity Academy in Loay. He was a university scholar at Far Eastern University in Manila, where he completed his studies in pre-medicine. He earned his medical degree from Far Eastern University's Institute of Medicine in 1967, graduating in the top ten percent of his class—and fulfilling his childhood dream of becoming a physician.

Internships and Residencies. Dr. Tejano completed internships and residencies at the United States Air Force Hospital at Clark Air Force Base in the Philippines and at St. Francis Hospital (now the St. Francis Campus of Via Christi Regional Medical Center) in Wichita, Kansas.

Memberships. He is a member of the Harvey Country Medical Society, the Kansas Medical Society, the Kansas Orthopedic Society, MidCentral States Orthopedic Society, Southwest Clinical Society of Greater Kansas City, the American Medical Association, and the American Academy of Orthopedic Surgeons. He is a fellow of the American Academy of Orthopedic Surgeons and a diplomate of the American Board of Orthopedic Surgery.

Scientific Papers. Dr. Tejano has published numerous papers and presented scientific papers at several prestigious conferences around the world. Conventions where he has presented his findings include those of the Kansas Orthopedic Society, the Asian Orthopedic Association, the North American Spine Society, the International Society of Spine Surgeons, and the Philippine Orthopedic Association. He has also presented papers at the University of Hong Kong.

One of Hobbies: Flying in His Own Plane. The surgeon's hobbies include spending time with his family, hunting, skiing, tennis, flying in his own planes, and ballroom dancing. He was selected as one of the 20 Outstanding Filipino Americans in 1994 and was featured in the book, *Filipino Achievers in the USA & Canada: Profiles in Excellence* by Isabelo T. Crisostomo.

Family. Dr. Tejano is married to the former Esperanza B. Buniao, D.D.M., a graduate of the University of the Philippines College of Dentistry and the dental exam "topnotcher" in 1968.

They have four accomplished children: Kristine, 27, a graduate of the University of Pennsylvania and now attending law school at De Paul University in Chicago, Illinois; Jennipher, 26, a graduate of Creighton University and a graduate student at Wichita State University; Neil, 22, a senior at Johns Hopkins University; and Victor, 20, a sophomore at Bethel College.

TING, JOSEPH K. Senior Mechanical Engineer and Adjunct Professor in Mechanical Engineering. Born in Manila, and raised in Little Baguio, San Juan, Rizal Province (now Metro Manila), Philippines, Joseph K. Ting is a senior mechanical engineer for the Dormitory Authority, State of New York (DASNY). He is also an adjunct professor in mechanical engineering at the Rensselaer Polytechnic Institute in New York, where he has been teaching since 1993. He attended the De La Salle University for his undergraduate studies, where he obtained his Bachelor of Science in mechanical engineering in 1972. Then he came to the United States and went to the Massachusetts Institute of Technology (MIT) for his graduate schooling and completed his Master of Science in 1974.

Dream. Ting's dream in life is to provide "comfort" to the human race either in terms of food, shelter, or clothing. His first involvement was in clothing when he had participated in the project at MIT through research grants of DuPont in the development of textile machinery to thermally and mechanically treat the continuous filament system for use with staple fiber in the creation of blended fabrics, thus provide the essential comfort clothing for human beings. He then got involved with the research in the conversion of the Rolls-Royce RB-211 jet engine into a gas pumping engine. This development led to the creation of the Trans-Canada Pipeline that provides the continuous supply of natural gas as one of the alternatives to fuel oil in order to provide the essential comfort shelter (housing) for residential homes, commercial offices, and institutional hospitals, as well as industrial plants.

Senior Mechanical Engineer. As a senior mechanical engineer for the Dormitory Authority, State of New York (DASNY), Ting oversees the design and construction of HVAC&R (Heating, Ventilation, Air-Conditioning & Refrigeration) systems for DASNY-financed buildings such as schools, colleges, hospitals, and other buildings for not-for-profit organizations. His involvement in ASHRAE (American Society of Heating, Refrigerating & Air-Conditioning Engineers) has been very helpful to his career.

Memberships. After completing his three-year term as director and regional chairman for ASHRAE, Ting is now serving as a member of the Nominating Committee. He is a member of ASME (American Society of Mechanical Engineers), CSME (Canadian Society of Mechanical Engineers); APEO (Association of Professional Engineers of Ontario); USNC-IIR (United States National Committee-International Institute of Refrigeration); NSPE (National Society of Professional Engineers), and NYSSPE (New York State Society of Professional Engineers).

He has served two terms as chairman of the board and president of MIT Alumni/ae Club of Capital District of New York from 1992 to 1994. He has been serving as an MIT educational counselor since 1992. He has also served as president of the Chinese American Community Center for the Capital District of New York.

Family. Married to Monique Crenn, Ting has a daughter, Audrey Adrienne, and a son, William Alexander.

TIZON, ALEX. Pulitzer Prize Winner. A reporter of *The Seattle Times*, Alex Tizon, received a Pulitzer Prize award at ceremonies held last year at Columbia University in New York City. He received the award from George Rupp, president of Columbia University under the category of investigative reporting. (Another reporter of *The Seattle Times*, Byron Acohido, received a Pulitzer Prize award under the category of beat reporting.)

Tizon headed an investigative team that included *Seattle Times* reporters Eric Nalder and Deborah Nelson, who also received Pulitzer Prize awards. In its series of articles, the team exposed anomalies allegedly perpetrated by some American Indian leaders who were reported to have made big money from certain housing projects financed by the Federal Housing and Urban Development (HUD).

An Immigrant at Age of 4. Tizon arrived in the United States at the age of four. His mother is from Pampanga Province, Philippines, and his father was born in Pampanga Province and raised in Cotabato Province in Mindanao.

Education. He obtained a bachelor's degree in political science and English from the University of Oregon and a master's degree in journalism from Stanford University. Even prior to his studying of journalism, Tizon did freelance writing, beginning at age 17.

No Talents, Except One. Tizon joined *The Seattle Times* in 1986 soon after he received his bachelor's degree. Referring to his profession, he said, "I grew up with no talents except one: writing."

TOMIMBANG, EMME. Hawaii TV Personality. When Emme Tomimbang was only three years old, her parents Eutiquio Tomimbang and Nina Tampon, divorced. Being an only child, her father raised her and sent her to school. She had a lonely and hard life.

Childhood Life. In an interview published in the *Filipinas* magazine issue of August 1995, she was quoted to have said: "The places we lived in never had hot water, not even running water. We had communal baths, no private baths." According to her, they didn't live in a "real" home until she was 16.

Award. Today, Tomimbang is president of her own company called Emme Multi Media Enterprise or EMME, Inc., producing the hour-long *Island Moments* that airs regularly on Channel 13. The program

Islands Moments profiles Hawaiian personalities, offering a taste of the Hawaiian culture and defines the true aloha spirit. In 1994, it was the only TV show that garnered the Kahili Award from the Hawaii Visitors Bureau for promoting the aloha spirit and tourism in Hawaii.

Flashback. Tomimbang, who was born and raised in Kakaako, on the island of Oahu, Hawaii, obtained a summer job at a Filipino radio station (KISA). This work made her desire to be a TV journalist. Moreover, her father, who was a pioneer broadcaster with the first Filipino radio and television program in Hawaii titled *Maligayang Araw*, might have also influenced her thinking into pursuing her TV broadcasting career. With a psychology major degree from the University of Hawaii, at Manoa, Tomimbang started her TV career at KITV 4, where she became a TV news personality. In 1987, she moved to the NBC affiliate KHON, where a program, *Island Style* was premiered as a feature part of the news show. In 1993, she quit her job to become her own boss. Using the *Island Style* concept, she produced her *Island Moments*.

Family. Tomimbang is married to James Burns, chief judge of the Hawaii Intermediate Court of Appeals.

TOMITA, TAMLYN. Movie Actress.

Now one of Hollywood's successful young actresses, Tamlyn Tomita is part Filipina. Her mother, born in the Philippines is part Filipina and part Okinawan. Her father, a U.S.-born Japanese American, as a child, was sent to an internment camp during World War II. She was born in Okinawa, but was raised in Los Angeles, California, from the age of four months. She grew up in Northridge, a suburb of Los Angeles.

The Karate Kid Girl. Tomita came to public attention when she played the part of an Okinawan girlfriend of Ralph Macchio in the film *Karate Kid II.* That was her first acting role. Since then, she has appeared in such theatrical movies as Four Room's *The Misbehavers, Picture Bride, The Joy Luck Club, Come See the Paradise, Vietnam Texas, Orange Curtain,* and *Hawaiian Dream.*

Never Dreamed to Become an Actress. Tomita never dreamed that she would become an actress. But fate intervened and she became one after she met Helen Funai, now her personal manager at the Los Angeles' Nisei Festival, where she won a beauty pageant. When she was invited, together with other young women, to see the casting director of *Karate Kid, Part II,* she didn't hesitate to go. Tomita was quoted to have said, "I came along. I figured I had nothing to lose. And I was curious enough and brave enough." And as they say, the rest is history.

People's Magazine Reveals Her Identity. Tomita was first written as part Filipina in *People's Magazine.*

She has also appeared on several television series, such as *The Sentinal, Chicago Hope, The Samurai,* and *Single Flame.* She also performed in TV movies such as *Hiroshima: Out of the Ashes,* and *Hiroshima Maiden.*

UNGSON, RAFAEL G, JR. Professor Emeritus, California State University at Northridge.

Now retired, Rafael G. Ungson, Jr., taught physics, astronomy, mathematics, etc. for about 13 years.

Flashback. From 1947-1949, Ungson was a U. S. Federal Government scholar at the University of California at Los Angeles (UCLA), where he acquired his B.S. in meteorology. Then he practiced as a meteorologist at the Kansas City Municipal Airport in Missouri. Later, from 1954-1955, Ungson Jr. as a university scholar, attended Oklahoma State University in Stillwater, Oklahoma, where he completed his M.S. in civil engineering, majoring in structures. After graduation, he worked as a structural engineer in the City of Milwaukee, Wisconsin.

To the Philippines and Back. In 1956, Ungson returned to the Philippines and worked as an engineer at the People's Homesite and Housing Corporation (PHHC) in Quezon City, in the suburbs of Manila, to build low-income housing projects. Afterwards, he joined the engineering staff of the Atlantic, Gulf, and Pacific Co., an American engineering company. He joined the Banco Filipino's construction of BF Homes Housing projects in Las Pinas and Paranaque, Rizal. Province.

Back to the United States in 1976, he taught civil engineering, mathematics, and physics at Southwestern College in San Diego, California. He also taught math and physics at the Naval Air Station (NAS), on Coronado Island, San Diego, California. In August 1983, he started teaching science subjects at California State University at Northridge, where he stayed until his retirement as a professor emeritus in 1992. As a teacher, he was rated as an excellent professor by his students in the official university survey.

Greatest Achievement. According to Ungson, his greatest achievement in life is "having helped the younger generation—the youth of the land." His formula for success is: "Hard work, honesty, and discipline."

UY, EMELIO Y. Outstanding Businessman and Civic Leader.

Of all the Filipinos in Guam today, Emelio Y. Uy is one of the most prominent, with a reputation for doing charitable work both on the island and in the Philippines. Although Uy has been residing on that island territory for more than 12 years, he continues to have a strong nationalistic feeling about the Philippines. Over the years, he has made countless invaluable contributions to the Philippine government's development efforts.

Presidential Awardee. For his contributions and other accomplishments, Uy was the recipient of a Banaag Award, one of the presidential awards given yearly to the most outstanding Filipino individuals and organizations overseas. (These outstanding Filipinos overseas received their awards at ceremonies held at the Malacanang Palace in Manila on December 13, 1996.)

Success in Business. Uy's success in business has inspired a lot of small businessmen in Guam to start their own businesses—businesses that now contribute a lot to the economy of the island in terms of jobs and services. Starting with only two employees in 1981, Uy, who is normally called "Emil" has transformed the National Office Supply into one of the largest retail stores on the island. Uy's success is one of the most remarkable Filipino success stories in Guam, and he has served as a model to many small entrepreners who came after him.

Honors and Commendations. Uy was selected by the U.S. Small Business Administration's as Guam's Minority Small Business Advocate of the Year for 1997. This highly prestigious award honors business owners for their outstanding achievements and special contributions to the economy.

Emelio Y. Uy is shown receiving a "Banaag Award" from President Ramos of the Philippines as one of the most outstanding Filipinos overseas in 1996.

In recognition of his humanitarian projects, he has received a lot of commendations. He was recipient of Guam's First Lady's (former First Lady, Rosanne Ada) 1990 Most Distinguished Volunteer Award and the 1990 Most Outstanding Adult Volunteer Award.

Achievements. Among Uy's notable achievements are:

■ He became president of the Guahan Lions Club which works on the beautification of Guam.

■ He was a recipient of the Golden Scroll Award for international relations sector given by the Young Achievers Foundation of the Philippines.

■ He produced and coordinated shows for a series of Philippine artists for various charities in Guam. These shows included entertainers such as Gary Valenciano, Dessa, German Moreno, and Moreno's young entertainers. All the proceeds were donated to various charitable organizations and causes.

■ He was the chairman of Ways and Means Committee of the Filipino Community of Guam, and was the fundraising chairman for various club projects.

■ He was president of the Metro Manila Association of Guam, and spearheaded fundraising campaigns for various charities in Guam, including victims reaching out, including the First Lady's war against drugs.

■ He was appointed by Guam Governor Carl T.C. Gutierrez as the fundraising chairman for the Guam delegation to the Pacific Arts Festival (FESTPAC). He was also appointed to assist in Guam's participation in FESTPAC to be held in American Samoa.

■ He was the adviser of the Lions Club International District 204 governor, and led the Guam and Micronesia delegation to the 35th OSEAL Forum (Orient Southeast Asia Lions) held in Taipei, Taiwan.

■ He received a presidential award on December

13, 1996, as one of the most outstanding Filipinos overseas for his exemplary community service through outstanding philanthropic fund raising activities, mobilizing resources, and organizing activities to support various humanitarian projects in Guam and in the Philippines.

■ In 1997, Uy was elected president of the Filipino Community of Guam (FCG) for 1998. FCG is the umbrella organization for the 67 various Filipino associations in Guam. He was also appointed by the Philippine Centennial Commission as the chairman for the Philippine Centennial celebration in Guam this year.

VALDERRAMA, DAVID MERCADO. Delegate, Maryland General Assembly. A staunch advocate of civil and human rights, David Valder-

rama was a David who fought against 10 Goliaths in his first try in American politics. David won in the Maryland General Assembly elections in November 1990 with a margin of 7,000 votes over his closest rival. He became the first Filipino American to be elected to a state legislature on the U.S. mainland, representing Prince George's county, whose 700,000 population is comprised of blacks (50 percent); whites (48 percent), and Asians, (2 percent). He was reelected for another four-year term in the November 1994 elections.

To Washington? Being one of the most powerful Filipino or Asian leaders on the U.S. mainland, Valderrama is considered to be the best bet to become the first Filipino American to be brought to the U.S. Congress in Washington, D.C.

How He Works. One of the significant times in Valderrama's life as a state legislator happened during Maryland's fight over the English-only bill. He and his followers were able to several times kill the vote in the Maryland House. However, the English only bill for Maryland was later considered and passed by the state assembly. Thinking that the law would strike a severe blow to the Asian Pacific American community, Valderrama helped launch a letter-writing campaign to President Clinton. Valderrama and his supporters also petitioned Maryland Governor Donald Schaffer to veto it, which the governor did.

As a delegate in the Maryland State Legislature, in 1997, Valderrama introduced a welfare reform bill on behalf of legal immigrants to qualify them for benefits. The proposed law filed by Valderrama with a dozen co-sponsors seeks to provide welfare assistance, including cash to legal immigrants who had been in the U.S. on or before August 22, 1996, the day President Clinton signed the national welfare reform legislation into law. It also provides food stamp benefits to certain legal immigrants, certain medical care services, and other benefits under Maryland's welfare program. Prince George's County, the district that Valderrama represents in the state assembly, has the highest concentration of the state's Filipino population.

Flashback. Valderrama, born in Siniloan, Laguna Province, Philippines, played the violin at the age of 7, and at age 13 joined a renowned Filipino symphony. At 16, he engaged in a cigarette wholesale business.

Valderrama graduated from the Far Eastern University in Manila, with a law degree in 1955. (He later obtained his master's degree in comparative law from the George Washington University in Washington, D.C.)

A former journalist in the Philippines, Valderrama left the Philippines as a bachelor at the age of 27. He first worked as a senior legal specialist at the U.S. Library of Congress in Washington D.C.

In 1982, he was elected vice-chairman for Prince George's County of the State Democratic Central Committee. He quit the position when he was appointed as a judge by Governor Harry Hughes of Maryland in November 1997. Five years later, Valderrama ran in the September 1990 primary elections. He was victorious in the primary elections, making him the official Democratic Party candidate for the 26th Legislative District of Maryland, which is Prince George's County. Then came the elections of 1990, during which he won as delegate to the Maryland General Assembly. As a member of the state assembly, he has sponsored bills that have been passed into laws.

Family. Valderrama is married to Nelly Perez of Pangasinan Province, whom he left as a fiancee in the Philippines in 1961. They were married in the United States several years later. Their daughters, Kriselda Vita and Emma Vida, are both attending college.

VELORIA, VELMA R. Washington State Representative.

Born on October 22, 1950, in the Philippines, Velma Veloria holds the record of being the first Asian American woman to be elected to the Washington State legislature and the first Filipina American to be elected to a state legislature on the United States mainland. She won her first election as a representative of the 11th District in Olympia, to the Washington State Legislature in the 1992 elections. She ran, won unopposed in the 1994 and 1996 elections.

Flashback. In 1984, Veloria, an activist, moved from New York City to Seattle, Washington, to help organize a Filipino cannery workers union marred by the murders of two union activists, Silme Domingo and Gene Viernes.

Upon her arrival in Seattle, she immediately became involved in local Filipino activities and in state politics. In 1987, she became the oral historian of *Alaskeros*, an oral history and photo exhibit of Filipino laborers who worked in canneries in Alaska in the 1920s and 1930s. Her other works that eventually pushed her to the political arena are as follows: 1988—acted as delegate of the Washington State Rainbow Coalition to the National Democratic Convention in Atlanta, Georgia; 1989—joined as a member of the transition team of Seattle Mayor Norm Rice, served as a field coordinator of then-Councilwoman Dolores Sibonga who ran and lost in her bid for mayor of Seattle, and served as an administrative assistant in the office of Representative Art Wang, Democratic-27th District (Tacoma); 1991-1992—became a member of the Filipino Political Action Group of Washington and member of the State Advisory Committee of the U.S. Civil Rights Commission.

International Trade Experience. In 1993, Veloria was the leader and organizer of the Washington State Trade and Investment Mission to the Philippines. She headed a delegation of small and women-owned minority businesses in order to find investment opportunities there. Governor Mike Lowry and Secretary of State Ralph Munro joined the delegation for the Philippines portion of the mission. The mission's accomplishments include the development of direct business links between small minority companies in Washington and the Philippines; $1 million in revenue for those businesses; a sister city agreement between Tacoma, Washington, and Davao City, Philippines; and the opening of the Philippine Trade Office in Seattle, Washington. In 1995, Veloria organized and led a similar mission, with similar goals, to Vietnam, Cambodia, and Thailand.

Committee Assignments. Currently, Veloria's committee assignments in the House of Representative are as follows: ranking minority member, Trade and Economic Development; Rules; and Education. Her previous committee assignments include assistant ranking minority member, Trade and Economic Development; vice-chair, State Government; Health Care; Labor and Commerce; Law and Justice.

Family. Veloria is the daughter of Apelino Veloria, a native of Bani, Pangasinan, who was a U.S. Navy man who decided to bring his family to San Francisco, California, in 1961. Veloria, who arrived there at the age of 11 and who graduated from the Balboa High School, attended the San Francisco State University, where she obtained a bachelor's degree in medical technology. She is married to Alonzo Susun and resides in Seattle, Washington.

VERA CRUZ, PHILIP. Labor Leader.

Philip Vera Cruz became involved in the Filipino and Mexican labor union activities in September 1965, after he learned about the Filipino farm workers' strike just a few miles from where he was working.

Vera Cruz helped in the merging of the Filipino and Mexican unions. In fact, he became a vice president of then-newly formed United Farm Workers

Union. However, in 1977, he resigned from his position in protest of Cesar Chavez's visit to the Philippines under the dictatorship of President Ferdinand Marcos. After quitting his post, he moved to Bakersfield, California, and devoted his life to continued labor activism. He often lectured on college campuses about labor issues.

Vera Cruz, who came to the United States in 1926 at the age of 22, died at the age of 89.

VILLA, JOSE GARCIA. Foremost Filipino Poet.

A recipient of the Philippine National Artist Award for Literature in 1973, Jose Garcia Villa died at age 88 in New York City after suffering a stroke.

The foremost Filipino poet, Villa has been known for his comma poems. An example of his poems:

> And, lay, he, down, the, golden,
> father,
>   (Genesis', fist, all, gentle, now)
>   Between, the, Wall, of, China,
> and,
>
>   The, tiger, tree, (his, centuries,
> his,
>   Aerials, of, light)...
>   Anchored, entire, angel!

Awards and Honors. Villa was named as a national artist, together with composer Antonio Molina, muralist Carlos V. Francisco, dance doyenne Francisca Reyes Aquino and sculptor Guillermo Tolentino. He was, besides a Philippine National Artist awardee, recipient of a Shelley Memorial Award, and a fellow of Guggenheim, Bolingen, and Rockefeller.

Villa was a self-exiled man of literature. He didn't go back to the Philippines and he lived in America for nearly seven decades. However, he remained a Filipino citizen until his death.

VILLA, PANCHO. Foremost Filipino Boxing Great.

Pancho Villa (Francisco Guilledo) is known as the foremost Filipino boxing great. He became the first Filipino champion when he knocked out England's Jimmy Wilde in seven rounds in a world flyweight title bout held in New York City on June 18, 1923. On September 15, 1922, he knocked out Johnny Buff to become the American flyweight boxing champion.

Born in Iloilo, Philippines, in 1901, Villa who was only five-foot one, came to the United States in May 1921. In 1925, when he was 21 years old, Villa decided to go through with his non-title fight on July 4 in Oakland, California, in spite of the fact that he had a wisdom tooth pulled the previous day. As a result of this fight, an abcess developed and he died from blood poisoning on an operating table ten days later in San Francisco. Villa, who had 108 fights with only 5 losses in his career, was elected to the Boxing Hall of Fame in 1961.

VILLARIN, MARIANO. Veteran-Author.

Mariano Villarin is the author of the book entitled *We Remember Bataan and Corregidor.* He also writes articles for magazines and newspapers. Examples of published articles are "I Saw the Fall of Bataan," "The Plight of the Philippine Veteran," and "The Massacre of 400 POWs at Bataan."

Education. Villarin received his Bachelor's Degree in Business Administration from the Far Eastern University. He then took post graduate courses at the University of the Philippines just to be enrolled in the ROTC Department for a four-year course in infantry. It paid off when he won a commission as a third lieutenant in the Philippine Army (PA) and a call to active duty on April 15, 1940.

War Breaks Out. When the second world war broke out on December 7, 1941, Villarin was the commandant of the ROTC Unit at De La Salle College in Manila. The entire armed forces of the Philippines was inducted into the U.S. Army Forces in the Far East (USAFFE) under General Douglas MacArthur. Villarin ended up as a second lieutenant with the 2nd Regular Division (PA) on the Bataan peninsula. All USAFFE troops surrendered on April 9, 1942, by order of the Bataan commander who wanted to prevent further bloodshed. Some 78,000 captives made the Bataan Death March, including 12,000 American troops. Only 54,000 reached the prison camp at O'Donnell in Tarlac. An estimated 7,000 to 10,000 POWS died on the Death March from starvation, disease, and atrocities. Another 29,000 PA troops and nearly 2,000 Americans died at Camp O'Donnell during the first four months alone.

World War II Ends. After the war in 1946, there was a shortage of U.S. manpower in the Philippines because the American GIs were being shipped to Japan as occupation forces. The U.S. Army needed officers and enlisted men for duty in the Philippines, Okinawa, and the Marianas Islands. Uncle Sam selected the first 300 highest scorers in the rigid physical and mental tests for a commission as second lieutenants in the U.S. Army for duty in the Philippine Scouts. Villarin was one of the lucky ones among thousands of applicants. But the Philippine Scouts, officers and enlisted men, were disbanded in 1949.

Korean War Breaks Out; Back to Active Duty. Villarin happened to be in the United States when the Korean War broke out. He was recalled to active duty as a first lieutenant. He was sent to Europe for a tour of duty and spent the best five years of his life in West Germany, where two of his three children were born in U.S. Army hospitals. He qualified for retirement as a lieutenant colonel after completing 20 years of combined active duty and participation in the Army Reserve Program. Following his discharge from the U.S. Army in December 1953, Villarin served as an auditor with the U.S. Army Audit Agency and the Department of Agriculture, starting as a GS-7 and ending up at the GS-12 level. He retired from the civil service in 1980.

Memberships. Villarin is a life member of the American Legion; Veterans of Foreign Wars, Disabled American Veterans; American Defenders of Bataan and Corregidor; American Ex-Prisoners of War; Reserve Officers Association; The Retired Officers Association; AMVETS and Philippine Scouts Heritage Society.

Family. Villarin is married to Margarett from Montana, and they live in Long Beach, California. They have three grown children: Corinne; 45; Larry, 43; and Jeanette, 42; and two grandchildren.

YUCHENGCO, MONA LISA. Magazine Publisher.

Mona Lisa Yuchengco publishes *Filipinas Magazine,* the most prestigious publication in the Filipino American community. She launched the glossy monthly magazine in 1992, after "years of wishing" for a high-quality publication and two years of feasibility study and foundation-building. The rest is Filipino American publishing history. *Filipinas* now has a circulation of 40,000 (as of year-end 1997) and is distributed in all fifty states. It is the only Asian American publication affiliated with the Audit Bureau of Circulation. Most importantly, the acclaim from readers shows no sign of abating.

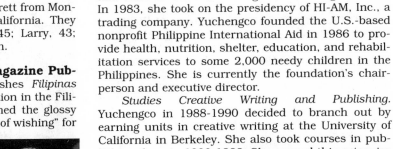

Education and Work Experience. Yuchengco, a scion of a respected Chinese Filipino family with a solid presence in banking, obtained her bachelor degrees in psychology and education at Assumption College in Manila in 1971. She studied for a master's degree in business administration at Ateneo de Manila University in 1979. In 1973, she was an assistant manager at Malayan Insurance Co., Inc. She then began a long career in banking with Rizal Commercial Banking Corporation, starting as a human resource assistant in charge of recruitment. She then trained in international banking. By 1975, she was supervisor for correspondent banking, and in 1976, she was pro-

moted to head the financial consultancy group. Yuchengco then became vice president and the assistant to the president in 1978, helping define bank objectives and guiding branch expansion, retail and corporate banking services, economic and business research, advertising, and public relations.

To the U.S. "To Start All Over Again." Yuchengco came to the United States in 1982 with her sons Paolo and Carlo to "start all over again," as a single mother. In 1983, she took on the presidency of HI-AM, Inc., a trading company. Yuchengco founded the U.S.-based nonprofit Philippine International Aid in 1986 to provide health, nutrition, shelter, education, and rehabilitation services to some 2,000 needy children in the Philippines. She is currently the foundation's chairperson and executive director.

Studies Creative Writing and Publishing. Yuchengco in 1988-1990 decided to branch out by earning units in creative writing at the University of California in Berkeley. She also took courses in publishing there in 1990-1992. She capped this extensive training by completing a professional publishing course at Stanford University in 1993. Meanwhile, she had become a columnist for the *Philippine News,* writing the weekly "Heart to Heart" column under her previous name, Mona Lisa Y. Abaya.

An Idea Comes Out of Her Brain. Increasingly becoming critical of the overall quality of community publications, Yuchengco began acting on the business proposition that "the Filipino community will support a publication that it can be proud of because it reflects the Filipino's best qualities and, in presenting them, follows a very high standard of journalism." She gathered a group of friends for a protracted examination of this hunch, and *Filipinas* was born as a result.

Awards. Yuchengco won third place in the 1990 PALM Short Story writing contest in Washington, D.C., and was given the 1993 Martin Luther King, Jr. Award by St. Paul of the Shipwreck Church in San Francisco, California. In 1996, *Filipinas Magazine* received the Kalampusan Award from Search to Involve Filipino Americans (SIPA) in Los Angeles, California, while Yuchengco received the Trailblazer Award from the Filipino American Women's Network (FAWN) in Minneapolis, Minnesota. ABC/K60-TV bestowed upon Yuchengco the Profiles of Excellence Award in San Francisco in 1997.

Bibliography/Recommended Reading

Abeleda, Jr., Alberto S. *Philippine History and Government.* Copyright 1992. St. Bernadette Publications, Manila, Philippines.

Agoncillo, Teodoro A. and Milagros C. Guerrero, *History of the Filipino People,* 7th Edition. Copyright 1977. R.P. Garcia Publishing Company, Quezon City, Philippines.

Andres, Thomas D. *Dictionary of Filipino Culture and Values.* Copyright 1994. Giraffe Books, Quezon City, Philippines.

Andres, Tomas D. *Understanding Filipino Values: A Management Approach.* Copyright 1981. New Day Publishers, Quezon City, Philippines.

Andres, Tomas D. and Pilar B. Ilada-Andres. *Understanding the Filipino.* Copyright 1987. New Day Publishers, Quezon City, Philippines.

Arcilla, Jose S., S.J. *Recent Philippine History 1898-1960.* Office of Research and Publications. Ateneo de Manila University, Manila, Philippines.

Bandon, Alexandra. *Filipino Americans.* Copyright 1993. New Discovery Books/Macmillan Publishing Company. New York, New York.

Blount, James H. *American Occupation of the Philippines (1898/1912).* Solar Publishing Corporation. Metro Manila, Philippines.

Brainard, Cecilia Manguerra, Editor. *Fiction by Filipinos in America.* Copyright 1993 by Cecilia M. Brainard. New Day Publishers, Queson City, Philippines.

Buchholdt, Thelma. *Filipinos in Alaska: 1788-1958.* Copyright 1996. Aboriginal Press, Anchorage, Alaska.

Bulosan, Carlos. *America Is in the Heart.* Copyright 1943, 1946 by Harcourt, Brace and Company, Inc. University of Washington Press, Seattle, Washington.

Constantino, Renato, *The Philippines: A Past Revisited.* Copyright 1975. Renato Constantino, Quezon City, Philippines.

Constantino, Renato and Letizia R. Constantino, *The Philippines: The Continuing Past.* Copyright 1978. The Foundation for Nationalist Studies, Quezon City, Philippines.

Cordova, Fred. *Filipinos: Forgotten Asian Americans.* Copyright 1983. Demonstration Project for Asian Americans, Seattle, Washington.

Crisostomo, Isabelo T. *Filipino Achievers in the USA & Canada: Profiles in Excellence.* Copyright 1996 by Isabelo T. Crisostomo. Bookhaus Publishers, Farmington Hills, Michigan.

de Grummond, Jane Lucas. *The Baratarians and the Battle of New Orleans.* Copyright 1961. Louisiana State University Press, Baton Route, Louisiana.

Espiritu, Yen Le. *Filipino American Lives.* Copyright 1995. Temple University Press, Philadelphia, Pennsylvania.

Friday, Chris. *Organizing Asian American Labor: The Pacific Coast Canned-Salmon Industry (1870-1942).* Copyright 1994. Temple University Press, Philadelphia, Pennsylvania.

Gochenour, Theodore. *Considering Filipinos.* Copyright 1990. Intercultural Press, Inc., Yarmouth, Maine.

Hunt, Chester L. and Lourdes R. Quisumbing, Socorro C. Espiritu, Michael A. Costelo and Luis Q. Lacar, *Sociology in the Philippine Setting.* Copyright 1987. Phoenix Publishing House, Inc., Quezon City, Philippines.

Kikuchi, Yasushi, Editor. *Philippine Kinship and Society.* Copyright 1989. New Day Publishers, Quezon City, Philippines.

Lasker, Bruno. *Filipino Immigration to Continental United States and to Hawaii.* Copyright 1931 by R.C. Carter. American Council Institute of Pacific Relations/The University of Chicago Press, Chicago, Illinois.

Machi, Mario. *Under the Rising Sun: Memories of a Japanese Prisoner of War.* Copyright 1994. Wolfenden, Miranda, California.

Mamot, Patricio R., Ph.D. *Filipino Physicians in America,* Volume I. Copyright 1981. The Philippine Heritage Endowment Publications, Indianapolis, Indiana.

Mayberry, Jodine. *Filipinos.* Copyright 1990. Franklin Watts, Inc., Princeton, New Jersey.

Melendry, Howart Brett. *Asians in America.* Copyright 1977. (The Immigrant Heritage of America Series). Twayn Publishers/G.K. Hall & Co., Boston, Massachusetts.

Takaki, Ronald. *In the Heart of Filipino America: Immigrants from the Pacific Isles.* Copyright 1989 by Ronald Takaki. Chelsea House Publishers, New York, NY.

Villarin, Mariano. *We Remember Bataan and Corregidor: The Story of the American and Filipino Defenders of Bataan and Corregidor and Their Captivity.* Copyright 1990. Mariano Villarin, Long Beach, California.

Publications:

Filipino Reporter, New York City

Filipinas magazine, San Francisco, California

Phippine News, San Francisco, California

Other Resources:

Internet

Electric Library

Index

D

Dado, Speedy 164
Dado, Speedy (Diosdado B. Posadas) 194
Dador, Denise 194
Dagohoy Revolt 34
dance halls 149
Dator, Denise 160
Datu Sumakwel 17
Dayao, Firmo S. 195
Daza, Eugenio 75
De Castro, Rolando A. 195
De Castro, Rolando A., D.D.M., 164
de Dios, Emiliano Riego 46
de Elcano, Juan Sebastian 28
de Figueroa, Captain Esteban Rodriguez 31
de Goiti, Captain Martin 30
de Goiti, Marshall Martin 23
de Grumond, Jane Lucas 106
de Izquierdo, Rafael 38
de la Cruz, Apolonio 42
de la Rosa, Fabian 160
de Lavezares, Governor-General Guido 30
de Legazpi, Adelantado Miguel Lopez 23
de Legazpi, Miguel Lopez 29
de Lome, Enriquez Dupuy 51
de los Reyes, Isabelo 39
De Los Rios, General 60
de Polavieja, General Camilo 45
de Rivera, Colonel Miguel Primo 49
de Rivera, Governor General Primo 51
de Rivera, Primo 48
de Saavedra, Alvaro 28
de Salazar, Father Domingo 33
de Salcedo, Captain Juan 30
de Tavera, Governor-General Primo 49
de Tavera, Trinidad H. Pardo 83
de Unamuno, Pedro 107
de Urdaneta, Father Andres 29
de Villalobos, Ruy Lopez 28
del Monte, San Juan 43
del Pilar, General Gregorio 69, 72
del Pilar, General Pio 47
del Pilar, Gregorio 53
del Pilar, Marcelo H. 39
del Pilar, Pio 46
del Rosario, Aguedo 43
dela Cruz, Pedro 195
Delacruz, Rosy C. Abarquez 196
Delgado, General Martin 68
Democratic Alliance 19
Democratic Party 84, 85
Dewey, Admiral George 79
Dewey, Commodore George 51, 91
Di Giorgio Corporation 135

dialects 14
Diario de Manila 42
Dichoso, Carmelo C. 196
dictatorial government 56
Diego and Gabriela Silang Revolt 34
diko 154
Dionisio, Juan C. (Johnny) 135
Dirige, Ofelia 197
discrimination and prejudice 147
discrimination in school 148
ditche 154
Dittmar, Melissa 197
diwata 18
Docusen, Bernard (Big Duke) 164
Dole, James 119
Douglas, William 136
Drakes, Vicky Manalo 164
Draves, Vicky Manalo 197
Duldulao, Julie R. 198
Duyungan, Virgil 141

E

ECFMG 114
education, system of 79
educational system 79
El Comercio 41
El Filibusterismo 40, 48
el Viejo, Cavite 44
Elcano 31
Eleanora 136
Elvambuena, Roland P. 198
encomendero 32
encomienda 30
Encomienda System 32
Enrile, Juan Ponce 21
Enriquez, Jocelyn 155, 162, 198
Escuela de Derecho 80
Espaldon, Ernesto M. 199
Espaldon, Ernesto M., M.D. 164
Espina, Marina 105, 108
ethnic groups 13
Europe 26
Europe-First Policy 93
Evangelista, Jose L, M.D. 164
Evangelista, Jose L. 200
Evangelista, Stella, M.D. 164, 201
exchange workers 108

F

Fabito, Daniel C., M.D. 202
Fair American 136
Fajardo, Juventino "Ben" 202
Fajardo, Pete 202

S

T

Author Veltisezar B. Bautista poses with his book
How to Build a Successful One-Person Business **at a**
Waldenbooks store in Madison Heights, Michigan.

The author, Veltisezar B. Bautista, is a multi-awarded Filipino American author, who has won seven book awards, including two Benjamin Franklin awards, the most prestigious awards in independent publishing. Bautista is the author of six nonfiction books, including the national bestselling *The Book of U.S. Postal Exams: How to Score 95-100% and Get a Job*, a Benjamin Franklin Award winner; *How to Build a Successful One-Person Business*, an Alternate Monthly Selection of the Month of Conservative Book Club; *Improve Your Grades*, the recipient of four book awards; and *How to Teach Your Child: Things to Know from Kindergarten through Grade 6*, a Benjamin Franklin Award Winner, and an Alternate Monthly Selection of the Homeschooling Book Club.

For being a successful author and publisher in the United States, Bautista was on the cover of *Business Monday* (January 20, 1997). The magazine is the Monday supplement of the *Detroit Free Press*, one of the largest newspapers in Michigan. Bautista is the recipient of the 1990 Small Press Publisher of the Year Award, a national publishing award. A native of General Tinio, Nueva Ecija Province, Philippines, Bautista is the only known successful Filipino American author and publisher whose books are sold through bookstores and to public and school libraries in the U.S.

A full-time writer and publisher, Bautista was a long-time staff member of the *Manila Chronicle*, one of the largest daily English newspapers in the Philippines. He started as a proofreader; then he eventually became a reporter and a deskman (copy editor). For a few years, he was a staff writer for *This Week Magazine*, the Sunday supplement of the *Manila Chronicle*.

He is a product of the University of Santo Tomas Faculty of Philosophy and Letters (major in journalism), in Manila, Philippines. A bilingual writer in the Philippines, writing in both English and Pilipino, he was a contributor to national publications such as the *Philippines Free Press* magazine. He was also a publisher of reference books for the country's Philippine Department of Education before he left Manila for the United States in 1976 with his wife, Genoveva Abes-Bautista, to pursue his own American Dream. A year later, their five children (Hubert, Lester, Melvin, Ronald, and Janet) followed them.